SPIKE MIKE RE

Spike Mike
Reloaded

A Guided Tour Across
a Decade of American
Independent Cinema

JOHN PIERSON

With the Conversational Collaboration of
KEVIN SMITH

HYPERION
NEW YORK

MIRAMAX BOOKS

"Critic's Notebook: For Sundance, Struggle to Survive Success" by Caryn James: Copyright © 1994 by The New York Times Company. Reprinted by Permission.
Drawing by Emily Breer

Library of Congress Cataloging-in-Publication Data

Pierson, John
   Spike, Mike, slackers & dykes : a guided tour across a decade of American independent cinema / by John Pierson—1st ed.
      p.   cm.
   ISBN 0-7868-6189-4
   1. Motion picture producers and directors—United States. 2. Low budget motion pictures. 3. Motion pictures—United States—History. 4. Motion pictures—Production and direction. I. Title.
PN1998.2.P56 1996   95-24979
791.43'0233'092273—dc20   CIP

Paperback ISBN 0-7868-8222-0
First Paperback Edition
10 9 8 7 6 5 4 3 2 1

Designed by Jessica Shatan

ISBN 1-4013-5950-7

FOR JANET
A great sounding board,
Although much softer

CONTENTS

Foreword by Kevin Smith ix

Out of the Jungle xiii

Introduction to the Original Edition: Stranger Than Fiction 1

Dialogue / Leaders 4

A Quick and Slanted Pre-1984 History 6

Dialogue / Starting Point 21

Stranger Than Paradise and the First Golden Age 24

Dialogue / Paradise 31

Parting Glances & The New Queer Cinema 34

She's Gotta Have It 45

Tube Socks and Tube Steaks 45
Black and White 56
Birth of a Salesman 66

Dialogue / Be Like Spike 79

Working Girls and Women 83

Inspector Errol Morris Walks The Thin Blue Line 103

D.O.A. 114

The Dance Part 1 114
Deceased 118
Quantity Not Quality 121

Dialogue / Batman and Sex 123

1989: The Year It All Changed 126

Dialogue / sex and Roger   133

Roger and Michael and Me   137

   The Cinderella Syndrome   137
   How to Make a Studio Deal   152
   The Morning After   165

Dialogue / Role Models   177

Slacking Off   185

Dialogue / Straight Outta Business   198

The Next Soderbergh   202

   Sundance 1990   205
   Sundance 1991   207
   Sundance 1992   209

Dialogue / Dogs   212

Sons of Mean Streets   218

Dialogue / $26,685   228

How Low Can a Budget Go?   234

Dialogue / Shannen   239

Amongst Jerks: Rob Weiss and the Dark Side of Overnight Success   249

   Toll Money   249
   Hitchcock: Who Needs Him?   257
   Murder Ink   265

The Odd Couple: Sundance 1994   279

In Hock and Staying There   299

Go Fiscal: Anatomy of a Back End   311

A Doc In The House   319

Dialogue / The Clerky Boys   330

Epilogue: It's A Wonderful Life, July 4, 1995   331

The Last Word   339

Appendix I   355
Appendix II   369
Appendix III   371
Index   373

FOREWORD: THE SEQUEL

When I was a child, my parents took me to the local drive-in to see *The Gumball Rally*, and for the next month, I tried desperately to organize an all-bike version with the other kids on my block. The only flaw in the plan? None of us had a gumball machine, not even a scaled down, plastic version, to offer the winner. No gumball, no rally.

I can recall a few years after that trying to mount a backyard staging of *Superman*, which fell through due to both lack of financing (Krypton *couldn't* be made of egg cartons, after all), and lack of a credible nine-year-old Man of Steel.

But the most tragic of might-have-been productions a young Jersey boy busied himself with as an outlet for an overactive imagination (until he'd discover masturbation a few moons later), had to be script for a Super 8 sequel he and his pals planned to shoot in the clay hills of their home town, entitled *Indiana Jones and the Lost Baal*. We'd had the budget (thirty bucks), the prize (a funky candle holder we bought in a head shop that looked demonic demi-godly enough to pass for an archaeological treasure), the lead (Ernie O'Donnell, he who would later become Rick Derris in *Clerks*, was only too happy to Ford it for us.), and a bull-whip purchased at Frontier Land, during one of many family vacations to Disney World. But our epic would forever remain on the page due to one crucial, missing element . . .

We couldn't find a fedora.

And so it would go for most of my childhood and teen years: promise went unfulfilled. Giving physical life to ideas and whims would elude me until my twenty first birthday, back in the summer of '91, when a Jersey boy drove a shit-box Pinto into New York City to see the film that would forever alter the course of his destiny: Richard Linklater's *Slacker*.

The power of that film, the impact it had on me and my life, can be measured squarely by where I sit, nearly thirteen years later. I, too, am now a filmmaker, with six movies under my belt. My films have been to Cannes and Sundance twice, and countless other film festivals multiple times. I've won some awards, and been praised by critics (taken a beating by some, too). I've met and worked beside actors and film-makers I've idolized, and become a recognizable fixture in the world of cinema, I've helped break some major movie stars, exec-produced a multiple Academy Award winner, and guided several smaller films through festival, theatrical and, video distribution. I've spent an inordinate amount of time building and maintaining a fan base with a surprisingly successful series of websites. I've written a shelf-full of comic books and opened a comic book store. I've seen my image adorn t-shits, key-chains, posters, and action figures. I've been at the center of far too many controversies and scandals. I've produced a quickly canceled cartoon, and shucked and jived more times that I should have been allowed to on the *Tonight Show*. I've gotten a ton of press that I didn't even court, and courted the press in a fairly intimate fashion, meeting my wife when she interviewed me for *USA Today*. I've had a beautiful daughter, lost my Father, and almost lost one of my closest friends to drugs. I've shilled for Nike, Coke, MTV, Hasbro, and been the pitchman for Panasonic. I've bought a really big house, made lots of money, made more friends (and an enemy or two), been beloved, been despised, gained and lost a ton of weight, and generally lived so dream-like a life, that most days, I'm sure a goateed Robert DeNiro's gonna show up and demand my soul, shortly after I have wild, blood-spattered sex with the chick from *The Cosby Show*.

Now, granted, I'm not the standard example of the effect one film can have on a person's life. However, I'm a valid example all the same. Had I not gone to the Angelika Theater that night to see Linklater's mini magnum opus, the paragraph above couldn't exist. That's the power of cinema. Sure, it's entertainment, but it can change the course of a life. Films (even so-called "bad" films; because every film is *someone's* favorite) have the power to lift the spirits, challenge perceptions, and most importantly, inspire.

Seeing *Slacker* filled me with "Let's Put On a Show!" gusto that directly led to *Clerks*. Linklater and Co. were able to succeed in doing what the young me never could: he took an idea and made it flesh. He finished what he started. Nothing stood in his way: not lack of funds, lack of stars, lack of anything traditionally associated with film production. He turned his debits into plusses; he made something out of nothing. And sitting in that theater, watching someone so far from the mainstream fulfill a dream I wasn't even sure I had yet lit a fire under my ass. *I* wanted to do what Linklater did. In *Slacker*, I'd found a kindred spirit. In *Slacker*, I'd found inspiration.

In *Slacker*, years after the fact, I'd found that elusive fedora.

But the *haberdasher* who got that fedora into my hands has been largely un-sung. He's the lynchpin shared by me, Richard, and so many other well-known once-Indie/now-established-y filmmakers. He's also the author of the book you hold in your hands.

That haberdasher's name is John Pierson.

Were it not for John, I might never have even heard of *Slacker*, let alone had my life changed by it. Without John, Spike Lee, Michael Moore, and *The Blair Witch Project* might never have impacted the cultural and pop-cultural landscape. Without John Pierson, the world of cinema (not to mention the world in general) would be far, far less interesting.

Years ago John invited me to play a role in his seminal tome about the Indie film community, by way of conversational chapter intros that cast us in what will forever be our respective roles: he as sage-like, cinema war-horse guru, and me as novice, mouthy filmmaker. I was as honored then as I am now to be a part of what became the Bible for Indie film. I can't tell you how many copies of this book I've autographed at all the colleges where I've spoken. And I always scribble the same inscription: on the title page, beneath my collaborative conversational credit, I write, "Look I helped."

But really, it was John who helped, and continues to help, *me*. With his blunt honesty, his passion for the medium, and his insightful wit, it's been John who's kept me on the straight-and-narrow for the last ten years. And whether it's a movie of mine he loves (*Clerks* and *Jersey Girl*) or a movie of mine he doesn't (he still scratches his head over why I felt the need to make *Jay and Silent Bob Strike Back*), he's always been there for me with advice, perspective, love and support. It's rare when you become friendly with your heroes. It's rarer still when, even after ten years of friendship and familiarity, they remain your heroes. And while all of you can't ever really know John as well as I do, you can get to know him through *Spike, Mike*—because this book has always been John laid out in page format (well, at least the cinema aspect of his life; for a better understanding of the man himself, you'll have to wait to read his upcoming, *Fiji Family Pierson: Adventures in Reel Paradise*). A more thorough or entertaining look at an important moment in film history you'll never read than *Spike, Mike*, I assure you. It's a book for people who love movies.

Just like John Pierson.

The British poet George Gascoigne once wrote "The haberdasher heapeth wealth by hats." If that's the case then Indie Guru/Haberdasher John Pierson is the richest man I know.

In the fall of '03, I took my four-year-old daughter to see Richard Linklater's *School of Rock*. And as the kids in the film took to the stage for the Battle of the Bands they'd worked toward the whole movie, Harley's face lit up. Swept up in the pure joy, the spirit moved her, and before I knew it, there was my kid, out of her seat, *literally* dancing in the aisle, air-guitaring and singing along at the top of her lungs (particularly the "KICK SOME ASS!" lyric of the song; she is, after all, *my* kid). And I couldn't help but get a little glassy-eyed and misty over it. Because there, years later, in a darkened movie theater, on the other side of the country, another generation of Smiths was profoundly affected by a film (a Richard Linklater film, no less). The notion hit home even further when she excitedly detailed her plans to start a rock band with her friends, for which it was my duty, she informed me, to provide the crucial Jack Black element. When I asked her if she meant that she wanted me to *be* the Jack Black-like chubby front-man in her band, she insisted—sounding ominously like every studio head in the business must have that Monday morning following an opening weekend box office that surpassed the sum total of every previous Richard Linklater film to date—"No—you gotta get me THE Jack Black."

Now my kid's got a fedora to chase. I just pray she'll find a haberdasher as good as the one I met.

—Kevin Smith
12/9/2003

OUT OF THE JUNGLE

I disappeared to Fiji for the better part of the last two years. What drove me away? First, there was the endless countdown to war in Iraq. Then the completely unexceptional, middle-of-the-road romantic comedy *My Big Fat Greek Wedding* began its slow climb to bump off the ingenious fluke phenomenon *Blair Witch Project* as the top-grossing independent feature in history. If ever there was a time to leave America and its much-vaunted off-Hollywood boom years behind, this was it.

Out of sight, out of mind. The end result is that I'm right back where I was when *Spike, Mike, Slackers & Dykes* was first published—a cipher. The original introduction (see page 1, as opposed to page *i*) played off those legendary "You don't know me" American Express commercials that featured names of well-known people whose faces you couldn't quite place. Back in the seventies, the first ad in the campaign focused on the man of a thousand animated voices, Mel Blanc. There is an independent-film angle to this story featuring the indie trinity: savvy, spunk and credit cards.

Thirty years ago, Warner Brothers had no idea how valuable Bugs Bunny and Daffy Duck cartoons would turn out to be. But sharp film programmers like Larry Jackson at the Orson Welles Cinema in Cambridge knew better. Larry got Warners to grant him the right to use nine classic cartoons in a feature compilation that would also contain documentary material on the creative geniuses who made them. He cleverly bankrolled the project with his American Express Card. Back then it was a charge card with a 30-day billing cycle, NOT a credit card, so he had to make sure that he ran up his highest costs—well beyond his limit—during a single month while he was completing post-production in the film lab. Somewhere around the thirty-first day, Amex caught on, tracked him down, and angrily demanded that he cut up his card and immediately submit payment in full. Somehow the inspired producer found out that they were desperately searching for Mel Blanc, a key figure in the film as the voices of Bugs, Daffy, Porky, et al, to kick off the aforementioned series of ads. Larry Jackson supplied the talent. American Express worked out a payment schedule for his budget. Mel Blanc finally had his day in the sun, and *Bugs Bunny Superstar* was the first credit-card movie to become a critical and commercial success.

Those were the days. As were the days, years and decade that I wrote about in 1996, when I was either a ferret, shaman or bagman. The subsequent exposure changed my life. I stopped representing first-time features. Instead, we put over a hundred unknown filmmakers, including the Blair Witch guys, to work on sixty-six episodes of *Split Screen*, an off-Hollywood, magazine-format cable television show I created on Bravo and the Independent Film Channel . For four years, people saw my mug on IFC every Monday night. In the last season, I chanced upon a memorable movie outlet at the edge of the world. Then I vanished. You don't know me . . . again.

Life in the Fijian bush, away from it all, was great fun. When you're eight thousand miles from New York on a small South Pacific island with no electricity, it's no longer possible to hear the drumbeat of Miramax's myriad Academy Award nominations and multiple victories. And the noisy media-fueled engine of the annual Sundance star-making machinery fades out a few nautical miles west of Santa Monica. It's quiet. You can almost hear the dalo (a popular tuber) grow. Perspective is available wholesale.

When my family decided to join the adventure, a veritable Fiji Family Pierson, we knew we weren't going to spend our time building a super-deluxe tree house. Nor would our hands be full taming the wild beasts of the rain forest, since, sadly, the largest native mammal on our island was the fruit bat. Instead, we decided we needed a family business and decided to operate a movie theater—a free movie theater where we had to tame the wild movie fans.

As you might imagine, the available onscreen fare at the world's most remote 35mm movie theater, the 180 Meridian Cinema, was a Hollywood hit parade. Packed houses rattled the walls laughing at Rob Schneider in a dress in *The Hot Chick* or cheering for The Rock's swordplay in *The Scorpion King*. I often thought about my buddy Jim Jacks, a producer of *Scorpion King*, who worked with the Coen Brothers, Sam Raimi, Richard Linklater and Kevin Smith looking for that indie/commercial nexus only to wind up with the billion-dollar worldwide *Mummy* franchise. As the Fiji free-movie king, I could relate. At first it was a flat-out joy to reject the higher, often flawed, aspirations of independent film in favor of the studio formulae that work all around the planet.

Lowest common denominator is an extremely dismissive term. It's very easy to deploy when you're not on the front line, or in my case the back row, watching 288 people go nuts for Jackie Chan, Jet Li, J. Lo, Eminem, E.T. or the Ents in *Two Towers*. They're all global superstars. On a media-free tropical isle starved for entertainment, aside from the nightly Catholic mass, Hollywood really doesn't seem so bad. It was a new diet for a guy like me, similar to the local food choices: fish and dalo, or dalo and fish.

Eventually you wake up one day, after seeing the rat in *Stuart Little 2*, or Martin Lawrence in *National Security*—genre films with absolutely no redeeming value—and realize that the daily fish is also getting old. Suddenly the edgier films like *Bend It Like Beckham*, *Rabbit-Proof Fence* and *28 Days Later*—British empire indies that made it to the jungle because Fiji is a former British colony—start to look better. And somehow the sun never sets on the Miramax empire either. *Gangs of New York*, *Chicago* and, better late than never, *Apocalypse Now Redux* all showed up on the rust-bucket ferry that chugs in on Thursdays delivering the weekend movies. And I'm still not sure how that print of *My Big Fat Greek Wedding* wound up on the projection-booth floor. I do know it stayed there without ever getting threaded up. It was bumped in favor of Mr. Bean, a Fijian favorite who is often mistaken as one of the Three Stooges, in *Johnny English*.

Chicago was a watershed. When we showed it, my opinionated son Wyatt called it one of the least-deserving Best Picture winners in Oscar history. I don't always listen to the wisdom of a 13-year-old who also thought that *Apocalypse Now* should have been "reduxed" by about 90 minutes, but this time I agreed. And yet, I was missing Miramax. I asked the 180 Meridian Cinema audience one of my patented pre-screening prize-giveaway questions: What world-famous award did *Chicago* win? Silence. Fijians are shy in public. They hate to stand out. Finally a hand went up and a very tentative voice said, "A Grammy." No one hates the modern-day proliferation of film awards more than I do. But after a year of liberation, it was time to go home.

From the moment we landed in Los Angeles, I couldn't catch up with enough indie films fast enough. It started with a string of wonderful documentaries including *Spellbound*, *Capturing the Friedmans*, *Winged Migration*, *To Be and to Have*, *Stevie*, and *The Fog of War*, then *American Splendor*, a brilliant fractured narrative that uses documentary techniques. It was exciting to see Steve James (*Hoop Dreams*) and Errol Morris (*The Thin Blue Line*), two key figures from my book, extending their mastery of the nonfiction form. The closest I'd come to any doc in Fiji was smuggling in a print of *Jackass*, or reading about Michael Moore's "Booing for Columbine" Oscar speech on the front page of the *Fiji Times*. I'd returned home just in time for the long-awaited year of the documentary to have finally arrived.

Man cannot live by fish, or studio blockbuster, alone. *Bad Boys 2*, *S.W.A.T.* and the return of The Rock in *The Rundown* seemed dumb and bloated back in the US of A, removed from the oohs and aahs of the 180 Meridian Cinema. But then I started to dream at night, and daydream during working hours, about the joy of being in another culture where movies meant so much, even if their content added up to just about nothing. While continuing to binge on the 2003 crop of almost-too-prototypical American indies like *Pieces of April*, *Thirteen*, *The Station Agent*, *Elephant*, and even *Lost In Translation*, I became more and more confused about what movies like these have meant to our culture. If you're not in the elite group seeing them in the festivals where they racked up the big awards (the first three at Sundance, *Elephant* dominating Cannes), the impact can get pretty defused.

That thought process was greatly accelerated one day while sitting at my friend Peter Biskind's kitchen table. His superb book *Easy Riders, Raging Bulls* was published a year after the paperback edition of *Spike, Mike, Slackers & Dykes*, and we cheered each other on. He called mine "the bible of independent film." For my part, I would argue with anyone who called his a gossipy amalgam of sex, drugs & rock 'n' roll by demonstrating that it was suffused with a love for, and keen appreciation of, the triumphant films of the seventies. Now I was sitting in his house in total secrecy under high security (Peter and his dogs) reading 500 manuscript pages of the book he'd been working on ever since, a book about independent film—my world.

In fact, I had to get past an early page where he actually wrote that I had forgotten more about independent film than he'd ever know—or some such. There's no doubt that *Down & Dirty Pictures*, as the book came to be called, portrays a world that I recognize, a world where Sundance and Miramax are the nine-hundred-pound gorillas, and Robert Redford and the Weinstein Brothers sometimes behave badly, and other times behave very badly. But it seemed to me, as I'd told Biskind early on, that there was little or no love for the movies (outside Quentin Tarantino), as there had been in *Easy Riders, Raging Bulls.* Nor was there much of any cultural—or even industry—context, as there had been in the earlier book.

I don't know how you can evaluate a company like Miramax and the dominant role it has played in the last decade without taking its measure against the decade-long run that United Artists had, starting around 1963, when David Picker became head of production. Both companies were based in New York, thus even if UA was technically a "studio" as opposed to Miramax, the studio (Disney) affiliate, they were both outside Hollywood. Both became Oscar factories by producing and acquiring higher-brow work, frequently with European directors, most often from England. The advantages of the New York/London connection (time difference alone) were many. For UA in the sixties, this meant Best Picture winners like Tony Richardson's *Tom Jones* and John Schlesinger's *Midnight Cowboy.* A little later, Bernardo Bertolucci's *Last Tango In Paris* changed the world. Fellini, Bergman, Truffaut, they all worked for UA because UA worked for them. Theirs was a filmmaker-friendly environment where the director ruled and, as a rule, even had final cut.

United Artists had another side. It was a superb cauldron where high and low culture, artistic forays and commercial genres were all mixed together. They put the Beatles on screen, released Sergio Leone's seminal spaghetti westerns with Clint Eastwood, and made a new comedy with Woody Allen every year. And of course they struck gold with

James Bond. Miramax also has its other side, Dimension. The Miramax/Dimension split seems a bit like United Artists, but really more like the cheesy side of New Line. Personally, I'd rather see three *Scary Movies*, three *Screams*, and three *Spy Kids* (all Dimension) than one *Texas Chainsaw Massacre* remake (New Line). But would you really rather see Leone's *The Good, the Bad and the Ugly* (UA) or Robert Rodriguez's tossed-off wannabe, *Once Upon a Time in Mexico* (Dimension)?

Picker and his bosses—Arthur Krim, Bob Benjamin, and Arnold Picker, his uncle—were able to comport themselves in a truly decent way and conduct their business in a most upstanding manner. The Weinstein modus operandi is more like a throwback—the "mogul operandi." Miramax is filmmaker-friendly in name, but a much more deadly minefield in practice. Both companies could make decisions much more rapidly than their competitors. Much of the UA talent kept coming back for more, while a majority of Miramax alumni try to slip out of the ankle bracelets. Some escapees, like Gus van Sant, remember the opportunity they were given; others, like M. Night Shyamalan, try to erase the bad memories. Kevin Smith, Tarantino, Rodriguez and Anthony Minghella are all in the family.

After United Artists' golden decade, a conglomerate without a clue called Transamerica bought the company. Life went on until a runaway train called *Heaven's Gate* bankrupted the studio. It was the same year as Martin Scorsese's magnum opus *Raging Bull*, and a year after Francis Ford Coppola mortgaged his house to finish *Apocalypse Now*. Many detractors believed that Scorsese's *Gangs of New York* might be the beginning of the end for the Miramax era, especially after Harvey Weinstein seemed to be spending his time starting magazines and trying to swing elections.

They're still here. And the United Artists name was briefly brought back to life as MGM's specialized wing under the able and still feisty leadership of distribution veteran Bingham Ray. As a result of the roadside wreck known as October Films, Bingham is the tragic hero of Biskind's tale. Fortunately, he lived to tell. At UA, he released both *Bowling for Columbine* and *Jeepers Creepers 2*. The earlier UA heyday overlaps with the last great Hollywood studio flowering described in *Easy Riders, Raging Bulls*.

How do the high-quality, award-winning movies from that era compare to the Miramax library? For me, *Good Will Hunting*, a story about two friends, is no *Midnight Cowboy*, and *Chicago* is not *All That Jazz*. Others might disagree. But I don't think anyone would pick *Shakespeare in Love* over *The Godfather*, *The English Patient* over *The Godfather*, *Part II* or *Life Is Beautiful* over *Chinatown*. But the world, the film industry, and audience sensibilities are very different now, compared to a time when life wasn't beautiful. It was Chinatown, Jake.

I come to bury Harvey, not to praise him. Wait, I mean I come to praise Harvey, not to bury him. Actually, I come not to quote Shakespeare (or *Shakespeare in Love*), but to weigh the scales. When last we visited Miramax, circa 1995, they'd progressed from *sex, lies, and videotape* to *The Piano* to *The Crying Game* to the $100 million breakout *Pulp Fiction*. At that time, they still had room for *Clerks*—just barely. These were exceptional films with spectacular marketing. The Weinstein passion for movies combined with an unerring gift for salesmanship and relentless drive is an undeniable reality.

Does the perfect mesh with current filmgoers' tastes lead to a soft, sentimental underbelly in many instances? Maybe for hardened critics like Peter Biskind the procession of feel-good art tearjerkers, from *Cinema Paradiso* to *Enchanted April* to *Like Water for Chocolate*, *Il Postino*, *Good Will Hunting*, *Chocolat* and, worst of all, *Life Is Beautiful*, constitutes a betrayal of quality control. But that's the other side of Harvey, the side that channels the weepy hearts of the world while adding a veneer of highbrow respectability. And who hasn't fallen under the spell of at least a few of these films?

Of course the relentless drive to try to "improve" Miramax films,—both productions and acquisitions—has grown and grown as test marketing permeates the entire industry. The acute gut instinct in an earlier era that told Harvey Scissorhands to lop forty dull, dull minutes out of *Cinema Paradiso* improved both the art and marketability. However, as the years went by, Harvey Scissorhands spent more and more time looking at the top two boxes on the preview cards and became Harvey Heavyhands. No problem if it's schlock like *She's All That*. But one size does not fit all.

Even if they do act a little bit like prima donnas, artists like Bernardo Bertolucci (*Little Buddha*) and Todd Haynes (*Velvet Goldmine*) should probably be spared his not-so-velvet-glove touch. Frankly, he might have helped both flicks. *Little Buddha* is no *Last Tango In Paris*. Then again, anal sex probably doesn't test too well nowadays. It's also pretty obvious that mucking around endlessly with films that nobody even remembers, like *54* or *All I Wanna Do* will never turn a sow's ear into a silk purse. It's the titles that Miramax tried and failed to shorten or change, but still pushed to the max in the marketplace, that are eye opening. These include the multi-nominated *Sling Blade, In the Bedroom* and *Frida*.

Here's what it comes down to. If you cannot find much of anything to treasure in the work, then any pattern of boorish, abusive behavior behind the scenes has absolutely no end that justifies the means. In Biskind's endless catalogue of avarice bordering on unmitigated greed, Harvey and Bob Weinstein become nothing more than a shrewd pair of brothers lining their own pockets. And there's always the implication that they've cheated somehow. The Go Fiscal chapter of this book is one of the few places where you can actually study up on how easily the "profits" evaporate, even on a successful low-budget film. Message to everyone out there: Get a gross deal like *The Blair Witch Project* did from Artisan. Saul Zaentz, producer of *The English Patient*, has been making noise for years about his missing net profits. He has the power, the money and the means to sue Miramax. Why hasn't he?

The saving grace in this litany of moral corruption is that Harvey, unlike elusive Sundance godhead Robert Redford, is in your face and bigger than life. Maybe he wasn't a good sport about losing *Shine* to Fine Line Features at Sundance, but he probably would have made it an even bigger success. He is exceedingly colorful. Does he poke a few chests and flick a cigarette in someone's face now and again? This was not *my* experience. Since I felt partly implicated in the dark interpretation, it was either time to take the slow boat back to Fiji or revise, reload and republish this book.

I was in love with the movies I wrote about in *Spike, Mike*. I still am. I believe that they matter. I am convinced that they did more than launch new talent, although with Spike Lee, Michael Moore, Richard Linklater and Kevin Smith, these fresh and original first features certainly did that as well. With verve, they brought thoughts about race, politics, sex, sexual politics, class and alternative lifestyles (thank you Blockbuster) into the culture. They did it through entertainment, but they continue to stick to the ribs.

In the memorable zombie horror classic *Night of the Living Dead*, a character describing the flesh eaters says, "They're dead, they're all messed up." Independent film isn't dead, but it's definitely all messed up. The only thing you can say with absolute certainty is that Sundance, Miramax and the rest of the indie infrastructure has been the primary farm team and funnel for new talent. And that talent has seen no shame, or even harm, in working within the studio system. Jon Favreau's *Elf* and former documentarian Terry Zwigoff's *Bad Santa* battle it out for your Christmas box-office dollars, while Bryan Singer's *X2* and Ang Lee's *Hulk* (as bad a crossover move as there's ever been) vie for your Christmas-gift DVDollars.

Now let me stop and point out that Ang Lee, aided and abetted by James Schamus, has been a model filmmaker. His bold choices and don't-box-me-in ambitions culminated in an artistically rich, gigantic crossover success with his previous feature, *Crouching Tiger, Hidden Dragon*. Nobody deserved it more. Following the current Steven Soderbergh rulebook (in partnership with George Clooney, no less), perhaps the very best directors can jump back and forth over the Hollywood fence until the fence flattens out to the ground. There's certainly nothing wrong with taking a studio's money and using its marketing clout for the right film, especially if it's subversive political dynamite like David O. Russell's 1999 *Three Kings* leavened with the star power of, once again, George Clooney. Russell's circle of new Hollywood filmmaker friends includes Alexander Payne, Wes Anderson and Spike Jonze. You can't do much better than *Being John Malkovich*, *Rushmore*, and *Election* if you are looking for reasons to be cheerful about the last decade.

On a certain level, the key action in the indie arena has shifted into the new-talent business. Who even remembers where the studios, major talent agencies, studio-affiliated production companies, and the Miramaxes of the world used to find directors? Now they can troll Sundance, MTV, film schools and short-film Web sites to liven things up—not to mention every other country on the planet with a film industry. It's not just that Hollywood films now colonize the globe. More than ever, Hollywood has become the ultimate brain drain, if that's not an oxymoron, on every other indigenous film culture, whether it's Germany (Wolfgang Petersen), Sweden (Lasse Hallström), Mexico (Alfonso Cuarón), the Netherlands (Paul Verhoeven), Hong Kong (John Woo), France (Jean-Pierre Jeunet) or Australia and New Zealand (absolutely everyone). Even in the semi-mythical mid-1980s golden age of American indies that I wrote about, some great filmmakers found their studio niche (Spike Lee, the Coens), and some stayed way outside (Jim Jarmusch, John Sayles). Today, everyone worth his salt still seeks some degree of control, but nobody wastes too much breath on quaint notions of independent purity anymore.

And at the same time Swingerman Favreau puts a nice edge on sentimental material and unleashes the charming antics of Will Ferrell with just the right amount of restraint, Richard Linklater does the same with Jack Black in *School of Rock*. Both hit #1 at the box office. In *School of Rock*'s second week, it was edged out by Tarantino's *Kill Bill Vol. 1*, with the Coen Brothers' *Intolerable Cruelty*, their second George Clooney vehicle (he's everywhere!), close behind. What the hell's going on here? Art trumps commerce? Commerce trumps art? Art and commerce happily coexist?

This particular weekend put a capper on the fall festival season and played out against a backdrop of intense protest over the banning of Academy screeners. Linklater, the original hardworking "slacker" and a long-time paradigm of independent virtue ,was on to his next film. In fact, it was already in the can before *School of Rock* opened. He'd gone to Paris to shoot a low-budget sequel to *Before Sunrise*, his two-character Ethan Hawke/Julie Delpy talker. *Before Sunrise 2* will need help from screeners; *School of Rock* doesn't.

It's no coincidence, nor is it totally a joke, that "Reloaded" is now in my book's title. ("Dykes" has disappeared for commercial reasons; I'm tired of losing bookings at Catholic schools.) When *The Matrix* came out in 1999, it was only the Wachowskis' second feature. I was standing in line waiting for *The Phantom Menace*, pondering the indie phenomenon. Hmmm, let me explain.

As I mentioned earlier, a few years ago I created a cable television show called *Split Screen*. At the beginning of the third season, in 1999, as a total goof we started waiting in line for the first entry in the new *Star Wars* trilogy—three months early. The initial concept was just dripping with irony. What could possibly be less "indiefilm" than George Lucas's juggernaut? Yet, ironically, as we were queued up at New York City's deluxe Ziegfeld Theater with way too much time to kill, Lucas began to loom larger and larger as the most independent filmmaker in history. After all, he self-financed the film, created his own special effects in-house, sold his own merchandise, selected a releasing studio as if he were hiring a butler, installed his own sound systems in theaters and even equipped four screens with the very latest technology: digital projection. Now that's autonomy, when you can preserve your increasingly stilted vision and control its presentation.

About halfway through our first-in-line vigil, another paradoxical event occurred. *The Matrix* opened. And it was full of surprises. It was visually inspired, unlike many of the current script-driven independents—and it was wildly original, even as it lifted ideas left and right from other movies and books. It was directed by a pair of palooka brothers from Chicago who had indie credibility from having made a lesbian-action-feminist-neo-noir genre film that was discovered at the Sundance Film Festival. That movie, *Bound,* was a total miss for me, a good example of a bad in die getting some unwarranted sympathy. Yet they made one of the most astonishing leaps from first to second feature ever. And from that unexpected peak, they bottomed out with one of the most disappointing sequels ever. Having run out of new ideas after one film, the only old, creaky one they seized on was to split one lame sequel into two even lamer ones. Let me assure you, there will be no *Spike Mike Revolutions.*

It's time to stop fretting about the death of independent film and start noticing the dearth of independent viewers. George Lucas may be acting like an indie, but his global audience is not. They just put on the feedbag. Well maybe not at our beloved 180 Meridian Cinema, a force-free zone. Viewers there don't go for *Star Wars,* or any science fiction, for that matter. To quote my favorite local expert, "They know it's bullshit." I'm not sure what they'd assign to the bullshit category in New York City, America's specialized film capital. More than two hundred off-Hollywood films have opened in each of the past two years, an average of four per weekend, with thirty-odd titles on screen at any given moment. That sounds diverse.

Maybe with any film, it's not the millions who watch and blank out who count. It's the one single, solitary viewer who sees an unexpectedly influential movie one day and is permanently changed as a result. But this is a costly proposition. The theatrical distribution gateway has always been a bottleneck, and marketing expenses have increased exponentially throughout the last decade. That's why it was cause for celebration at Miramax in July 2000 when *Scary Movie* had a $42.3 million opening weekend. If you haven't abandoned your core business, that pays for a lot of *Station Agent*s and maybe an army of Confederate soldiers running around in Romania giving *Cold Mountain* that extra authenticity.

So many choices. So many devoted screens. So many pages of ads in the papers. People often claim that theatrical releasing is a loss leader. Most of these films quickly fall by the wayside and are nearly forgotten outside the film community because the specialized audience is exceedingly finite and—despite wishful thinking—not really getting any larger. It's getting older and maybe even a little less smart. Theoretically, word-of-mouth had weeks and weeks to build in days of yore (1981), when *My Dinner with Andre* could gradually find its audience. Back then, there weren't sixteen films lined up right behind it.

It's a bitter pill to swallow, but the competition is more intramural than indie David vs. studio Goliath. It's a hit-driven, cannibalistic, opening-weekend business mirroring the Hollywood philosophy. Miramax blazed the trail. Others with deep pockets followed. Now, the smartest distributors with far less capital squeeze through the cracks. Nancy Gerstman and Emily Russo at Zeitgeist Pictures garner a Best Foreign Film Oscar for the crowd-pleaser *Nowhere in Africa* and nurture it all the way to a $6 million box office. Eamonn Bowles, with his one-man band at Magnolia Pictures, pushes all the right buttons on the difficult doc *Capturing the Friedmans*, just as he'd done at The Shooting Gallery for the major sleeper hit *Croupier*.

And just where does this leave the true down & dirty, up-from-the-bootstraps first-timers that populate *Spike, Mike, Slackers & Dykes*? Basically they're in a pretty tough spot due to their overpopulation. The most common outcry is directed at the distribution bottleneck, which backs up all the way to key film festivals. Even Sundance, "our" debutante ball, fills many, many slots in the line-up with name-brand merchandise: Tom DiCillo returns with his fifth straight film, or Christina Ricci slums in a small movie, or iconoclastic uber-producer Christine Vachon has several new features ready to premiere. Sundance always carefully tallies and proudly touts the new filmmakers. Yet it's really not the same to be a "first time" director anymore if you've got Holly Hunter, Katie Holmes or Patricia Clarkson in your cast. *Clerks* wouldn't be *Clerks* if it starred Mark Ruffalo and Macaulay Culkin.

Of course it's never completely hopeless, since the established media machine requires that complete unknowns bubble up from the depths—the next Neil LaBute, Todd Solondz, Ed Burns, or Kevin Smith. But there's only so much room at the inn. Clearly the odds of finding distribution greatly increase with a high-profile, award-winning festival run.

It's been years now since distributors have been ready, willing or able to deal with the volume of over-the-transom submissions. And since I watched thousands of undistributed films in my former career, I can't fault them too much. They can sap your life force faster than an anthrax spore. On the other hand, in a film democracy, why would anyone want to give Sundance dictatorial power?

How are the last decade all-stars doing? Linklater linked arms and rocked out with legendary producer Scott Rudin, as described above, after struggling to make two exceptional films that nobody saw: the digital *Tape* and the animated *Waking Life*. The Austin film production scene has grown by leaps and bounds from the roots he laid down. And don't blame him for the locally shot *Texas Chain Saw Massacre* remake.

Kevin Smith, who will reappear for a Last Word with me at the end of this new edition, continued to build a major body of work as the New Jersey/Jay & Silent Bob trilogy grew to five feature films. He sells a lot of action figures too. Now the excellent, more adult *Jersey Girl* is on the runway, awaiting that perfect release date when the Bennifer backlash has subsided. (Fiji is so ready.) Ben and J. Lo generated great publicity while he was shooting the film in 2002. Now the worm has turned, big time, due to the media over-saturation that this country has perfected.

If you start with *Joe's Bed Stuy Barbershop*, Spike Lee has reached the two-decade mark in his prolific, provocative career. He's started to mix in fascinating documentaries with his features. He actually had his biggest box office success in years with *The Original Kings of Comedy*. His advertising, speaking, media empire is firing on all cylinders. But as with the white Spike Lee, Woody Allen, movie production money can be a little hard to come by because crowds don't line up for his films. Pathe, in conjunction with Tom Bernard and Michael Barker at Sony Pictures Classics, funded his modest current project *She Hate Me*. Here's a director who has never backed down from a challenge, or stopped challenging his audience. After two failed projects, Spike wants nothing whatsoever to do with Miramax.

All of which brings us to the future president of the United States, at least in his own mind, Michael Moore. Fact: He made the most successful documentary, *Bowling for Columbine*, in history, not counting *Jackass*. Fact: Counting *Jackass*, he made the second most successful documentary of the last year. Fact: He wrote the most successful nonfiction bestseller, *Stupid White Men*, of the last two years. Fact: He campaigned for Ralph Nader, a former nemesis, in the 2000 election. Fact: He indirectly helped George Bush win. Fact: If Bush and his Republican cronies hadn't won, there would have been no *Stupid White Men* or *Bowling for Columbine.* Fact: Michael Moore owes everything to "W." In these pages, much to his chagrin, I wrote, "[H]e is not defined first and foremost as a filmmaker." He is first and foremost a persona. Is he an effective voice from the left? I often hear people say "better him than nobody." I say better him than Al Franken.

Not a word has been changed in the following text from page 1 to page 337. Any adjustments and corrections that needed to be rendered from the hardcover edition already appear in the original paperback and are retained here. The coda from that edition has been dropped to clear out some more room for The Last Word, an extension of the Kevin Smith/John Pierson no-holds-barred conversational collaboration. So all acknowledgments, new and old, appear right here.

This book wouldn't exist without Janet Pierson. I know I already dedicated it to her, but that's still not enough. She lived it with me, she heard it from me, and she helped me get it on paper. Plus she was willing to go to Fiji.

Susan Dalsimer, an invaluable editor, set me on the right path at Miramax Books in 1995. She had a young assistant named Kristin Powers. Kristin has been at Miramax Books ever since, and was instrumental in shepherding this new edition. Donna Daniels would not take no for an answer during months of publicity, when all my dreams of being treated like a real writer came true.

Then, in the end, there's always Harvey Weinstein. He did not tamper with one critical word in the original book even as he was quoted in the *New York Observer* saying, "John spares no one, including us. He is an equal opportunity killer." I'm still trying to call 'em how I see 'em. Let's hope he takes it all in stride again. I wouldn't have had nearly as much fun in the last fifteen years without him.

For more information about Fiji or Split Screen, please visit our Web site: www.grainypictures.com.

INTRODUCTION TO THE ORIGINAL EDITION: STRANGER THAN FICTION

A busybody neighbor of mine on MacDougal Alley once went to see *The Thin Blue Line* just to report back to the block that I had nothing to do with it. Not only is my name not found above the title, it's never been anywhere in the head credits. Sometimes if you sit patiently to the very end of the end credits you just might find sketchy evidence in the alphabetical thank-yous that I exist. And that's as it should be.

My local Hudson Valley art exhibitor once introduced me as a "bag man" for independent movies. Now I've been called a lot of peculiar things in print—guru, dealmeister, scout, shaman, veteran angel, ferret, Johnny Appleseed, kingmaker, a filmmaker's best friend, icon—almost always preceded by the adjective "indie." I think of myself as a film lover who got married in a theater while showing the wedding guests a movie. But "bag man?" I guess I forgot about the secret cash deliveries to the set in the middle of the night.

I did write Spike Lee a check for $10,000 to finish *She's Gotta Have It*, close a $3 million deal with a major studio for Michael Moore's documentary *Roger & Me*, help make *Slacker* a household word, unleash

Quick Stop clerks and fishy lesbians on screens all over the world, and take fifteen films to the almighty Sundance Film Festival. But I doubt that you know my name.

This book is really about the two dozen first-time filmmakers I've helped make a name for themselves, and a hundred others whose success stories I've observed at close quarters, and a thousand more whose work may not have ever gotten too far beyond the VCR in my office. This is their story, warts and all.

But it's also my story, one pilgrim's progress from 1984's *Stranger Than Paradise*, a film that pushed many new directors into production, to 1994's *Pulp Fiction*. These two films frame a remarkable decade for the American independent low-budget film, a decade whose third benchmark, Steven Soderbergh's 1989 debut, *sex, lies, and videotape*, neatly divides things right down the middle. His debut radically and demonstrably changed the business for all newcomers. Where it had been the exception for a first timer to have follow-up opportunities, it became the rule for the door to swing wide open for anyone who made the smallest splash in places like Sundance.

Kevin Smith made a big splash with *Clerks* and a bit of a belly flop with his second studio feature, *Mallrats*. At the tender age of twenty-four, he is the voice of "the filmmaker" throughout this text. His forebears provided the dance steps, but he still has his own distinct sense of rhythm. After spending hour upon hour talking with him and enjoying every minute of it, I invited him to collaborate on audiotape between Thanksgiving 1994 and Easter 1995. He would mock me if I described him with phony catchphrases like "generational spokesperson" or "postmodern totem" of indie filmmaking. But he *is* very young, although wise for his years, in an era where the median age for new videophile filmmakers keeps dropping all the time. (How young? I recently got a handwritten note on a work sample that said, "My mom urged me to contact you.") And he did emerge at the tail end of this decade with an acute awareness of his predecessors. Seeing *Slacker* on the day he turned twenty-one changed his world.

This book is not a how to, it's a how come. Even having said that, I don't necessarily have all the answers. When avant-garde filmmaking giant Stan Brakhage taught at NYU in the summer of 1975, I loved to hear him talk although I often felt befuddled. Luckily I didn't interrupt his obscure flow. One day a foolish film student broke in with a question and Brakhage responded cryptically with one of his trademark 2000 Year Old Man-style etymologies. He pointed out that the roots of the word "question" were "quest" and "shun." Consequently, he suggested, if you ask one, you're shunning the quest—not to mention bugging him. Unlike the impatient Mr. Brakhage, I welcome queries, disagreements, and, above all else, dialogue.

Leaders

JOHN PIERSON: In *Clerks*, you have an end credit thanking Spike Lee, Jim Jarmusch, Rick Linklater, and Hal Hartley for "leading the way." The other day you described yourself as a "movie brat." Michael Moore used to say that he would see every damn movie that was released except for Ninjas and Neil Simon. You seemed to use the expression to mean someone who is really a constant, frequent viewer of *Hollywood* films.

KEVIN SMITH: That's my understanding. First off the connotation really is on "brat" because that's what I did as a kid. All I did was watch studio movies. At first, it sprang mostly from my father. It wasn't until I became "a man," you know, in my twenties, or nineteen, somewhere along that line, that I started getting inclinations toward the independent field. So "movie brat" to me has more emphasis on the brat part because I was younger. I don't think I was trying to learn anything. Let's turn it around. Do you consider yourself a movie brat?

JP: Well, I certainly wasn't a mass-movie consumer. When I had my religious experience it was partly triggered by a fantastic show on PBS called *Film Odyssey* when I was in high school. I saw things like *The Seven Samurai*, *L'Avventura*, Ingmar Bergman. I guess I was more of an art-film brat. I became a consumer of specific directors, specific national cinemas, and smart Hollywood movies, of which there were plenty in the seventies. I guess *The New Yorker*'s Pauline Kael led the way for me.

KS: One person that mentioned being left out of the *Clerks* end credits was Martin Scorsese. When I sat down with Illeana Douglas, I said, "Did he see it? Did the man see it?" and she said, "Yes, we watched it on video," which means it must have been the old crappy video copy but they watched it nonetheless. And I'm like, "What'd he say? What'd he say?" She answered, "Well, he laughed, and he liked it, but at the end when you mention those four names and thank them 'for leading the way,' he said 'Oh, *they* led the way.' "

JP: Scorsese's been very generous in crediting John Cassavetes as *his* leader. Hey, my theory is we're living in a world of ten-year cycles.

KS: Sorry, Martin, you just missed the cutoff.

A Quick and Slanted Pre-1984 History

Moviegoing was a very rare occurrence in my childhood home. That's why I vividly recall the Friday night when I slept over at my best friend's house, and his older brother took us to see not one but *two* films. The first was the briny adventure saga *The Vikings* with Kirk Douglas, and the second was the racy circus melodrama *Trapeze* with Burt Lancaster and the voluptuous Gina Lollobrigida. Two decades later, I was programming two films a day three times a week to make up for the lost early years.

In the summer of 1981, the venue was the 102-seat Harold Clurman Theater on Manhattan's wild West 42nd Street, on a rehabilitated block called Theater Row. We regularly crammed 120 customers into every nook and cranny with cavalier disregard for any fire regulations. Our gang of seven film "professionals," collectively known as Roadmovies, was having a rocking good time. We programmed all of our favorite rock 'n' roll movies, both the great ones and the cheesy ones. Instead of Gina L., we had the equally well-endowed Jayne Mansfield in the ultimate guilty pleasure, *The Girl Can't Help It*. It was a time of devil-may-care innocence, and very few working filmmakers.

One hot afternoon, Amos Poe walked into the Clurman's projection booth as I was rewinding a reel of *Jimi Plays Berkeley*. At that moment, Amos was probably the most notable independent feature filmmaker in New York City with several underground features under his belt. He wore his Jean-Luc Godard and Andy Warhol influences on his sleeve. His latest film, *Subway Riders*, starring John Lurie, had been a triumph at the Berlin Film Festival earlier in the year. We had just shown his seminal 1977 punk rock documentary *Blank Generation*, as part of a comprehensive Rock 'n' Repertory program. Amos had persuaded one of my partners to sponsor the idea of having a complete retrospective of his other films. He explained that he didn't just want to make movies in New York; he wanted to make a *movement* in New York like the French New Wave—a whole "film generation" of cheap, 16mm, black-and-white features. Amos was definitely ahead of his time. Ten independent features a year then has turned into four hundred a year now. It fell to me to let him down easy by explaining how we were trying to make a buck on a short-term lease where every day's grosses counted. I was relieved that he took the rejection well, but then he threw me when he asked, "Well, if you're not going to show my films, could I be an usher?"

Since the Lumières and Thomas Edison invented moving pictures at the end of the nineteenth century, the American cinema has gone through all kinds of trends and cycles involving new independent talent. Even D. W. Griffith had his own studio on 14th Street in New York City and shot his innovative two reelers all over town before he made his epic features. Why do I know this? I'm a member of the art-film brat generation. We're not the movie brats who ended up redefining Hollywood in the seventies with their wide multiplex releases. And we're not the multibrats who saw those films when they were kids and are crowding all around the edge of Hollywood in the nineties. We're the tweeners, the last generation to have a keen interest in our worldwide, century-long film history. A distributor like Harvey Weinstein at Miramax, a festival director like Geoff Gilmore at Sundance, an exhibitor like Scott Dinger at the Dobie in Austin, Texas, or a journalist like J. Hoberman at the *Village Voice*—all art-film brats.

During a semester at Yale in 1972, where I spent my evenings hopping from one film society to another seeing self-invented double bills of Fritz Lang's *You Only Live Once* and 007 in *You Only Live Twice*, I accidentally learned of the existence of "film schools" and the die was cast. I went to NYU in 1974 after the Two Martys Era (Scorsese to Brest) but before the later arrival of Jim Jarmusch, Spike Lee, Joel Coen, Susan Seidelman, et al. In my time, fewer people graduated from film programs and not all of us wanted to make our own movies. For one thing, there weren't enough successful role models yet and it seemed almost futile. Equally important, the studios were at a creative peak—not exactly the lowest common denominator mentality of today, which is far more likely to foment rebellion.

It's well documented that the period in Hollywood from 1969's *Easy Rider* to the mid-seventies was a free-swinging, artistically inspired renaissance. A number of raw-edged films really pushed the envelope and still managed to fare quite well commercially. Sam Peckinpah's *The Wild Bunch* pushed the boundaries on screen violence in a far more substantial way than *Pulp Fiction* would a quarter century later. Melvin Van Peebles gave the world a black stud hero who fathered the blaxploitation movement in *Sweet Sweetback's Baadasssss Song*. Robert Altman was turning out terrific films, sometimes two per year, culminating in *Nashville*. Many directors learned the ropes under the crank-'em-out tutelage of exploitation king Roger Corman. Graduates like Bob Rafelson and Jack Nicholson teamed up for films like *Five Easy Pieces*, while Peter Bogdanovich left his film criticism behind to make *The Last Picture Show*. I cut out of a high school Broadway field trip to see the Bogdanovich film the day it opened on Manhattan's East Side, then went downtown to the Elgin to see the entire François Truffaut/Antoine Doinel trilogy. My understanding teacher looked the other way.

The seventies' movie brats like George Lucas, Steven Spielberg, and Francis Ford Coppola might have started small. (Please see the superb Michael Pye/Lynda Myles book, *The Movie Brats*.) However, they quickly found themselves creating the blockbusters that permanently changed the studio system. Coppola led the way with *The Godfather*, then reached back to help Lucas get over with *American Graffiti*. For the ultimate New York filmmaker, Martin Scorsese, the independent underpinnings of his breakthrough *Mean Streets* carried through masterworks like *Taxi Driver* and *Raging Bull*. His fellow brats' leaps from *Sugarland Express* to *Jaws* or *THX 1138* to *Star Wars* were a bit more disjunctive and pointed the studios in the ultimately disastrous direction of sequels and wider and wider openings.

Film school did not make me a director. I tried being a documentarian for a brief spell after graduating at the end of 1976, probably feeling encouraged by the Library of Congress's selection of a blues videotape I produced for its Folk Archive. I teamed up with a co-producer to profile a legendary physicist (not Stephen Hawking) who lived in a Westchester suburb. We filmed hours of precious interview material in his lovely yard on a peaceful Saturday afternoon. Having brought the wrong omnidirectional microphone, I should have known that planes landing at LaGuardia, lawn mowers buzzing, and birds chirping might provide a deafening ambience. After transcribing an hour of the interview two days later, I retired as a filmmaker.

Needing a real job, I answered an ad in *The New York Times* for an Upper West Side "art film distributor" with "German films." The office was an apartment on 72nd Street off Broadway, the owner was a young Cuban anti-Castro emigré named Ray Blanco, the German films were mainly by Wim Wenders, and the company was first called A.J. Bauer, then Bauer International since it seemed more impressive. The name, it turned out, had been selected out of a phone book because it sounded German. Blanco, like many others in the seventies, took his inspiration from John Cassavetes even if he looked to Europe for his product.

With his 1960 feature *Shadows,* Cassavetes is often credited as the inventor of the American independent cinema. Martin Scorsese has made it a point all along to testify that it was Cassavetes who made it possible for him to think that *he* could actually make a movie. Cassavetes' insistence on doing his own movies his own way with an ensemble group of actors was very instructive. Of course he did have the distinct advantage of being able to pick up substantial paychecks as a Hollywood actor to fund his personal work. Those roles ranged from the ridiculous (*The Dirty Dozen*) to the sublime (*Rosemary's Baby*). Early on, after seeing *Boxcar Bertha*, Cassavetes had warned Scorsese to escape the Corman trap and make a personal film. That advice spawned *Mean Streets* in 1973, a year before Cassavetes found his largest audience as an off-Hollywood director with the release of *A Woman under the Influence.* Perhaps it's Scorsese's oft stated admiration for John Cassavetes along with his own gritty, urban environment that kept him rooted as his peers soared into outer space.

Cassavetes cast an even longer shadow over future distributors. In a move that's not entirely unfamiliar today, Paramount recruited Cassavetes to make inexpensive, high-quality studio pictures after the success of the low-budget *Shadows*. He did one for them that they disowned (*Too Late Blues*), and another for United Artists that was drastically recut (*A Child Is Waiting*). Consequently he became a bigger hero by setting up a distribution company, Faces Films, to own his films and *control* how they were released and shown. (Jim Jarmusch owns his copyrights and Spike Lee owns half of Fort Greene, Brooklyn, with his burgeoning 40 Acres and a Mule Filmworks, but neither one self-distributes.) Both Jeff Lipsky and Ira Deutchman entered the film distribution business through their involvement with the 1974 Faces release of *A Woman under the Influence*. Over the next twenty years, the two of them would be intimately involved in the release of literally hundreds of independent films at ten different distributors.

Ironically, Cassavetes' iron control of his own rights provides a crucial explanation for his waning influence on filmmakers in more recent times. The films were simply hard to see before and after his death. Theatrical exhibition consisted of the very occasional career retrospectives at places like the 1989 Sundance Film Festival. Astonishingly, until early 1994 the titles were completely unavailable on video. This was a difficult proposition for the typical twenty-three-year-old filmmaker who eats tape for breakfast. Admittedly the somewhat older Alexandre Rockwell did get a great *In the Soup* performance out of Cassevettes mainstay Seymour Cassel. The Cassavetes influence is primarily available as an echo that resonates beautifully in Scorsese's work but sounds clamorous via Henry Jaglom (who does in fact self-distribute).

Bauer tried to wedge its way into the expanding ranks of indie distributors, among them New Line Cinema. In the years after 1969, several key New York distributors had set up shop in order to take advantage of the peak baby-boom college audience, which ravenously consumed specialized movies both in theaters and on campus. New Line started in a fifth-floor walk-up apartment with one title, Godard's *Sympathy for the Devil*, which they sold as a Rolling Stones concert film, and kept rolling with the marijuana goof *Reefer Madness*. The moment when a 300-pound transvestite ate an all-too-real dog turd on camera back in 1972 really put New Line on the map. Baltimore's baron of bad taste John Waters devised this ultimate gross-out climax for *Pink Flamingos* and the rest was midnight-movie history.

The seventies did have genuine cult movies that played midnights before the advent of *The Rocky Horror Picture Show*, and Waters was responsible for several of them. Long before Freddy Krueger, Ninjas, or Ted Turner arrived on the New Line scene, Waters helped launch founder Bob Shaye's quarter-century run as the head of the most successful independent distributor. The Waters combination of amateurish performance, primitive visual style, and rampant grotesquerie was almost innocent. Waters probably set more independent standards than anyone would think. He had an attitude/vision, which he got on screen through primitive means with virtually no money by assembling a support group in his home town and capitalizing on their meager talents through a combination of charm and shock value. Baltimore's my home town too!

Although Bob Shaye's public-domain research (*Reefer Madness* had no copyright protection) and keen grasp of cultish college film society preferences served him well in his company's early days, it was the maniacal Don Rugoff who was on top of the theatrical heap. Unlike Shaye, Rugoff purveyed quality as the not-so-benevolent despot of Cinema 5, a New York exhibitor that segued into distribution with high-impact results. Rugoff's integration of distribution and exhibition was invaluable in an era when the Bloomingdale's Third Avenue cluster of theaters were dominant. (Before Reagan-era deregulation, the consent decree still prevented major studios from owning theaters.) Rugoff's key showcases, Cinema 1 and Cinema 2 launched Cinema 5 titles like *Z, Seven Beauties, Swept Away, Harlan County, U.S.A., Putney Swope, Monty Python and the Holy Grail, Scenes from a Marriage*, and *The Man Who Fell to Earth*. Those theaters also played many classics that Cinema 5 didn't distribute itself, such as *A Clockwork Orange, The Conformist*, and *Mean Streets*. On Scorsese's opening day, there was an unofficial holiday at NYU Film School celebrating its first successful graduate. Rookies like Ira Deutchman stepped into Cinema 5 jobs where they had to learn fast, making things up along the way. They also got a ringside seat to Rugoff's self-destruction. Even with the cautious voice of even-keeled key booker Fran Spielman in his ear, he was one of the first casualties of uncontrolled overspending . . . although certainly not the last.

Dan Talbot of the smaller New Yorker Films had a set-up similar to Cinema 5, but avoided the Rugoff hubris. Dan owned and programmed the New Yorker Theater on Broadway at 88th Street on the Upper West

Side. Throughout the sixties and into the seventies, it was a hub of foreign, independent, art, and repertory film activity. After showing Bertolucci's *Before the Revolution*, Talbot became its distributor by necessity because no one else would. Thus began New Yorker Films distribution, perhaps one of the *highest* quality libraries ever assembled with the work of Fassbinder, Ozu, Bresson, Herzog, Sembène, and a host of the greatest international directors. Jeff Lipksy became sales head at New Yorker Films after working for Cassavetes, as the stakes were getting higher and Rugoff was about to crash and burn. Between Faces Films and New Yorker Films, Lipsky made a stop to help producer Ray Silver and writer/director Joan Micklin Silver self-distribute *Hester Street* with profitable results. (Sadly, Joan, Claudia Weill [*Girlfriends*], and Lee Grant were just about the only American female directors in the seventies.) When Dan Talbot sold the New Yorker Theater, he opened Cinema Studio 1 and 2 about twenty blocks south. Fassbinder's *The Marriage of Maria Braun* played there for an entire year in 1978, grossing about $700,000 on one screen.

The New German Cinema was at its peak in the late seventies. New Line, Cinema 5, and New Yorker had all jockeyed for R. W. Fassbinder and Werner Herzog titles, but the six Wim Wenders features through 1976's *Kings of the Road* had fallen through the cracks. Bauer International, my first employer, grabbed them for a song. The mighty Bauer was in a state of failing almost from the moment it was founded, but that didn't stop its principals from adopting the distributor/exhibitor model. In 1977, we opened the Jean Renoir Cinema in the Actor's Playhouse Theater just below Sheridan Square. Renoir, who was still alive, granted permission to use his name in a lovely letter that was posted in a showcase in the lobby. When Ray Blanco's mom came home from her sweatshop job around 5:00 p.m. each day and started frying bananas while Sparky the chihuahua barked frantically, that was the signal to go downtown and open the theater. So for about $75 a week (a living wage in NYC then) I got to learn hands-on distribution by day and exhibition by night.

There were two major hurdles to overcome in that distribution era. First of all, there was no overnight delivery for shipping prints. Federal Express was only a dream. In 1978 you had to hand deliver cargo to the airport. Secondly, cash flow was exceedingly tight, so Bauer often put new titles in its catalogue without having the money to strike even one print. If enough exhibitors booked it and paid an advance the lab order went in. Given this high-wire act, we probably should have moved the office to Kennedy Airport.

On the exhibition side, there were some real triumphs at the theater, with Wenders's *Alice in the Cities* and several unreleased Mexican films by Luis Buñuel. One of these Buñuels, *Illusion Travels by Streetcar*, was about ten minutes from the end of a sold-out final show of the night when the projection lamp blew and, unforgivably, there was no spare on hand. We couldn't refund any money because our employers had been in earlier to stuff all the evening's cash into their jean pockets and walk out. They returned during the breakdown, but the cash was long gone. I panicked. But Blanco's partner actually stood on stage, calmly explained why it was impossible to resume, described the action in the film's last ten minutes, and offered passes to come back another time. No one grumbled; fewer than half a dozen customers took passes. I immediately began to understand that it really is the bold who shall inherit the earth. One night the theater's ceiling collapsed and there was no recourse. We shut down.

My fellow employees at Bauer included Donna Gigliotti, who became Scorsese's assistant, then teamed up with Tom Bernard and Michael Barker first at United Artists Classics and then at Orion Classics. Tom Prassis trained me. He was another Cassavetes disciple who later ran Wenders's distribution outfit, Gray City Films. As Bauer started moving around to evade creditors, I made a grab for the brass ring by offering to drive Wenders cross-country on his spring 1978 college/museum tour just before he signed up to make *Hammett* for Coppola's Zoetrope.

New Yorker had released *The American Friend* the previous fall, and it made Wenders a much bigger name. I was trying to hitch my wagon to his star as we hopscotched around the Midwest. In Pittsburgh, we argued about Chuck Berry lyrics. In Ann Arbor, Wim bought a box of Kinks LPs, and one of our on-campus hosts was future ace entertainment attorney John Sloss. In Chicago, Wim claimed that the Rolling Stones stole the song "No Expectations" from him, and Scott Levine, who became East Coast publicity head for Fox, took us to Junior Wells's South Side blues bar. In Minneapolis, where Al Milgrom runs the University Film Society to this day, I was left waiting while Al dined alone with Wim. I've known these characters as they've plugged away through the years, more art-film brats.

I couldn't get to second base with Wim. In the car, he would only look up from his reading to ask me to find a Kinks song on the radio. I was ready for in-depth discussions about those Van Morrison essays he'd written years earlier. I'd given him my Blind Willie Johnson slide guitar records hoping to get involved with *Hammett* in some capacity, all to no avail. During a hearty truck-stop breakfast one morning, he looked at my plate and asked, "What does the sausage have to do with the pancake?" He stayed in America long enough to learn, since *Hammett* was eventually four years in the making. I followed Wim to San Francisco where, unbeknownst to me, my future wife was heading the Canyon Cinema distribution co-op and unsuccessfully angling for a job on *Hammett* herself. I bailed out after about a month and drove back to New York fast. Wenders later wound up being a key link in the chain that led to *Stranger Than Paradise.*

I answered another newspaper ad, this time in the *Village Voice*, and found myself helping Sam Kitt organize an event called American Misfits. It was the first American independent film festival. Kitt made a crucial adjustment in his event's title to send out more positive psychological vibes—American Mavericks. Sam had been involved with a filmmaking commune that was trying to complete a touchy/feely feature called *Getting Together.* When funds ran out, they decided to make a quick killing with a *Shampoo* porn parody called *Blow Dry* which the *New York Daily News* would advertise only under the title *Low Dry.* In all this mayhem, his partners acquired a huge old Second Avenue Yiddish theater and rechristened it Entermedia (it's now the Village East). As you might guess, their definition of independent encompassed many genres. In the eclectic lineup, documentarian Warrington Hudlin (who later produced *House Party* and *Boomerang* for his brother Reggie) was side-by-side with Les Blank, Mark Rappaport with Henry Jaglom, the Maysles with George Romero. Once again as associate director I had to do a little bit of everything including changing the Entermedia Theater's ancient marquee on a precarious ladder in the dead of winter. Attendance and media attention were great. John Carpenter had just revitalized the horror genre with *Halloween.* We had a sellout for his first feature, a sci-fi parody called *Dark Star.* One film we did not include was Abel Ferrara's first feature *Driller Killer*, which was shooting right around the corner.

Although you could count total new production on the fingers of two hands, 1979 was a watershed for the infrastructure. The year started with the renamed American Mavericks in January. By early 1980, the Independent Feature Project (IFP), American Playhouse, and First Run Features had all been founded. The IFP grew out of Sandra Schulberg's American Independent sidebar at September's New York Film Festival, which included a mix (à la Mavericks) of that year's serious output and a few historical titles. In fact, Sandra had suggested earlier that Sam Kitt should fold his event into hers. Sandra's most notable new films were John Hanson and Rob Nilsson's *Northern Lights* (which she produced) and Victor Nunez's *Gal Young Un*. First Run Features started as a distribution collective specifically for feature-length American indies, four of the originals being *Northern Lights, Gal Young Un,* Barry Brown and Glen Silber's *The War at Home,* and Maxi Cohen and Joel Gold's *Joe & Maxi*. PBS started funding American Playhouse, which would back more indie features over the next fifteen years than any other source. And the Miramax of its day, United Artists Classics, came into being.

For us art-film brats, it just seemed like it was important to find ways to support the movies we loved. Rugoff and Talbot in New York and Mel Novikoff in the Bay Area were elder statesman, not young turks. In an unusual turnabout, a bunch of fresh-out-of-school types went to work for them and then quickly came to dominate the system in the early eighties, and maintained their power into the mid-nineties. As the opportunities for becoming a filmmaker grew stronger throughout the decade, the instinctual movement toward distribution and exhibition faded away.

I discovered over the next few years that my peer group included people like Tom Bernard and Michael Barker, both of whom worked at Films, Inc. Tom, who got off on films like Frank Zappa's *200 Motels,* quickly became a sales executive. Michael started as a lowly billing clerk. His legacy, once he moved up and out, was a quote from Nicholas Ray's moody noir *In a Lonely Place* that Michael wrote on the wall: "I was born when she kissed me. I died when she left me. I lived for a few weeks while she loved me." Bingham Ray managed the Carnegie Hall and Bleecker Street Cinemas. (He's no relation, but he did name his son Nick.) These two repertory houses along with the Elgin and Thalia (earlier), Regency and Metro (later) were irreplaceable gathering spots for cineastes in the "dark" days before home video. The convivial, collective atmosphere and chance to see noir pairings of *Screaming Mimi* and *Bedlam* or new prints of films like Howard Hawks's *Rio Bravo* made late-seventies pilgrimages to those theaters one of the brightest experiences I can remember. As a manager, Bingham had to strive to maintain that atmosphere. One Saturday at the Bleecker, he opened the doors at noon for a day-long Akira Kurosawa/Toshiro Mifune double bill featuring a "new" print of *Yojimbo*. Every seat was filled. The "new" print was gorgeous—and dubbed! There was a near riot. Audiences were serious about these things. Bingham wasn't too happy himself when his future wife came to see *Lolita* at the Carnegie and just happened to sit next to the theater's most notorious pervert. He flashed, and Bingham ran him out of the building.

Ben Barenholtz, who later helped discover Joel and Ethan Coen, operated the legendary Elgin Theater in Chelsea, birthplace of the midnight movie—most notably *El Topo* and *Pink Flamingos*. It was a thrill to be there for those discoveries, but it was even better to have a yearly opportunity (normally in February) to see the complete silent works of Buster Keaton, the greatest and most original filmmaker in history. Ben didn't become a distributor/exhibitor. He started Libra Films after his theater's demise. The Elgin's 1978 closing was almost like a canary in the coal mine given the eventual fate of all rep houses as a genuine endangered species. After directing American Mavericks, Sam Kitt worked with Ben Barenholtz at Libra, noted for its release of David Lynch's *Eraserhead* and John Sayles's *The Return of the Secaucus Seven*. Sam also joined up with a seven-person company we formed to find a movie theater and program it *our* way. Five of us had met in film school. This collective was called Roadmovies in honor of Wenders's German production company, to celebrate a genre we loved, *and* because we had no home.

In 1981, we settled back into the Clurman, having failed to take over the legendary, run-down Thalia on upper Broadway. That deal collapsed when a key investor rejected an operating budget because I had failed to leave a sufficient contingency for broken flushometers. The truth is I'd never even heard of a flushometer, although I think it's found on a urinal. It was back to the Clurman for the third consecutive summer. This was already my third exhibition venue following the Jean Renoir Cinema and Entermedia Theater. As a fringe operation, our programs steered clear of the official classics and featured newly invented genres like Hard Boiled Hollywood and Outlaw Cinema with titles like Russ Meyer's *Faster Pussycat! Kill! Kill!* We highlighted the complete works of directors like Brian De Palma and George Romero. It was a great treat the night that Duane Jones came downstairs from his Black Theater Alliance office and slipped quietly into the back of the theater to watch himself fend off the zombies only to be killed by a white cop in the always creepy late-sixties landmark *Night of the Living Dead.*

When Amos Poe came in to interview for his career retrospective/ushering job, I was in the midst of repertory heaven. Even ushering at the Clurman could be great fun. You got to throw out kids who lit sparklers in the back row on the Fourth of July when they realized that the Rolling Stones weren't going to get past the first eight notes of the title song in Godard's *Sympathy for the Devil.* And of course, Screamin' Jay Hawkins might come in with his walking stick and Monster Movie Club ID card to watch himself rise out of the coffin in *American Hot Wax.* Unfortunately for Amos, the board members of our corporation already held all those desirable in-theater jobs.

Throughout the period from 1980 to 1983 the pace really picked up. United Artists Classics led the way as Tom Bernard, Michael Barker, Ira Deutchman, Donna Gigliotti, Linda Beath, and Sam Irvin (the last two later of Spectrafilm) all wound up working together. The company started with Truffaut's *The Last Metro,* peaked with *Diva,* and more or less ended with Diane Kurys's *Entre Nous,* demonstrating its emphasis on foreign-language films, which were at a peak in quality and popularity. The UA Classics executive finishing school eventually spun off Cinecom, Orion Classics, and Spectrafilm, while other studios like Fox and Universal formed their own classics divisions so they wouldn't feel left out. As this all happened, a handful of scattershot successes from the American independent ranks broke out. In 1981 New Yorker had *My Dinner with Andre* (if Louis Malle counts) and Wayne Wang's $20,000 debut *Chan Is Missing.* In 1982 New Line acquired Susan Seidelman's *Smithereens* after its surprise selection at Cannes, Cinecom released Paul Bartel's *Eating Raoul,* and First Run had the first-ever hip-hop feature with Charlie Ahearn's *Wild Style.* In 1983 UA Classics released Sayles's second feature *Lianna;* Cinecom, which always made a point of focusing on America indies, had a hit with Gregory Nava's *El Norte;* and Cinevista let the truly bizarre *Liquid Sky* play for months on end in the Village at the Waverly—a midnight show that played all day.

There was no particular pattern or common thread to these films. Wang and Seidelman had no money and were pretty light on story too.

Nava and Bartel were better financed, and far more script-driven. In fact the social realism of *El Norte* and outrageous comedy of *Eating Raoul* were almost mainstream. In the latter case, if you trace a line from John Waters through Bartel to Kevin Smith, Bartel is clearly the most tasteful. *My Dinner with Andre* was adapted from a play featuring Andre Gregory and Wallace Shawn and directed by a Frenchman. It grossed nearly $5 million, proving a point that many young filmmakers would discover on their own; you can have two characters in one room talking for ninety minutes if you have the right dialogue and actors. The invaluable (if a bit outdated) *Off-Hollywood,* written by David Rosen with Peter Hamilton, is an excellent source for case studies of many of these earlier films. And John Sayles plays a major role in that book.

Bridging three decades, John Sayles remains a much admired modern-day maverick. Like Cassavetes, he also serves the Hollywood beast—but, rather than as an actor, by writing scripts for hire (first for Roger Corman). This money fueled his own work outside the system. His first success, 1980's *Secaucus Seven,* was also the first indie feature to make serious hay out of promoting the low, low budget—$60,000! He's made nine features in the fifteen years since and will undoubtedly continue to do more of the same. Having started as a writer, he's taught himself, slowly but surely, the elements of visual style, although it still seems secondary to his literary concerns. His name will come up repeatedly in subsequent chapters, but he's held up more as an example by disgruntled distributors than as a filmmaking influence or creative spark for young filmmakers. Independent distributors who see new talent moving on to make studio films for larger budgets just love to wag their fingers at those youngsters and bemoan the fact that none of them has the integrity and purity of John Sayles. Frankly, while many distributors praise him as a role model, they have suffered through marginal attendance when releasing his features. Since his scripts often start with an issue, it's appropriate that he's stuck to his guns. In their film *My Life's in Turnaround,* Don Ward and Eric Schaeffer had Sayles play hilariously against type as a sleazy Hollywood producer who knows "all the stories."

Like Cassavetes and Waters before him, Sayles really stands outside of any trends or cycles. I think of "The Three Johns" more as independent paradigms. Cassavetes had a shoestring budget phenomenon with his first feature, and was then courted, seduced, and screwed by the studios. He seized control of his own fate through self-distribution and had a major success with *A Woman under the Influence*, which helped unleash a whole new generation of distributors. In a strange mid-career turnaround, John Waters made his two most recent films at the studio level with stars Johnny Depp and Kathleen Turner. But from *Pink Flamingos* to *Hairspray*, he stuck with one distributor, New Line, and his production scale grew organically as Bob Shaye's New Line distribution and production machine grew. His vision stayed remarkably consistent. John Sayles has sold his films one by one resulting in his nine features being distributed by six different independents, one so-called mini-major (Orion), and one major. The major, Paramount, virtually abandoned *Baby It's You*, his third and least successful feature. None of the others have become crossover hits, although *The Secret of Roan Inish* topped out at a surprising $6 million domestic gross. But the critics always seize upon his latest release to declare him the ultimate independent for staying outside and steering his own course. Although a handful of other filmmakers, like Ed Burns, are quick to cite his influence, Sayles hasn't been a catalyst like Cassavetes, Scorsese, Spike Lee, or, in a decade-launching moment in 1984, Jim Jarmusch.

Entering the mid-eighties, there was one enormous change afoot in the business, which would enhance the prospects for all English-language features while fatally wounding specialized repertory exhibition. After a halting start, home video was exploding and the video distributors were beginning to throw cash around to acquire rights as if there were no tomorrow. The specialized *theatrical* audience didn't seem to differentiate that strongly between American, British, or foreign titles, but far more money became available to the former.

I was acting old-fashioned, looking backward instead of peering into the future during this turning of the tide. I did manage to show some foresight by getting married to the assistant director of the Film Forum, Janet Perlberg. I met her when I was house manager during Herzog and Fassbinder retrospectives; we both loved *Aguirre, the Wrath of God*. We courted during the premiere engagement of *The Atomic Cafe*, the hilarious antinuke send-up directed by Pierce and Kevin Rafferty with Jayne Loader. Before we said our vows in the theater, we showed Buster Keaton's *Seven Chances*, a classic silent comedy in which he's chased by five hundred angry brides.

I didn't want repertory to die. When I programmed the Bleecker, I would show the cutting edge Super-8 serials of Scott and Beth B one week, then reopen Godard's *Breathless* on the same day as the Richard Gere remake. It sold out for months and ran for half a year. Finally I joined the club at United Artists Classics in its waning days when Sam Kitt ran the division, and I became repertory sales head. When Classics was shuttered I landed on my feet at Films, Inc., where we hatched reissues of Warners cartoons, the four-hour *1900, Jules and Jim*, and the restored director's cut of Sergio Leone's *Once Upon a Time in the West.* In 1984, there were still eight thriving rep screens in NYC and nearly a hundred others around the country—places like the Brattle in Boston, the Castro in San Francisco, the NuArt in Los Angeles, and many others in the Landmark art-theater chain. Aspiring filmmakers were still hanging out at them all the time. But this late renaissance was to be short-lived as the modern era of first-run, off-Hollywood features was about to become dominant. As Landmark switched over, art-film brats who'd grown up attending classics on these screens soon saw their own films opening there.

Starting Point

KEVIN SMITH: So you had repertory theaters, Rick Linklater had his Austin Film Society. . .

JOHN PIERSON: And you invited people over to watch your thousand laser disks, so that was like your film club. Does that easy access change everything?

KS: If anything you can file it under "how to win friends and influence people." We were driving around on a *Mallrats* location scout with our producer Jim Jacks. Scott Mosier [*Clerks/Mallrats* co-producer] and I started doing lines from *Raising Arizona* to the point where Jim Jacks said, "My god, you guys really watched that movie . . . I forgot that line." And here's a guy that lives and breathes the Coen Brothers.

JP: What if you went back fifteen years ago and could only see the movies once when they came out?

KS: I guarantee you I'd still be quoting them, just not as well. Paraphrasing. Instead of the *Jaws* line, "We need a bigger boat" it'd be like "We need something bigger to catch that shark with" or something like that. The influence is still there.

JP: Have you ever in your life been to a rep house to see an old-fashioned double bill like we used to?

KS: Yeah, and it was the best double bill in the world, in Vancouver, during my only semester at film school. I tried to get everybody else to come.

JP: What were the films?

KS: *Slacker* and *Trust*.

JP: Once *Slacker* turned you into an aspiring filmmaker, you had a blizzard of catching up to do with earlier independents. So let's go back to that *Clerks* "Spike, Jarmusch, Hartley, and Linklater" end credit.

KS: *Slacker* is the movie where I want to be a filmmaker and realize "I can do this." Jarmusch's *Stranger Than Paradise* is "This is what it's going to look like, I can pull this style off visually." *Trust* and *Unbelievable Truth* are the movies where I say, "This is my dialogue model." Hartley's a guy that's playing with dialogue and his audience doesn't seem to mind. And that just leaves Spike. He gets all the credit because *Do the Right Thing* was such an influential film. It's a very character-driven piece that takes place all in the span of one day, in one block. *Clerks*, it's a block of stores, but in *Do the Right Thing* it's a block. And there was the perfect model.

JP: Did you span the globe or stick to the Americans?

KS: I stuck to the Americans—with a Canadian or two like Atom Egoyan for good measure.

JP: Some critics like J. Hoberman have compared *Clerks* to early John Waters films. And you do have an "egg man" like his "egg lady" in *Pink Flamingos*.

KS: I've only seen later films—*Hairspray* and *Cry Baby*. What does his egg lady do?

JP: Sits around in a crib all day eating eggs and waiting for the egg delivery man. So how far back did you go?

KS: The earliest I go back is *She's Gotta Have It* and *Stranger Than Paradise*, in that order.

JP: Is it pretty much catch as catch can?

KS: Yeah from Choice Video in Jersey, Kim's for the obscure stuff, and a few bootlegs. I read Spike's books, never finished *She's Gotta*, but *Do the Right Thing* is a great read. I went far enough in the first one for a mention of Jim Jarmusch.

JP: But you didn't get to my name. I assume you saw *Stranger Than Paradise* on tape, which is too bad since it's a great big screen, audience experience.

KS: You can't miss what you never saw. For me, that film exists solely on videotape and subsequently laser disk—a great laser disk too. It's a brilliant film that makes it all seem even more approachable.

Stranger Than Paradise and the First Golden Age

One afternoon in late April 1984 I slipped away from my Films, Inc. office for a pre-Cannes screening of the completed *Stranger Than Paradise*. We all knew it was headed for the Director's Fortnight, but virtually no one had seen anything since the original half-hour that now comprised the first act of Jim Jarmusch's 90-minute feature. The atmosphere was mildly expectant when the lights went down, wildly enthusiastic after the film's final blackout. It was hilariously dead-pan with pinpoint comic timing from its letter-perfect nonprofessional cast. Yet the film's minimalism was also strangely poignant. It was elegantly shot in black and white by Tom DiCillo, who finally made his own mark as a director a decade later. The best thing about it was that the mastermind of this surprising triumph was one of our own, the epitome of cool with his silvery hair, Jim Jarmusch. And all for a little more than $100,000. It was too soon to worry about the commercial distribution prospects.

When the lights came up at the Magno Penthouse screening room before Jim and his producer Sara Driver were scheduled to fly off to seek their fame and fortune in France, the fledgling New York film community had been galvanized. It's a near perfect, organic film completely true to its own aesthetic, which was identifiably European and quintessentially American at the same time.

One of Jarmusch's crucial contributions to hundreds of future low-budget films was his casting concept. His cast did not come from the Screen Actors Guild; they weren't exactly actors acting. He chose John Lurie, Richard Edson, and Eszter Balint to inhabit characters not unlike their everyday personalities. Lurie, Edson and Jarmusch all traveled in the same downtown New York scene. Balint's parents had an experimental theater group whose nude performances in storefront windows sometimes brought out the police. The three of them were the characters, and the characters were them. Jim's plan was no accident, which is not to suggest that he didn't write a finely honed script. It was just impossible to imagine the effectiveness of the delivery until his cast spoke the lines. Spike applied precisely the same technique in *She's Gotta Have It*.

Jim's travails through the pre-*Stranger* years intersect with a number of supporting roots characters. In the NYU graduate film program, he met Sara Driver and Spike Lee, who worked together in the equipment room. He was also Nicholas Ray's teaching assistant before working on Wim Wenders's film about Nick, called *Lightning over Water*, in 1980. Jim then completed his own Lower East Side, existential, guerilla, student feature *Permanent Vacation*, which was not exactly a harbinger of things to come. Throughout those years, he moved freely between punk music and avant-garde film circles where he knew Amos Poe, the Bs, Charlie Ahearn, Eric Mitchell. He was Eric's soundman on the feature *Underground USA*. He sang and played keyboards in a band called The Del Byzanteens while his future actors John Lurie (Lounge Lizards) and Richard Edson (Konk) also dabbled in music. Jarmusch has often suggested that underground film was like punk rock; it wasn't about virtuosity. It was about having something to say with feeling. However, in the same way that John Lurie got quite serious about his music as the years went by, Jim developed deft filmmaking skills.

Wenders gave Jim a finite amount of leftover black and white raw stock from *The State of Things* on which he shot the initial 30-minute short in one weekend. Jim and Sara mounted a portable 35mm projector in the middle of the dance floor at the club Danceteria one night early in 1983 to show the short and try to generate interest and cash for the remaining two thirds of the film, which had been scripted. I got to know them because they were completely broke and would come to the Bleecker Street Cinema, which I was programming, for free movies. I tried to evade their requests for more four-hour Jacques Rivette movies. They did come to the U.S. premiere of the Wenders film at the Bleecker along with Spike Lee and Errol Morris in February 1983. Jim and Sara also attended our Film Forum nuptials where they got to see Buster Keaton with a slice of wedding cake on the side.

Since the power of *Stranger Than Paradise* is cumulative, the initial half-hour segment left an unfinished impression. However, when it was shown in Germany's Hof Festival, Jarmusch found two angels. Director Paul Bartel gave Jim money to extricate himself from a soured connection with Wenders's Gray City Films. Then liqueur-filled-chocolate impresario Otto Grokenberger stepped forward as executive producer with money to finish the film. When *Stranger* was invited to Cannes, it didn't seem that earthshaking, because the work certainly emerged from the European tradition. Any excitement was also tempered by the fact that previous American invitees like *Northern Lights* and Robert Young's *Alambrista* hadn't really gotten any stateside boost from Cannes.

The response in France was avid and Jim was the first American to bring home the Camera d'Or for best first feature as a meaningful selling tool. Distributors weren't entirely convinced, thinking that the enthusiastic reaction might be unique to foreign filmgoers. The next stop was an increasingly prominent Los Angeles event called Filmex. Although Cinecom had already passed on the film, two other indies, the Samuel Goldwyn Company and Island/Alive, used Filmex to monitor the domestic audience very closely. They loved it. So Goldwyn, with strenuous pushing from the recently relocated Jeff Lipsky, stepped up and aced the deal. During the negotiations, I became aware of the fact that my old friend Sam Kitt was assisting the producers, although I wasn't sure how. After American Mavericks and Libra, Sam had headed UA Classics in its final year. Now without coining the term, he was acting informally as a producer's rep.

Scorsese claims that the greatest impact of John Cassavetes' 16mm *Shadows* was simply this: There were *no more excuses* for aspiring directors who were afraid of high costs or unmanageable equipment. That was then, and this was now. His statement, when applied to Jarmusch, rings totally true for the first three New York filmmakers I worked with,

Bill Sherwood, Spike Lee, and Lizzie Borden, and continues all the way through to Kevin Smith. Gregg Araki assured me that the West Coast impact on filmmakers like him, Allison Anders, and Gus Van Sant was equally strong.

An earlier downtown New York movie like *Smithereens* was okay. You go with it; it's got a few good moments and lots of attitude. Plenty of movies had attitude. *Stranger Than Paradise* was both brilliant and attainable. The camera doesn't move for artistic reasons. Conveniently that made it *much cheaper* to make. When the budget drops, the profit potential rises. *Stranger Than Paradise* grossed $2.5 million in North America and was a hit all over the world—especially in France and Japan.

Goldwyn did an exceptional distribution job under Jeff Lipsky's guidance. He captured the right combination of very hip and very funny in his marketing plan. Jarmusch was of course a complete unknown yet the ad campaign said, "A new American film by Jim Jarmusch." The trailer took full advantage of the film's one song, Screamin' Jay Hawkins's "I Put a Spell on You" which had cost an extra $10,000 to license correctly at the last minute. Despite its Filmex showings, the film was invited to the Telluride festival, which normally requires a U.S. premiere. Wenders and his producer, Chris Sievernich were there with *Paris, Texas* and the potentially awkward politics of the situation were ameliorated with a *Stranger* versus *Paris* softball game. I pitched for Wim's team for old times' sake and we prevailed with the help of Werner Herzog's unique batting grip and lively cheerleading by festival tribute subject Janet Leigh. Jeff Lipsky's super competitiveness, which serves him well in distribution, struck out this time when he tagged Ry Cooder's nine-year-old son way too hard at third base. Both sides booed.

The New York Film Festival was the next stop for both films with the higher-profile *Paris, Texas* scheduled for closing night. *Stranger* played on the first Saturday, so the all-important *New York Times* review was out in the early edition during the opening night party at the rather dark and unglamorous New York State Theater. Otto Grokenberger came in with the paper under his arm and a big ol' grin on his face. Vincent Canby had discovered Jim Jarmusch in a big way, as Roger Ebert had before him. Three months later, the National Society of Film Critics voted *Stranger* Best Film of the Year. Having been there from the get go, Canby remained a very constant Jarmusch fan for years to come. One of the essential strategies that this film, and many since, benefited from is the magic trick of making as many people (critics are people too) as possible for as long as possible believe that they are discovering something that almost no one else knows about. You can keep this going for months before the theatrical release, but if, at some point, the film has grossed millions it becomes a bit ludicrous. Lipsky and ace publicist Reid Rosefelt worked this angle to perfection, keeping all hype in check. The motto was hip, not hype.

Stranger Than Paradise opened in early October 1984 and played in key cities for many months. It was hardly the only American independent choice of the remarkable fall/winter of 1984/85. John Sayles's most commercial film to date, *The Brother from Another Planet*, opened in late September and also stuck around well into the following year; it was Sayles's "black" film, starring Joe Morton and photographed by Ernest Dickerson. Cinecom had great success with both *The Brother* and Jonathan Demme's Talking Heads concert film *Stop Making Sense*, which they co-distributed with Island/Alive. Island/Alive also had a second significant release that fall with Alan Rudoph's career-best *Choose Me*, which featured their trademark sexy, irresistible artwork. These films were all going strong in January when Ben Barenholtz's new company, Circle Releasing, opened the Coen brothers' *Blood Simple* which they had picked up at the Toronto Film Festival. Joel Coen was an NYU Film School graduate like Jarmusch, but he worked a different vein by putting a wickedly funny spin on a classic American genre—film noir. Ted Pedas and Barenholtz ran Circle Films, and later produced several features with Joel and Ethan Coen. Their staffers Jim Jacks and Chris Zarpas parlayed their involvement into Hollywood executive posts with Universal and Disney respectively. Last but not least (maybe it is least), in February 1985 a small company called Angelika Films, which later opened the country's top-grossing art complex, New York's Angelika Film Center, released Martin Bell's "narrative documentary" *Streetwise* on homeless kids in Seattle. All of these theatrical releases, including the European/American hybrid *Paris, Texas*, grossed between two and five million dollars, making it a veritable golden age for independent films.

Despite the new conceit that home video would be the goose that laid the golden egg, the ancillary results were much spottier. The best example is the black-and-white *Stranger*, whose video release was held up for over an entire year so as not to intrude on sustained theatrical runs. Leon Falk of CBS/Fox paid a couple of hundred thousand dollars for video rights, but the initial shipment was a pathetic five thousand units. Buyer beware: It was the theatrical experience which made that film click.

As 1985 rolled along, there were a few theatrical disappointments like Spectrafilm's release of the second Victor Nunez picture, *Flash of Green*, Cinecom's failure with Horton Foote's *1918*, and *Pumping Iron 2*. However mid-summer brought the biggest surprise up to that moment in the eighties. Island Pictures, which had jettisoned Alive as its partner, went completely against the grain of conventional indie distribution strategy and opened *Kiss of the Spider Woman* in late July. This now looks like bold Hollywood counterprogramming, but it was unprecedented then. The result: $17 million and Academy Award nominations. Because it starred William Hurt and Raul Julia and wasn't exactly cheap, *Spider Woman* did not directly inspire no-access, low-budget directors. However, its performance as a nonstudio production made the entire industry take note and made Island Pictures the preeminent quality independent. (Declassé New Line had already begun to print money with the *Nightmare* franchise.) Island didn't rest on its laurels. Cary Brokaw and Russell Schwartz planned a December opening for *The Trip to Bountiful* so that Geraldine Page would qualify for a Best Actress nomination. She did, and she won. So did William Hurt as Best Actor for *Spider Woman*, giving Island a remarkable, stunning one-two punch in the face of the studios. Their marketing was tasteful, yet very aggressive and they began to spend money pretty freely—especially when a film was in profit and earning overages, since any money spent at that point is really producers' money.

Distribution deals for completed independent features generally involve two pages worth of substantive deal points and another twenty, or more, of boilerplate. Since it is a license agreement, the first three issues are the territory, the term, and which rights are included. Even simple things change over the years. The standard term used to be seven, ten, or twelve years; now it's twenty, thirty-five, or (*gasp*) perpetuity. It's always been extremely hard to segment theatrical, television and home video rights. Producers might win a negotiation to exclude sequel/remake rights, books, merchandise, or, looking ahead, interactive rights.

Ideally the distributor pays a significant, nonrefundable advance which is recouped from any future producer net profits. They earn distribution fees for releasing the film theatrically (30 to 35 percent) and sublicensing the other ancillary rights (25 to 35 percent for home video, pay cable, syndication). When it comes to prints and advertising (P&A) and other distribution/promotion costs, the smart producer is looking for a strong show of distributor support without careless or frivolous overspending. After the fees are earned, the costs are covered, and the advance (with interest) is recouped, the film has entered the promised land of overages. This normally means it's either done quite well, or had a modest purchase price. As costs have steadily risen, overages have become rarer.

After the fact, producers David Weisman (*Kiss of the Spider Woman*) and Sterling Van Wagenen (*The Trip to Bountiful*) bitterly complained about Island's credit-claiming, spendthrift ways. Weisman captured the producer attitude perfectly when he described Island as having had "the *privilege* of distributing *Spider Woman.*" The *Bountiful* gripes zeroed in on the $2 million P&A expense, a large final chunk having gone toward the successful Oscar campaign, which pumped up the home video release. Obviously, the time to object to draining profits is while the money is excitedly being spent, not a year later.

Shortly after *Kiss of the Spider Woman* came out and received enormous support from the gay community, I got a call from an old NYU schoolmate of mine who had also been a partner in Roadmovies. He wanted me to come and screen a gay feature that was close to completion.

Paradise

KEVIN SMITH: You watch *Stranger*, you think "I could really make a movie."

JOHN PIERSON: So it's been having that impact for ten years now. What was it in particular that gave you that confident feeling?

KS: First thing, the camera doesn't move. Jarmusch sets it up and things happen. His really sparse dialogue is not my forte, but visually he's it— at least for the first film. If I'm going to do a movie, I'm going to do it like this and just add dialogue.

JP: Did you know the budget?

KS: I don't know exactly what the budget is on *Stranger*, but I know I'm gonna go for that price if I can do it for that.

JP: The whole idea of $110,000 in 1984 was bargain basement, nearly unimaginable. It's funny now to have $20 to $30,000 be the ballpark for low budgets.

KS: So I go on to see his other films and read whatever I can about him.

JP: What do you do when he says, "Hey, Jacques Rivette was a major influence?"

KS: I'm a student of American independent cinema, and I'm not the best student in the world, but I was good enough to do what I eventually did. I don't feel that I have to go back and view European or other foreign films because I feel like these guys have already done it for me, and I'm getting filtered through them. That ethic works for me.

JP: So *Mystery Train* [Jarmusch's third feature] for you is like *Rashomon* for me in terms of a cultural reference point?

KS: You mean the fact that it covers three different stories from different points of view?

JP: Yeah, anytime somebody in my generation had a multiple point of view story, even Spike in *She's Gotta Have It*, it would be described as "*Rashomon*-like."

KS: And now a *Mystery Train* reference is too obscure?

JP: *Rashomon* has a general cultural currency. It could be in an editorial in *The New York Times* or it could be cross referenced in a review in *Entertainment Weekly*. There's a certain part of film culture that's the equivalent of the library shelf of the Fifty Great Books. These would be the standard texts if you dealt with film classics.

KS: That's the way my dad feels about *Navy Seals*.

JP: What else did you pick up from Jarmusch's later films?

KS: The one shot that really got me every time I watched *Mystery Train* is when the Japanese couple walks with the suitcase on the stick and the camera is moving for one of the first times in a Jarmusch film other than the car shot at the beginning of *Down by Law*. Wow, a moving camera, but still it seems utterly attainable. I'm sitting there watching before I'm "film knowledgeably whizzy," as Flavor Flav would say. I'm watching saying, "All right, it's gotta be maybe some tracks and a dolly—something I could do. If you have to move the camera, you could do it like that."

PARTING GLANCES
AND THE NEW QUEER CINEMA

B ill Sherwood came to the Upper West Side of Manhattan from Battle Creek, Michigan, to train as a classical musician at Juilliard. He soon reached a point in his life when he decided to compose with images instead of notes. Having failed to raise money for an earlier script set in the downtown art world, he turned to *Parting Glances* in 1984. Bill teamed up with producer Arthur Silverman, a former NYU schoolmate and Roadmovies partner of mine. We had shared two great pleasures in life: cleaning up the sunflower seeds after the Grateful Dead movie at the Clurman and listening to future *48 Hours* screenwriter Larry Gross spar with the daunting film semiotician Professor Annette Michelson in a Cinema Studies course. Bill and Arthur were soon joined by another producer, Yoram Mandel.

The three of them formed a traditional limited partnership, Rondo Productions, for the purpose of raising $300,000 to produce an independent feature right around the time that *Stranger Than Paradise* was invited to Cannes. In essence the arrangement gives investors 50 percent of the profits of a film in return for which they have no liability, no artistic say, and no guarantee that they'll make back one thin dime.

Although Rondo fell short of its fully capitalized goal, the partnership raised enough to begin production the very week that *Stranger Than Paradise* opened in New York across the street from Juilliard. During post-production, Paul Kaplan (of the Stanley A. Kaplan—SAT Preparation—Institute) stepped forward with $60,000 to bridge the gap to full completion in return for which he was named executive producer. Some investors were gay, others straight; almost all of them had a direct connection to one of the movie's principals.

Parting Glances, which takes place in a compressed twenty-four hours, was the first theatrical feature to deal with the threat of AIDS in a world where all the gay characters behave in an extremely recognizable, normal, everyday manner. Being gay is neither an issue nor a problem. The relationships in the movie are filled with the struggle for honesty and commitment just as in the heterosexual world.

For the hidden world of homosexuality embedded in the subtext of Hollywood films, Vito Russo's book *The Celluloid Closet* is comprehensive. Most of the previous *overt* gay films from Hollywood and around the world featured bitchy banter like *The Boys in the Band*, broad physical farce like *La Cage aux Folles*, or freak shows like the infamous *Taxi zum Klo*. In the latter, a German schoolteacher cruises public restrooms looking for dangerous anonymous sex, or ultimately, a golden shower of urine. *Taxi* became a prurient sensation before AIDS was widely recognized in 1981. It was admittedly a lot more fun than watching undercover cop Al Pacino go *Cruising* as a male hustler or repressed doctor Michael Ontkean fear *Making Love* with *Mr.* Right, two notoriously unconvincing studio concoctions.

Oddly enough, the most earnest attempts to portray gay life in a serious, unsoapy, nondegrading manner came from two straight, male writer-directors. One worked in Hollywood, one worked off-Hollywood. Both chose to portray lesbians in the early eighties. Robert Towne created *Personal Best* with Mariel Hemingway as a gay athlete, and John Sayles went into the low-rent world of Jersey academia to tell the story of *Lianna*. Both movies focus on one avowed lesbian and one metamorphosing wannabe surrounded by a straight world.

Bill Sherwood turned the tables by making that straight world secondary. He also had the acute judgment to cast downtown performance artist Steve Buscemi in his first featured role as the charismatic, sardonic rock musician Nick. The other two male leads in the central triangle were adequate. Richard Ganoung had a serious sweetness reminiscent of Tom Hulce while John Bolger played the serviceable "hunk" character in a manner that betrayed his soap opera roots. As a manly father in real life, he kept his distance afterward and was not to be found at events such as the gala closing night screening of the 1986 New York Gay Film Festival.

The whole of *Parting Glances* was always greater than the sum of its parts. Other than being blown away by Buscemi's performance, I didn't know quite what to make of the film when I saw it for the first time in double system (meaning the picture and sound elements have not yet been joined together on a composite print) in the summer of 1985. Since *Parting Glances* was shot in the unreleasable Super 16mm format, it would not have a finished answer print until it was blown up to 35mm. The structure and editing rhythms of the film were beautifully realized, like the mix of Bronski Beat and Brahms that Bill Sherwood used through the score. However the film had an unresolved ending that couldn't be rationalized away as "lifelike:" it was a dramatic fizzle.

When my friend Arthur Silverman asked me what I thought, I told him my feelings about the ending, and other relative strengths and weaknesses. I assumed he just wanted my opinion, but he then asked if I could help sell the film to a distributor. I suggested that he do it himself, which probably would have been his intention if not for the fact that he was on his way to Alaska for at least a half year. Arthur had years of experience as an independent distributor with films like *Best Boy* (1979) when he decided to go back to law school. As his third-year assignment, he was on his way to be a clerk in Alaska State Supreme Court—4,000 miles and four time zones away. He needed somebody else. When I asked, "Why me?" he simply pointed out, "You know all the distributors." I thought about it and said, "You're right." Since everybody agreed that the film needed a reshoot for a new ending, I agreed to sign on.

Now the problem became timing. Between the reshoot and 35mm blowup at the filmmaker-friendly DuArt Film Lab, the September festival trilogy of Telluride-Toronto-New York was out of the question. It wasn't even worth screening for them. The U.S. Film Festival in Utah (later Sundance, of course) was not such a big deal that it was worth waiting until January 1986. These days it certainly would be worth the wait.

The only practical answer was a screening at the Independent Feature Film Market in mid-October. That event has grown to include over 400 films each year, but the 1985 lineup had only forty-three titles, most of them quite reputable. When I called the latter-day IFFM with its undistinguished mass of hopelessly unreleaseable films a "a toxic dump," the Independent Feature Project's executive director became quite incensed. After a volatile discussion, we both agreed that I would henceforth refer to it as a "dump," not dangerous to your health. The untarnished 1985 market became our target.

Fortunately Sam Kitt had become IFP market director, vastly improving the organization and raising the profile of the annual event to its highest level yet. He gave *Parting Glances* the red-carpet treatment as he threw me a few tips on deal points and representation. I realized that I knew the distributors and understood the art of negotiation (since I once bought a television from Crazy Eddie, New York's most notorious electronics discounter), but I would have to fake my way through the actual details. I still had a nine-to-five job in repertory sales at Films, Inc. at this point, and this sideline activity posed a serious conflict. I had the good sense to invite the company's president and executive V.P. to the IFFM screening, on the assumption that they wouldn't get it. They didn't. Based on the questionable assumption that it wouldn't take much of my time to sell it, they effectively gave me their blessing.

Our program note used the word "gay" three times and mentioned AIDS once. The turnout of domestic buyers at the one and only screening was a little disappointing. On the foreign side, both the U.K.'s Channel 4 and Germany's ARD made excellent television offers. In the mid-eighties, half of the key indie distributors were L.A.-based, most importantly Island Pictures and Goldwyn's home office. But Richard Abramowitz and Shelby Stone of Cinecom were in the house. The response was very enthusiastic and Cinecom immediately arranged for a follow-up screening for Ira Deutchman, the full staff, and their then publicist, Steve Seifert.

Seifert was just about the first film publicist to focus on the independent side out of a deep love of movies. He was also extremely bright, very feisty, and openly gay. When he had left a staff position with Nancy Seltzer to start his own company, the first client he had was our Roadmovies summer program at the Clurman. Shortly thereafter he established a tight link with United Artists Classics via marketing head Ira

Deutchman, which carried over to Cinecom. As his business was growing in 1982, Steve and I had a dispute over a fee that he felt I owed him.
Although it was only about $300, he worked out a monthly payment
schedule. He was so adamant and I found it all so goofy that I sought
out bizarre ways to pay him. Once my wife and I drove from San Antonio, Texas, to Telluride to give him a $20 check at the festival's open-
ing-night party. Finally wanting to retire a debt that was questionable
in the first place, I had a shoebox full of $200 in nickels and dimes de-
livered to his office—maybe not as memorable as a horse's head on satin
sheets, but symbolic nevertheless. Seifert got into the spirit and sent back
one nickel taped to an index card asking me why I had overpaid him.

Steve Seifert's excitement about *Parting Glances* helped bring
Cinecom's interest to a boil before anyone else had even turned the
burner on. Starting with their very first 1982 release, Robert Altman's
Come Back to the 5 & Dime Jimmy Dean, Jimmy Dean, Cinecom had
established the closest identification of any distributor with American
independent films. They'd already released eight in their three-year history. These films reflected Ira Deutchman's taste, and they suited the
company's ancillary dealmaking needs. Their CEO, Amir Malin, made
a self-described preemptive offer with a $125,000 advance. This rapid
first strike created two immediate problems for me. I had to learn the
literal meaning of "preemptive," and then make a moral judgment about
how to behave in those circumstances.

A preemptive offer is meant to halt any further screening or negotiation with other parties while the seller decides whether or not to accept the stated offer. Since Cinecom's offer for North American rights
was less than half the film's budget, we certainly weren't going for that.
In a slightly broader interpretation, preemptive strongly implies a period of exclusive negotiation when the seller may strive to improve the
sole buyer's offer. This strategy is very difficult without the leverage of
other interest and the threat of competitive bidding. So in my first slick
move in a career where I've adjusted my professional code of conduct
for the benefit of my producers to the detriment of some distributors,
I asked Amir Malin to up his offer and give me three days to run through
the numbers with Bill Sherwood and his producers. Our ploy was to
take that small window of opportunity and cover the waterfront with
New York–based distributors.

We wedged in a number of screenings. Since each company has an incentive to maintain secrecy, the main anxiety about leaks comes from the operators in various screenings rooms. That's one of the reasons I started with Orion Classics, the only place with a private screening room. In that case secrecy was no problem, but Michael Barker told me years later that the crusty old projectionist wanted to stop the screening after the second scene of two men kissing. Barker himself found the film a bit "too slick" and, aside from Buscemi, not that well acted. On a macrocosmic level, he said, "we live in a homophobic nation and *Parting Glances* will have no crossover." By the time the clock had ticked off seventy-two hours, the rest of the New York distribution community— Circle, Goldwyn (NY office), Spectrafilm—had also shown no great interest in *Parting Glances*. We scurried back to Cinecom acting bold and confident, and I brought Bill Sherwood into Amir's lush thirtieth-floor corner office, with its sweeping views from the Battery to Pennsylvania, to make the pitch that he absolutely "needed" to get a $200,000 advance if we weren't going to test the waters with competing distributors. They went for it. Ira said it could be the biggest word-of-mouth hit since *El Norte*.

Now this approach didn't feel like a hustle to me, and I believed that everyone would come out well on the deal. Bill and his three producers expected more and were disgruntled about the distributors who passed. Cinecom would have been happy to pay a bit less. The context then for advances on desirable first-time features like *Stranger Than Paradise* or *The Great Wall* was in the $200 to $250,000 range. The bigger problem was the fierce struggle for positioning between *Parting Glances* and two other soon-to-be-released gay films. Suddenly it was the *Gunfight at the Homosexuals 'R' OK Corral*.

Just prior to *Parting Glances*' debut at the IFFM, Goldwyn had taken on Donna Deitch's lesbian-themed *Desert Hearts*. When that film premiered at Telluride I had three distinct memories: The final sex scene in the last reel was worth the wait, Donna Deitch carried her own seventy-pound film cans around, and co-star Patricia Charbonneau didn't want anyone to mistake her for a real-life dyke. She had her new baby glued to her hip.

Slightly before then, Orion Classics had come across a 16mm, BBC television movie written by Hanif Kureishi, directed by Stephen Frears, starring the then unknown Daniel Day Lewis. It was called *My Beautiful Laundrette*, and its extremely modest acquisition price was $100,000.

Since they saw it in London, they hadn't had to worry about their squeamish New York projectionist turning the film off when Daniel Day Lewis shares his tongue and a mouthful of champagne with another man.

Both Goldwyn and Orion Classics were now prepared to wage a three-way spin-control battle with Cinecom. Goldwyn, with Jeff Lipsky leading the charge, sold the eroticism of *Desert Hearts*. Tom Bernard and Michael Barker were particularly clever in emphasizing that the gay content in *Laundrette* was just *one* component of a very rich film that touched on a long laundry list of issues in a dramatically compelling manner. When talking to conservative exhibitors, they tended to describe *Parting Glances* as that *gay* film. Of course, Tom and Michael always savored a head-to-head conflict with their former UA Classics colleague Ira Deutchman.

I had not fully understood the severity of their split back when Ira left United Artists Classics to join the newly formed Cinecom with Amir Malin and his pipe-smoking partner John Ives. United Artists Classics was bidding on a Gillian Armstrong punk musical film called *Starstruck*. So was Cinecom. While Ira was still employed by UA, he helped Cinecom lock up the deal they had made that was contingent on the producers sitting down with the individual who would be responsible for marketing their film. That meeting took place in a Los Angeles hotel restaurant on a Friday when Ira was not at work in New York. Tom Bernard became suspicious and smoked Ira out with a hotel page. To this day, Deutchman insists that Cinecom had already acquired *Starstruck* and points out that he immediately resigned from United Artists Classics. The feisty Bernard sees it differently, although he resists pinpointing this incident as the trigger to the fiercest, longest-lasting feud within independent film's "permanent government." Cinecom wound up with the movie, which is long forgotten. Of course, it wasn't that much later that Bernard, Barker, and Donna Gigliotti left UA Classics en masse to start Orion Classics. The war carried over.

Back at Cinecom, Ira and Steve Seifert began to work out their release and marketing strategy, while I struggled to finish off the long-form contract so that the producers could be paid. Tom Rothman, expert attorney at Frankfurt, Garbus, Klein, and Selz, had been my choice for legal counsel since he represented Jim Jarmusch and knew Amir Malin quite well. Once we'd signed a binding two-page deal memo that triggered no instant payment, the wheels slowed right down. The first prototype contract draft that came over had been used for some upcoming Cinecom release called *A Room with a View*, and I remember wondering if that film would be any good.

The discussions about release strategy began to get a bit weird. It was easy to agree to open in New York and Los Angeles first in February (1986) after taking the film to the U.S. Film Festival (now Sundance) in January. Discussions about grassroots campaigns at the level of gay bartenders and hairdressers consumed too much time. One day Steve Seifert brought in a fairly extensive press book which he'd written. The entire emphasis was on *Parting Glances* as another quality low-budget American independent film. It wasn't immediately apparent that it was gay, and there was absolutely *no mention* of the fact that the Steve Buscemi character had AIDS. It was still early, people were afraid, the Aidan Quinn first-ever AIDS television movie *An Early Frost* hadn't even been on yet. But this whole attempt to reach some crossover audience without scaring anybody off didn't quite seem like the bold, outspoken Steve Seifert that I knew. It was clear that Buscemi should go on the poster and ad art and Ira Deutchman added some subtle, almost coy, suggestions about its content with a pink triangle background and the tag line "An American *very* independent film." So while Orion Classics was painting *Parting Glances* as faggy, Cinecom was selling it as ho hum, another indie. "Whether it's a small group of college friends in *Secaucus Seven*, a Chinese-American family in *Chan Is Missing* or a clan of misfits in *Stranger Than Paradise* . . ."

This was around the time that the New York City Council passed the first gay rights bill on the same day that Congress denied any further funding for the so-called Nicaraguan Freedom Fighters. The *New York Daily News* front page headline read: GAYS YES, CONTRAS NO!

Everyone hoped that the film would open in New York on one of Dan Talbot's screens. Dan (then) programmed his theaters entirely based on his own taste, and he didn't care for the film. He actually told me it lacked the "narrative drive" of *Taxi zum Klo*, especially the public toilet scene when the director/star Frank Ripploh stuck his penis through a hole in the wall. The backup theater became the now destroyed Embassy 72nd Street Twin, where ironically it ended up playing side-by-side with *My Beautiful Laundrette*.

The initial Los Angeles run was at the Beverly Center Cineplex, which was the first "multimultiplex" (fourteen screens) in the United

States and also the premier art complex in L.A. at that time. In a bizarre coincidence, Richard Ganoug, the film's lead actor, had moved out there after completing the film, and needing some income, was working in a shoe store on a lower level of the Beverly Center. He would take breaks and hop on the escalator to see himself on screen in the trailer even before the film opened.

When the tally came in, *Parting Glances* was a distant third. *Laundrette* drew rave reviews and long lines of straight and gay viewers, grossed $4.5 million and established three careers—writer, director, and star. *Desert Hearts* was effectively marketed as erotica and grossed $2.5 million. *Parting Glances* was a very mixed bag. Excellent reviews from places like *Variety* (Todd McCarthy at U.S. Film Fest), Seattle (John Hartl), and L.A. (Michael Wilmington in the *Los Angeles Times*) never quite made up for a mediocre Janet Maslin review in *The New York Times*. The best quote that Ira could pull was "relentlessly upbeat," which isn't what most people are looking for on a Friday night. Nevertheless the film's gross approached $1 million, it shipped about 15,000 home video units via CBS/Fox, and sold to pay cable services like Cinemax, where it was widely seen. Cinecom essentially broke even, which illustrates that the deal was ultimately fair for both sides. Rondo's world revenues exceeded $600,000—double the budget!

Cinecom of course would have preferred the Sherwood picture to perform like the mystery title on the prototype contract they sent us. A month after *Parting Glances* came out, they released Merchant-Ivory's *A Room with a View*—their first (and last) megahit, and the first quality independent release to gross over $20 million. Sales head Richard Abramowitz pushed the seal of the indie distribution envelope when he hooked in with Neil Blatt at the gigantic Cineplex Theater circuit, where *Room* thrived. Blatt secured the Los Angeles showcase run at the Century Plaza for an unprecedented $150,000 advance, and a 70 percent film rental floor for the first three weeks. Rich kept a copy of the check on his wall.

The legacy of *Parting Glances* is both impressive and heartbreaking. I solved the mystery of Steve Seifert's uncharacteristic conservatism when I learned that he had AIDS, a lightning bolt that had struck him out of the clear blue sky a month after Cinecom acquired the film. He died in 1988. Bill Sherwood was never given an opportunity to make another feature, although he wrote a number of disparate screenplays.

He was always a catalyst for the people around him, although he himself became embittered about the success of other writers like Hanif Kureishi. When Bill died of AIDS in 1990, his memorial service was the first time I'd seen executive Paul Kaplan in years. He was very sick, his mouth was too dry to speak, and he didn't last much longer. Buscemi was also there, having become a mainstay of the American independent film—an honorary position that has grown since then. Co-producer Yoram Mandel has gone on to produce a half-dozen features, some gay (*Grief*) and some not (*Johnny Suede*).

Parting Glances has grown in stature through the years. Distributors like Michael Barker now praise its artistry. Bingham Ray speaks for many people when he admits that he had to get over a remnant of homophobia to prepare for later in-your-face queer films like the 1992 October-distributed Gregg Araki feature *The Living End*. Unfortunately *Glances*'s stature hadn't grown enough to prevent *Longtime Companion*, an American Playhouse production which entered wide release via the Samuel Goldwyn Company at the time of Bill's memorial service in the spring of 1990, from promoting itself as the first theatrical feature about AIDS. Without dwelling too much on the point, it was quite unseemly of them to make that claim in light of several tragically shortened lives in the *Parting Glances* family. Of course one must credit everyone involved with *Longtime Companion* for boldly calling a spade a spade, even in a watered down drama. It was four years later, and it did more than four times the business of *Parting Glances*.

One of the lowliest members of the *Parting Glances* crew may have been the most effectively inspired progeny. Christine Vachon is often described as the queen of the New Queer Cinema, having produced Todd Haynes's *Poison* and *Safe*, Tom Kalin's *Swoon*, Steve McLean's *Postcards from America*, Nigel Finch's *Stonewall*, and Mary Harron's *I Shot Andy Warhol*. Unlike many other independent producers who've merely sought a springboard to the more commercial realm, Christine has remained true to her gay and lesbian, often experimental calling. Yet she's too smart and funny to be an ideologue. In 1985, she started as an assistant editor for Bill Sherwood.

As for me, *Parting Glances* changed my life. No, I didn't buy into a Blockbuster Video franchise, although they opened their very first store in Dallas just when we sold the film. And it's not just that I realized the excellent opportunities for gay cinema, although I did wind up collaborating with Christine Vachon as the key investor in *Go Fish*. *Parting Glances* provided me with a taste for deals, more confidence in my poker-face abilities, and an unexpected windfall of $10,000. The actual cash wouldn't pass from Cinecom to Rondo Productions to me for six months, but I knew I could count on it as my 5 percent fee on a $200,000 sale. Five days after signing off on the Cinecom October 25 deal memo, I saw a rough cut of another first feature in the Bijou Theater at NYU. Walking down the street afterward I told my wife, Janet, and Bingham Ray, "I have seen the future of cinema and his name is Spike Lee."

SHE'S GOTTA HAVE IT

*"In thirty years, you'll be able to tell
your grandchildren you were there."*
—SPIKE LEE,
March 28, 1985 9:30 A.M.

TUBE SOCKS AND TUBE STEAKS

Spike Lee is my hero. Oddly enough, I can't remember the first time I met him. It must have been the winter of 1983, when I was programming the Bleecker Street Cinema, a legendary repertory site in Greenwich Village. Although it may seem impossible to believe now, he was the invisible man. He wasn't sitting courtside at Madison Square Garden, he wasn't selling sneakers with Michael Jordan, he wasn't lecturing at Harvard, and he wasn't debating Bryant Gumbel or Ted Kopple on television. He was sitting unobtrusively, with his Mets cap pulled down low, inspecting the scratches and splices on 16mm prints at a small, independent distributor called First Run Features in the Bleecker building, a stone's throw from his alma mater, NYU.

I think Spike decided to start talking to me for two reasons. I wore my Baltimore Orioles baseball jacket just about every day making it pretty clear that I liked sports as much as movies—a feeling he shared. A further inducement was that First Run, which was basically a filmmaker cooperative, had a staff of about ten squeezed into an office space that was identical in square footage to one that I had all to myself. First Run's mom and pop were Fran Spielman, formerly of Cinema 5, and Seymour Wishman, formerly a defense lawyer. Spike's future editor, Barry Brown, was one of its founding filmmakers.

It's no secret that Spike is short and slight, but he still felt cramped. So he would wander next door for some elbow room, then proceed to tease me about the Orioles, who were on their way to a World Series win in 1983, or occasionally ask me to show something like *Blue Collar* or *Rashomon*. Unsurprisingly Spike's requests weren't nearly as obscure as those of his NYU classmate Jim Jarmusch, so I tried to accommodate him. Then one day he asked me to show his own hour-long thesis film *Joe's Bed-Stuy Barbershop: We Cut Heads*.

In March 1983, *Joe's Bed-Stuy* was the first student film ever selected for the high-profile New Directors/New Films series at the Museum of Modern Art. I played it on the smaller, second screen at the Bleecker for a couple of weekends in April just around the time that Jim Jarmusch was screening his *Stranger Than Paradise* short at Danceteria. Spike got an agent at William Morris, but no further work. I stopped running the beloved Bleecker just before the Orioles clinched the championship in October. I passed Spike on the street from time to time as he geared up for a self-produced feature called *Messenger* with Larry Fishburne and Giancarlo Esposito. That film collapsed during preproduction in the summer of 1984. Spike was invisible all over again, collecting a paycheck back at First Run for inspecting prints of movies like Lizzie Borden's *Born in Flames*.

The next time I heard from Mr. Lee, I was wheeling and dealing with *Parting Glances*. He told me that he planned to screen a double-system rough cut of his new feature, *She's Gotta Have It*, at the end of October. Of course I laughed when I heard the title. Everyone does the first time. I immediately wanted to repeat it to other "virgins" and hear them laugh. I wondered why I hadn't heard about this one while Spike was shooting in the summer. After the previous year's humiliation with *Messenger,* he didn't want to shout it from the rooftops until the right moment this time. The monumental struggle to attempt to raise money to shoot *She's Gotta Have It* is documented in excruciating detail in his book. As far as money for principal photography was concerned, two funding organizations played critical, contrasting roles. The New York

State Council on the Arts provided an $18,000 grant and became a hero, while the American Film Institute withdrew a $20,000 grant made to *Messenger*. Spike showed no mercy in trashing them for years afterward.

Despite the two and a half years that had passed since *Joe's Bed-Stuy*, Spike reassembled his core support group. Monty Ross switched over from actor to production supervisor and all-around right hand man. Tommy Hicks was back to play the earnest, loving teacher instead of a slick gangster. Spike's dad, Bill Lee, composed another wonderfully effective jazz score. Spike's key collaborator since NYU days, Ernest Dickerson, had further improved his cinematography skills by shooting John Sayles's *Brother from Another Planet* and the first studio rap feature, *Krush Groove*. That Michael Schultz film, whose producers included George Jackson, Doug McHenry, and hip-hop impresario Russell Simmons, was one of the tiny handful of black films in the eighties. Starting years before with *Cooley High*, Schultz was just about the only black director carrying a very dim torch after the blaxploitation movement died out. *A Soldier's Story* and *The Color Purple* may have been heavily marketed to black audiences, but they were directed by white men. After the *She's Gotta Have It* screening on October 30, 1985, it seemed like that situation might change very soon.

Spike invited an audience of potential investors, writers, and other industry types to an evening show at NYU's Bijou Theater. Spike was all dressed up with his pants hitched high, and the atmosphere was quite lively. The sound in a rough cut screening is quite crude, production dialogue only, no effects, no automated dialogue recording (ADR, done later in the studio), almost no music. Consequently the atmospheric Brooklyn Bridge shots at the beginning of the film and Nola Darling's introduction could not fully work their magic. The crowd perked up with Jamie Overstreet's introduction followed by the first sex scene. But there was an absolute explosion of laughter about ten minutes into the film, when a succession of twelve black men in all shapes, sizes, and skin tones demonstrate their most uproarious pick-up lines. Monty popped up on screen first with the irresistible come-on, "You so fine baby, I'll drink a tub of your bathwater." The sequence ended with the most lascivious statement: "Girl, I got plenty of what you need, ten throbbing inches of USDA, government inspected, prime cut, grade-A tube steak." It turned out that the "dog sequence," which also featured Ernest, rapper Fab Five Freddy, and director Reggie Hudlin, was the very first thing

FORTY ACRES AND A MULE   presents   A SPIKE LEE JOINT

"SHE'S GOTTA HAVE IT"

Rough Cut Screening: Wed. October 30th at 7:30 p.m.

PRODUCER   SHELTON J. LEE
PRODUCTION SUPERVISOR   MONTY ROSS
ASSOCIATE PRODUCER   PAMM JACKSON
PHOTOGRAPHY   ERNEST DICKERSON
MUSIC   BILL LEE
PRODUCTION DESIGNER   WYNN THOMAS
WRITTEN,EDITED AND
DIRECTED by   SPIKE LEE

                         PLAYERS

Nola Darling   TRACY CAMILLA JOHNS
Jamie Overstreet   REDMON HICKS
Greer Childs   JOHN TERRELL
Opal Gilstrap   RAY DOWELL
Clorinda Bradford   JOIE LEE
Sonny Darling   BILL LEE
Dr. Jamison   EPATHA MERKINSON
Mars Blackman   SPIKE LEE

Ships at a distance have every man's wish on board. For some
they come in with the tide. For others they sail forever on the
horizon, never out of sight, never landing until the watcher
turns his eyes away in resignation, his dreams mocked to death by
time. That is the life of men. Now, women forget all those
things they don't want to remember and remember everything they
don't want to forget. The dream is the truth. Then they act and
do things accordingly.

ZORA NEALE HURSTON- **THEIR EYES WERE WATCHING GOD**

that Spike shot, and he shot it right there in NYU's Bijou Theater. Not too long after the dogs, Mars Blackmon, a part Spike decided to play himself about halfway through writing the script, made his first crowd-pleasing appearance leaning into the camera importuning Nola with his "Please baby please" repetitions. Was this destined to be the legendary first public showing where absolutely everything goes right? Spike described it in his book as an overwhelming response that "rocked the house."

My memory is markedly different. Near the end of the first reel, the double system projector slipped out of sync and then a splice broke, stopping the show. It wouldn't be the last time. There was so much good-will toward the film that it didn't really matter until the infamous color sequence. Conceived as an homage to Vincente Minnelli and *The Wizard of Oz*, the nearly five-minute dance sequence featuring Spike's ex-girlfriend brought the movie to a dead stop. Previously, when Spike proudly had shown the sequence to his father, Bill Lee reportedly said, "It could make a glass eye cry." Like father, like son, like no one else. The film certainly recovered with more Mars, the Greer Childs pixilated sex scene, and Thanksgiving dinner, but the sex psychologist was another dead spot and Jamie's near-rape of Nola at the end really threw people for a loop. It looked and sounded especially brutal in this primitive presentation. This version of *She's Gotta Have It* ended with Nola's fantasy wedding, a scene that was never again seen.

In screenings like this, there are lots of viewers, even film educated viewers, who can't see the forest for the trees. The color sequence and the rape were two big trees. None of the black cadillac dealers or other outside investors came through with any money. *Village Voice* critic David Edelstein didn't get it at all, a confession he made publicly in giving the film its first great review when it opened nine months later. Friends of Spike, like the writer Nelson George and Earl Smith, who had already put money in, added some more. Long after the official limited partnership was tossed aside, I became the sixth and largest individual investor in *She's Gotta Have It*. It was the best business decision I ever made in my life. I announced my intention walking over to the Great Jones Cafe, a popular New York film-community hangout, and repeated myself at the bar inside, explaining that I would simply roll over my $10,000 fee from the sale of *Parting Glances*. One of my old Roadmovies repertory partners, who was still distributing Wenders's films, belittled my excitement about stepping into the brave new world of independent American features by gays, blacks, and other unheard voices. I tried to laugh it off, but we were never really friends again.

The first distributor to see *She's Gotta Have It* was Cinecom. Spike was tight with Wayne Salazar, who designed the elongated head credits for the film. Wayne also worked at Cinecom, distributor of John Sayles's *Brother* and Jonathan Demme's *Stop Making Sense*, two Spike favorites by mentor directors. They passed, in part, because Ira Deutchman did not find Tracy Camila Johns sexy as Nola. Through the years, I've tortured Ira by reminding him of this opinion. His usual response is to point out that my investment in the movie was really Cinecom's *Parting Glances* money. Spike retaliated by accusing Cinecom of refusing to put Joe Morton's black face in the ads for *Brother*.

I thought I could assist Spike in three ways aside from my financial contribution. First and foremost, I expected to act as producer's representative on the picture as we mapped out a sales strategy. Of course, we needed a finished film to show. The second step was to help convince Irwin Young at DuArt that Spike deserved a deferment on the $30,000 cost of a 35mm blowup. Now Irwin's a fervid supporter of independent film, but the myth surrounding his initial encounter with Spike is a bit distorted. He did not immediately offer a full deferment. He did not immediately offer a 50 percent deferment. He took me aside and expressed his serious concern about black films that were neither commercial nor specialized, citing as his only example the roller boogie epic *Get Rollin'*. The lab had extended credit as an investment in that film. It had opened at a very commercial screen in Times Square, the Embassy, and gotten an astoundingly good *New York Times* review from Vincent Canby. But nobody went and DuArt dropped a bundle. I assured him that the two films were hardly comparable and that Spike was a man of his word. Irwin eventually agreed to a substantial short-term deferment, a strong inducement to move quickly on selling the picture.

That was good news, because the third way I tried to help Spike involved an outside $15,000 investment that fell through. Although there was no particular advantage for me, I thought I would bundle my money with an additional sum from *Parting Glances* producer Yoram Mandel. Unfortunately for Yoram, he failed to grasp the essence of Spike Lee. He tried to dictate unacceptable conditions regarding cuts, and to secure an executive producer credit for himself. Spike sat in our tiny tenement apartment suffering through Yoram's critique while our two cats, Spike (named for a West Texas bar) and Salem, were under his feet. I later discovered that he has a terrible fear of cats. He needed the money badly, but he had his principles. So he said, "No, thanks." I had no conditions. I could even live with the color sequence, although I did suggest shortening it. Spike's response was that the choreography *and* his father's song were four and a half minutes long; therefore the color sequence must be that long. Other money trickled down, but the big lump sum was a $10,000 Jerome Foundation grant administered by the Film Forum. When my wife, Janet, handed Spike the Jerome check, she actually told him, "John wants to give you all of our money. He thinks you are the future of cinema."

Spike finally came calling for my check after a daylong recording session. I made it out to Shelton J. Lee, his real name and the one he used as producer of the film. He figured that people would tire of the nickname his mom gave him as a toddler after reading "Spike" Lee three times as writer, director, and editor. On the contrary, most people wondered who the hell Shelton could be. Shelton handed us a pair of his precelebrity Knicks tickets (middling yellow seats) and a tape of the "finished" score featuring his father and an exceptional jazz quintet. We listened. Vocalist Ronnie Dyson (remember *Hair*?) sang way off key. I told Spike "He's flat." He said, "No, he's not." I repeated, "He's hopelessly flat." Spike shook his head, "No way." They rerecorded two days later. Spike wrote, "I guess our ears were fatigued, because if he's flat now, he was flat when we recorded it."

The final days of January saw a flurry of activity. *The New York Times* ran a feature by Gary Bradford on the difficulty of raising money for an independent film, that started and ended with Spike. He led off with his already standard story about the credit office at DuArt, run by a very unpleasant man named Howard Funsch, threatening to auction off the *She's Gotta Have It* negative for nonpayment. Spike took the threat quite seriously, as anyone in his shoes would, not realizing that Howie's role, which he savored to an unsettling degree, was to be the aggressive bad cop to Irwin Young's good cop. More significantly, the article concluded with Spike repeating a wonderful line that he'd used at the Bijou rough cut screening: "If I don't raise some money, I'll be selling tube socks on 14th Street." He never became a street vendor, but this idea came in very handy later when we were brainstorming the trailer.

SHE'S GOTTA HAVE IT - FORTY ACRES AND A MULE

TOTAL BUDGET FOR COMPLETION

Outstanding loans, bills and deferred crew salaries	$23,871.21
Actors salaries	$ 6,550.00
Post - production	$83,912.00
TOTAL	$114,333.21

ACTORS SALARIES

Tracey Camilla Johns	$2,000.00
Tommy Redmon Hicks	$2,000.00
Raye Dowell	$ 500.00
John Canada Terrell	$1,000.00
Joie Lee	$ 100.00
Bill Lee	$ 100.00
Aaron Dugger - Dancer	$ 100.00
Cheryl Burr - Dancer	$ 200.00
Stephanie Covington	$ 100.00
Renata Cobbs	$ 100.00
Cheryl Singleton	$ 100.00
Epatha Merkinson	$ 150.00
TOTAL	$6,550.00

POST PRODUCTION

Music	$15,000
Titles/Credits	$ 1,500
Opticals	$ 1,000
Lab-Blow up Super 16 to 35mm	$32,812
Negative cutting	$ 3,000
Sound Editing-incl. 8wk rental of 6 plate	$ 2,000
Sound Editing by SOUND SHOP	
ACCESS	
MIX	
FOLEY	
ADR	
OPTICAL TRACK	
MATERIAL STOCK	$11,600
Pick ups/additional shooting	$ 2,000
Spike Lee-script, directing,producing and acting salary	$15,000
TOTAL	$83,912

FUNDING GRANTS RECEIVED SO FAR

New York State Council of The Arts	$18,000
Brooklyn Arts Cultural Association	$ 500
Jerome Foundation	$10,000

The morning after the *Times* piece ran, Island Pictures chairman Chris Blackwell was passing through New York on the way from Los Angeles to London and asked for an 8:30 A.M. screening which we arranged at DuArt. George Jackson, a producer who could be a very effective word-of-mouth tub thumper, had recommended the film to Blackwell, who arrived bright and early with his black girlfriend. I was impressed with his film company, but I was in awe of Island Records, the label he started with next to nothing in Jamaica in the early sixties, which had discovered Traffic, Bob Marley, and U2. Originally I half-expected to wind up in the music business after investing most of my savings in a blues and jazz record company while I was still in high school. Company founder Tom Pomposello tempted fate (and proved himself a prophet) by naming the label Oblivion Records. I lost everything, had fun doing it, and learned a valuable lesson; music is a good hobby. Blackwell was fairly reticent before and after seeing the film, and absolutely nothing happened with Island at this point. Consequently George Jackson's later suggestion that he initiated the Island deal is a stretch.

As postproduction entered the home stretch, mid-March was the absolute deadline for having a 35mm release print for Filmex, the L.A. festival that had locked up the deal for *Stranger Than Paradise*. Spike wanted to follow in Jarmusch's exact footsteps: Cannes, Filmex, New York Film Festival. The one small problem was that Filmex was canceled forever that year. San Francisco, which started later in March, was the next viable domestic festival. They wanted the film badly. We weren't going to know about the Cannes Directors' Fortnight until the week of March 17. Even with an invitation in hand, it's extremely, almost prohibitively, costly for a low-budget film to go there for the purpose of selling rights. It made sense to have a supportive distributor in place ahead of time.

No matter how cocksure you feel about an unseen movie, its first public exposure is still a time for nail biting. And to enhance the value of a low-budget, no-name first feature, especially a comedy, you have to put in in front of an audience. Every single word that's written and every laugh from that audience winds up under a magnifying glass. Therefore, even when you believe a movie has good genes, you still need to raise it in a nurturing environment while it's a baby.

San Francisco and its well-run festival had several factors in their favor.

Joe's Bed-Stuy Barbershop had been well-received there in 1983. This time, Program Coordinator Laura Thielen wrote a terrific program note that mentioned the past connection and set the tone for the new feature by irresistibly describing Spike's Mars Blackmon character as "the hip hopper in high tops whose primary aspiration is to keep Nola laughing." The regional film press also seemed like a fairly good, if not completely safe, bet. The local *Variety* critic, Herb Michaelson, and the long-time lead critic from the *San Francisco Chronicle*, Judy Stone, had both shown a predisposition toward innovative independents. The first trade review always carries more industry weight than it probably should, especially in terms of predicted gross box office. However the first major consumer newspaper reviews are far more telling. Stone was a slightly tricky call as an old Jewish lefty and strong supporter of women's films. She could get very emotional about hard-hitting political documentaries like *The Battle of Chile*. In fact, when I worked for Tricontinental, the distributor of that and other landmark third-world films, I was told that she was the unofficial litmus test for our potential acquisitions: "When Judy Stone cries, Tri-Con buys." One would have expected her to respond very favorably to a film about a strong, self-determined, sexually active black woman, but the fact that it was written and directed by a black man created a wild card.

A final benefit of playing the film in the Bay Area was the proximity of a large black population in the East Bay—especially Oakland. Spike was ready to go out and start promoting a week before the premiere, as soon as the blowup came out of the lab and the Cannes screening was over. DuArt blew it, falling a week behind schedule. But by now *She's Gotta Have It* had entered a remarkable state of grace where nothing could stop it. The Directors' Fortnight selection duo of Pierre-Henri Deleau and Olivier Jahan had to see the film in less than ideal 16mm double-system conditions the night before Spike's twenty-ninth birthday. At least they heard the fully mixed soundtrack. About half an hour in, they decided to invite it. At that time, it was the only American film they chose for the 1986 Quinzaine, although they would eventually select Lizzie Borden's *Working Girls* as well.

Spike left town with the same unfinished print in tow for the San Francisco press screening. Herb Michaelson, Judy Stone, and twenty other journalists were shoehorned into a stuffy, ridiculously cramped postproduction suite. No one fainted, and the result was pretty electrifying. Judy's minor qualms about the sexual politics disappeared after talking to Spike. You could just feel Spike's confidence growing throughout the week leading up to the prime-time Friday-night curtain raiser. Shortly after his arrival, he appeared on a black filmmaker panel with Danny Glover and Stan Lathan, where he made his first dig at a black celebrity (Bay Area native Whoopi Goldberg) trying to be white (by wearing blue contact lenses). No one had even seen *She's Gotta Have It.* Later we listened to another seminar on distribution featuring Laurie Parker from Island Pictures and the producer's rep for *Blood Simple* and *Desert Hearts,* Jeff Dowd. Dowd suggested that you need to set aside $25,000 above and beyond your production budget to sell your film. Spike leaned over and muttered, "If I had another $25,000, I'd make another motherfuckin' movie." We had about a hundredth of that.

Various *She's Gotta Have It* postcards featuring David Lee's photographs were circulating all across the land and throughout the offices of every distributor. I've always believed that a good postcard is a great method of cheap promotion. These images of Tracy Camila Johns and Spike were particularly intriguing and sexy. As the world premiere, San Francisco was the first golden opportunity for distributors, especially those based in L.A., to check it out knowing full well, because I'd told them all, that it was heading to Cannes. Island's Laurie Parker had come with postcard in hand, along with her colleague, Jesse Beaton. Laurie was just starting a successful career that has seen her become a producer for Gus Van Sant and Tim Burton in the nineties. The 1986 festival marked her return to San Francisco, where she'd started as a cashier in the offices of the Renaissance Rialto art theater chain. From the beginning, her ambition exceeded her job responsibility which led her to complain to her boss Ray Price one day. When he asked her which position at the company might better suit her, she said, "Yours." She became a crucial player in the Spike deal.

Twenty-four hours before the show in the 900-seat Palace of Fine Arts, the black audience had not yet been mobilized to buy advance tickets for *She's Gotta Have It.* The finished blowup hadn't arrived yet either. Friday morning I woke up at Ray Price's house, read two very good reviews in the *Chronicle* and the *Examiner,* then sat down with a cup of coffee to listen to the virtually unknown Spike Lee give his first major radio interview on the morning drive-time show on Oakland's top-rated R&B station. After two entertaining, occasionally tongue-tied hours during which Spike kept saying the word "ideal" when he meant "idea," the smooth-talking DJ, Lee Hildebrande, asked if he had any final words. Spike said, "You're going to want to be at the show tonight so you can tell your grandchildren in thirty years you were there." Ray Price almost fell off his chair. Over 600 tickets sold that day, right up to the 7:30 showtime. The final late arrivals made it a sellout. When Janet and I picked up Spike at the Diva Hotel, he volunteered another astonishing prediction when he said, "I guess my life won't ever be the same after tonight." When I encouraged him to share a couple of his goals, aside from making a movie a year, he mentioned two things. He wanted Stevie Wonder to do a soundtrack for him. Stevie, who is known for being perpetually late, came through four films later on *Jungle Fever*. He also wanted to do sneaker commercials with Michael "Air" Jordan and Mars Blackmon, a character he didn't have other plans to resuscitate. Those ads were on the air at the next NBA All-Star game—in black and white, no less.

BLACK AND WHITE

When I woke up the next morning, I realized that my life had changed too. For starters, the knot that had been in my stomach all week had disappeared. And in my foggy San Francisco half-sleep, I remembered something about blackouts and blank checks.

It's a pretty good indication that you've primed the sales pump effectively when distributors start picking up the tab before they've even seen the film. The Samuel Goldwyn Company, spearheaded by the ultra-enthusiastic Jeff Lipsky, flew up a team of six for a prescreening "let's get acquainted" session. Lipsky already had the Jarmusch seal of approval for his expert handling of *Stranger Than Paradise*. When Spike walked into the restaurant and laid eyes on Jeff's New York Mets warm-up jacket, Goldwyn immediately had the inside track. Although Dwight Gooden hadn't yet thrown the first pitch of opening day, 1986 would turn out to be the year of the Mets. There were only a few black faces on that team—Gooden, Darryl Strawberry, Mookie Wilson. *She's Gotta Have It* had nothing but black faces, and 1986 would also turn out to be the year of Spike Lee.

The Palace of Fine Arts, which had been built long before for a world exposition, had a classic look along with an out-of-date building code. As the auditorium filled up with industry types, regular festivalgoers, and a substantial black middle-class audience dressed for a night on the town, I suddenly realized that no one had seen the 35mm print that had finally arrived earlier in the day. When the lights went down, everyone was ready. I groaned when the show started with a lousy short with a minstrel show feeling. It's a standard festival nightmare to have the programmers put an inappropriate short, which they've decided is a perfect companion piece, before the feature. Once the New York Film Festival put a Peter Greenaway film about people who had been struck by lightning in front of Wim Wenders's *Lightning Over Water*. Really amusing. I escaped to the lobby and hoped that spirits inside wouldn't sag. Finally a quotation from Zora Neale Hurston rolled down the big screen, signaling the start of the feature.

The newly struck 35mm print looked and sounded great. The audience of nearly a thousand was clearly caught up in the film from the moment the 40 Acres and a Mule production credit appeared. But like the crude screening at NYU five months earlier, it was the "dogs" at the ten minute mark that brought down the house. It was Spike's joint from that moment on, which was a very fortunate development when the screen went dark about twenty minutes later. The Palace was pitch black because it had no emergency lighting. No one knew exactly what had happened, but immediately it was clear that it wasn't a simple projection failure. The power in the building, throughout the neighborhood, across the entire Marina District of San Francisco was out for no explicable reason, just when the crowd was under our command.

I took a deep breath and screamed silently. But I noticed that no one was leaving. No one was even moving—except for one person, a distributor. Ben Barenholtz of Circle Films found me in a dark aisle, pulled out a checkbook, and asked me how much we wanted for the movie. He'd only seen one third, but he made both a bold and smart move. I didn't have time to think about whether he was serious or not because the festival's artistic director Peter Scarlet was conferring with me about what to do next. After an eternal ten or fifteen minutes, we decided to give Spike and Tommy Hicks flashlights to shine on their faces and sent them up on stage to answer questions. Obviously you wouldn't normally do this after thirty minutes of a feature, but we were desperate to hold the crowd while we found out when the power might be restored. The very first question was, "What happens next?" and Spike nearly threw his flashlight at the lunkhead who asked it. After about ten minutes of them buying time, a SWAT team showed up to help empty the theater. No one was leaving, although the room had now been dark for as long as the movie had been on. The police became impatient and were just about to forcibly evacuate the crowd, effectively ending the premiere of *She's Gotta Have It*, when the lights flashed on followed immediately by a great cheer. Barenholtz again flashed what appeared to be a checkbook and pen.

The film resumed at the beginning of the second reel, and the response kept building and building to a tumultuous standing ovation. I got tremendous feedback from the Goldwyn contingent and three key exhibitors. One was Gary Meyer, co-founder of the extremely influential Landmark Theater chain, and another was Ray Price who realized that Spike had made good on his audacious morning prediction, and the third was elder statesman Mel Novikoff, who had recently ceded control of Surf Theaters to Ray. Somehow the Island Pictures duo slipped away before we could talk, and I made a note to track them like a bloodhound on Saturday morning. Then I collapsed in utter elation.

Spike was scheduled to leave for Los Angeles the next afternoon with his associate producer Pamm Jackson. After I sniffed out Island's Jesse Beaton and heard her voice added to the chorus of raves, I called him to report that the vote was unanimous. I also asked him if he'd seen the blackout story on the front page of the *Examiner*. The paper gave the film its first hilariously mistranslated title, *She's Got a Habit*, and went on to add that "it's quite graphic and it's not about a nun."

We stayed on in San Francisco through the weekend to savor the last taste of a vintage festival. The buzz on the street was Spike, Spike, Spike. Earlier in the week, we'd all gone to see *Salvador*, Oliver Stone's ballsy directorial breakthrough. America's two most controversial filmmakers—together for the first time at the 1986 San Francisco International Film Festival. Stone wasn't there, of course. He was off making *Platoon*. (No one could guess then that their careers would dovetail so perfectly when Warners released *JFK* and *Malcolm X* as consecutive, prestige, year-end Oscar contenders in 1991 and 1992, respectively.) We'd also seen six of the unreleased BBC features of the superb, then unknown British director Mike Leigh. San Francisco also had a locally famous pair of animation programmers called Spike and Mike, whose latest anthology was about to play at the Palace of Fine Arts. So the town was taken over by Spike Lee, Mike Leigh, Spike & Mike. More seriously, the festival honored Akira Kurosawa with a lifetime achievement award. I'd recently programmed a complete Kurosawa retrospective at New York's Film Forum. No matter how thrilling the success of *She's Gotta Have It* might have been, I was truly awestruck to sit down, ever so briefly, with the great Kurosawa.

We finally pushed on to L.A. to have follow-up screenings and meetings with the distributors there. It was my first trip to that city as an adult. I was the only driver in our group and had to instill confidence in the troops by pretending that I knew my way around. We had one Hertz rental car with one print in the trunk. What more could you need? That print ping-ponged between screening rooms, including the private one at Sam Goldwyn Jr.'s house. Although George Lucas and Quincy Jones requested screenings, there was *no* studio interest in Spike. It was a different world then. On Tuesday there were back-to-back make-or-break conferences with Goldwyn and Island. The Goldwyn session was a bust. Spike described their $50,000 offer as an insult. I took it as a lowball opening bid, but felt as if Sam Jr. probably hadn't gotten the film. I told their acquisitions V.P. Larry Jackson that the offer was "missing a zero." Thinking that he had a gift for repartee, Larry asked where the zero would go. Business affairs head Norman Flicker looked like he was ready to hit the tennis court. We traded looks of condolence with Jeff Lipsky, who had prepared an enormously detailed eight-page distribution and marketing plan that was clearly not going to be put to use.

Years later Jeff confirmed his monumental frustration and explained that he had talked himself blue in the face until he finally stared at his colleagues and told them never to look back and say, "We should have bought *She's Gotta Have It.*" Maybe they paid too much attention to the *Variety* review, which called the movie "a worthy but flawed attempt."

Island was a completely different story. Film division president Cary Brokaw and distribution/marketing V.P. Russell Schwartz got it and wanted it. They didn't blink at a domestic advance of at least $250,000 and they were interested in world rights in Cannes as well. They already had *Mona Lisa* and Jarmusch's second feature, *Down By Law,* scheduled for the Cannes Competition, giving them enormous profile. Island also planned to presell its first significant production, *Nobody's Fool*—a dark cloud on the horizon.

To _____ All Concerned _____ **Date** _____ 3/31/86 _____

From _____ Jeff Lipsky _____ **Re:** _ "She's Gotta Have It" - Page 1_

What is "She's Gotta Have It?" It is the first work of a
talented hyphenate (director-writer-actor-editor) whose style
is so unique, direct, and appealing that he is definitely
someone whose future work we, and the rest of the cinema world,
should certainly be on the look out for. He is the first young
black filmmaker to break out into the pantheon of media darlings
like Jim Jarmusch, Susan Seidleman, Donna Deitch, John Sayles
and Marty Scorsese. More importantly his debut feature is not
a social issue movie; in this case the talent of an individual
is speaking rather than the individual trying to speak for an
entire race or for an entire cause. The cause Spike addresses
is both the oldest and the freshest and, at once, identifiable
to all people: sex, love, power and sex. It is ironic that a
white filmmaker made "Sounder" and that another white filmmaker
made "The Color Purple," in both cases perhaps out of liberal
guilt. Spike·doesn't suffer from guilt he suffers from talent
and a great sense of humor.

What is "She's Gotta Have It?" It is a pull yourself up by your boot-
straps movie. It cost $20,000 cash and $100,000 in deferments. It
was shot in 14 days in July 1985. It is a popular and critical
success in San Francisco (as well as a success with the local
exhibitors) and has been chosen to compete in the Director's
Fortnight in the upcoming Cannes Film Festival. It is a film
featuring total unknowns, some of whom are sure to go on other
notable projects, and all of whom live in the United States and
will be able to tour with the film once it opens.

What is "She's Gotta Have It?" "She's Gotta Have It" is one of
the sexiest and most erotic mainstream films (in a non-self
conscious way at that) in recent years. More significantly
they are satiric and humorous at the same time they are being
exciting. It is a rarity in current films dealing with the subject:
it is a film unafraid of sex. In these days of AIDS, homosexuality,
safe sex, puritanism and Jerry Falwell it sticks its neck out and says
that the only problem with sex is that it can fuck up your love life.
It is an entertainment; no time-outs for medical precautions or social
messages. This is its strength, this is how the film must be positioned
(using all of the above, as well) and this is why the film will succeed.
We must take advantage of the controversy that will be stimulated by the

Having just won the Best Actor/Best Actress Oscars in March, Island was releasing films with style and gusto. It was immediately clear over lunch with Russell and Jesse Beaton that Island wouldn't tiptoe around the blackness of the film. Before arriving at Island, Russell had an extensive bicoastal resume ranging from repertory exhibition (Regency in New York) to production (Bogdanovich's *They All Laughed*) to art distribution (Landmark Films). I originally got to know him when I played Landmark's reissue of Kurosawa's *Seven Samurai* at the Bleecker. Like her colleague Laurie Parker, Jesse came out of the San Francisco art exhibition scene, where she worked for Ben Myron. After Island she produced Carl Franklin's films starting with *One False Move*. Their boss Cary Brokaw was just about the whitest man I ever met, and a surfer dude to boot. Somehow even with his studio background and his teeth, Cary got the spirit on Spike's movie. Island Pictures was the place to be.

Circle Releasing remained willing to match their every move. Spike's former boss from First Run Features, Fran Spielman, had become Circle's distribution head. Since we felt like we had another two weeks to play out the negotiation and still leave nearly a month for Cannes preparations, we scheduled an open distributor screening at the Film Forum in New York. The day of that screening we agreed to allow the Orion Classics triumvirate (of Barker, Bernard and Gigliotti) to see it in their own screening room. Their recent acquisition of Peter Wang's *The Great Wall* was one of our deal benchmarks. Although they promptly joined the race, their evaluation really seemed to be "art film" all the way. They ran at half-speed.

Three of the distributors at the afternoon show had very diverse responses. Bill Quigley from Vestron, an extremely successful home video company that had recently tapped him to run a theatrical division, was the first to pass. They were looking for "comedies and thrillers" and *She's Gotta Have It* didn't qualify. Jonathan Olsberg from Spectrafilm was the first distributor to pound away on the "black Woody Allen" comparison. In our one and only painful meeting, Spike said about two words and pulled his cap down lower and lower as Olsberg went on and on about how the Woodman's name *must* appear on the poster. As we left, Spike summed up the meeting under his breath: "bush league." All that blather made us forty-five minutes late for an Italian dinner meeting with Michael Rosenblatt from Atlantic Releasing. He told Spike that Atlantic had a movie for him to write, a movie for him to direct, and a movie for him to star in. He also bragged about their success with *Teen Wolf* and may have even expressed regret over not having *Soul Man*. Get the hook! Spike had already launched his missiles at Rae Dawn Chong for appearing in that white man in black face anti–affirmative action crock.

For the rest of April we kept moving toward the Island deal, but sometimes it was two steps forward, one step back. Russell Schwartz dropped two bombshells during a trip through New York. They wanted three cuts: Two were acceptable to Spike, but the third was a *dealbreaker* (I remember being impressed the way Spike said that word). It was the controversial near-rape scene at the end. They also wanted an option for another picture—not exactly an unreasonable position. In the meantime, I hand-carried the print (which was still the one and only print) to Ben Barenholtz's partner, Ted Pedas, in Washington, D.C., where he owned Circle Theaters. Ted eventually sold his theater chain to Cineplex for $30 million plus. Even before then he was loaded. Circle was looking to re-create the kind of relationship that it had established with Spike's NYU compatriot Joel Coen and his brother, Ethan. But we had fully concluded that Island's ability to release the film domestically, sell the film internationally, highlight it in Cannes, make another movie with Spike, and pay a $400,000 advance really clinched it.

We verbally accepted Island's terms on April 28 with ten days to go before Cannes. When the contract came over, Chris Blackwell and Cary Brokaw had pulled a dirty trick by making the option clause for *two* additional pictures. On the one hand, it would be dramatically impressive to announce a three-picture deal at Cannes. Trade ads were ready to go along with thousands of buttons and jerseys and postcards, and the whole cast was about to leave for Paris, pick up the freshly subtitled print and jump on the overnight train to Nice. No one had *ever* discussed the second option. I felt utterly manipulated as we caved in. I had trusted Russell Schwartz and failed to devise a protective shield against this stunt.

It was a great year in Cannes for a groundbreaking new American independent director like Spike to burst upon the world film scene. Almost all of the big Hollywood celebrities were scared off by two huge geopolitical events. The United States had just bombed Qaddafi's Libyan compound right across the Mediterranean, and it was expected that he would exact some revenge through a terrorist bombing. As if that weren't enough discouragement, Chernobyl had blown up and the prevailing radioactive winds resulted in a warning not to eat any leafy vegetables.

FILMS INCORPORATED
INTEROFFICE CORRESPONDENCE

TO _____ OFFICE _____ DATE _____

FROM _____ OFFICE _____

SUBJECT   DEAL POINTS: "SHE'S GOTTA HAVE IT"

Term: 15 years, all rights world-wide

Advance: $400,000 payable as follows:
1. $100,000 on delivery, but:
   a. $27,000 to Duart Film Lab now, deductible from first payment
   b. $10,000 for Errors & Omissions Insurance deductible from first payment
   c. $63,000 balance on delivery
   **d. $25,000 advance for all Cannes Festival expenses (print,subtitling, travel for 6 people, housing,per diem,promo materials) to be taken off the top upon release as a distribution cost.
2. $100,000 on opening day or October 1, 1986, whichever is first
3. $100,000 90-days after opening or January 1, 1987, whichever is first
4. $100,000 on July 1, 1987

U.S./Canada Advance	Foreign Advance
$250,000	$150,000
30% distribution fee,costs off top	17.5% sales fee, costs off top
30%/70% paycable	(up to recoupment of advance)
35%/65% syndication	20% sales fee after recoupment
15%/85% network (ha,ha)	
HOMEVIDEO: we get 100% of standard 20%	MAXIMUM OF 50% CROSS-COLLATERALIZATION
royalty on the wholesale cassette price	BETWEEN FOREIGN AND DOMESTIC

Consultation: on all marketing,sales,trailer,ad & poster design, etc.

Delivery Condition: Two scenes to be removed from the negative completely totalling less than four minutes, those being:***
1. Final scene between Nola & Opal at Opal's house
2. Nola & Clorinda moving day flashback.

No other cuts or changes are conditional, except that it is understood that the film must receive an R-rating from the MPAA

***The cost of cutting these two scenes shall be advanced by Island Pictures as a distribution cost.

Big strong men like Sly Stallone and Clint Eastwood stayed home. The biggest American star was probably Griffin Dunne who was promoting *After Hours* alone since Martin Scorsese also kept his distance.

Going to the Cannes Film Festival for the first time is one of the most disorienting and surreal experiences you can have in your life. For me it all started with an early morning arrival at the Côte d'Azur Airport, where Lou "Incredible Hulk" Ferrigno was waved straight through customs. The rest is a blur—exorbitant cab ride to Cannes, stepping out on the curb into baking sunlight and festival fever, wading through a bureaucratic maze to pick up accreditation. It's an impossible situation if you don't have a job to focus on and a comfortable place to stay. I arrived in 1986 with the first, and thought that Spike's digs would provide the second. Within minutes I determined that there wasn't even an empty corner on the floor. Fortunately after hours of drifting about on the first night, Ray Price took me in. I found a room at the Jarmusch-endorsed Hôtel Univers the next day and slept for twelve hours. Island spent $40,000 on *She's Gotta Have It* in Cannes that year, a fairly modest amount. My country boy upbringing told me not to raise that tally on my account. If only I'd had enough confidence in my high school French to ask for toothpaste (dentifrice) in a pharmacy (pharmacie), I would have been all set.

Spike and his exotic black cast were in the spotlight even before *She's Gotta Have It* premiered. The French title was *Nola Darling: N'en Fait Qu'a Sa Tête*. The translation and subtitle spotting were done by the gifted Pierre Cottrell, who'd produced Jean Eustache's masterpiece *The Mother and the Whore*. A former French New Wave producer transplanted to Berkeley, Pierre was in on the secret that Spike had looked to that movement as one of his stylistic sources. The first screening at the beautiful Old Palais was the crowning achievement after Spike's many struggles. He was practically carried down the massive steps when he emerged after the show. Later that night glamour turned back to reality when he returned to a modest apartment that he was sharing with Tracy Camila Johns, Raye Dowell, Tommy Hicks, John Canada Terrell, and Pamm Jackson. I think Tommy was sleeping in the bathtub. I've often been asked if the actors were like their characters. Of course I answer yes. When queried further on how John Terrell could be an egomaniacal womanizer like Greer, I usually point out that he surpassed Greer in every way in Cannes. Tracy and Raye promenaded topless, which undoubtedly helped the French press dub Tracy "the new Josephine Baker."

It was a watershed event for American indies. Sara Driver's *Sleepwalk* opened the International Critics' Week. Eugene Corr's *Desert Bloom* and Glenn Pitre's *Belizaire the Cajun* both played in the "un certain regard" section (as someone once pointed out, only the French could say they have "a certain regard" for your film and mean it as a compliment). Lizzie Borden's *Working Girls* was Spike's compatriot in the Directors' Fortnight. Finally Jim Jarmusch returned to the scene of his triumph two years before with the competition entry *Down by Law*. Although there was some immediate competition over the international sales figures for the two new films, Jim remained a crucial role model for Spike. Goldwyn had a promotion going throughout the week for their upcoming *Chipmunk Adventure* with four or five people in furry costumes. Spike wanted to know if it was okay to be photographed with the chipmunks without looking stupid. Jim nodded his approval.

Although the French press couldn't get enough of Spike, many American journalists had also been scared away from the 1986 festival. In fact, of the two key articles that appeared in the consumer press in the United States, one in the *New York Post* called Spike the "black Woody Allen" and another in the *Washington Post* suggested that *She's Gotta Have It* would probably play only at college film societies. At least Roger Ebert filed a piece that described it as "filled with life and funniness." The Island deal announcement was major industry news. The trade stories featured an illuminating photograph of the very tall and white Cary Brokaw standing next to the very short and black Spike Lee—the ultimate odd couple.

For the last weekend, I hunkered down with Russell Schwartz at the Island business suite in the Gray D'Albion Hotel and helped to close $400,000 in world sales, in the process giving *Down by Law* a run for the money. The results were sensational and enormously rewarding for our producer's share because Island had agreed to take a low foreign sales fee and cross-collateralize only half of the revenue. In other words, only $200,000 could be applied toward any future costs in North America if *She's Gotta Have It* failed to make money. Unsurprisingly, the biggest single territorial sale involved France. A brand new company run by Jean Labadie called Bac Films took the prize. Some people questioned that sale at the time. Bac Films has subsequently grown to be the Miramax of France. Jeff Lipsky kept tabs on our foreign tally as it soared so that he could rub it in back at Goldwyn. When I saw Goldwyn's Larry Jackson on the Croisette, I mentioned that I could hardly keep track of the zeroes.

I flew back to New York on Monday morning with Russell and Jesse Beaton several hours before the names of the award winners were released. Spike coveted the Camera d'Or for best first feature. He'd already won a prestigious French prize called the Prix de la Jeunesse on Saturday, but we didn't believe that this precluded anything else. We all thought that the stiffest competition would come from a well-received Japanese comedy called *Comic Magazine*. As we were leaving the hotel, Dave Kehr walked by. He was then a Chicago film critic and a knowledgeable member of the New York Film Festival selection committee. So we asked him for a hint. He said enigmatically, "I can't tell you, but it's black and white." Since the Japanese film was in color, we were celebrating on the drive to the Nice airport. There was still a twinge of doubt when we landed at JFK hours later so Jesse called France to confirm the victory. The French publicist said that "Black and White" had won. Jesse, doing her best "who's on first" routine, told her to stop teasing and say which black-and-white film had won. At that point the publicist grasped our misunderstanding and explained that an obscure French film that nobody had seen called *Noir et Blanc* had won. I was angry at Dave Kehr (no big fan of Spike it turned out) for years for skewering us like that. Spike had his first Cannes letdown which he summed up in two ways. He said, "We wuz robbed" and started calling the Prix de la Jeunesse the "booby prize."

BIRTH OF A SALESMAN

Everyone was back home by late May. The New York Film Festival committee had already invited *She's Gotta Have It* before Cannes ended. We shifted onto a completely different track, despite Spike's years of wanting to be the homeboy in his hometown festival. Island had a bold new initiative. Let the artiste Jim Jarmusch wait for the fall; Spike's movie was going out in early August. The release of *Kiss of the Spider Woman* the previous summer had broken the outdated commandment "Thou shalt not open non-Hollywood pictures in hot weather."

Preparations needed to proceed with all speed. The immediate complication was that the international buzz had not carried back to the

United States that strongly. Island's longtime publicity firm Clein & Feldman quickly scheduled a long-lead screening for a handful of people—Bruce Williamson from *Playboy*, Stephen Schiff from *Vanity Fair*, Stephen Schaefer from *US*, and Judy Doren from the *Village Voice*. The best comment any of them could muster was the man from Playboy calling it "amateurish but sexy." Schiff has never liked Spike's work. Doren who was, and is, in charge of the *Voice*'s monthly ticket giveaway screenings apparently found the sexual politics offensive and inappropriate for *Voice* readers. Clein and Feldman panicked, thinking Island had acquired a real turkey after a string of highbrow pearls. Of course they had no clue about the black audience. On top of that, their tiny, all-white first screening demonstrated the common blunder of extrapolating too much from too few.

We spent the month of June cutting the trailer and devising the print and poster campaign. Using the images from a lively color photo shoot where Spike almost forgot his Mars gold chain, Island had their enormously gifted design agency Concept Arts work up 4-color comps on six different campaigns. Each one was strong in its own way, ranging from a musical approach to sexy Nola alone to goofy heads on cartoon bodies. *Stranger Than Paradise* may have had black-and-white graphics, but *She's Gotta Have It* was going to look like a splashy, colorful film. The Keith Haring–style title treatment was clearly a great choice, and the tag line "a seriously sexy comedy" easily defeated the runner-up "a mighty black comedy." The debate about key art was much harder. Cary Brokaw stepped in forcefully as final arbiter and declared that the design in which heads of Nola and her three suitors pop in from the edges of the frame was Island's choice. Although poor Tommy Hicks had to suffer many Chicken McNugget forehead jokes, that campaign was letter-perfect for newspaper advertising. It leaped off the page.

The collaborative trailer went back to Spike's "tube socks" quote from October 1985 and January 1986. Island cut the middle of the trailer using black-and-white footage from the film proper. Spike wrote and directed a color wraparound shot in front of a Keith Haring mural on East 7th Street. He plays himself hyping the movie, begging people to see it so that he doesn't have to go back out on the street selling "tube socks, tube socks, three for $5." As soon as the trailer was done and on screen at Dan Talbot's theaters near the Clein & Feldman office, we walked publicist Susan Jacobs and the whole staff over to give them a morale boost. Whenever that preview showed in front of any film, the audience went wild. Of course we still needed some critical support for *She's Gotta Have It*, but its populist appeal was undeniable.

As with all Spike's subsequent features, his contract required that he deliver an R-rated picture. The Motion Picture Association of America (MPAA) slapped an "X" on *She's Gotta Have It* for the first time in late May. Much has been said and written about the ratings board having a bias against black sexuality and/or independent distributors like Island Pictures. This may very well have been true then, and it may be true now. Nevertheless, they definitely do not give R ratings to studio movies in which you can see an erect penis of any color. In the Greer/ Nola pixilated jungle-drumming sex scene that appeared in the original version of *She's Gotta Have It*, you could most definitely see a black man's (John Canada Terrell) erection. That was the original problem, which Spike then compounded. He removed some, but not all, of that erection before resubmission. At that point it might have seemed subliminal, but the MPAA panel members were probably annoyed at the attempt to slip one through.

In many cases, it is seemingly impossible to figure out exactly what to recut. The studios can wear the board down by going back again and again, but this takes both time and money. In a break with established tradition, MPAA ratings board head Richard Heffner explained his theory to me and suggested specific cuts. He said the board tries to look "with the eyes of a parent" and found the film "sexually saturated" even if part of that effect was "film illusion." More specifically he referred to the penis in question as a "smoking gun." Although it may have been removed, it opened the door to explicit complaints about how there were "three thrusts too many" from Greer, not to mention what he called "multiple rear entry" in a fantasy sequence in Nola's near-rape scene. He practically drew a road map.

Opening day in New York had been set for Friday, August 8, at the Cinema Studio across from Lincoln Center. The Black Filmmaker Foundation, under the leadership of Warrington Hudlin, had set up a gala benefit premiere ten days before, the first time the film was seen by a nearly all-black audience. A solid promotional foundation was in place and Spike had insisted on hiring separate black publicists in New York and Los Angeles. Given Clein & Feldman's anxiety level, you couldn't blame him for forcing the issue. The New York special interest publicist took one look at Tommy's truncated face on the poster and suggested some nefarious plot to cut him off at the nose. The film was set to open exclusive engagements in New York followed one week later by Chicago, followed a week after that by L.A. and Washington, D.C. The sequence was a bit odd but Chicago had an important black film festival called Blacklight just prior to the scheduled opening. Island got the trailer on screens all over the country where it was making new converts every day. In a very unusual coup for a low-budget independent, they actually spent $13,000 for a huge billboard on Sunset Boulevard a few blocks from their offices. Suddenly there were big black faces (half a face in Tommy's case) in between images of *The Fly* and *Aliens*.

As we entered the final week before the opening, two question marks were in the air. The MPAA had refused to grant an R rating three more times after very slight additional trims. The response of the white film press also remained an enigma. One of the very first favorable features had been written by Anne Thompson, another former schoolmate and Roadmovies partner, in the *LA Weekly* under the headline THE BLACK WOODY ALLEN? (at least it had the question mark). Spike explained to Anne that they had two things in common: "We're both from Brooklyn, and we're both funny." Just two days before the opening, the *Village Voice* finally gave Spike the full star treatment—front cover, review, and interview all under the headline BIRTH OF A SALESMAN. In his review, David Edelstein acknowledged having been at the previous fall's rough cut screening: "I had a hard time responding to anything except Lee's performance; and I wasn't sure I even wanted to go back for seconds. . . . I couldn't believe how fluid and ingratiating it had become." The circle was closing.

The twenty-four hours after the Thursday evening gala premiere were still a bit unnerving. Friends found it presumptuous that Spike Lee's name was above the title on the marquee when he was just an unknown. Russell Schwartz and I grabbed an early edition of *The New York Times* on our way to the Sneaker Jam at Spike's Joint, aka the Puck Building. This review, normally a key break for specialized films, was written by a fourth-string book critic who called *She's Gotta Have It* "technically messy" undercutting its "serious, even poignant" message. It wasn't exactly a bad review, and Spike always asserted that the film wasn't a comedy. It definitely wasn't the sort of "money" review that sells tickets to white, arty filmgoers. The first matinee at noon on Friday had only about twenty-five customers. There was no time to worry too much about that humble start because the MPAA had threatened Island with a full-fledged lawsuit for displaying a poster with an R rating (their copyright) while the film was unreeling unrated. They sprang their devious trap. Either we cut the entire second half (thirty seconds) of pixilated sex or the MPAA would go to court. I called editor Barry Brown at his weekend house in Bucks County, Pennsylvania, to beg him to hustle into town, go to the projection booth at the Cinema Studio and physically cut the offending footage out of the very print that was showing. He left his newborn baby and made it in time to cut and splice between the second and third shows. Spike always resented the pressure tactics, but he had tempted fate in the first place.

Somehow the word of mouth needed one afternoon to spread. When I looked up at the 6:00 P.M. screening, the Cinema Studio was full. It stayed that way for the next three weeks, each one surpassing the previous week's house record. We entertained ourselves by counting the number of turnaways. Spike was selling and signing T-shirts outside whenever he was in town. I was inside helping Carlos Canessa, the manager, fill every last seat. The Cinema Studio was *the* place to be in New York City in August 1986. The Broadway sidewalk was always congested. One night Eddie Murphy and his entourage took all fourteen spots in the last row. Robert Townsend, known then as an up-and-coming comic and supporting actor in *A Soldier's Story*, checked out the scene one sultry evening when Janet and I were eating outside at a nearby cafe with Spike's lawyer, Loretha Jones. He was finishing a film with Goldwyn's postproduction backing called *Hollywood Shuffle*. He'd shot the comedy skit material on his own with his credit cards. Despite blowing it with Spike, Sam Goldwyn Jr. had black film credentials, having produced one of the very best films of the early seventies, *Cotton Comes to Harlem*. He aggressively corrected his Spike slight by grabbing the Townsend project. It was even in color. Later on, Loretha backed the wrong horse when she became Robert Townsend's producer on the commercially unsuccessful *Five Heartbeats* and the inane *Meteor Man*. She disappeared from my life without a trace.

By the end of the first weekend, Spike had earned his marquee credit. He couldn't just hang around New York to savor it because he had three weeks of publicity roadwork. The rest of my life stopped. I often camped out at the theater with another investor, Earl Smith, who saw a fleet of cars in his future. Then we went to Chicago for two days for the opening at the Fine Arts. Dave Kehr wrote a dismissive two-star review in the *Tribune*, but it still sold out. The official company line always described the *She's Gotta Have It* audience as 50 percent black/50 percent white, but crowd composition throughout the run was more than 75 percent black and the degree of celebration, identification, and pride was really palpable. Spike always said you never get to see black people kissing. He gave them a lot more. Even the 40 Acres logo got a rise out of black viewers. Los Angeles was the third stop for an opening weekend sensation. We were reunited with Spike, Monty Ross, Pamm Jackson, the whole cast, and all the Island staffers. Monty was holding court like a cross between Martin Luther King and Barry White. "You so fine baby I'll drink a tub of your bathwater" indeed! The Royal Theater in Santa Monica didn't set a house record until the second week of the run, but a teenager named John Singleton showed up right away and talked to Spike in the lobby. Spike didn't really seem taken aback by any of this instant success. Later the most he would admit was that it all happened faster than he expected.

I went to Telluride over Labor Day while the film's playoff expanded. It was nearly the only thing everyone was talking about, and I didn't once remove my "Please baby please" T-shirt. I remember standing with Boston's George Mansour, just about the savviest specialized film buyer anywhere, as he phoned Beantown for the terrific grosses. Before long, *She's Gotta Have It* was playing on twenty-five screens in the New York area, and over a hundred nationwide. Island had won the rights to the film by claiming that it wouldn't be an art release. Now they were pushing it. Spike was worried. Russell convinced me. I convinced Spike. Even if we'd protested, Island wasn't about to stop the train.

The New York break became a golden opportunity to tour the five boroughs and surrounding suburbs that had always been mysterious to me as an art film guy. In Bloomfield, New Jersey, *She's Gotta Have It* played in a twin with *Women's Prison Massacre* on the other screen. In Valley Stream it played in a theater the size of an airport hangar, and it actually looked great—and people went! With Island spending quite liberally, the grosses rose from one to two to four million dollars by mid-October. Spike was on *Today*, the *NBC Evening News*, and most important, the cover of *Jet* before you could say Jack Robinson. One of

TOWN AND STATE	THEATRE	CONT.# DATE APP. DATE	SUBJECT AND TERMS	PLAYDATE	SUN.	MON.	TUES.	WED.	THUR.	FRI.	SAT.	GROSS TOTAL	LESS 2ND FEAT.	NET GROSS	GROSS FILM RENTAL	LESS ADV.	NET FILM RENTAL	INV. NO. B.O.S.	AMOUNT BILLED	AMOUNT PAID	BALANCE DUE
		WEEK #13	NEW YORK	8/8-14	9858	7134	6709	7365	7206	8682	9933	57,086									
		21,810		8/15-21	10,857	7485	7668	7992	7809	9108	11133	61,992									
		19,887	Cine INDIO	8/22-28	10785	7800	7623	8361	8193	8934	10,896	62,592									
				8/29-9/4	9300	10,251	5424	5751	5856	9543	7849	55,771									
				9/5-11	8916	4423	4116	4323	4203	7806	8835	42,722									
				9/12-18	6198	2859	2913	2826	3727	7689	7923	33,537									
				9/19-25	5536	2001	2163			6753	7818										
		102,406	NY AREA BREAK	9/12-18	33,732					(25,926)	42,748										
		122,406	16 SCREENS 20 "	9/19-25																	
		21,559	NYC (QUAD)	8/29-9/4	8664	7665	3733	3925	4204	7932	8319	43,882									
		20,612		9/5-11	7707	2968	3568	4080	4751	7191	8568	38,833									
				9/12-18	6252	2935	5198	2820	3245	7201	8106	37,757									
				9/19-25	5740	2469	2522			6617	8055										
		13,335	NYC METRO	8/29-9/4	5885	4905	2148	2202	2478	4332	5076	27,026									
		13,296		9/5-11	4446	1281	1461	1608	1767	4386	6126	21,075									
				9/12-18	3209	1338	1305	1122	1254	4254	5772	18,354									
				9/19-25	3492	963	1071			3887	5922										
		19,307	NYC RKO 86 ST	9/5-11	4738	1703	2277	2429	2522	5709	5815	23,193									
		20,151		9/12-18	5651	2128	2211	2420	2991	6389	7267	28,857									
				9/19-25	5706	2088	2115			6594	7851										
		178,947																			

CUMULATIVE GROSS = 1,621,743 (9/15)

TOTALS:
8/8-14 57,086
8/15-21 94,415
8/22-28 168,453   { BAM = 101,645
8/29-9/4 419,731   { NYC = 126,808
9/5-11 724,457
9/12-18 649,000

Spike's first talk appearances was on the short-lived *David Brenner Show*. Spike got off his line about Woody Allen having no blacks in his New York movies, and Brenner retorted with "I don't see too many Jews in yours." He was always the serious filmmaker in this setting, not Mars Blackmon the clown. That's why Letterman passed on him. He did trot out Mars briefly on a *Saturday Night Live* appearance introducing Run-DMC. On the show, Mars complained about rap's false violent image while the group pulverized Lorne Michaels backstage.

The runaway phenomenon was quite unprecedented and definitely not review driven. The critics recognized a force of nature, but they were sometimes grudging in their praise. Many called the film awkward and threadbare. In a strange way, the universally panned color sequence turned out to be a useful lightning rod. Having an easy target to attack and deride as an example of the movie's flaws spared other lesser imperfections. The issues surrounding Opal as a predatory lesbian and Spike's overall sexual politics escaped criticism. One night about three weeks into the run, an audience at the Cinema Studio actually broke into spontaneous applause at the end of that sequence. I decided if they ate that up, a $10 million gross seemed possible. I also decided it was time to pull selected color sequence quotes for Spike's amusement:

"It thuds along . . . Stops dead in its tracks"
"In every way, an amateur blotch. . . . Sticks out like a bludgeoned digit."
"The jolt just may be the best argument against colorization."
"An inane salute to *The Wizard of Oz*."
"The amateurish sequence must have Vincente Minnelli twirling in his grave."

Ironically, Spike couldn't get the MGM musicals he saw at Radio City Music Hall as a child out of his system.

Inevitably within moments of a first-time success, everyone wants to know what's next. The savvy filmmaker starts pushing the follow-up project immediately. Since Spike was no slouch, he dusted off an ambitious old screenplay set on a black college campus called *Homecoming*. He spruced it up between interviews and retitled it *School Daze*. The second feature was designed to be both a hard-hitting look at racism *within* the black community and a singing and dancing extravaganza. It was inspired by his own experiences at Morehouse College in Atlanta, especially the events of homecoming weekend every fall. While *She's Gotta Have It* chugged along to a $5 million gross, Island began to finance development of his second picture—specifically a twenty-five person field trip to Morehouse on the weekend of November 7 for the real-life event.

The talent pool was very deep and very black. The actors included Larry Fishburne, Giancarlo Esposito, Jasmine Guy, Phyllis Stickney, Kadeem Hardison, and James Bond III, all of whom wound up in the movie. All eyes kept shifting to the unfairly scandalized Vanessa Williams. The former Miss America eventually spurned a very unappealing female leading role. We all attended an outrageous sorority coronation ceremony and talent show, which was marked by much high-spirited whooping and woofing. In a vast sea of black faces, there were three pale visages—Janet, me, and Island's Laurie Parker. Laurie felt right at home because she'd studied dance at Howard University on a minority scholarship.

Aside from pageants, step shows, parades, and football (the home team was massacred just as in the movie) on the surface, there was more than one hidden agenda throughout the weekend. Most of the key production department heads were clearly defined, but the issue of who would produce this film and future Spike Joints was muddled. Spike's lawyer, Loretha Jones, and Laurie Parker were both exceedingly ambitious. Monty Ross, who had organized the weekend, was the longtime sidekick. Everyone must have wondered what I was doing there since I hadn't yet defined myself as the eternal seeker of the next first-time filmmaker. Loretha and Laurie both went out of their way to ingratiate themselves to me and Janet with sweet nothings. Laurie used the phrase "between you and I" as if it was going out of style. I knew Spike was the one, but I wasn't looking for a position in his world. I was white, and I would never be a yes man. *School Daze* seemed like a mighty big challenge.

At the Atlanta airport, Larry Fishburne told me in no uncertain terms that his wife, Hajna Moss, was the model for Nola Darling. It wasn't the first nor was it the last time I heard someone make that claim. I was a little surprised that a husband would identify his spouse with such insistent pride. Spike always stuck to his story that Nola was a composite.

She's Gotta Have It was beginning to tail off very slowly, but the core ongoing runs were unflagging. Filmmakers normally get the most excited when a film plays most widely. Sometimes it almost seems like a macho competition. For black filmmakers, the competitive spirit is further stoked by a belief that their films are, quite literally, being ghettoized. The truth of the matter is that the vast majority of the box office gross for a specialized film, especially one that attracts a primarily black audience, comes from a finite number of markets. I sent a chart to Spike and Island showing that an amazing 87 percent of the first $6 million gross on *She's Gotta Have It* came from only twenty markets, half from the Northeast Amtrak corridor, and a full third from the New York metropolitan area. Even more remarkably, half the total gross was generated by just twenty individual theaters. Several of those venues— like the Sunrise in Valley Stream, the Grand Lake in Oakland and the Baldwin Hills in L.A.—drew almost exclusively from the African-American community. This kind of pattern emerged again and again in the years to come with *School Daze, House Party, Menace II Society*, and many other films.

Going up to 150 prints and eventually having over 500 play dates should have enhanced the value of *She's Gotta Have It* in the ancillary markets, especially homevideo. Here's where the racial bias really hurt potential revenue. *She's Gotta Have It* was a black and white comedy made by, for, and about black people who in the mid-eighties were still deemed to be moviegoers but not videocassette renters. They were still buying audiocassettes instead of CDs. *She's Gotta Have It* came along and grossed $7.5 million in North America with Island spending a splashy $1.9 million to release it. Through their efforts and his, Spike became practically a household name. The setup should have been ideal for a big push from Island's home video partner. The only problem is that their partner was CBS/Fox and they didn't have a clue.

CBS/Fox also didn't have the slightest incentive to get a clue because of the underlying output deal they struck with Island about a week before the New York release of *She's Gotta Have It*. At the time Russell excitedly described the freshly minted eight-picture deal as being advantageous because Spike's movie had an allocation of $300,000 as an advance versus the 20 percent royalty deal we'd already structured with Island. If *She's Gotta Have It* had stiffed, that advance for an "unknown, first feature" would have been great. In one of life's perverse reversals, the seven other higher guarantee, marquee-name Island titles in the package went down in flames while *She's Gotta Have It* soared. The timing of the deal one week before our release was also extremely unhelpful since you might as well wait for the actual opening results once you've gone that far.

The CBS/Fox shipment of first 25,000, and eventually 30,000 units was derived from a strict mathematical equation for them to recoup their allocated advance. Video rental does not operate on normal laws of supply and demand because wholesalers call the tune. If a retailer winds up with two copies of a title that are always out being rented for months on end, that retailer could have easily ordered two more. But once they don't order more initially, they're happy to let fewer copies fulfill the demand more slowly. *She's Gotta Have It* was on the rental chart for half a year. It was one of the top 100 video rentals for 1987 (one of only four non-Hollywood releases) and it was competing with movies that had three to twelve times more copies in the marketplace. The year before, CBS/Fox had even managed to ship more units on Kurosawa's Japanese-language *Ran*. The producer's share works out to about $10 per unit on a 20 percent royalty deal, so we conservatively lost about $200,000 on the underperformance. Spike eventually sued Island over the original allocation in the output deal (and the litigation is ongoing).

Island hit some serious turbulence in the late fall as Spike and Loretha moved to close the $4 million *School Daze* production deal. *Down by Law* was a quiet commercial disappointment given the fact that it cost ten times more than *Stranger Than Paradise* and grossed less. *Nobody's Fool*, their in-house production with Rosanna Arquette and Eric Roberts, was a flat-out disaster on every level when it opened, eating up all the *Spider Woman* profits and more. Their next co-production *Square Dance*, with Jane Alexander and a fourteen-year-old named Winona Ryder, looked like more of the same. Cary Brokaw resigned unexpectedly when Chris Blackwell wouldn't give him an equity interest in the company. It wasn't clear how much more capital Blackwell would throw into the film division. Island went from being the hot shop to being on the hot seat in six months, and *School Daze* hung in the balance. Four million dollars was a serious risk for them. After all, Spike's script did have pages that read "Straight and Nappy (MGM style musical number with thirty Jigs and Wannabes)."

The film was scheduled to start early in March 1987. In the third week of January, way beyond the eleventh hour, Island decided to pass. Chris Blackwell didn't call Spike. Russell Schwartz didn't call Spike. They had

Laurie Parker do it in the middle of the night. Spike found studio backing to the tune of $6 million in less than a week from David Puttnam and David Picker at Columbia Pictures. Picker was tight with Spike's law firm Frankfurt, Garbus. In fact, Tom Rothman, a partner there, had just joined the Puttnam team. Spike didn't even break his confident stride. Laurie had to give up her hope of producing for him. She threw in her lot with Brokaw's new company, Avenue Pictures, and found Gus Van Sant instead. Loretha Jones became his producer/lawyer this one time only. *School Daze* had some production problems. Morehouse kicked the production off-campus, the music hadn't been fully cleared when the film opened (thus delaying the soundtrack), and no one caught Spike's oversight when he inadvertently shortchanged Tisha Campbell on her singing and songwriting credits.

She's Gotta Have It was the best investment I ever made. Even so, no matter how profitable a film becomes, it always seems like it could have earned even more through higher revenue and lower distribution costs. In addition to the video shortfall, foreign performance did not match the excellent advances, except in the U.K. Island could have spent less than $1.2 million on advertising and gotten the same results. But then again, it was Spike who pushed for the $85,000 Academy campaign for his father's score and the screenplay! The eventual producer net revenue was just about $1 million. He maintained close to two thirds of the equity himself—not bad for a first feature. Tommy Hicks, Tracy Camila Johns, and Ernest Dickerson had small participations. Janet and I were thrilled with our ten points. Janet left the Film Forum the week the film opened, knowing that she had to go from the moment that her boss, Karen Cooper, had proscribed her from joining me, even briefly, in Cannes. Karen's program has been a crucial part of this country's film culture for two decades, but it was time to make a change. I quit my last day job at Films, Inc., vowing not to work for anybody else ever again. I also gave up programming the Film Forum 2, since I lost my focus and started making suicidal moves like three weeks of Laurel and Hardy movies. We ate out almost every night, moved into a charming building next door to Matthew Modine on a semiprivate Greenwich Village cul-de-sac, and had a baby on July 14, 1987.

A few weeks after the baby was born, we took her with us to Spike's one-year-after-the-opening anniversary party at the Puck Building, site of the premiere. Patrick Ewing was towering over the crowd. We spotted Larry Fishburne, who told us that Hajna (or should I say Nola?) gave birth on exactly the same day Janet did. We counted backward through the months to homecoming weekend in Atlanta, and realized that we'd both been expecting without knowing it. In fact, we named our baby Georgia: They named theirs Langston.

Spike Lee's career has been exemplary: hardworking, disciplined, inspired, experimental, rabble-rousing, committed, and marked by steady growth. He's stumbled occasionally. Even those imperfections seem to play an essential role in his process. He's far more evolutionary than revolutionary. The color sequence in *She's Gotta Have It* begins the trail to the large-scale musical numbers in *School Daze* without which Spike never would have learned how to stage the extraordinary climactic riot sequence in *Do the Right Thing*. *Joe's Bed-Stuy* and the five features after it all laid the foundation for his epic career summary *Malcolm X*— which of course has a musical number at Roseland. Spike has used his stature to support and advance the careers of a very long list of black talent. My life changed when his life changed. I don't believe Tawana told the truth. I can't stand New York Knicks guard John Starks. I would never call Warners "the plantation." Spike Lee is still my hero.

Be Like Spike

KEVIN SMITH: If one wanted to emulate a career it would be Spike's. He did exactly what he always wanted to do, first in the independent arena and then with the studios. I think he's got it easier in dealing with the studios. I don't think I could use the media the way Spike does. I don't think I could kick and scream like him. I'd be too scared to have the people turn around and say "Screw you—we're not going to do your movie." But Spike's got courage, and he can do that and it works to his benefit.

JOHN PIERSON: You go out of your way to credit Spike, but you've never articulated his specific influence on you.

KS: All one has to do is look at *Do the Right Thing*. It's probably the most key influence over *Clerks*. It's a great way to tackle a movie, you don't have to span time. *She's Gotta Have It* took place over a certain amount of time, and I'm no good at time. In fact, it spanned seasons. There were pictures of winter in there.

JP: It was filmed in just twelve days in the summer of 1985 but his brother David took the opening sequence still photographs for months.

KS: It's not just the still photographs, Spike actually wears a parka, and there's also Thanksgiving. That dinner scene became the defining clip for the movie. It does take place over time. I'm not confident enough as a writer to do that yet. I can do one day in the life just like in *Do the Right Thing*.

JP: Obviously working in a contained time and/or place has been a trademark of probably more independent films than not.

KS: True. Someone pointed out that the ones which have been influential to me have the three Greek unities: time, place, character.

JP: Even *Reservoir Dogs*.

KS: And there's another level on which *Clerks* strives to be *Do the Right Thing*. It's evident in our first cut. *Do the Right Thing* was a movie to me that was funny, funny, funny, funny, character driven, and then at a certain point turns and leaves you on your ass. You're like "What the hell happened?" All of a sudden there's a very serious message driven home here. I tried to do that with *Clerks* but failed when I had Dante shot at the end. The thought was, "Let's make it a comedy up to this point and then just turn it in the last three minutes." People will consider that a real film because that's what I consider *Do the Right Thing*; a real film.

JP: But the way that played in *Clerks* is much more of an existential statement. The way that played in *Do the Right Thing* is much more rooted. It was motivated by recent actual history. It was almost an inevitable result of a racially tense situation.

KS: That's why Spike's a better writer, because he can be political and I can't. It's not so much content as tone. The tone of that movie was humorous and then it turned. And I thought I'd like to do that in a movie. Humorous, and then turn it.

JP: Did Spike's books give you any writing pointers?

KS: I had a black marble notebook back when *Clerks* was called *Inconvenience.* I kept notes, just like Spike kept his line ideas in the *She's Gotta Have It* book. He'd write down a line of dialogue with a wavy, curly line underneath. The first scene I wrote down was Randall's "I don't appreciate your ruse, ma'am." I think the scene is exactly the same as it was when I wrote it. I never made any changes. I didn't do the wavy, curly line.

JP: One of my favorite first-time filmmaker stories about the early days with Spike and *She's Gotta Have It* is from when we were traveling around together as the film opened in its initial markets. We were all with it in New York. Then I went to Chicago and we were all together again in L.A. for the third opening. When that weekend ended, at the end of Sunday night at the Royal Theater in Santa Monica, Monty Ross, Spike's longtime co-producer turned to me and said, "We're going home now John, so what do they do with the money at the end of the night when you're not there?"

KS: Which is a question we might have asked if you hadn't told us this story.

JP: Here's another of my favorite illustrations in the category "rude awakenings." In *She's Gotta Have It,* one of the other five individual equity investors besides me was Spike's longtime friend Earl Smith. They'd gone to high school together. Earl'd been a big college basketball prospect and then bounced from school to school, allegedly being a malcontent who couldn't fit in. He'd do things like turn over every ketchup bottle with the cap off in a junior college cafeteria. He was deemed to be "uncoachable." Earl took the biggest risk of any individual by far to help back the film because he used his life's savings after his mother's death. So since he took the biggest risk he was probably the most delighted when it opened to sellouts. In New York, for the first month, it was basically sold out every show every day, and I don't mean just 8:00 P.M. at night. I mean from noon on. After about a day and a half of this, in his mind Earl had already bought three houses and a fleet of cars and . . .

KS: Champagne was flowing.

JP: He saw every one of those ticket sales and thought all that money was going to come straight back into his wallet. He was due a rude awakening and it was my job to explain it to him.

KS: Rude awakening but was he belligerent about it? Like, "son of a bitch?!!" Was he like the dude in *GoodFellas,* "I want my money, give me my money." Was it your job to put the screwdriver into the back of his head?

JP: If you go to the theater at the end of the night, like Monty says, and hold it up like the Lufthansa heist in *GoodFellas,* you could in fact know exactly what your take was supposed to be . . .

KS: You're not a safe guy. You pop ten grand into a movie, a black movie, where at the time black movies weren't really big. You'd be hard-pressed to find something other than *A Soldier's Story.* Why didn't you stick with Spike on *School Daze?*

JP: The hawks were circling. He wanted to "uplift the race." I found some other first timers. It was a crucial crossroads for me, and I know I chose the right road. Eventually it took me to people like you.

WORKING GIRLS AND WOMEN

So now I had a gay film and a black film under my belt. They were both by men. The dominant personalities in the next group of films were all women. They were the writers, directors, and/or producers of four diverse features, all of which were released theatrically in 1987—a chronological coincidence.

On a half-empty Pan Am flight back from Cannes after *She's Gotta Have It* took the world by storm, Island Picture's Jesse Beaton asked me if I was officially hanging out my producer's representation shingle. She had a professional interest in my career crossroads because she'd been the sales rep for *El Norte* a few years before. She warned me that she'd been deluged by other filmmakers of meager talents before following *El Norte* to a job at Island. I told her I was thinking more along the lines of a selective solicitation. In fact, the first six films I represented turned out to be the first six films I considered. The third and fourth were already right under my nose in Cannes, although I backed into both of them.

Lizzie Borden was a perfect example of a political, experimental film-maker from the downtown New York arts scene who moved toward more accessible, although still provocative, form and content. Before *Working Girls*, she had made quite a mark with a feminist quasi-narrative. I met her through Janet when *Born in Flames* opened at the Film Forum in 1983. It was distributed by First Run Features. Lizzie's credentials from her debut enabled her to raise almost $100,000 in grant money for *Working Girls*. The balance of her $300,000 budget came through a lesbian-owned commercial production company called Alternate Current, which normally acted as a liaison for Japanese shoots in New York. Co-owners Andi Gladstone and Margie Smilow became feature-film producers. Lizzie built the one claustrophobic brothel set in her edge-of-Chinatown loft and moved out while filming there.

The intersection of Lizzie and Spike's stories made for an affectionate siblinglike rivalry. It seemed like she had a head start, but they wound up on equal footing in March, 1986. *Working Girls* and *She's Gotta Have It* were shot in Super 16mm and blown up to 35mm at DuArt. Both films were screened for the Directors' Fortnight on the same day. Not only was Spike's debut selected on the spot and sold before the festival started, it almost sold before Lizzie's feature was even invited. Olivier Jahan needed nearly a month to convince his boss Pierre-Henri Deleau that she deserved a slot. The selection was so late that Pierre Cottrell did the *Working Girls* subtitles after finishing up on *Nola Darling*.

Whether you're picked first or last doesn't really matter. Once you get to the party, anyone can cut the rug. *Working Girls* went over very well at its initial screening, and two very insistent rug merchants cornered Lizzie and her co-producers afterward. These were the Weinstein brothers, Harvey and Bob. In the mid-eighties, they were a unique hybrid combining the competitive yet collegial world of Cinecom and Island with the dealmeister approach of Golan and Globus at Cannon. I'd heard of them and their oddly named distribution company Miramax, but they'd been missing in action a month before when *She's Gotta Have It* was up for grabs. They'd distributed a good Ruben Blades vehicle called *Crossover Dreams*, the Brazilian *Erendira*, and a very small Danish picture called *Twist and Shout*, but their approach seemed slightly uncommitted and scattershot. They'd been to Cannes before, when they had successfully acquired two separate Amnesty International concert/comedy films called *The Secret Policeman's Ball* and combined them into one subdistributed American release cleverly retitled

The Secret Policeman's Other Ball. The Weinsteins might have acted like hustlers, but they seemed to have much better taste than your average hustler. They certainly deserved credit for not being intimidated by the clinical depiction of sex, power, and money in *Working Girls.* Other men, especially certain male distributors, definitely felt threatened. In fact Harvey and Bob might have been *too* unintimidated, because they'd already determined how to sell the sex in a film that was utterly, demonstrably unsexy.

Lizzie and her colleagues resisted the importuning of the brothers thinking that there'd be other offers from more upstanding buyers. Their foreign sales agent, George Pilzer, the elegant, older French gentleman who'd done a fine job internationally on *Parting Glances,* made steady progress on foreign territories. Eventually *Working Girls* earned almost $400,000 overseas. But the American distributors were holding back. Although I was tied up with Spike, I sat down with Lizzie on the hood of a car very late one night to offer moral support. We were across the street from the Petit Carlton bar, the cool filmmaker hangout where Alex Cox would sit astride the motorcycle that he'd ridden all the way from London for the Cannes premiere of the superb *Sid and Nancy.* I didn't know exactly what to tell Lizzie about Miramax, but it didn't really matter. As suddenly as the Weinsteins had materialized, they disappeared . . . for months.

In the meantime *She's Gotta Have It* wasn't consuming every minute of my time so I began to think seriously about representing *Working Girls.* Shortly after Cannes, Janet had a chance to see the film and liked it enormously. At her urging, I signed on, knowing that we needed a key domestic festival to reignite the sales possibilities and garner some critical support. The Toronto Film Festival had already invited the film, but it hadn't yet become a force. Nor had the Ontario censors chilled out. When *Working Girls* played there, Lizzie had to block out a handjob scene with tape. The New York Film Festival decided that their Lincoln Center crowd wasn't ready for middle-class prostitutes inserting diaphragms and floated the idea of us waiting for the less visible, more cutting-edge New Directors/New Films Series at the Museum of Modern Art. Telluride was our last hope. After a long wait reminiscent of Cannes, the film was invited by the skin of its teeth and interest was rekindled. The press also started to perk up although perhaps in a fit of overweening political correctness, Kevin Thomas of the *Los Angeles Times* called the film *Working Women*.

Sara Driver's *Sleepwalk* was not invited to Telluride after playing in Cannes as the opening-night film of the then obscure section called Critics' Week. After a very fine forty-minute film adaptation of the Jane Bowles story *You Are Not I*, Sara had chosen a very whimsical, slight, enigmatic story with an incredibly unappealing female lead for her first feature. As payback for her enormous contribution to *Stranger Than Paradise*, Otto Grokenberger fully financed it and Jim Jarmusch was one of the cinematographers. When Sara asked me to help find a U.S. distributor, I knew it was a lost cause but I couldn't possibly say no. At first, I couldn't even bear to tell Sara that I had also agreed to represent her downtown New York neighbor, Lizzie Borden. I felt like I was two-timing her. Friendship can't really alter theatrical distribution reality: *Sleepwalk* had slim prospects in Europe because it was artfully made, but none here. We did accept a New Directors offer for this film. When it played there in March 1987, it received an excellent *New York Times* review that really predisposed the sellout audience at MOMA to embrace the mysterious dreamscape. Afterward, 400 people stayed for Sara's Q&A. Normally the first query at these sessions is "How much did it cost?" In this case, the film had cast its spell so effectively that someone started by asking "What does it mean?" Now Sara could have answered earnestly, responded with a riddle, or cracked a joke. But she completely broke the spell by saying "Whatever you want it to mean." More than half of that audience got up and went home feeling a little bamboozled.

By the time *Sleepwalk* played New Directors, *Working Girls* had been setting house records a few blocks away at the 57th Street Playhouse. Although the two films had wildly divergent fates after Cannes, they would dovetail one last time at the end of the year in home video.

Selling *Working Girls* after Telluride wasn't as easy as one, two, three, although there were three distributors making modest bids: Ben Barenholtz at Circle Releasing, who was last seen pulling out his checkbook in the San Francisco blackout; Janet Grillo at New Line, which was trying to reestablish its art credentials; and Joy Pereths at IFEX, normally an importer of Soviet films. Ben was the preferred choice, although each offer got stuck at no more than a $100,000 advance in mid-October. These companies had capital, but they were holding the line. It was almost more impressive when Seymour Wishman at First Run Features, the distributor of *Born in Flames*, made what was for him an astronomical $70,000 offer. We needed some external leverage to break the logjam.

Five months after their disappearing act, Miramax returned to the scene as if they'd just gone out for a pack of smokes. The Weinsteins had been making like the Taviani Brothers, co-directing a feature for Universal Pictures called *Playing for Keeps*. It is the pits, although they did call in some chits from their years as rock 'n' roll concert promoters in Buffalo, to assemble an impressive soundtrack album with artists like Phil Collins, Pete Townshend, and Eric Clapton. Having quickly realized their limitations as filmmakers, Bob and Harvey jumped back into their distribution company with a vengeance. Harvey flew off to the fall's major film market in Milan (MIFED) where he saw Cathy Doyle of Embassy Home Video, who promptly told him how much she wanted the rights to *Working Girls*. He phoned Bob and instructed him to get it. We were caught off-guard by their sudden return. New Line raised their offer to $125,000 and Miramax leapfrogged to $150,000, but we had decided that Circle was the best home for the film. Lizzie and her cast had bonded with Ben Barenholtz in a hot tub. I probably felt a twinge of guilt about spurning him with Spike, and *Raising Arizona*, their next Coen Brothers production, sounded like a winner. At the end of October, I told Ben verbally that we had a deal.

When I conveyed the news to Miramax, they freaked out and raised their bid to $200,000 (twice Circle's). Bob arranged a lunch for us with him and their distribution head, Mark Lipsky, the next day. My twinge of guilt with Barenholtz turned into a flood when I realized that for the first (and as it turns out, only) time in my career I was going to renege on a deal. The Miramax offer was just too compelling. Of course it turned out that they had Cathy Doyle's $375,000 video guarantee to back it up since the mid-eighties was a free-spending era for those rights. Doyle and Sydney Levine at Karl Lorimar were spending piles of money on art films as if there was no tomorrow. (Two years later, there was no tomorrow for them. Levine returned with a useful tracking guide.)

Working Girls went on to bear the trademark Miramax marketing touch and become their first real direct distribution success. We didn't just jump in bed for the money. They had an instinctual grasp of how to walk the tightrope between sensationalistic come-on and classy intellectual tease. They put this technique to use time and time again over the next decade, perfecting it on films like Peter Greenaway's *The Cook, the Thief, His Wife, and Her Lover* and, more recently, Atom Egoyan's *Exotica*. Somehow it must relate to their seminal teenage experience of going to see *The 400 Blows* under the misapprehension that it would be semipornographic, then being transformed by great art—a regular beauty and the beast tale. It doesn't always work. When the Weinsteins put a topless peasant girl in the ads for the flagging *Pelle the Conqueror*, they were ridiculed. More important, business didn't improve, so they reverted to Max von Sydow looking grim.

Lizzie may have been new to the theatrical feature game, but she had well-established highbrow credentials. She could complain about the sex sell as if she wasn't an accomplice, and reap the commercial benefits at the same time. Harvey acted as second unit director on the studio photo shoot where the cast looked like they were naked under black velvet. He and Mark lifted the tag line directly from the dialogue: "The two things I love most in life are sex and money, I just never knew until much later they were connected." The line came from the yuppie madam Lucy, whose character name was originally Susan. It was relooped when the "real" Susan at the real brothel where Lizzie Borden had done her research got touchy. The uncomplicated trailer stole the film's biggest laugh by highlighting a scene where one of the "girls" buys a variety of contraceptives for everyone at work as if she were ordering lunch. The film was being released unrated, but a big, black box in the ads screamed NO ONE UNDER 17 ADMITTED. None of this was designed to attract the raincoat crowd, although a few showed up, and usually walked out. It was much more a matter of titillation for the curious, not the prurient.

Miramax made an odd decision to give *Working Girls* an out-of-town tryout in San Francisco right after it played at the January 1987 U.S. Film Festival (Sundance). That was a banner festival for me because *Sleepwalk* also played in the Dramatic Competition as did a third feature that had been banging on my door since the previous summer. Producer Lynn O'Donnell had sent me a tape of a rough cut of Steven Okazaki's wry portrait of a green card marriage, *Living on Tokyo Time*. The Bay Area film had some charm and a very appealing female lead, Minako Ohasi, who tried to learn English by reading record reviews of the Red Hot Chili Peppers. The problem was the somnambulant male lead. The character was written to be dull in a droll way, but the movie didn't convey that joke. It was a bore. I told Lynn how I felt, and she seemed to take it to heart. When the finished film reached the festival, it was much tighter and some funny scenes had been added, which made it clear that the other characters were in on the joke of his dullness.

Living on Tokyo Time played well in Utah. Although I seemed to have a full plate, I really liked the production team, especially Lynn. The deadpan Okazaki had obviously drawn partly on himself for the lead character, Minako was very charming in person, and the writer, John McCormick, was a regular pistol who turned out to have a record collection numbering about ten thousand titles. Since *She's Gotta Have It* was wrapping up, *Working Girls* was set to open, and *Sleepwalk* was going nowhere fast, I agreed to sell the film. I immediately arranged bicoastal postfestival distributor screenings in the best available 16mm facilities. This was a film whose mood was so gossamer that even a break for a reel change could hurt it. Everyone turned out since the movie had received strong trade reviews and my star was rising. The most enthusiastic response by far came from our old friend in the Mets jacket, Jeff Lipsky.

To retrace Jeff's distribution résumé to this point, he'd started with John Cassavetes in 1974 at Faces Films, helped Joan Micklin and Ray Silver distribute *Hester Street*, then become head of distribution at New Yorker Films, before moving to Los Angeles in 1983 to take the same position at the Samuel Goldwyn Company. He stayed there until late 1986, when he jumped to the command post at Skouras Pictures, an operation owned by the extremely wealthy and well-connected Tom Skouras, and used as his playground. Jeff's oversized glasses made him look like the white Mars Blackmon. The fact that he doesn't have a hair on his body made him look like the white, bald Mars Blackmon. This was long before Michael Jordan made the shaved head a fashion statement. Lipsky was also known to wear purple bell-bottoms without a trace of self-consciousness. No one worked harder, although his brother Mark might have been his equal.

Jeff wanted to make his first acquisition for Skouras. He was passionate about *Living on Tokyo Time*. Lynn and the gang loved his spirit. Once again other offers were lagging, but Jeff believed his main competition was Goldwyn. Jeff's right-hand man, Bingham Ray, had followed in his footsteps from New Yorker to Goldwyn, from New York to L.A. Bingham, who could be a truly hilarious dinner companion, took charge when Jeff jumped ship, displaying an equally combative temperament. In fact Chris Zarpas, president of Ridley and Tony Scott's production company, once suggested that if you locked Bingham up alone in a closet, he'd pick a fight with himself. The truth is that Goldwyn wasn't really in the running this time around, but I fueled Jeff's sense of competition with his former company. He made a very handsome $215,000 offer (plus the blowup). I had a brief summit with the producers between the pool tables at Barney's Beanery and quickly closed the deal.

I was convinced that the Skouras advance guarantee for North American rights was as much as the market would bear. What I didn't know was how profitable this might be for the producers. I knew that *Living on Tokyo Time* was a low-budget film, shot in conventional 16mm on weekends with great equipment deals. But from the beginning, I told Lynn not to tell me exactly how low. Distributors sometimes use a film's budget as a measure of its market value. You can undercut your negotiating position by revealing too much, except of course where there's heavy competitive bidding. The prototypical, glib producer response when asked how much a film cost is "under a million." I wanted to be able to tell distributors quite honestly that I simply didn't know the *Tokyo Time* budget, then editorialize that it was irrelevant anyway. After the sale, Lynn admitted that the film cost only $70,000, an ultralow amount in that era. I almost fell over. Obviously the producers made out great.

February was action packed from beginning to end. The Circle-produced *Raising Arizona* was released by Fox. Joel and Ethan Coen's hysterical second feature, starring Nick Cage and Holly Hunter, made the brothers look like the independents with the most commercial appeal. *Working Girls* had opened a bit softly at the far-from-ideal Opera Plaza in San Francisco, even with a predictable rave from Judy Stone in the *Chronicle*. It was sitting there like a lump for three full weeks before the next scheduled opening in its hometown, New York. I kept getting phone messages from some producer with the exotic name Zanne about some film that was about to be completed called *Anna*. The messages said the director was Yurek somebody, it was written by Agnieszka somebody, and it co-starred Paulina somebody and Sally Kirkland . . . and why wasn't I calling back? I was going from New York to Los Angeles to Utah to New York to Los Angeles. Before heading home after *Tokyo Time* was sold, I was still in L.A. the morning the 1986 Academy

Award nominations were announced. Anne Thompson invited me to go with her in person to the Academy in the pitch-black predawn hour. I thought it would be a kick to see if Spike had lucked out. The astonishing news that morning was that Cinecom received *eight* nominations for *A Room with a View*, their $21 million grossing Merchant-Ivory film. This recognition followed Island's triumph the year before. The independents were on the march playing on Hollywood's homefield. Confirming my suspicion of their abilities with nonstudio titles, CBS/Fox shipped only 125,000 units on *A Room with a View*, despite the multiple nominations. This was less than half their total on *The Fly*.

When we got back to our hovel in Soho, I finally spoke to Zanne Devine and made arrangements to screen *Anna*. It was the kind of movie that was compelling, yet at the same time overly melodramatic. Polish filmmaker Agnieszka Holland had written the script, which she'd given to Polish theater director Yurek Bogayevicz. He found twenty-five-year-old producer Zanne who, with her partner Deirdre Gainor (Yurek's ex-wife), raised the $800,000 budget from a single source, Julie Kemper of the Kemper Insurance Group. They had cast Czech supermodel Paulina Porizkova and New York stage legend Sally Kirkland as the immigrant ingenue and fading expatriate actress. Sally cut her teeth in the sixties with Andy Warhol, then became the first actress to disrobe on the New York stage. Speaking of teeth, she was such a method fanatic that she had insisted that an older actress actually bite her on the arm through several takes of a crucial scene of the play within the film. At one point Zanne got a call on set from the Screen Actors Guild asking what the hell was going on? When she asked what they meant, she was told that one of their members had reported a health insurance claim. She had broken her bridge biting another actress.

I was already busy, the film's ending was some absurd *Persona* ripoff, and Zanne kept pounding on me to drop my already paltry 5 percent fee. I could have walked away in a second, but there was something about her feisty, know-it-all attitude that was refreshing—even if her total previous movie experience was producing an industrial training video for a western Canadian restaurant chain. I determined that we could slip *Anna* into the 1987 San Francisco Film Festival at the last second. The idea of returning to the scene of Spike's breakout was hugely seductive. This would be a relative high-budget feature for me—still "under a million" but not by that much. Maybe it was just the thought of hanging out with Paulina and her geeky boyfriend Ric Ocasek (of the Cars) that led me to represent *Anna* for a 3 per cent fee.

Zanne and I shook on our agreement a couple of days before *Working Girls* opened at the 57th Street Playhouse. Once again, Miramax had little or no clout at that time and this was not the first or second choice for a theater. The campaign was provocative and the reviews generally strong. One exception was the *Daily News,* which gave the film half a star and suggested that Lizzie Borden couldn't cut as well as her ax-wielding namesake. Vincent Canby's *New York Times* review really gave the work serious respect. It was quite amusing to be reading that review in the early edition at Café Un Deux Trois the night before *Working Girls* opened. On the other side of the restaurant, New Line entrepreneur Bob Shaye was doing the same thing for *Nightmare on Elm Street, Part 3.* That sequel was a huge success. Lizzie's feature also cleaned up that weekend. There were lines down 57th Street long before Planet Hollywood arrived on the scene. Everyone with a vested interest had a different response that opening Friday. Lizzie kept her distance in a little café across the street. Mark Lipsky was wound tight as a drum and simply couldn't relax and enjoy the moment. Andi and Margie were happily drunk in the lobby. Zanne and Yurek were imagining how it would soon be their turn. I felt greatly relieved and quite vindicated about going with Harvey and Bob. They had mentioned to me at one point that the company was named for their parents Miriam and Max. I thought loving sons would never put the screws to me.

Exactly one month later, on March 27, which was coincidentally the one-year anniversary of the *She's Gotta Have It* premiere, *Anna* did have its moment in the spotlight back at the Palace of Fine Arts. Zanne, Yurek, and Sally Kirkland received a standing ovation and critical accolades. In fact, the reviews from the *Chronicle*'s Judy Stone, who turned out to be a gigantic Agnieszka Holland fan, and *Variety*'s Herb Michaelson, who predicted box office glory, were actually much better than Spike's had been. Sally made herself the centerpiece right away by wearing a canary yellow, thigh-high opening-night dress, which appeared to be painted on.

The distributor turnout had grown from the year before because Vestron and Miramax had now fully jumped into the game, and everyone was hoping that lightning would strike twice. It felt almost eerie when it did and the two newcomers got into a pitched battle over distribution rights. Other studios and larger independents entered the fray a bit tentatively over the next week of follow-up screenings. Michael Barker told me that the Orion Classics screening was going along fairly well until a long dramatic scene in which Sally's character humiliated her lover by telling him to get down on all fours and bark like a dog. He barked as the Orion execs howled with laughter. But the main event quickly boiled down to a tag team match of the Weinsteins versus Dan Ireland and Bill Quigley of Vestron. Both companies sought world rights, although Miramax did not have a foreign division at the time. My goal was to get them out of under $500,000 advance terrain, and have them leapfrog toward the million-dollar mark. That becomes easier in two-party bidding when both have something to prove. Vestron seemed like they had all the money in the world just from the profits on *The Making of Michael Jackson's Thriller* video release. Their fledgling theatrical division was still learning to walk through its first few failed releases. Division head Bill Quigley kept asking everyone for distribution advice since his previous experience had been as an exhibitor—head buyer for New York's Walter Reade Theater chain. His acquisitions VP Dan Ireland also had exhibition roots; he'd run the Egyptian Theater, Seattle's premiere art screen, as well as the Seattle Film Festival.

In other words, Vestron's capital exceeded its distribution expertise. They compensated by copying successful models. Island used the Concept Arts agency for its ad campaigns. Vestron did too. Unlike Island, they foolishly let them write copy, each line worse than the one before. At least Vestron passed on "*Anna*: You should meet her if *she* has the time." A year later, Island was on the skids and had the River Phoenix film, *A Night in the Life of Jimmy Reardon,* based on Bill Richert's novel. The same agency designed the cover for the tie-in paperback. It said: "Jimmy Reardon . . . you should meet him if *he* has the time."

Miramax was just back in action itself and hardly needed some new kid on the block to steal away a picture. They were off to a good start on *Working Girls* and Harvey in particular seemed pretty obsessed with Paulina's role in *Anna*. She had a rather discreet bathtub scene from which Harvey hoped there were some racy outtakes to add back in. You can't blame a man for trying. Nowadays he has a first-look deal with Elle Macpherson.

The phone calls flew back and forth at a furious pace. At one point I said to Bob Weinstein, "We're almost there." I probably shouldn't have. The final round of bidding occurred fairly late one evening. When distributors aren't interested in your film, it can be hard to get them on the phone anytime. When they're in avid pursuit, it's a twenty-four-hour business day. I had absolutely no separation between my personal and professional lives because I worked from home. The good part of that arrangement was that I could field these offers in my underwear drinking shots of bourbon. The bad part was that there was no escape when I crossed the Weinsteins. With Vestron's international division making the difference, their advance jumped to $900,000 and we closed. At least I thought we did.

On one level, I'm convinced that I wanted to spread the films around: five titles, five distributors. And Vestron did seemingly land a knockout blow with their bid, a bid that was based on their unofficial credo: "If it's worth out time and trouble, it's worth about a million bucks." But the Weinsteins weren't finished. Being denied redoubled their interest. They got tough. This turned out to be typical behavior.

Bob and Harvey have a gift for finding a person's most vulnerable point in any negotiation. They already knew I'd broken my word before with Ben Barenholtz over *Working Girls*. Why not a second time? Bob, who already had Embassy's Cathy Doyle on the hook for home video again, kept accusing me of misrepresentation when I said, "We're almost there." In fact he claimed I never said "almost." Zanne didn't appreciate the strong-arm tactics, but she did want the largest possible advance. I almost called her greedy since I found the Vestron deal enormous. With millions in video funny money, Quigley and Ireland were blissfully unaware of these hard-hitting pressure tactics. We kept our word and closed for real with Vestron.

By the end of April, I'd also managed to help Sara Driver secure an extremely modest deal with First Run Features for *Sleepwalk*. The advance was $7,000. Sara took me to dinner as the entire sales fee. *Sleepwalk* was the fifth film I sold in a one-year span. Coincidentally it was also the third out of the five for which Embassy/Nelson Entertainment acquired home video rights; they wanted all five! We had our first "Please baby please" baby due in about ten weeks. It occurred to me that I had just gone through the male equivalent of a pregnant woman's well-documented nesting instinct just before giving birth, marked by an energetic burst of last minute activity.

Now I just had to nurture an infant and a litter of films through release. *Sleepwalk* and *Living on Tokyo Time* were the ugly ducklings. The former sank without a trace, taking Otto Grokenberger's money with it and undermining his sunny investor confidence from *Stranger Than Paradise*. Jeff Lipsky was typically relentless in his *Tokyo Time* efforts, but the critics had my original problem: They found the musician/lead boring rather than seeing him as a witty commentary on boredom à la Jarmusch. One writer said that the film alluded to Led Zeppelin, but played like a lead balloon. The domestic gross was a disappointing $400,000. (Measurement standards became lower in the nineties; Hal Hartley's first three features each grossed less.) Lipsky took comfort in two developments. Embassy Home Video kicked in another sizable advance for the title, and Skouras scored its grandest success that year with *My Life as a Dog*. For a while, that triumph made up for a string of disappointments. Producer Lynn O'Donnell started work a year later on a documentary about Robert Crumb, directed by Terry Zwigoff. I didn't know exactly how long she thought that might take, but I sold the finished film for her in the fall of 1994.

Working Girls wound up grossing about $1.8 million theatrically and, with the help of a hot new photo on the box, shipped 35,000 videocassettes. The film eventually earned about $750,000 for the producers, half domestically, the other half in foreign revenue. This result was surprisingly close to *She's Gotta Have It* at the end of the day. Profits might have been somewhat less if Lizzie Borden hadn't insisted on auditing Miramax when she thought the "publicity and promotion" column on their producer report was way too high.

Lizzie had covered quite a bit of the country promoting her film. Her presence had resulted in some serious coverage in backwater nonmedia centers like Cleveland. She was used to it, since she'd gone wherever she was invited with *Born in Flames*. That previous experience had also trained her to be very frugal—coach air fares, no limos, low per diem. She did her job uncomplainingly. The only thorn in her side was the fact that her travels in the spring of 1987 often intersected with Robert Townsend's tour. *Hollywood Shuffle* got off to a great start and Townsend got enormous mileage out of his "I made it for $100,000 on my credit cards" story. Of course he was stretching the truth since Goldwyn's completion financing had been many times that amount. Lizzie, like Spike, had consistently stated the full and accurate budget of *Working Girls*—$300,000. So if she got to a market before Robert, it was no

NOTE 5   FILM REVENUE

The Partnership received revenues from the following distributions and/or countries:

	1989	1988	1987
Miramax	$ 50,473	$121,352	$180,410
Japan			26,520
Germany		600	52,583
Uruguay			16,500
England	21,611	15,866	63,907
Switzerland	29,961		7,490
Finland		1,190	16,920
Australia		17,500	54,795
Holland		5,000	10,840
Israel		7,323	3,320
Portugal			1,400
Miscellaneous	2,461	12,300	70
Vestron		17,500	
	$104,506	$198,631	$434,755

NOTE 6   CONTINGENCIES

On March 16, 1988, the Partnership retained an independent certified public accountant to review the books and records of the U.S. distributor, Miramax Company.

The report issued by the accountant has disclosed discrepancies, which have been fully resolved and received during 1989.

problem. But if he got there first, journalists wanted to know why her film cost so much. Lizzie wanted to know why her promotional tour cost so much, and the audit provided an intriguing inside view of distributor accounting.

First and foremost, distribution costs on an independent film should always be *only* direct, out-of-pocket costs—the cash spent on that one, specific movie. Secondly those should be real, documented, invoiced expenses. Consequently *Working Girls* items like the ski rental in Utah and the $1,000 Mark Hopkins Hotel bill from San Francisco raised a red flag. The Hopkins stay would have been justifiable when the film opened in the Bay Area, but it dated from two months later when Harvey came in pursuit of *Anna*. The rest of the stuff was more mundane, like multiple Weinstein trips to Buffalo (their old rock 'n' roll promoter stomping grounds) during the run there, so we managed to settle. It was hardly shocking, but Lizzie felt a lot better.

Miramax was undoubtedly relieved not to have shelled out big bucks for *Anna* after seeing some of its key reviews when it played in the New York Film Festival in early October 1987. Janet Maslin got the *New York Times* assignment. I sat behind her in Alice Tully Hall unobtrusively waiting for the screening to start. Unexpectedly, Vincent Canby joined her at the last minute. She had her notebook out. He didn't, so I figured he was just along for the ride. Anyway, about ten minutes in, he started twirling his umbrella, looking mightily impatient. When the film finally ended, they ran out together, and Maslin composed one of her most scathingly funny pans. It listed sixty ludicrous moments in the film by number. Maybe he pitched in.

Anna's total domestic gross was only slightly more than Vestron's advance, and it probably ended up losing about $1 million. Vestron didn't have to worry too much because like Skouras (times ten), they were in the midst of releasing their biggest hit. *Dirty Dancing* grossed $63 million and created a whole cottage industry in soundtracks, stage shows, and dance contests. I bought stock just prior to the film's release and watched the price climb. The days of Vestron soliciting everyone else's opinion came to an instant stop. Now they knew better. If Bill Quigley said the sun rose in the west and set in the east, it must be true. The one unqualified *Anna* winner was Sally Kirkland. The film could never suffer neglect with Sally around since she effectively promoted herself twenty-four hours a day for months on end. She wrote, she called, she sent flowers to the voters, and consequently she won a Golden Globe and even received a Best Actress Academy nomination. She didn't win the Oscar, but she did win roles in about a dozen lousy movies over the next few years—not to mention frequent appearances on Howard Stern's show where he would taunt her to remove her clothes.

In the end, I was annoyed that Zanne had jawed my fee down. She resented the fact that I still made more on the movie than she did. I held onto my Vestron stock too long and broke even. She sold hers at the 52-week high and made out well. Everything evens out over time. Zanne and I hooked up again on *Prisoners of Inertia*, written and directed by my friend Jeff Scher. It had the same budget and backer as *Anna*, yet it never sold—except to *American Playhouse*. Amanda Plummer, usually a fine actress, was miscast in this romantic comedy. Zanne had to go to work after that. She went on to be a production executive at Universal, where she's been involved with several of my first-time filmmakers, including Nick Gomez and Kevin Smith. She's a rarity: independent filmmaker turned studio executive, young turk turned wizened warrior.

Through the luck of the draw, I did not become involved with another woman filmmaker for over four years—or just slightly longer than it took Lizzie Borden to make her follow-up feature *Love Crimes*.

One of the films along the way that passed me by was *Daughters of the Dust* by Julie Dash. I read once that she believed that "white male gatekeepers" were blocking her film and ignoring its waiting audience, and wondered if she put me in that category. I couldn't stay awake through the film, and I had no feeling for her following. Nevertheless, I found it incredibly encouraging and exciting that she was absolutely right that the college-educated, black, middle-class, female, Toni Morrison–reading audience would line up for her feature. Starting at New York's Film Forum (via Kino International), its $2 million box-office gross with almost no paid advertising support was a genuine triumph. Between the unremarkable premiere of the Julie Dash film at the Sundance Film Festival in 1991 and its theatrical opening a year later, I found a more contemporary project written and directed by a black woman.

Leslie Harris seemed more uncomfortable than just about any filmmaker I'd ever met when she dropped off a tape of her short in the spring of 1991. I think she always had a sense of trying to be the first black woman to have a theatrically released feature, and the black-and-white short was meant to be the first third of it. By this time I had a fund to provide completion money for first-time filmmakers, but her principal photography was only partially completed. I knew Spike wanted to start sponsoring other black filmmakers, and I knew some people still questioned his attitude toward women. So I thought that Leslie's film, *Just Another Girl on the IRT*, might be his perfect point of entry in a collaboration with me. It seemed like the fix was in when I learned that Leslie lived nearby in Fort Greene and that her producer, Erwin Wilson, had known Spike since kindergarten. He'd even been scheduled to be one of the *She's Gotta Have It* "dogs," but he never showed up that day. Too bad for him.

Spike evaluated the short and script and decided to pass for four reasons: He didn't like the lead B-girl actress; he hated the camerawork with its obtrusive zoom shots; he thought the film should be in color; and he believed that it should be shot in Super, not regular 16mm, for blowup to 35mm. He told me all this, and except for the Super 16mm comment, I thought he was dead-on. I advised him to give Leslie some direct feedback, and he made a questionable decision. He chose not to discuss those details with her. Leslie told me that Spike simply declared that he "didn't have the money"—a fairly preposterous notion at that point in his career since 40 Acres was scheduled to kick in only $50,000 with my company's $100,000. He'd just come back from running with the bulls in Spain for a Levi's jeans spot. I conveyed Spike's real opinions and Leslie seemed to disagree pretty vigorously. Spike started to develop a feature with Darnell Martin.

Leslie Harris forged ahead on her own. The next time I heard from her she'd reshot the entire feature in seventeen days in color, in Super 16mm, with a new cinematographer, and, most crucially, a much improved new lead actress named Aryan Johnson. We reentered financing negotiations and seemed to be moving in a positive direction. Two disagreements tripped things up. Her film climaxed with a home-birth scene, of a very premature baby no less. This posed a particularly daunting challenge for a low-budget film. Having been present at actual births, I demanded to see that footage and was denied. Then I asked Leslie to prepare a list of her deferments so we could structure them into the deal recoupments. She handed me two pages. The first was quite ordinary, about $27,000 for her essentially unpaid cast and crew. The second page was producer deferments—$80,000 for Leslie, and $20,000 for Erwin.

Now Leslie had written, directed, produced, and partially edited her own film, but this was not uncommon in our world. She was a driving creative force on a $250,000 first feature, and in such cases you look for a deferment in the $30,000 range, maybe a bit higher or a lot lower but never $100,000. When I pointed out this established precedent, I became "white oppressor man" and there was a brief rumour about my "rip-off" deal. We agreed to disagree and went our separate ways. I talked about the film with Amy Taubin at the *Village Voice* and Nelson George, another one of Leslie's Fort Greene neighbors. Amy wrote a column that captured the attention of Mark Tusk at Miramax. Nelson invested some money to keep Leslie going.

Eventually Leslie got to a fine cut on her own in the spring of 1992. By this time Julie Dash had beaten her to the punch theatrically; *Daughters of the Dust* was thriving. But Miramax had kept up their pursuit of *Just Another Girl*, and Leslie called me back in to help close a deal. We did. The film was energetic and spoke its mind, but the story of Chantal, the black teenager who's smarter than everybody else but still has an unwanted pregnancy that she will not abort, was not entirely coherent. The movie tends to split into two halves that don't quite fit together, and the birth scene turned out to be laughable, sort of like the old John Belushi "stunt baby" skit from *Saturday Night Live*. The delivery may have lacked authenticity, but there's no question that more than a few New York City newborn babies have been found in the trash. Toronto Film Festival programmer (and *IRT* supporter) Kay Armatage demonstrated the amazing innocence of Canadians when she expressed disbelief because it had never happened there. I showed her some clippings, one of which I even carried around in my wallet to tease her. Eventually I realized that Toronto is so clean, you couldn't even find any trash in which to discard a newborn.

Despite these problems, Leslie made a bold attempt to portray a character that hadn't been seen on film before. There's an ongoing debate about whether it's harder for a black filmmaker or a woman filmmaker to make a first feature. It might seem that a black woman would have the hardest time of all. I know two things. First, making an independent feature is torture for anyone. But once a black woman manages to make a passably good film, the media just run wild with that story. Most of Leslie's sympathetic coverage jumped off from that point—the poor, oppressed, struggling black woman angle. Leslie sometimes sounded like

DEFERRED PAYMENTS
CREW & TALENT

PRODUCTION PERSONNEL
16 SHOOT DAY

	Quantity	Flat Fee	
Cameraman/DP	21 dys	2000	
Assistant Cameraman	16 dys	1200	
Sound Mixer	20 dys	1350	
Boom Person	16 dys	1000	
Gaffer	16 dys	900	
Grip	16 dys	750	
Production Designer	10 dys	750	
Location Manager	10 dys	1000	
Location Assistant	16 dys	750	
Makeup/Hair Artist	16 dys	750	
Wardrobe/Stylist	12 dys	1000	
Driver w/van	16 dys	900	
Driver	16 dys	750	
Production Asst.	16 dys	1000	
Still Photographer	4 dys	600	
Production Coordinator	4 wks	2000	
Prop Person	16 dys	750	
PA	16 dys	500	
Camera Intern	16 dys	-0-	
Intern		-0-	
Intern		-0-	
TOTAL			**17,950**

	Quantity	Fee	Subtotal
TALENT			
Lead Actress	20 dys	200	4,000
Supporting Actor	14 dys	125	1,750
Supporting Actress(1)	12 dys	100	1,200
Supporting Actor(1)	6 dys	100	600
Supporting Actress(3)	4 dys	100	1,200
Supporting Actress(4)	2 dys	75	600
Supporting Actor(4)	1 dy	75	300
TOTAL			**$9,650**

TOTAL DEFERMENT
CREW/TALENT: $27,600

DEFERMENTS ABOVE THE LINE PERSONNEL

	Quantity	Fee	
STORY & SCRIPT			
Story & Script	In perpetuity	20,000	
Writer: Leslie Harris			
SUBTOTAL:			20,000.00
TALENT			
Executive Producer/ Producer:			
Leslie Harris	2 yrs	40,000	
Co-Producer: Erwin Wilson	1yr	20,000	
Director: Leslie Harris	15 wks	20,000	
SUBTOTAL:			$80,000.00
TOTAL:			$100,000.00

a tape loop. A year and a half later, Darnell Martin wrote and directed the first major studio feature by a black woman. Darnell rejected Columbia Pictures' affirmative action sell and insisted that *I Like It Like That* stand on its own merits.

As a studio director, Darnell Martin was unique as a black woman; she was also quite rare as a woman. The problem isn't as pronounced in lower-budget independent ranks, but you won't find parity. (Women come closer to holding their own in the supporting role of producer.) This doesn't really make sense since independent film is an equal-opportunity employer—or, more precisely, self-employer. Filmmakers of every race, creed, gender, sexual orientation and color invent themselves every day. One of their most essential personality traits is an aggressive self-confidence—perhaps a more common male trademark. Is it a conspiracy that Sundance has included only a handful of dramatic features by women each year? Do potential investors see a woman coming and close their checkbooks? Do women writers/directors have to throw in guns and blood squibs to even the playing field? Nancy Savoca or Allison Anders might respond differently, but I answer no to these questions when it comes to *first timers.*

Once directors like Darnell, Lizzie Borden, Sara Driver, Leslie Harris, and Julie Dash or producers like Lynn O'Donnell or Zanne Devine have a foot in the industry door, the problems begin. The elapsed time between their first and second features (or between their first and 1995, if they haven't yet had a follow-up) has averaged more than four years.

This feels like a pattern of bias. Traditionally, documentaries have been a safe female haven; yet except for Barbara Kopple, all the recent theatrical breakthroughs have been made by men—men like Errol Morris.

INSPECTOR ERROL MORRIS
WALKS THE THIN BLUE LINE

In the last week of 1986, I heard from Errol Morris for the first time in four years. Someone had told him what I'd done for Spike Lee. When I saw him on New Year's Day, 1987, he was buried in an editing room above the Ed Sullivan Theater. Errol was so completely immersed in his own work, which seemed to consist of about four different features from what I could tell, that he actually referred to my involvement with *Skip* Lee. Talk about the absentminded professor. Given the myriad projects swirling in the brain of Errol Morris, I'm surprised he knew what year it was. He also had a baby on the way.

In one long afternoon he told me about Einstein's missing brain and showed me footage of Dr. Death, a lion trainer, a giant chicken, and a dog accused of murder. He had already devised the tag line for the story of King Boots, the homicidal sheep dog: "Only two people knew what happened. One was dead. The other was a dog." Despite the diffuse enthusiasm, it was Dr. Death and his "patients" to whom Errol kept returning. Dr. James Grigson was a Dallas psychiatrist who consistently appeared as a very friendly witness for the prosecution in death penalty cases to confirm the likelihood of the defendant killing again, if given the chance. Errol had received money from PBS to make a film about "Dr. Death." That project remained (and still remains) unfinished because he was distracted by the case of one particular convict who had been on death row courtesy of Grigson—Randall Dale Adams. I saw footage in which Grigson pointed out that sociopaths like Adams would always profess innocence. Then Errol showed me Randall Adams, who came across as a fatalistic, none-too-bright victim. Yet he showed flashes of insight. For example, he accurately described Dr. Death as "that ostrich-looking dude."

On that New Year's Day, Errol's passionate yet cerebral narration of the story that became *The Thin Blue Line* was way ahead of the visual realization. But you couldn't bet against his ability to make it a film. German director Werner Herzog had learned that the hard way almost a decade earlier. Having met Errol at the Pacific Film Archive (PFA) and collaborated uneasily with him on the final American sequence of *Stroszek*, Herzog stated that he would eat his shoe in public if Errol ever finished his own film *Gates of Heaven*.

I knew everything about Errol's earlier career. I had seen his brilliant documentary (for lack of a better word) *Gates of Heaven* several times when it finally opened at the Bleecker in 1981. Inspired by the closing of one failed pet cemetery and the transfer of its disinterred residents to another one, his first movie was hilarious, heartbreaking, and utterly unseen. Even less available was a second, hour-long feature called *Vernon, Florida*. Originally titled *Nub City*, it evolved out of a failed attempt to probe a town-wide, limb-severing insurance scam. Once again Errol's tag line preceded the film: "It's about people who in order to achieve the American dream literally become a fraction of themselves." Morris was like the thinking man's Samuel Z. Arkoff: Make the poster, then worry about the film later.

Errol showed up at the Bleecker the night of the premiere of Wim Wenders's *The State of Things* early in 1983. He seemed interestingly weird as one might expect from his work. I was concentrating on preventing Wim from seeing the negative early-edition reviews of his new film so I didn't really have time to talk to Errol. Then he disappeared for years. He didn't even appear in Les Blank's legendary short *Werner Herzog Eats His Shoe*, a film documenting the preparation and public consumption of an appetizing boot in Berkeley as Herzog pays off his earlier bet with Morris. The vast array of movies, especially film noir, shown at the Archive had saved Errol while he pursued, but never got, his doctorate in philosophy at Berkeley in the seventies. Maybe the town just wasn't big enough for the two of them. Errol ardently pursued the offbeat. But Herzog had stood at the foot of a volcano waiting for it to erupt and thrown himself on a cactus to atone for setting a dwarf on fire. Errol also considered Herzog guilty of "stealing a landscape" from him (Plainfield, Wisconsin, home of serial killer Ed Gein) for *Stroszek*.

So where had he gone? The simple answer was midtown Manhattan. Errol had become a private detective for an agency that investigated Wall Street security fraud. Janet unknowingly had helped him crack an international financial swindle. The Film Forum had come up with a print of Andrei Tarkovsky's great Soviet film *The Stalker* for its U.S. premiere. The print source was quite strange, an Eastern bloc "importer/exporter" who usually handled commodities like tractors, not art films. He seemed a bit shady, and apparently he was. Errol called to request a front-and-back copy of the canceled check with which the Film Forum paid the film rental for the engagement. It had been deposited in Bank Leumi. The account number became a crucial clue in Errol's investigation.

Two careers intersected. Errol Morris director met Errol Morris detective just in time to return to filmmaking and clear an innocent man who had been on death row. Spike was once asked if films like *Do the Right Thing* can change history. On the broader social scale, his answer was no. Then he added that *The Thin Blue Line* proved that a movie could change one man's history. Errol accurately described his film as "the first murder mystery that actually solves a murder."

Randall Adams was arrested and railroaded through the Dallas courts early in 1977 (right around the time that I was graduating from film school). Ten years later, Errol was honing in on the story with truly amazing interviews with the principals and a whole cast of eccentric supporting characters. Three lines from that first day's footage kept ringing in my ears. The first was the chief prosecutor's boast that "anyone can convict a guilty man, but it takes a genius to convict an innocent one." Then there was Dr. Grigson's comment that Adams was the type of person who could "work all day and creep all night." Finally the judge in the case could hardly remember any of the trial except for the prosecutor's summation about "the thin blue line" of police that maintain the social fabric. Errol was a great listener and his unblinking-eye interviewing technique seemed to make people willing to talk and talk.

Eventually even David Harris, the real killer, wound up effectively confessing on audiotape one day when the camera malfunctioned.

As the months ticked by, Errol was trying to craft his material into a film, not a court brief. Dramatic re-creations (production designed by Ted Bafaloukos), inserted close-ups of objects that became almost fetishistic, film clips from grade Z detective and soft-core porn movies, a relentless score by Philip Glass—these were the extra added ingredients. As a notorious slow worker, he needed someone to crack the organizational whip and help raise the substantial budget. I wasn't a producer, and I hadn't yet started my completion fund. So my involvement couldn't really go beyond moral support and endless word-of-mouth; his film was my juiciest conversation piece for months on end.

Mark Lipson stepped in very effectively as Errol's producer, and quickly moved to close a deal with American Playhouse to complete the picture. I thought that was great news for Errol *and* a fantastic new direction for Playhouse. Lindsay Law was their executive director and his motto up to that point seemed to be "When in doubt, make another Horton Foote movie." Lindsay's background was theater with a capital "T". We both served on an Independent Feature Project Program Committee, which met monthly in a Playhouse conference room whose walls were filled with Horton Foote posters. About an hour into every meeting, like clockwork, we would have our standard disagreement about the primacy of the script for independent films. Lindsay was a structured, three-act traditionalist, and I believed that most of the best independents violated all screenplay guidelines and only read well after the visual goods were on screen—e.g., Spike, Jarmusch, the Coens. We never managed to reconcile our difference. Then suddenly and audaciously, Lindsay put a bundle on the line for *The Thin Blue Line*.

A full year went by as Errol painstakingly crafted the finished film with editor Paul Barnes. I was deep on the sidelines throughout 1987 with my four openings and the new baby—not to mention the fact that Mark Lipson, a control freak, didn't want or need my help. There was still a financial shortfall at the beginning of 1988, and Mark and Errol decided they had no choice but to commence a series of double-system distributor screenings. We took five-month-old Georgia along to one of these screenings and cringed at the many loud gunshots in the multiple reenactments of the murder. It wasn't her first film; she'd already been to Douglas Sirk's *Written on the Wind* at the Public Theater. For a film with an eventual seamless flow and hypnotic effect, which was partly dependent on the final Philip Glass score, these unfinished screenings may have been futile. Bingham Ray came very close to getting Shep Gordon and Alive Pictures to cut a deal. He'd just gone over there from Goldwyn and was preparing for the release of Alan Rudolph's *The Moderns*. Jeff Lipsky had bad memories of Errol as an extreme pest from his New Yorker Films days where Jeff had distributed his earlier work. Whenever the subject of *The Thin Blue Line* came up, he would say "tick, tick, tick, tick." That was his shorthand description that it belonged on *60 Minutes*. Years later, when Bingham and Jeff formed October Films and had an almost identical opportunity during postproduction to acquire D. A. Pennebaker's *The War Room*, a documentary about the 1992 Clinton campaign, they jumped.

Trend spotters are often off the mark when they attempt to characterize various good and bad eras for theatrical documentaries. Documentaries were in the doldrums right then. Ross McElwee's *Sherman's March* (1986), an enormously charming and moving personal essay film, was just about the only theatrical breakthrough during those two years. Diane Keaton's vanity trifle *Heaven* had the distinction of being the only documentary ever invited to the Directors' Fortnight of Cannes in 1987. Unbelievably, Keaton didn't show up. It was acquired and released very marginally by slumping Island Pictures. Marcel Ophuls's Klaus Barbie epic *Hotel Terminus* was on its way to the Un Certain Regard section of Cannes, where Goldwyn would pick it up, but that was about it for documentaries.

Sometimes the only way to force a perfectionist like Errol Morris to completion is to set up a deadline that you cannot break. I suggested premiering the film in March at the San Francisco Film Festival, a place where Errol was very well known (even if he'd skipped the shoe eating), followed by an April U.S.A. Film Festival showing in Dallas, site of the actual case. There were always two different sides to this film. The first festival showing would be for esthetics, the second for front-page news. Of course, the two were indelibly intertwined.

Once these festival programs were in print, Errol had to stop tweaking and let go. *The Thin Blue Line* occasioned my third consecutive March trip to San Francisco for a high-profile Friday-night world premiere. The venue was no longer the Palace of Fine Arts, but an ordinary multiplex called the Kabuki. The other far bigger change was that

I had been demoted to sideline cheerleader and observer. It felt strange and unfulfilling. There was no mistaking the cold eye that Mark Lipson gave me. Although Errol didn't look the part, he was an avid rock climber who was intimate with the vertical cliffs of nearby Yosemite National Park. The response to the film was excellent and the weather was unusually warm so I decided to get my thrills in Yosemite for the weekend while Lipson peddled the picture. Afterward I went straight back to New York without even thinking about going to the subsequent Dallas show.

In the meantime, Miramax had gotten the scent and immediately grasped the sales hook for the film. The first words out of Harvey Weinstein's mouth at the initial marketing meeting were "Never has Miramax had a movie where a man's life hangs in the balance." Mark and Errol put me in my absolute least favorite position by asking me to be their rep *after* they'd already agreed to a worldwide deal with Miramax for a $400,000 advance. That's sort of like being the policeman on patrol instead of precinct captain. They were certainly eager to earn every dollar of revenue they could, since *The Thin Blue Line* had eventually cost over a million dollars. Mark hadn't called on my sales expertise, but he thought I could carry a big billy club to keep the Weinstein boys in line. I always loved the film and thought Errol a near-genius, so I said yes. It didn't immediately seem like a mistake.

Miramax was bubbling over with excellent ideas and strategies, even if it wasn't Harvey's greatest brainstorm to suggest that Francis Ford Coppola, whose name was on everything then, should "present" the film. The broadest stroke was to label the film a nonfiction feature rather than a documentary. One key element in this ruse was a truly brilliant film noirish trailer created by the Glass, Schoor production house under Harvey's supervision. It didn't use a single talking head shot, but did use objects like the extreme close-up of a swinging watch to suggest mystery and drama. While every attempt was being made to avoid the D word, the miscarriage-of-justice hard-news angle was just as important as selling it as a "movie movie." The names of justice-seeking journalists like Anthony Lewis, Pete Hamill, Bob Woodward, Mike Wallace, and Jimmy Breslin were flying around the table at the marketing meeting. After all, the film itself had now been entered into evidence in the Federal appeal. I think this was also the first time that Harvey raised the name of the publicity-hound defense lawyer Alan Dershowitz.

The next public showing of *The Thin Blue Line* took place in Cannes at the market, the vast bazaar where hundreds of titles play that have not been officially selected. Miramax had assigned the foreign rights to a sales agency called J&M International, a company that walked a fine line between art and commerce. Errol's earlier films had a cult following in the United States, but no name recognition anywhere else. Harvey used Cannes primarily to position the film with the American critics, none of whom had been in San Francisco or Dallas. At the very top of everyone's list was Roger Ebert, a man who had reportedly seen *Gates of Heaven* more than fifty times and designated it as one of the ten greatest films ever made. Ebert may have been Errol's biggest supporter, but after seeing *The Thin Blue Line* he planted a terrible seed. Walking down the Croisette with Harvey, Ebert whispered that the film had too many repetitions of the reenactment of the crime itself with its multiple gunshots—the ones that had made Georgia squirm. That's market research: A five-month-old baby and America's most recognizable thumb had voted for change.

Pandora's box was about to be reopened. Errol had already spent years editing his film. Miramax had acquired it "as is," without any contingencies as to running time. Harvey now suggested that it should be five to ten minutes shorter, and Errol didn't slam the lid closed. He was completely willing to go back in and fiddle some more. I saw a nightmare develop from which nobody would wake up because no protocol was put in place. The deeper cuts that Miramax desired and the slight trims that Errol offered were out of sync for most of the summer, a summer marked by a record-setting, truly disgusting New York heat wave.

The film was scheduled to open in late August rather than waiting for the New York Film Festival, where Errol's previous two films had played. This plan provided more lucrative playing time before the late fall. It also accelerated the focusing of attention on the Randall Adams appeal. By early August there was still no reedited film. Under some duress, Errol signed an agreement that gave him back book rights, which had inadvertently been granted to Miramax, in return for which he agreed to deliver a shorter film by a set date. If he failed to deliver, he was subject to a monetary penalty clause. Now, I couldn't believe he signed it, but his legendary entertainment lawyer, Arthur Klein, told him to go ahead. The delivery date came and went. All the long lead advance screenings used the original version. The week before the scheduled August 26 opening in New York, the new materials finally made it to Miramax's chosen lab, Film House in Toronto, where twenty-five prints were to be struck. Sound One sent a mono optical soundtrack instead of the Dolby stereo optical that featured the Philip Glass score in its full glory. The lab didn't spot the mistake. Mark Lipson went to Toronto but couldn't hear the problem when he checked a print because the lab's screening facility had no Dolby stereo capability. These eleventh-hour prints were worthless.

What's more, the daily and weekly critics were just going to have to make do with the original version of *The Thin Blue Line*. This became a moot point since the film appeared on more 1988 year-end ten best lists than anything else. The paying public did see the shorter, less repetitive new cut. So one could argue (and Harvey did) that the word of mouth improved. The whole exercise seemed to me like a lot of sound and fury signifying nothing—except of course there came a time to pay the piper when Miramax attempted to collect on the penalty clause. Although the Tim Burton feature wasn't out yet, the older Weinstein would soon earn the soubriquet "Harvey Scissorhands." I have nothing but praise for his improvements in films like *Cinema Paradiso* and *Farewell, My Concubine*, but this first instance (not counting the two-for-one splicing of *The Secret Policeman's Other Ball*) was not a proud moment.

Since lifelong fan Roger Ebert had catalyzed the whole recut, Errol could never quite understand why he gave the film 3 1/2 rather than 4 stars. There were plenty of other raves and quite a bit of news coverage as well. When other inmates asked Randall Adams why his case was being argued in the arts section, he said, "I'll argue it anywhere I can." During a controversial film's theatrical release, there is always a danger in being at this entertainment/news nexus. The Lincoln Plaza run in New York got off to a solid if unspectacular start and went on to constitute nearly a third of the total national box office gross. Openings in the next few key markets were also respectable, although San Francisco suffered some damage when the *Chronicle* changed its policy and refused to rereview films that had played in the festival. The most telling return came in from Dallas, where the story truly was front page news. Business there was strictly mediocre.

Soon after the opening, I gave Errol my prediction of the film's final gross—$1.2 million. Although he kept mum, he turned out to be quite irritated with me for selling it so short. Undoubtedly I could have improved my bedside manner, but I couldn't have guessed any better. That's pretty much what it grossed, and you couldn't fault the relentless efforts of Miramax distribution head Mark Lipsky. The real success story of the *The Thin Blue Line* as a movie "product" was in video and on American Playhouse, where it had a large viewing audience. The video was tricky because of a tiny window between January 1989 and the April PBS broadcast (less than five months after the theatrical release). Playhouse had already waited for two years and just couldn't delay its showing anymore. HBO Home Video did a phenomenal job with a real pulpy-looking new box as opposed to the almost cerebral, graphically beautiful Miramax campaign. That design with its haunted eyes and the big clockhands at one minute to midnight remains a personal favorite. (If you look closely at the credit block, you'll see that Miramax buried "An American Playhouse Presentation" in an attempt to avoid the frequent dull association.) The real secret to the enormously successful 35,000-unit videocassette shipment comes back to the news angle and great timing. In December, Randall Adams had finally gotten his appeal hearing—before Dallas County's one and only black Muslim judge no less.

I may not have sold the film; but after two years, I felt far more connected to the fate of Randall Adams than I did to my other pictures. I think Mark Lipson also understood this bond when he suggested that we fly down to Dallas together for the hearing on December 4. When we slipped into the courtroom in a building off Dealey Plaza, everything snapped into focus. There was the Kafkaesque victim Adams in his orange prison jumpsuit looking really aged after twelve years in maximum-security prison, the first two on death row. There was Errol, a little rumpled as always, sitting between Randall's mother and sisters. Somehow his presence dominated the proceedings, although he never took the stand. In fact Errol's Boswell, Mark Singer, was sitting behind him working on a long (and truly wonderful) profile for *The New Yorker*.

There was no doubt that Judge Baraka commanded this court of law. He was in a position to recommend a new trial if he found in favor of the plaintiff, represented by Randy Schaffer, on even one of the thirteen claims in his writ. By the end of the first morning, baby-faced killer David Harris had, for all intents and purposes, confessed. I flashed back to the very first time I'd seen his face, the picture of innocence, on Errol's

editing table. Halfway through that interview, David lifted his mana-
cled hands into the frame, and it was chilling to realize he was in federal prison for killing again. Often audiences would gasp at that moment
in the finished film. By the end of the second day, the credibility of every
original prosecution witness had been destroyed and the behavior of the
DA's office was seriously impugned. It almost was like a Perry Mason
moment when homicide detective Gus Rosen directly contradicted his
own interview in *The Thin Blue Line* and Schaffer waved a videocassette
in his face. Generally Errol had performed an enormous service to Randall Adams with the documents and evidence that his investigation had
uncovered. But the actual movie was tainted because, after all, it *was* a
movie. We'd been calling it a nonfiction feature all along, a kind of *Twilight Zone* episode, a meditation on truth and chance. Even as it became
clearer and clearer that Randy Schaffer was going to prevail, Errol seemed
troubled by this double-edged sword. The prosecution nearly always referred to him as "the filmmaker from New York."

The court granted relief to Adams on *six* points—five more than necessary. Errol was pleased, but one failed argument still bugged him, as
it always had. From that first day back in January 1987, I knew how ob-
sessively important it was to him to prove that David Harris's timetable
of events the night of the murder was transparently false—off by two
hours. Errol's research had shown that the sleazy drive-in where Harris
and Adams had seen *The Swinging Cheerleaders* had closed long before
midnight, a moment brilliantly memorialized in the film with a screen
full of gigantic popcorn. The judge ruled against the plaintiff on that
point. Errol thought Randy Schaffer had let him down.

Adams still had to await a new trial, but Judge Baraka's final words
echoed through the courtroom and rippled across the national media:
"If the defendant were to be retried, considering all the testimony elicited
and what would be presented to the jury or a court, more likely than
not the defendant would be found not guilty." On that note we all returned to a celebratory dinner with Randall's family in the plush restaurant at Dallas's ritziest hotel, the Adolphus. Around a large banquet
table, we ran up an astronomical bill on Miramax. Mark Lipson and I
had conferred and decided that everyone should eat, drink, and be
merry since there wasn't much likelihood of the film ever earning an
overage anyway. Surprisingly in the end, it did—mainly because the increased media hoopla fueled the video release the next month. The tele-

vision audience also peaked in April because Randall Adams was finally released from prison around Easter, just before the airdate.

In between the hearing and his release, *The Thin Blue Line* had *not* won the Best Documentary Oscar. In fact it had not even been nominated. In fact, the documentary committee, in the first of a string of publicly derided decisions, had not even watched the entire film, having concluded that it wasn't really a documentary. That was unfair, but ironically we had taken great pains to deny that it was a documentary. So it didn't pass muster with the film purists, nor was it admissible as evidence in court.

Errol settled a threatened lawsuit from Randall Adams without any money changing hands since the perceived success of the movie generated only imaginary dollars. Adams wanted to recover the rights to his own life story presumably so that his own book, *Adams v. Texas*, could potentially become a television movie. Everyone believed that Adams had suffered a terribly unfair fate. Yet some of us always wondered why he spent a whole day in the car with David Harris in the first place, especially after Harris started waving a pistol around. Randall wrote, "Why had I not dumped David Harris early in the day? Why had I let him suck me into this mess?"

Errol deservedly won a MacArthur Foundation genius award. He moved from New York to Cambridge, Massachusetts and eventually dipped into his bag of visual tricks from *The Thin Blue Line* to make the costly study of Stephen Hawking, *A Brief History of Time*. Errol is truly one of a kind. I'll never forget the way he described the pattern of his relationships to Janet in our final Boston visit with the Morris clan: "I only have ex-friends." Perhaps that's because his mind is always filled with so many current ideas.

D.O.A.

1988 was an extreme lull for the independent film movement and a terrible shakedown period for distributors. The stock market crashed in October 1987 and the indiscriminate video boom started to crash soon thereafter. The impact of *The Thin Blue Line* and the slow but steady rise of Miramax were notable exceptions to the downbeat rule. The year started poorly at Sundance and never quite snapped out of it. In retrospect you could call it the calm before the storm or the restorative sleep before the next growth spurt. However, living through this slump after four years of exciting action seemed like death.

THE DANCE PART 1

The first stumble occurred in Park City, Utah in January. Although Robert Redford had taken over the U. S. Film Festival from originator Lory Smith and the Utah Film Commission in 1985, he didn't fully rename it Sundance until 1991. For simplicity's sake, I will refer to the event as Sundance before and after the official name change. In 1988, it was still the U.S. Film Festival, and it hit its nadir. After my Dramatic Competition triplets the year before, festival director Tony Safford had asked me to join the selection committee. I instantly said yes, thinking that the only hard part would be turning down some very good features because others were even better. This wasn't quite the case.

The initial film I'd sent off to Sundance was the first I was involved with, *Parting Glances*. The class of 1986 included many other films I've already mentioned, including *Desert Hearts*, *The Great Wall*, and *Smooth Talk* as well as Wayne Wang's second feature *Dim Sum* and the Horton Foote based *On Valentine's Day*. The festival was an extremely manageable size and remained the same the next year. You could easily park on Main Street in the evening. Every member of the film community in attendance was invited to a sit-down closing-night awards dinner. The whole atmosphere was so quaint and low-key that a major Cinecom honcho like Ira Deutchman still took the festival shuttle bus around town. In fact I remember driving around an icy corner one night and nearly knocking him into a snowbank as he stood waiting patiently in subzero weather. There were admittedly more than a few mediocre and long-forgotten entries in 1987 but in addition to my trio you could have seen Tim Hunter's harrowing *River's Edge*, Robin Williams in *Seize the Day*, and Ross McElwee's *Sherman's March*.

At the awards dinner, which was nearly devoid of agents, lawyers, and young studio executives, there were only the two Grand Jury prizes. The documentary award went to *Sherman's March*, which I couldn't understand at first because I always thought of it as fiction. The dramatic prize was split two ways with *Working Girls* also receiving a runner-up Special Jury Prize. The winners were Jill Godmilow's *Waiting for the Moon*, inspired by Gertrude Stein as played by Linda Hunt, and Gary Walkow's forgettable fantasy *The Trouble with Dick*. The second feature and its director disappeared for eight years, thus beginning a grand tradition of the Grand Jury Prize being poison (until, of course, Todd Haynes's *Poison* won the prize). When Jeff Lipsky arrived at Skouras Pictures, he inherited the turgid Godmilow feature. He gave it the old college try, including a smart attempt to work the lesbian angle. Lizzie Borden thought she'd blown her chances with the jury when she gave a particularly suggestive, yet ditzy introduction at the *Working Girls* screening attended by juror Randa Haines, the very serious director of *Children of a Lesser God*. There were five dramatic features (out of sixteen) by women that year. Unfortunately, that remains a festival record. The average is three.

Leading up to the January 1988 festival, I knew we were in trouble

when September rolled around and I couldn't find a single film to recommend. Time was running short, since programming used to be completed by early November. So I dropped Tony Safford a line hoping that
he'd found better films than the absurd desert allegory *South of Reno* or
the ultrabland, small-town little-people American Playhouse title *Rachel
River*; they were both invited. The second American Playhouse film in
Sundance, *The Silence at Bethany*, was actually an Amish story involving a crisis over delivering milk on Sunday. The third was a low-rent
adaptation of Lanford Wilson's memory play *Lemon Sky*. At least that
starred Kevin Bacon. All in all, it was a Playhouse kind of year! The Sundance Institute itself had sponsored a "saga about the darkened souls of
this country's heartland" called (surprise) *Promised Land*. It was shot in
Utah, and obviously it was slated for the festival. When Vestron acquired
it beforehand, they tried to impose their imperious new festival policy:
only opening- or closing-night slots. Sundance has never had a "closing
night." Tony Safford told me that he informed Vestron that he'd be
happy to show the film at the end of the final Sunday after everyone had
already left town.

I'd been very excited, along with everyone else, by a fourth Playhouse
title, *Walking on Water*, when it showed at the 1987 IFFM and was invited to Sundance. At the behest of East Coast development V.P. Susan
Dalsimer, Warners pursued this feature with Edward James Olmos as
an East L.A. calculus teacher extraordinaire, Jaime Escalante. The studio was known to occasionally experiment with this kind of image-en-
hancing, modestly profitable pickup. They bought it, changed the title
to *Stand and Deliver*, and pulled it from the festival—reportedly because
the Adam Ant title song couldn't be ready in time.

I added to this dreadful plight as well by endorsing a feature directed
by Peter Hoffman called *Valentino Returns*, a quirky coming-of-age
story from central California. Hoffman had made an exceptional half-
hour short, *Pilgrims*, which I'd never forgotten from American Mavericks a decade earlier. He'd spent years editing his feature, spending millions of dollars of family money in the process. Occasionally he'd call
me up to let me know that he'd trimmed a few frames from the opening shot and thought that it changed the entire film. Once invited to
Sundance, I assumed he'd settle down and meet the deadline. But Hoffman was so possessed that he couldn't stop tinkering. He pulled out—
a *second* cancellation. Nobody would blow that golden Sundance op-

portunity today (although *The Picture Bride* did it in 1994 and was reinvited the next year.)

By 1988, attendance had only grown incrementally and cellular phones were still a dream (or nightmare, depending on your vantage point). There were two terrific films that brightened that year's gloom, and I expected one of them to take the Grand Jury Prize at the awards ceremony. The festival unintentionally created a mob scene by cramming everyone into a cramped, smoky hotel conference room and serving a buffet dinner that seemed to consist of three hunks of beef jerky. Then Sundance Institute director Tom Wilhite dyspeptically moderated the ceremony. The two standout titles for me were John Waters's inspired and hilarious kitsch classic *Hairspray* and the uproariously obscene David Burton Morris film *Patti Rocks*. Admittedly *Patti Rocks* could easily seem sexist and wasn't designed to win over a jury. At any rate, to a chorus of "huhs" the Grand Jury Prize went to Rob Nilsson's experimental, black-and-white, video-shot confessional feature *Heat and Sunlight*. This was serious stuff; New Line's *Hairspray* was frivolous, commercial, and didn't need any help. In fact it went on to become Waters's biggest success. The jury recognition couldn't help the impossibly anticommercial *Heat and Sunlight*. Tony Safford quickly resolved to add more prizes in future years—especially an audience award. In the meantime, we were all left with a very sour taste.

One additional delight throughout the 1988 festival was an eleven-feature retrospective of the films of Sam Fuller, with Fuller in person. His punchy, straight-to-the gut narratives cut through the flabby independent also-rans. One of his key lessons that shouldn't have been lost on that year's crop of filmmakers was how to take a serious subject and make an energetic, entertaining picture like *The Steel Helmet* (war), *Underworld U.S.A.* (organized crime), and *Shock Corridor* (mental illness.) He was small. He was getting old. But he was still a kind of white-maned lion, larger than life. I understood why Wenders had cast him in two of his films. Luckily Fuller flew back to New York on a nondirect flight to which all documentary filmmakers and lesser luminaries had been consigned. Dramatic filmmakers and greater luminaries were flown direct. When I queried Tony Safford on this caste system, he tried to deny it then 'fessed up. Democracy in Sundance was on the way out. I'd helped program the single worst festival in history and traveled in steerage—but at least with the great Sam Fuller.

DECEASED

As 1988 progressed, some of the newly arrived go-go distributors of the eighties appeared ready for a tumble. I'd already been an eyewitness to this phenomenon from the moment I entered the business. Within two months of my arrival at financially shaky Bauer International in 1977, one of my bosses gave me a special assignment. One morning he sent me on an errand to Fulton Rubber Stamp, New York's leading rubber stamp emporium, where he instructed me to get the largest possible stamp that said just one word: D-E-C-E-A-S-E-D. I was young and I didn't mind getting out, so I didn't ask any questions. When I returned with a very big stamp, the office mail had just arrived. I was an eyewitness to a demonstration of how we would use the new device. We pulled out all the letters that looked like bills and stamped DECEASED over the addresses. Then we dropped them back in a mailbox. Needless to say, this couldn't work indefinitely. Bauer eventually changed its name to Liberty Films and moved to Plainfield, New Jersey.

United Artists Classics was formed out of the void left when Don Rugoff's Cinema 5 overspent and collapsed. I was inside UA Classics when it splintered and fell apart in less than four years, having spawned other studio classics divisions (which were also rapidly disassembled after an average life span of only about two years). Small companies run out of capital; studios just lose interest. Of the smaller companies that spun off UA Classics, only Spectrafilm utterly failed to make a dent. They printed a poster listing their original seventeen releases. None became a genuine hit; some were never even released. They had one marginal American indie success with Laura Dern and Treat Williams in *Smooth Talk*, and two reasonably successful European films, Paul Verhoeven's *The Fourth Man* and the French thriller *La Balance*. Distribution is no cakewalk. But at a certain point when a company has failed over and over again, one can't help but think about the great Mel Brooks comedy *The Producers* and wonder if they'd have done better by trying to fail.

Spectrafilm had just about fizzled out before 1988. Other companies that couldn't seem to find a hit, and then saw their protective home video money dry up, included Cineplex, Circle, Film Dallas, and Skouras. Gone were the days when Ben Barenholtz could secure a quick $300,000 advance from Karl Lorimar Home Video for a tough title like the Liverpudlian *Letter to Brezhnev*. For Jeff Lipsky and Skouras, life after *My*

Life as a Dog was problem plagued. They were partly shackled by serving as the theatrical conduit for American Playhouse titles, a situation that was exacerbated by a run of bad acquisitions (like *Dogs in Space*) from the normally reliable Jeff. I had a vivid illustration of the overall blight one day when I visited video buyer Cathy Doyle at the spectacular new Nelson Entertainment complex in Beverly Hills. Posters of *Living on Tokyo Time*, *I've Heard the Mermaids Singing*, and half a dozen of her other fairly expensive acquisitions were leaning against the wall. I wondered why they weren't hanging, but I didn't say anything. Cathy mentioned at one point that none of the titles on display had shipped more than 7,000 units. I felt a chill and suddenly understood the feeling of impermanence inside a multimillion-dollar edifice.

A company like Spectrafilm might have simply died a slow death as a distributor. They decided to go out in a blaze of glory by doing the very thing that was beginning to topple the big boys like Atlantic Releasing, Cinecom, and Vestron—production. It's a nearly irresistible step. In Spectrafilm's case, *Sticky Fingers* and *Tokyo Pop* closed the candy store for the last time. Island was already close to belly up, having typically been ahead of the curve. *Square Dance* and *Slamdance* (Wayne Wang's third feature) had added to their woes. Sales head Rob Schulze told me late in 1988, "A year ago I wondered if we just screwed up on our own. Now I look around and see that Island has lots of company."

The story was slightly different for each company. Atlantic became addicted to the big profits of a fluke Michael J. Fox vehicle like *Teen Wolf* and lost interest in the smaller margins of films brought in by acquisitions ace Bobby Rock like *Wish You Were Here*. Ironically they occupied a building on Sunset Bouvelard that Casablanca Records had built with its disco-era booty before going bankrupt. They followed in those footsteps. Cinecom's first major production premiered in Cannes in 1988. It was the costly, save-the-farm flop *Miles from Home* starring Richard Gere, Kevin Anderson, and a bull. Company head Amir Malin continued to make overpriced ICM-packaged literary adaptations for a couple of years until the $20 million rent came due. For quite some time, he kept claiming that no Cinecom film lost money because of foreign sales and such. Vestron really spread its riches around after cleaning up with their first in-house production, *Dirty Dancing*. With the notable exception of *The Dead*, John Huston's critically acclaimed swan song, they produced and released a dozen straight duds by the end of 1988, with more to follow. These films all cost less than $5 million, but losing a million here and a million there really adds up when you're not a studio. Even former Hollywood high-flyer Julia Phillips benefited from Vestron's largesse with her rehab/comeback production *The Beat*. In a familiar pattern of soaring overhead, Vestron also had a vast and spiffy office complex in Stamford, Connecticut, with regular Friday afternoon bowling parties for the staff. New Yorker Films veteran publicist Suzanne Fedak landed a job out there in the 'burbs and remarked that corporate life felt like one long committee meeting.

I should stop, but there were others. Despite Bingham Ray's efforts, Alive Pictures didn't come out of *The Moderns* that well. In fact Alan Rudolph's only commercially successful film of his entire career is still 1984's *Choose Me*. For their follow-up, Alive gave playwright Sam Shepard millions for a film starring Jessica Lange and a metaphorical herd of wild horses called *Far North*, but the grosses went far south. The soon-to-be casualty list would also include that peculiar pair of mini-major-wannabes DEG and WEG, for De Laurentiis Entertainment Group and Weintraub Entertainment Group. I never understood these companies. To me a "group" was the Rolling Stones.

It's not as if there weren't any decent films from anywhere that year. For starters, the extremely shrewd brain trust at Orion Classics had traditionally steered clear of American independent films. It almost seemed like a house rule, except for the occasional failed attempt with Marissa Silver's *Old Enough* (1984) or the tedious Arkansas railroad tale *End of the Line*. In 1988, Orion Classics scored four times in a row on the foreign-language side with Louis Malle's *Au Revoir les Enfants*, the Danish *Babette's Feast*, Wim Wenders's one and only "hit" *Wings of Desire*, and Pedro Almodovar's New York Film Festival opener *Women on the Verge of a Nervous Breakdown*. Video was basically a nonfactor for these subtitled films; it didn't confuse the issue. No one expected much more than 7,000 units. Tom Bernard, Michael Barker, and Donna Gigliotti had a consistent game plan throughout the eighties based on intelligent conservatism and savvy taste in world cinema. They left it to their parent company to get in way over its head by being "filmmaker friendly" with the Woody Allens of the world.

Even in these doldrums, Goldwyn managed to produce a surprise crossover hit at year's end. Mainstream audiences responded very well to the commercial romantic comedy *Mystic Pizza*. The secret to that film's near $20-million grossing success was an extremely appealing ensemble cast featuring the then unknown Julia Roberts. *Mystic Pizza* was a Goldwyn production and its profits graphically illustrated the seductive appeal of *making* movies rather than acquiring them. I had a more modest goal. I just wanted to find a few undiscovered first features. That had now become my official mission.

QUANTITY NOT QUALITY

Although it was the worst of times, I was receiving far more unsolicited work than ever before. Every single low-budget film seemed to have a story behind it—a story that was often more compelling than the film itself. I'll never forget the director who offered my dentist a point in her film in return for some fillings and a crown. I doubt I'll shake the memory of the director who, while slowly recovering from the brain damage sustained in a mugging, decided he wanted a 400-theater four-wall release of his revamped San Francisco psychedelia film. Then there were dozens of films that seemed to be competing in "The Most Misconceived Movie of the Year Sweepstakes." Yaphet Kotto, a fine character actor, set aside his acting fees so that he could direct himself in a sexorcism film featuring a possessed basketball. Some energetic producers from the northwest made a high school musical starring the thirty-five-year-old composer of the score as a teenage student. One director made a "general audience" picture about a city slicker on a ranch, and was careful to tell me he was trying not to make a "sick" film like *Blue Velvet* or an "amateurish" one like *She's Gotta Have It*. He needn't have been concerned. And did you hear the one about the first Lebanese-American film featuring a stand-up comic mining Beirut for material?

Being hopelessly out-of-touch was no worse than being a clone. Every breakthrough film had the effect of inspiring other independents to try to emulate, or in some cases just imitate, that model. Horton Foote's rural roots made Waxahachie a household name. Jim Jarmusch's deadpan downtown deadbeats became familiar figures. The Coens' genre-skewing black comedy sensibility seemed to pop up time and again as a substitute for real comedy. But it's never the same the second (or third, or fourth) time around. Spike Lee preached that he wanted black artists to seize control of their own destinies, but his congregation didn't realize how much pure talent, hustle, and originality it took to invent *She's Gotta Have It* out of thin air. The pioneers had demonstrated not only that low-budget feature filmmaking was possible but that there was also a market for it. Suddenly, there was no excuse not to make a feature film, and the desire to make a film, *any film*, replaced the need to express a vision.

Over 560 filmmakers were in attendance at the 1988 Independent Feature Film Market. Fifty-seven completed features were shown, plus a similar number of works-in-progress. Nothing in the lineup of completed films received a meaningful domestic distribution offer at the time. A few were given extremely marginal releases later on. When I moderated an acquisitions panel at the start of the market, I suggested that the title should be "The Pickup Artists: Why Won't They Buy My Film." In the interest of trying to sound more positive, the subtitle was changed to "Will They Ever Buy My Film?" The difference eluded me; apparently it eluded the distributors as well.

School Daze, Spike's second feature, had come out early in the year. He hadn't wanted it to premiere in Sundance because the audience was lily-white. Some critics groused that he used his $6 million to make a sprawling, large-scale college musical instead of sticking to the intimate Brooklyn neighborhood that he knew best. I found it to be a simple case of sophomore slump, where he attempted to cram together incoherent elements. Nelson George provided a kinder description: Spike Lee's dictionary of soul. Fortunately for Spike, the black audience didn't care where he made the film or how much he spent and it grossed more than $14 million domestically—this despite the fact that Dawn Steel's Columbia Pictures spent less money releasing *School Daze* than Island had on his debut. If he'd been in Park City in January, he would have gotten a big laugh from the dead-on, icy portrayal of a Dawn Steel–like studio executive in Christopher Guest's film à clef, *The Big Picture*.

Steel's imaginative memoirs claim that a frustrated Spike called her "white, bitch, ho" when she asked for a definition of a Spike Lee Joint. I find that rather dubious. However he did take the time to write to *New York Times* critic Janet Maslin when her review suggested that *School Daze* was beyond his "technical abilities." Spike's response: "I bet you can't even dance." Then, as always, he moved on. He was setting up shop at Universal Pictures and preparing to shoot one of the essential films that would make 1989 a lot better.

Batman and Sex

JOHN PIERSON: Where were you in 1989 anyway?

KEVIN SMITH: It was the year of *Batman*. That's where my head was.

JP: You bet it was the year of *Batman*. *Roger & Me* and *Batman* were side by side on the Great Wall at Warners' Burbank studio. Did you see *Batman* the day it came out?

KS: I knew they were having a sneak preview before the Friday opening. At this point I'm not even considering filmmaking. I must have just left the New School for Social Research since *Batman* opened June 23. I left in May, so I'm just getting home and I'm going out with my girlfriend and I'm working at Domino's for one day for two hours and quitting and going to see *Batman*.

JP: Wait . . . the girlfriend whose mother wrote the sign on your desk?

KS: Yeah. It says, KEVIN SMITH WILL NEVER BE A FAMOUS WRITER BECAUSE HE LACKS THE DRIVE, BUT I WISH HIM WELL ANYWAY.

JP: What were the circumstances?

KS: Can you imagine that? A woman who's so spiteful that I'm breaking up with her daughter? At the time I was just a layabout, a slacker if you will. She said, "Wait here." I was at the door, leaving, saying goodbye. I thought she was bringing me something her daughter had written and she brought me this piece of paper, and it was folded up and she hands it to me and holds my hand like this, holds my hand and won't let me open it and she goes, "If I'm wrong about this find me, and I'll eat this." And I've had it on my desk ever since, wherever I write.

JP: I assume you saw *sex, lies, and videotape* a couple of months after that incident.

KS: I have a very Harvey Weinstein–like story, just like Harvey went to see *The 400 Blows* (in his most famous publicity story I guess) because it sounded much racier than it was. It's like "hey man, *sex*." It has it right in the title. *Lies* does nothing for you, but *sex* and *videotape* scream "Come see me, come see me!" I'm nineteen. I can get into seeing this. I'm definitely going. But there's no naked Andie MacDowell. If you look real hard, you'll see maybe some breast, no nipple of Laura San Giacomo so . . .

JP: How about the plant on Peter Gallagher's member?

KS: That's it. Unless you're a Peter Gallagher fan it just doesn't do it for you. So you're in there, and on one level you're disappointed. On the other hand it's like whoa . . . this is a different sort of narrative. Especially coming in the same year as *Batman*.

JP: Did the film play at the mall?

KS: The Loews, now Sony, Red Bank where *Clerks* played. *Sex, lies* was the film that started the process of Red Bank becoming the town's "alternative" theater. My friend Walter's wife asked him where *Clerks* was gonna play when it opened, and he said "It'll probably play at Red Bank, that's where all the movies that you never hear about play—nowhere else." It's a euphemism for independent films.

JP: This raises a big question: what it means to "hear about" a movie. Does that mean it's got some exposure on television?

KS: Oh God. Who in my milieu, where I grew up, reads the *Village Voice* or *The New York Times?* Who reads anything but the *Asbury Park Press* and the *Monmouth Courier?* Maybe if you're lucky, *the Ledger.*

1989: The Year It All Changed

n January 1989, the corpse stirred. Throughout the previous fall, I was searching for Sundance titles again as the New York member of the selection committee. I felt that the field was at least a little stronger this time around. If not, Sundance would have been in serious trouble. Since I'd been involved in a second feature co-produced by Zanne Devine called *Prisoners of Inertia*, I recused myself during its selection. The strongest film I screened was Nancy Savoca's *True Love*. The producers didn't seem happy that in my program note for that ensemble film, I singled out newcomer Annabella Sciorra as a "sultry screen presence." Savoca was the only female director represented in that year's Dramatic Competition, and she was home having a baby. Her true-to-life Italian neighborhood story was eventually picked up for big bucks and woefully released by MGM. They actually put a toilet stall in the ad campaign. Through its lengthy gestation, *True Love* had gotten some financial backing from indie stalwarts Jonathan Demme and John Sayles. When it won the Grand Jury Prize I thought it a bit questionable that Peggy Rajski, a long time John Sayles collaborator, chaired that jury.

Nobody had time to notice. We were all too busy trying to dream up ever more laudatory plaudits for the film of that or any festival, *the* film that put the capper on one decade and jump-started the next one, Steven Soderbergh's *sex, lies, and videotape*. *Heathers* was fiendishly satirical, *Apartment Zero* was well acted, *The Big Dis* had grainy charm, *Powwow Highway* hit the offbeat road, and *For All Mankind* captured the awesome majesty of space. *Sex, lies, and videotape* caught the popular imagination with its unerring delineation of that moment's zeitgeist. The veneer of the eighties was cracking; the devastation of AIDS discouraged promiscuous coupling. The film presented a rare portrayal of a sensitive, vulnerable male, along with a beautiful, neurotic wife, a sexpot sister, and a crass, cheating husband. It was serious, thoughtful, funny and it pushed the edge of what was allowable on screen. Early on, Soderbergh admitted a strong autobiographical element, but he soon played this down since the film spoke very directly to its viewers' own relationships—a kind of yuppie Rorschach test.

Made for $1.2 million with domestic (RCA Columbia) and foreign (Virgin) home video financing, *sex, lies, and videotape* had slipped into Sundance quietly. Tony Safford hadn't been that wild about it, so Marjorie Skouras (of Skouras Pictures) wrote the underwhelming program note, which featured all-purpose phrases like "elegantly paced and sparsely framed." That doesn't exactly sound like a movie that would shake up the entire industry. By the end of the first weekend, it seemed like a clarion call had gone out to both coasts and flights to Salt Lake City suddenly started to book up. Park City's sidewalks got crowded for the first time in the second half (Package B) of the festival. Tickets for the fourth and final *sex, lies, and videotape* show were being scalped as a huge throng assembled in the suddenly sardine-sized lobby of the Holiday Village Cinemas. I snuck Columbia's Tom Rothman into a seat with a phony ticket stub. Soderbergh immediately resisted the instant prophet role. The twenty-six-year-old chose to drive a shuttle van back and forth. To this day, he describes *sex, lies, and videotape* as a fluke that should never have been used as a financial benchmark of the breakthrough potential for an independent film. He seems enormously uncomfortable with his early success.

Whether Soderbergh likes it or not, he changed the industry landscape and Miramax helped. There was very spirited bidding from most indie distributors for this film. Many of the failing companies made a last-ditch grab, hoping Soderbergh could be their savior. Because home video rights had been presold to finance *sex, lies, and videotape*, the North American offers topped out around the $1 million advance level. The Weinsteins edged 10 percent higher and demonstrated their consuming passion in a myriad of forceful ways to Soderbergh, his five producers, and Larry Estes, who was riding shotgun, having greenlit (along with Gina Resnick) the film for RCA Columbia. Miramax had been growing in stature ever since *Working Girls* although none of their films had crossed the $2 million mark at the box office. The Palace-produced *Scandal* (a perfect Miramax title) would soon become their first true hit. Their acquisition team was captained by Charles Layton, with swarming support from Trea Hoving, Mark Tusk, and Alison Brantley. Layton's short-term predecessor, Michael Spielberg, once told me how much he wanted to buy the Hemdale title *Vampire's Kiss*, in which Nicolas Cage gives his all-time over-the-top performance. When I mentioned this desire to Harvey, he wondered out loud if he should put a revolving door on Spielberg's office to give him a sense of job longevity. Layton himself (and Mark Silberman before Spielberg) didn't last much longer in the Miramax world. Personnel turnover actually started to settle down in the nineties; Mark and Trea remain integral today.

Even with Ira Deutchman's input as producer's rep, the trailer and ad campaigns on *sex, lies, and videotape* weren't that remarkable. Harvey's single smartest move on positioning this film was his mold-breaking Cannes strategy. It would have been conventional wisdom to play a first feature in the Directors' Fortnight, which wanted the film very badly. With the help of the film's French distributor, AMLF, Harvey shrewdly used the intense hidden strife between the Quinzaine and Gilles Jacob's main event to leverage this small film into the main competition with the big boys. I thought it was risky. So did almost everyone else. We were wrong. Soderbergh won the Palme d'Or. On stage he half-jested, "Well, I guess it's all downhill from here."

Sex, lies, and videotape wasn't the only absolute sensation at Cannes that year. Spike hit his stride both artistically and politically with his third feature, *Do the Right Thing*. Both Sam Kitt, who had landed at Universal as acquisitions director after his indie decade, and production head Sean Daniel, were responsible for getting Spike to the studio after the Columbia *School Daze* fiasco. He was back on the block in Brooklyn showing the consequences of tension building up over one long, hot summer day. Inspired in part by a terrible act of racial violence in the

Queens neighborhood of Howard Beach, the first draft of the screenplay had Spike's lead character, Mookie, actually shouting "Howard Beach" as he threw the garbage can through the window of Sal's Pizzeria, inciting a riot.

My old touring mate Wim Wenders, coming off *Wings of Desire*, his biggest success in a twenty-year career, was Cannes jury chairman. Fassbinder was dead; Herzog was walking across Europe. Young filmmakers hadn't even heard of them, much less seen their work. Wenders had prevailed. He played an instrumental role in pushing the more internal Soderbergh, thus denying the more external Spike his prize once again. (Proving that the chickens do come home to roost, Spike's original nemesis, Whoopi Goldberg, thwarted him on the 1991 jury, which chose the Coens' *Barton Fink* over *Jungle Fever*.) Perhaps Wim overstepped his bounds when he complained that Mookie was no hero, and, eerily echoing my old *She's Gotta Have It* prediction, described Soderbergh as "the future of cinema." Spike became livid and suggested he had a Louisville Slugger bat with Wim's name on it, before returning to his milder "we wuz robbed" refrain. He did have the presence of mind to point out that James Spader's video-viewing, masturbating character in *sex, lies, and videotape* wasn't exactly heroic either. As combative as Spike can be, he's funny.

I had seen *Do the Right Thing* twice before Cannes and saw it again there. I was at the festival on assignment with a first timer, who had started making shorts long before Spike's discovery, and had perhaps even been a small inspiration. Charles Lane's truly original *Sidewalk Stories* had come my way in February. He was a SUNY/Purchase film school graduate. In an audacious move after years of frustration, Lane decided to expand on an idea from one of his student shorts to make a feature length, black-and-white, 35mm, *silent film*. It starred Charles Lane himself as a Chaplinesque homeless man who has to care for a lost little girl. She was played by his real-life daughter, although we concealed that fact. As one of only a handful of early eighties black filmmakers, he actually had a little chip on his shoulder about Spike's success. I was relieved that *Sidewalk Stories* came along when it did because the Pierson family was running out of money after the 1988 famine. The Quinzaine invited it on the spot, and when it arrived in Cannes the French and the other Europeans really loved it. Best of all, it didn't need subtitles.

The film had two flaws. It dragged at 103 minutes. Michael Barker, astutely pointed out that there was a reason that Chaplin's features were only seventy minutes long; silent films take great concentration. Charles had actually tricked me during the rushed editing by saying that it was down to 98 minutes. When I timed it in Cannes, I thought my watch was broken. The second flaw was a hasty and ineffective synthesized music score that may have cost it the Camera d'Or. Spike can be very direct. He made a point of seeing *Sidewalk Stories* right away. When he came out, he raved about the great visual storytelling and Bill Dill's cinematography, but he condemned the music. He actually recommended using the great jazz saxophonist Wayne Shorter to rescore it and offered to help get him. Charles wasn't too happy to hear this. His producer Howard Brickner got angry because he hated the idea of spending any more money because he'd already mortgaged his weekend house to raise $200,000. I made it easier to swallow by selling world rights to Chris Blackwell and Island Pictures for $500,000—not bad for a black-and-white, silent film with a grating score.

Sidewalk Stories would go on to become the *last* title Island directly distributed later in the year. I'm particularly proud of this deal. Harvey Weinstein had really helped me by pretending that Miramax was aggressively in the hunt when they weren't. I loved the fact that Blackwell got into *Sidewalk Stories*, but I almost felt as if he bought it partly as a payback for some of the lingering bad feelings about Spike. When Spike went to Universal, Island had actually gotten some concessions with ongoing *She's Gotta Have It* royalties in return for releasing him from the original deal's "second option." Island signed Charles Lane for a single-option picture, then released him from that obligation when he wanted to step into the lion's den at Disney to rewrite, direct, and co-star in the wretched *True Identity*. Since the story involved a black man (Lenny Henry) in white face, Disney decided they needed a black filmmaker to avoid *Soul Man* attacks. Charles thought he could fight the power; instead he proved that, contrary to popular opinion, a black movie *could* lose money—millions.

The American independent impact in Cannes 1989 even exceeded 1986, the year of *She's Gotta Have It* and *Down By Law*. Having originally spotted him a two-year head start, Spike had caught up with Jim Jarmusch's career pace. The 1989 competition marked the premiere of Jim's third feature, the JVC/Japanese-financed *Mystery Train*. Tom Bernard kicked in a door to sneak into an early press screening and tried to wave me in with him. I hesitated just long enough to be shoved aside by a gendarme. I saw it soon enough, and Orion Classics wound up acquiring the film. It's beautifully made, but I couldn't help feeling that Spike was taking giant steps forward while Jim was inching over the same ground. Of course the French critics in the *Cahiers du Cinema* had invented the concept of auteurism to celebrate just this sort of thematic and stylistic repetition.

In the three-time Jarmusch tradition, *Mystery Train* waited for the fall's New York Film Festival to open stateside. *Do the Right Thing* was an explosive, hot-weather film and it jumped right into the thick of the summer releases. *Sex, lies, and videotape* waited just a bit for that now established early August slot when the studio juggernaut is beginning to wear down and intelligent viewers are getting desperate. Then Miramax boldly took it wide. When the smog cleared, Spike and Soderbergh did a similar amount of business ($25 to $30 million) and both generated tons of discussion. Spike demonstrated the possibilities of a sustained career for a newcomer working with a studio and growing in stature. It's not as if Universal ever gave Spike an open checkbook. In order to do his movies his way, he had to make them within budget limits or, in studio lingo, "for a price." When Spike once complained about films like *Uncle Buck* getting big budgets without a fight, Universal Chairman Tom Pollock told him he'd give him millions more if he wanted to make *Uncle Buck 2*. By the time of his third and fourth features, *King of the Hill* and *The Underneath*, Steven Soderbergh had also joined the Universal family. He still seemed to want to make subtle art films.

Sex, lies, and videotape on the other hand showed just how far a first feature, released by an independent no less, could go all over the world. By using videotape both in the title (a controversial choice before Sundance) and in the film itself, Soderbergh almost literally ushered in the new era of the video-educated filmmaker. It wasn't just a smash in the United States, but virtually every foreign territory as well. If I had a nickel for every prospectus that I've received that highlighted the $100 million dollars in worldwide gross on a $1.2 million budget, I'd be a rich man. Although I had no direct involvement, I always wondered how the actual profit participants in *sex, lies, and videotape* made out. In the realm of hearsay, outsiders want to believe that there was a small fortune to go around. Whatever Columbia/TriStar (née RCA Columbia) made, it wasn't enough to keep Larry Estes' indie production boutique in business indefinitely. After more than twenty features over the next few years, it went the way of Vestron.

I subscribe to the Old Mother Hubbard theory of producer net revenue: The cupboard is nearly always barer than you think. For one thing in this case, an overstretched company called MCEG bought Virgin Video and assigned many foreign territories to Goldwyn before promptly falling into bankruptcy, thus entangling millions in foreign revenue for years. Domestically Miramax obviously went whole hog with their print and advertising (P&A) spending. And of course there were multiple producers involved in sharing the wealth. I've gotten to know one of them, Nancy Tenenbaum, quite well. She has a great passion for producing distinctive movies. Her subsequent films have included Michael Tolkin's *The Rapture*, John Turturro's 1992 Camera d'Or winner *Mac*, and Greg Mottola's *The Day Trippers*. Having started as an executive as CBS/Fox Home Video, she now makes movies she cares about because it's in her blood. But I know that even if she'd wanted to retire to Tahiti with her *sex, lies, and videotape* profits, the money wouldn't have lasted that long.

Collecting money after a film's success can be quite difficult. We got it *up front* on *Roger & Me*. And unlike Steven Soderbergh, Michael Moore was not averse to becoming a star.

Sex and Roger

JOHN PIERSON: Seeing *sex, lies* didn't immediately make you think, "Oh, look what this Steven Soderbergh did"?

KEVIN SMITH: His backstory wasn't that familiar to me, and I didn't know the budget. I knew it had Andie MacDowell, who didn't do her own voice in *Tarzan [Greystoke]*.

JP: So for the last time, this film was not an influence?

KS: No, because it was too glossy. Later in life, when I do get into the independent arena, it's not the glossy independents that do it for me. It's the ones like *Stranger Than Paradise* that make it seem achievable, that make it seem doable. Soderbergh pulled together this really good looking movie. I mean it looks like a movie, as they say in this part of the world. And that's why when we're done with *Clerks* we're not even thinking about Sundance because by now I've caught up on my independent film history from the last five or six years, and I know that *sex, lies* is the kind of movie that comes out of Sundance, not *Clerks*.

JP: I'm not sure you had that figured out quite right.

KS: Anyway, let's break it down—glossy movie, more esoteric than anything I'm used to, not enough dick jokes, and stars—way out of my league. Especially for a first timer.

JP: But that movie changed the business which, in the long run, was a benefit for you. Although the script kicked around for a while, Soderbergh started out fairly well connected. He had some savvy producers, a respected agent, a strong casting director—ways of getting to Andie MacDowell and James Spader. Spader was the "star" and deal lynchpin.

KS: I absolutely agree with you on where it fits in the time line. It's seminal. It also has one direct effect on me because it kind of gave Sundance the significance it has. *Sex, lies* provides the high-profile lift so that suddenly a lot more people know what Sundance is. The industry's paying more attention. So when *Clerks* gets accepted, the astute people know what you're talking about.

JP: *Roger & Me* is the film that everybody thought was my "big deal." Well, it is my biggest deal in terms of just money, and it's the only film I've sold to a studio. But I've never heard you talk about it. Why is that?

KS: It's a documentary . . . and while I feel it's an engaging and entertaining documentary, it's nonetheless a documentary, so it just doesn't enter into my milieu. It's on a par with *Star Wars*. I can never do it.

JP: Warners must have booked it in your neighborhood . . .

KS: Yeah, Middletown. But as a documentary, no matter how much it's praised, it's not going to get me in the theater.

JP: Hey, you're the problem. You asked me on the way over here how much it grossed, and I gave a double answer—$7 million, which is great unless your expectation is $20 million.

KS: What's it about? On the surface, it's about the auto industry. Cars and me just never go together. But my uncle, who doesn't go out to the movies, he sees it cause he's a huge, huge car guy. My father's father worked for Ford somewhere in Jersey forever, worked for them for years and never got my dad a job in the business. But he got my father's sister's husband, my uncle, a job, and I think my dad kinda resents it. My father never works in the auto industry so he never goes to see it. My grandfather's dead so he doesn't see it. Years later when I bring it home from the video store, Dad watches it and loves it. If more people like my old man had gone to see it and dragged their son, well then you would have had your $20 million. Or at least $10 more from us.

JP: Your mother, your sister? I'm in Chinatown, Jake. [Ed. Note: We suggested "you've lost me."]

KS: Didn't *Roger & Me* turn the documentary world upside down?

JP: Every post-*Roger* feature documentarian has been obsessed with the film. But even people who make very successful dramatic films who think that they should get big deals tend not to refer to it, although they have no equivalent dramatic substitute made for that little that sold for that much.

KS: When you read up on indie history, you find out what things go for—what little info you can—on what sold to whom and for how much. Three million for a first film, unless it cost millions is just a one-in-a-million shot.

JP: A fluke where every single, solitary thing went right. . . .

KS: The key factor is that it was worth it. It's a brilliant documentary, a brilliant *film*.

JP: And because of *Batman*, which you pointed out in the first place, Warners had money to spare—"the dabbling fund."

KS: And later on, Michael Moore set aside his "idiot grants" for other people to dabble.

JP: You know when Michael was on *Tonight* for the first time with Jay Leno as guest host, Leno asked him if he would ever make a sequel to *Roger & Me* which he kinda did three years later with the short *Pets or Meat*. Michael said he would never do it unless Warner Bros. combined the *Roger* and *Batman* sequels into one film where Batman would come to save Flint, dangle Roger Smith from a tower, and everyone would go back to work to build BatMobiles.

KS: Was he ever on Letterman?

JP: Yes. You know how you were talking about those fake-sounding rags-to-riches stories before? Mike was on Letterman when the film first opened—Dave told him that his success was really another version of the American dream and Mike shot back, "Except this one's a reality." Letterman looked annoyed like he'd been one-upped, and didn't look any happier when Mike added something like "to most people the American dream is just a dream."

KS: The top ten reasons why Kevin hasn't been on the show. Number one: Afraid he would make some American dream reference.

ROGER AND MICHAEL AND ME

THE CINDERELLA SYNDROME

His walk looked suspiciously like a waddle. But when the big man from Flint, Michigan, walked into my life in August, 1989, he was definitely in the right place at the right time with the right $3 million movie. Michael Moore's *Roger & Me* was financed in part by bingo, promoted with lint rollers, acquired by multi-national Time-Warner for nineteen times its cash budget, and went on to become one of the most successful nonconcert documentaries in history. Unlike *She's Gotta Have It*, Michael's film was no simple Cinderella story. He's a complex character with a penchant for attracting and amplifying controversy.

One year earlier, *Roger & Me* had first seen the light of day as a work-in-progress at the Independent Feature Film Market. The laborious working title was *A Humorous Look at How General Motors Destroyed Flint, Michigan*, perhaps in a nod to fading hopes for nonprofit funding. Michael claims he would have sold the film for lunch at that point. A mere half-dozen "buyers" signed in for the screening. My name wasn't on that list, thus beginning a grand tradition that I continued the next year with *Slacker* and capped off with *Clerks* three years later.

I filed the press book and tuned out. Fortunately, Derek Hill from Channel 4 in London actually saw the film and paid a crucial $35,000 for British broadcast television rights. His bold move kept Michael and co-editor Wendey Stanzler moving toward completion. Razor-sharp editing was always the key for *Roger & Me*.

In the time between Roger-in-progress and Roger-ready-for-the-world, one remarkable event had totally redefined the off-Hollywood world at mid-decade. That of course was the triumph of *sex, lies, and videotape*. The independent distributors that hadn't bid high enough and the studios that had categorically refused to consider acquiring any title without home video rights were suddenly staring straight in the face of a $25 million gross and a mushrooming cottage industry in more little indies like Steven Soderbergh. In certain later cases this led to semihysterical behavior such as Samuel Goldwyn's purchase of John Sayles's *City of Hope* at Sundance (1991) for $2.5 million without video. Like the Soderbergh film, *City of Hope* was financed by RCA Columbia Home Video. The similarities end there. Its performance fell short by about $24 million.

Back in August 1989, the moment was ripe for *Roger & Me*. The Reagan/Bush backlash was gaining momentum, just begging for a scathingly funny, unforgivably entertaining, deadly serious rallying cry. The only problem was that I still hadn't had any contact with Michael Moore. Over the summer while he was in his postproduction homestretch, I was away in Rockport, Maine, for a month teaching at the Photographic Workshop. I learned later that Michael called my phone machine at the urging of IFFM director Karol Martesko (later publisher of *Filmmaker* magazine). Upon hearing the Maine getaway message, he quickly concluded that I must be privileged yuppie scum. In a lucky break for me, Michael called back the very day I returned to New York, and scheduled a screening of his first answer print at DuArt the next morning.

Picture this setup: one closet-size room, several metal chairs, one 16mm Bell & Howell projector necessitating several breaks for reel changes. Michael, Wendey Stanzler, and Judy Irving, director of the hard-hitting antinuclear documentary *Dark Circle* were there. I didn't have a Spike Lee "I have seen the future of cinema" reaction. Although I found it funny, I laughed less than I did at any of the fifty public screenings of *Roger & Me* that I saw over the next six months. I didn't have enough political passion to get worked up into a high dudgeon. My mind turned to more surgical strategic issues. In fact, when we all went to lunch at a nearby Thai restaurant, I immediately demonstrated my dispassionate unflappability by dropping a bowl of shrimp soup in my lap. It didn't take much longer for me to realize that the spiciest food Michael eats is the secret sauce on a Big Mac. Coca-Cola and ice cream turned out to be his midwestern staples.

Knowing that the film would soon be starting the "Big 3" September festival circuit from Telluride to Toronto to New York, we cut to the chase and discussed its market value. Using the recent experience on *The Thin Blue Line* and knowing the approximate $160,000 *Roger & Me* budget, I predicted that a $200,000 advance would be great if all went well. Judy Irving, a traditional documentarian, looked amazed. Michael, on the other hand, looked unimpressed—almost as if he had a greater faith, like the Catholic priest he could have become who knows that heaven awaits. It was impossible to think of him as a typical deluded novice filmmaker because of his considerable achievement as a rapier-wielding journalist with a keen sense of story. We agreed to work together. So I was *in* for the cost of an uneaten lunch, the seasoned industry pro, the only member of Michael's circle who was not his acolyte from Flint.

As my pants slowly dried, I sang the generic documentary blues. Then I systematically explained the obstacles with each of the major independents: Orion Classics had never distributed a documentary and paid low advances, Goldwyn had been doc-gunshy since the low-grossing Oscar winner *Hotel Terminus*, Avenue was still struggling to get started, Cinecom was reaching the end of its rope, and Miramax was ultimately a bit disappointed with the performance of the Errol Morris picture, given all the publicity. Little did I know how much ribbing I'd get for my puny prediction. But the big bucks didn't come by accident. You must first devise a campaign even as you savor every moment of serendipity. Living through the thirty days of *Roger & Me* in the month of September was like opening the little windows on an Advent calendar, counting down the days until Christmas. Inside each window was a pleasant new surprise—another rave review, a major press feature, another bigger offer, a first-class ticket to Hollywood, a prolonged standing ovation. And then Santa arrived.

9/13 MMX
9/22 OC
9/27 ANE
9/28 SG
10/6 WI

SEPT.
1 - 5   TELLURIDE   ⎫ NO J.P.
6 - 8   FLINT → TOR ⎭
9 - 13   TORONTO: EBERT 10 SHEILA 13
14 - 15   LA/DISNEY (+ UNIVERSAL)   DAY 14
16 - 18   MM IN DC
17   TORONTO PRIZE
19 - 21   NYC SCREENINGS: NYT 21 VOICE 20 F,C,KS 21
22   NYFF PRESS + OPENING: NYT 22   ORION 150-1M
23 - 24   GBH IN ST. VINCENT
25 - 26   NYC DIST. MEETINGS
27   NYFF PUBLIC #1: NYT 27   AVENUE - 1.1M
28   "   "   #2: NYT 28   GOLDWYN - 1.2M
29 - 30   HARVEY (REACTIVATE UNIVERSAL)   DAY 28
30   MYSTERY TRAIN
OCT. 1   HELLER + GIGERMAN (CAP)
2   PROSP. DEAL MEMO
3   IFP OPEN: SUNDANCE STORIES   DEAL MEMO
5   CANBY SHARY TIMES ADVANCE
6 - 7   LA/UNIVERSAL (+ WARNERS)
7   VANCOUVER
8   IFP KEYNOTE: NYT 8
11   IFP SCREENING/SUNDANCE PARTY
12   HARVEY ENCOUNTER
13 - 14   DENVER IFF + SUNDANCE + IFP CLOSING
15 - 18   LA/WARNERS   QUAKE 17
★   19   WB TERMS + HARVEY'S HOUR   DAY 49
20   ST. LOUIS. UAW/NEW DIRECTIONS (HOLLYWOOD REP)
21 - 22   MONTREAL
23   FF FOTOS
26   MORAL CRISIS
★   27   WB CLOSED   NEW CUSS
28   FT. LAUDERDALE
29   CHICAGO/SISKEL
30 - 31   FLINT ANNOUNCEMENT   PTL
NOV. 1   MM/LA
2   "
3 - 4   VA. FILM FEST.
5   PHILA. INQ (DET. NEWS/LA TIMES
9 - 13   MM/FLINT PHOTO
14 - 16   LA   DAY 77
16 - 19   LONDON
25   AMPAS/LA SCREENING
24 - 27   LEIPZIG
DEC. 1   TRAILER + BLOW-UP + ONE-SHEET
2   EBERT & SISKEL

Week 1

Roger & Me had its world premiere at Telluride on opening night, Friday, September 1. Telluride is a wonderfully pure festival for cineastes, held in a stunningly beautiful setting high up in the southwestern Rockies. Although *El Norte* and *The Great Wall* found distributors in earlier years, this festival was becoming less and less noted for business. Two of the reasons no deal has been sealed there in years are industry skepticism of the Telluride elitist audience, and *very* finite press turnout as opposed to the Toronto Festival's populist crowds and a press corps in the hundreds. Because I believed that Toronto held the key for selling *Roger & Me*, I skipped out on Telluride for the first time in eight years.

Michael Moore–lookalike Roger Ebert is one of the Telluride regulars. Before Michael and the economy-size posse from Flint headed off to Colorado, I pointed out that one early goal in Telluride should be to get him to see the film. At the kickoff party, the posse surrounded Ebert as Moore got in his face and persuaded him to dump the Peter Greenaway tribute that night in favor of *Roger & Me*.

The film eventually had six packed screenings, each more tumultuous than the one before. There were several small bumps. Festival director Bill Pence pulled Michael aside at one point and bluntly observed that his retinue was taking up too many seats at each screening. (Telluride always described itself as "filmmaker friendly.") One person walked out of the Friday debut during the rabbit skinning: Goldwyn's V.P. of Acquisitions Anne Templeton, whom Michael spotted wearing fur in the chilly mountain air. The first viewer from Warners, V.P. of production Lisa Henson, saw a later show, praised it, but concluded that it was way too small for the studio. The foremost studio film maven, Jim Jacks, reached the same initial conclusion for Universal, although he courted Michael for future projects. In my absence, Ira Deutchman, who between his stints at Cinecom and Fine Line acted as a producers' rep on films like *Metropolitan*, put the moves on the newly coronated Michael Moore. Even in the thin atmosphere at 9,000 feet, Michael stayed loyal. By the end of the four-day weekend, no offer for *Roger & Me* had surpassed $100,000. The extraordinary response was deemed to be aberrant, "festival fever," of no validity in the real world. But the word was out, and it was on to Toronto.

Week 2

Finally I joined the troops from Flint, numbering over twenty, in Canada. They had buttons, T-shirts, caps—but their Helmac lint rollers had been seized by Canadian customs at the border. The first public showing in Toronto was scheduled for Saturday night, September 9, at 9:00 P.M. in the Cumberland 3—a 300-seat theater. *Roger & Me* was shot in 16mm, and snuck into this festival under the wire through the good graces of print trafficker Noah Cowan. (He now programs the Midnight Madness program.) Let's just say that the screening slots were a bit weird. The first of Ebert's several great reviews was out that day. By 8:00 P.M. Saturday, it appeared that the entire population of Ontario was heading east on Bloor Street in the general direction of the Cumberland in numbers that could have filled it many times over. The only slight problem was that not a single significant distributor could get in, although the ever enterprising press corps did a little better. The magical mix of uproarious comedy, biting satire, powerful emotion, and hard-hitting politics snapped into sharp focus for me in these surroundings.

On Sunday, the Canadian Film Centre had its annual afternoon barbecue. It seemed clear that the time had come to start pushing harder, especially after Michael's then girlfriend, now wife Kathleen Glynn took me aside and asked, "What have you done for us lately?" I felt confident enough to guarantee a $500,000 advance before heading off to another table occupied by the Avenue Pictures contingent, where I begged on bended knee that they go to the Monday evening screening at the Royal Ontario Museum. They had their current release *Drugstore Cowboy* at the festival, so Cary Brokaw, Bingham Ray, and Claudia Lewis were hanging with producer Karen Murphy, director Gus Van Sant, and stars Matt Dillon and Kelly Lynch.

New York Times reporter Glenn Collins arrived in town on assignment to follow Michael around for twenty-four hours. The Monday show went through the roof. Actually the floor nearly collapsed as a result of overcrowding since every square inch of the aisles was filled with bodies. I felt goose bumps, but I didn't forget that Toronto is the festival where even Henry Jaglom is a god. By now I knew where all the big laughs drowned out the dialogue. The ovation was deafening and, as usual, Michael was wickedly funny in the post-screening Q&A session. He acknowledged breaking a cardinal rule by making a documentary that was actually entertaining. In discussing the film's less than stellar production values, he said he didn't know the difference between an f-stop and *F Troop*. The intensity of the response made me ratchet up my mental price. Matt and Kelly claimed that if Avenue didn't buy the picture, they would. Tom Bernard of Orion Classics crashed through a door and high-sticked a couple of helpless ushers, like the hockey player he is, to see the film a second time.

All of the advance guard from Miramax, a company known for its waves of hyperaggressive acquisition executives, had now seen the film; but Harvey was still missing. As it turned out, they were also successfully pursuing the other notable American indie debut at the festival, Hal Hartley's *The Unbelievable Truth*, along with Peter Greenaway's *The Cook, the Thief, His Wife, and Her Lover*. The simple fact, then and now, is that the brothers Weinstein are the generals who make the decisions. Bob Weinstein sat in a screening of the Greenaway film, observed nearly half the audience walking out in disgust, and called his brother to insist they must buy the film. It's a standard chapter in the annals of Miramax. The point man for us was Harvey and, as of the Monday night triumph, he was missing in action.

The standing-room-only Museum screening spilled directly over into a hot-ticket industry party sponsored by the festival sales office—all the film buyers in one medium-size room. Crack *Variety* reporter Richard Gold was closely monitoring every move. There was a throng of people clustered around Mike for hours waiting for their moment. I wasn't doing so badly myself in this courting ritual. Back in New York, David Dinkins was winning the Democratic primary for mayor. The following morning, Sheila Benson's favorable *L. A. Times* review was out and she was already lecturing Michael over bacon and eggs about the evils of going Hollywood. This was *exactly* where we were heading the next day on Disney first-class tickets, but we had to finish several pieces of business first.

Harvey Weinstein had arrived in Toronto and needed a private screening—something we had vowed not to do. He's very persuasive and has always carried a bulging wallet when it comes to acquiring films. Between *Scandal, sex, lies, and videotape, My Left Foot* and *Cinema Paradiso* (released early in 1990), Miramax was having a vintage year. The Cineplex Screening Room had to jerry-rig one 16mm projector propped up with a paperback. I flashed back to my DuArt experience and wondered if he would laugh without an audience. He sat alone in serious silence, pounded his chair in anger at GM's evil ways, and came out insisting he wanted to buy the film without delay, but never went north of $500,000. We booked that L.A. flight.

Andrew Hersh was the Disney acquisitions V.P. on whose dime we were traveling. Over an unexpectedly volatile lunch in a dark room across the street from festival headquarters, Michael grilled him about Disney's shared board members and corporate ties with GM. He suggested that there was a conspiracy afoot to buy his film and then permanently shelve it. I couldn't tell how much of this was a test or an act, and how much resulted from enormous stress or pathology.

Earlier in the day, the film critic for the *Detroit Free Press,* a paper that had frequently and favorably covered Michael and the film, had asked to use a plug-in phone jack in Moore's hotel room for her modem. Somehow there had been a misunderstanding in which she wound up accused of trying to steal a *Roger & Me* videotape from the room, presumably to hand over to Roger Smith. The contretemps escalated to the point where she volunteered for a strip search. I guess it's safe to say the pressure was building—and there was no tape on her person, not even in her zebra stripe bikini briefs.

The storm blew over. We claimed the Disney tickets, which was a good thing since we'd already arranged for a Universal screening and an open show at the Aidikoff screening room on Sunset for all the independents. Disney's Andrew Hersh drove us from LAX to the Burbank lot, with a brief stop at his home to freshen up. During the five minutes we were left alone, I discovered another one of Michael's secret talents. The skills involved in investigative journalism and plain old gumshoe work must not be all that different, since Michael could have told many private details of Andrew's life. I couldn't help laughing, but made a note not to leave this documentarian alone in my apartment.

Week 3

The L.A. screenings were fairly uneventful—aside from meeting Michael Eisner, Jeffrey Katzenberg (after pacing outside on Goofy Lane), and Tom Pollock who kept asking Mike why Universal's *Sea of Love* wasn't doing better in Michigan on its opening Friday. Disney actually tried to have a preagreed low-rent deal on the table before their dynamic duo watched. They seemed very gracious when discussing the movie, but nothing substantial ever happened (and we all know what became of the Eisner-Katzenberg relationship), which goes to show that I had lots to learn about studio behavior. Studios have pathetic 16mm facilities, and when a film looks like hell, sounds even worse, and nobody's shouting "bravo," it's hard to convince people that it's transcendent.

The Aidikoff open-call screening had one definitive result. Jeff Lipsky, then president of Skouras Pictures (where he released *My Life as a Dog*), was already a huge fan of *Roger & Me*. He pushed Tom Skouras to make that screening. Halfway through, the projectionist came out of his booth and shouted, "There's a call for Tom Skouras. It's your wife." Although he was in mid-row, Tom Skouras took the call in the booth and never came back. Later Lipsky told me somewhat sheepishly that it was no emergency, then added, "You're nuts if you don't sell this film to Bingham at Avenue." One down, two dozen to go, since everyone else in the room wanted to buy the film. Like Tom Skouras, Mark Burg and Chris Zarpas from Island saw only half the picture. Unlike him, they orchestrated a massive Chris Blackwell offer. In the *She's Gotta Have It* era, Island was the leading indie distributor. Although I was glad Island was about to release *Sidewalk Stories*, the company was a shell of its former self and was not about to get *Roger & Me*.

Although Mike was long gone, and despite the fact that only about 600 voters actually saw *Roger & Me* in Toronto, it won the festival's one key award—the John Labatt Audience Prize.

After a brief trip "home" to Washington, D.C., Michael rejoined me in New York, where we resumed distributor screenings and negotiations fairly calmly as if in the eye of a hurricane. Press was accumulating—a full page in the *Voice*, the first arts feature by Glenn Collins and a business section piece by Doron Levin in *The New York Times*. Whenever Michael came to New York, he stayed in a comfortable Upper East Side guest apartment owned by Stewart Mott, a sort of black sheep General Motors heir and longtime backer of Michael's alternative paper the *Michigan Voice*.

Week 4

The fourth Friday in the short public life of *Roger & Me* was the most crucial day yet. In an extremely advantageous scheduling fluke, the one and only New York Film Festival press screening fell on the afternoon of the gala opening-night party. Alice Tully Hall was buzzing like a beehive. Stewart Mott climbed on stage with his video camera at one point and made an eccentric, jumbled statement of support. No one had a clue who he was, and program director/festival selection committee chairman Richard Pena asked if he should alert security. It was more crowded than any press screening in memory, except when Jimmy Stewart appeared with the *Rear Window* reissue to explain that "Hitch had no dark side." Taking *our* cue from Hitchcock, we added the extra drama of a ticking clock by telling all distributors to have their best offers on the table at Tavern on the Green by midnight.

Vincent Canby of *The New York Times* was the key individual we were tracking at Alice Tully from the moment of his arrival. The most important reason that we had set our early deadline was that we did not want to face the possibility of a less-than-glowing review from him on the following Wednesday. Having an advance sign from the utterly professional, poker-faced Canby would be a godsend. He never fraternized with filmmakers like the Roger Eberts and Sheila Bensons of the world. He had the highest standards and a real affinity for independent film. Everyone always tried to monitor his reactions. My wife, Janet, who got to know him during her five years as assistant director of New York's Film Forum, laughingly explained their code; if Vincent said good-bye on the way out, he liked the film, if he didn't, the news was bad. He was a great voice for many films that needed and deserved extra attention.

Canby stayed for most of Michael's press conference and looked pretty happy on his way out. It seemed obvious that at the very least he wouldn't take the film down a notch. On the steps outside, one of Roger's Rangers attempted to give him a free lint roller (in violation of Lincoln Center policy!). He stayed in character as the consummate pro and turned it down, but whispered "Great movie." Now we were sitting pretty if I could just trust this hearsay. But a little further confirmation would be reassuring.

We got two surprises, one pleasant and the other less so, as the clock approached midnight at the Tavern on the Green party. As I fielded offers on the phone and in person from the inebriated, tuxedo-clad distributors, I realized that no one was willing to break the $750,000 barrier. Somewhat shockingly, the ever stingy Orion Classics would not budge past $100,000, according to acquisitions V.P. Donna Gigliotti. The pleasant surprise was that none of this mattered because a secret

Canby confidante confirmed that we had "nothing to worry about." That source was Carrie Rickey, film critic of the *Philadelphia Inquirer*. So we had some more champagne and turned off the ticking clock for now. After all, Hitchcock always said the bomb should never actually explode.

As if there wasn't already enough tension in the air that weekend, my two-year-old daughter was hospitalized with her first acute asthma attack. I had to blow off a Miramax meeting. They had several dozen balloons and a teddy bear at St. Vincent's hospital almost before she was admitted. Give them a humanitarian award. We made up for the lost Sunday rendezvous by visiting their 48th Street office regularly. At one point Michael and I sat down in their office with Team Flint (numbering about seven by now, since some people had had to go home) and opened our new presents—Bauer hockey skates. I must have been thwarting the "Weinstein will" somehow because my note said, "You're skating on thin ice." Those skates were never the right size, but I still have them hanging over the bathroom door in my office.

The skates were given in good humor, but we did have a serious altercation earlier in the year. In May, the *L.A. Times* Calendar section ran its first profile of Miramax. It was the proverbial puff piece except for a few comments by some despoiler named Pierson. I got a stereo conference call after midnight from the Weinsteins reading me my nasty quotes like "The campaign was a model of how to be intelligent and sleazy at the same time," or "It's unfortunate, but a lot of their competitors would like to be able to dismiss them as a pair of crooked, former rock 'n' roll bookers from Buffalo." They asked me how I would like it if they exposed some of my devious techniques for selling films. Bob pointed out that I often got great reviews from *Variety* when I took films to the San Francisco Film Festival, where Herb Michaelson had been the local staffer until his recent death. I was a little mystified. Then Harvey asked how I'd like it if they called Herb and told him that I made these calculations that he might like my films. I told Harvey that even *he* might have a hard time calling Herb since he was dead. I believe I heard Bob laugh. Later when I needed a favor, I made three promises to Harvey: I promised that I would never use the word "sleaze" again, never publicly mention the *Working Girls* audit (oops, see the chapter on *Working Girls*), and never, ever say that Marvelous Marvin Hagler defeated his homeboy Sugar Ray Leonard.

In addition to all the typical concerns that one might address in meetings with Miramax and other distributors, Michael had a serious laundry list of his own. So, for example, when any distributor asked about his willingness to travel extensively to promote the film, he offered to go to twice as many markets as anyone had before—as long as he never had to fly union-busting Continental Airlines or cross a picket line. Then of course we had to add that on top of his touring, we expected the distributor to fund a roving, grassroots field promotion office to keep five of his Flint cronies employed. One of the assignments they would have was to mobilize auto assembly plants, so of course we also needed 25,000 free tickets for unemployed auto workers. We quickly laid out the fact that for anyone who was buying world rights, British television was unavailable. Then Michael added that the film must never be sold to or shown on PBS. And turning back to the foreign side, he decided that both South Africa and Israel were territories to which the film could not be sold. The Israel exclusion immediately ruffled some feathers, but Michael quickly moved to quash anti-Israeli allegations by explaining that he was standing up for Palestinian rights. All distributors agreed to absorb the cost of errors and omissions insurance (a basic liability policy that covers unanticipated lawsuits after you've secured all obligatory releases, licenses, etc.), but Michael insisted that they agree to release the film uninsured if necessary and warrant that they would bear the responsibility and cost of defending any lawsuit. The consensus was that the film should open in a timely fashion, but Michael wanted a guaranteed opening date before Christmas where the winning distributor would provide a one-month window on other releases before and after that date. The general strategy on securing an Academy Award nomination for Best Documentary was crucial, but Mike added that nontheatrical rights must not be sold until after the announcement so that documentary committee kingpin Mitchell Block of Direct Cinema could think he had a chance to add it to his catalogue. The final capper was a $25,000 distributor housing contribution to the five evicted families.

I did believe that Michael Moore was sincere about all these demands, although I made fun of the Roger's Rangers field office. In fact, years later, I felt flattered when he described me to *Premiere* magazine as "someone who can get you the best deal—not just in the sense of dollars but in all the other protections you need to make sure that your work isn't tampered with." Oh, I forgot . . . distributors also had to promise that one empty seat would be available at every single show at every single theater for Roger Smith.

Despite all the activity, the five-day wait from opening night to the two New York Film Festival public screenings on Wednesday and Thursday was nerve-racking. For the second time, all distributors were on notice that their best offers should coincide with these shows. How often could I cry wolf? The *Times* review was set for Wednesday so the Flint brigade made the ritual trip to the lobby at 9:30 P.M. the night before to grab copies of the early edition. Canby raved even more than expected, comparing Mike to Mark Twain for the literate crowd. Much more useful to a crass schemer like me, he wrote, "the movie leaves the audience roaring with laughter." We floated around the corner to the somewhat shabby Sardi's for a victory drink. In the midst of the revelry, Michael pulled me aside to show me that editor Wendey Stanzler's name was missing from the credit box whereupon he practically leapt into an old-fashioned, hinged-door phone booth. Somehow he talked his way up the late-night editorial food chain, and magically her name appeared in the next edition. He was still unfazed by all the acclaim. The rest of the New York reviews the following morning were also great. It was unanimous.

The L.A.–based distributors had to make a serious commitment to fly cross-country for this auction. For Goldwyn, Worldwide Production V.P. Tom Rothman and President Meyer Gottlieb showed up. Cary Brokaw and Bingham Ray were back for Avenue, and since they arrived earlier in the day we sat down with them first. I soon realized that there was a misapprehension afoot that their 3,000-mile trip implied a position of exclusive, deal-closing negotiation. Actually that wasn't impossible. To this point no company had jumped ahead of the curve in its offer, or the deal might have closed. Avenue pushed us to name a price. For the first time, we did—$1.1 million. Given the first opportunity to clinch, chairman Cary Brokaw made a terrible blunder. He could say yes, or he could say no. But knowing that Mike was not exactly a friend of corporate culture and expected to deal with people one-on-one, he should have known better than to say, "I have to go back to my board for approval" and expect to get away with it. End of meeting. I gave them seats for the screening. On to Lincoln Center where ABC's *Prime Time Live* had sent a camera crew to shadow Mike.

All the usual suspects were circling around Alice Tully Hall before the Wednesday evening show. There were certainly no seats inside, although I briefly entertained the thought that GM might have bought up all the tickets and left the theater empty. I gave a pair of tickets to the just arrived Goldwyns, and as they wandered off I had a sinking feeling that they were right next to the Avenue seats. I wanted every distributor to feel the competition, but that was going too far. Once the movie started and the laughter exploded, the action moved to the backstage "green room." Cinecom and Orion Classics were hanging out. The latest Miramax ploy was to bring in my old Island Pictures friend Russell Schwartz months ahead of schedule as their new head of marketing, and have him report for duty at Alice Tully Hall. Russell had shown perfect judgment time and time again on the release of *She's Gotta Have It*.

Carrie Rickey later described this cast of characters, in a somewhat embellished manner, as "representatives from seven major studios and seven independents" hovering in the "green room." Festival selection committee member Wendy Keys called Michael "a debutante at the fox hunt ball." Michael and I slipped away to a hidden office to marvel at it all, but the bloodhounds tracked us down. Mike returned to the director's box for the end of the show. The audience roared and applauded and then stood and applauded. The spotlight illuminated Michael. *Prime Time Live* taped it. The standing ovation went on and on. I remembered the reception for Akira Kurosawa after *Ran* in 1987. That was amazing, but nothing like this. Finally after more than seven full minutes, the soon-to-be-legendary ovation died down. How could you possibly quantify the value that had just been added to *Roger & Me*?

As the crowd streamed onto the sidewalk outside, *Prime Time*'s camera recorded reactions to the film. Tom Rothman proved a good sport by giving them his two cents worth and an even better sport when he shared a table across Broadway at the Saloon with Bingham and Brokaw. They all looked beat, and I felt a twinge of guilt when I walked in and met their stares. *Roger & Me*'s production company was Dog Eat Dog Films. A full five years later, Bingham told me how much he resented being forced to put on a dog-and-pony show. I was feeling a lot more like the elusive fox that had the hounds chasing their own tails.

The next day, *The New York Times* ran its third *Roger & Me* feature in eight days. We met with Goldwyn and had a long discussion about the Israeli rights. Meyer Gottlieb told a story about the exclusive golf club behind the Goldwyn office building that has no Jews. Michael said he would go there with Meyer and walk a picket line, but still wouldn't allow his film to show in Israel until Palestinians could see it anytime, anywhere without a curfew. We gave them a clean shot at $1.2 million, but they hemmed and hawed and protested having been dragged cross-country. We parted company and zigzagged to Cinecom before the 6:00 P.M. show. Although the company was self-destructing, Amir Malin took us into his well-appointed office, twisted his precious Mont Blanc pen top around, and told us in a monotone how deep his passion for the film ran. His offer went to $1 million. I returned a phone call to Orion Classics, in which they shocked me by jumping to the $1 million mark. This was one zero more than the Friday before, an amount that would have gotten them the film at Tavern on the Green.

All of Miramax's competitors had bad words to say about them even if it wasn't "Go back to Buffalo." There were suggestions of profligacy and transience. For the record, Avenue and Cinecom were both in bankruptcy within two years, although Cary surfed on with Altman's *The Player* and Amir became one of four partners in October Films. Avenue's original launch money came from Harvard's endowment fund, whose managing partner summed up the failed investment this way: "If no one goes to see the pictures there is only so long you can go even if you have low overhead." And to demonstrate that a bad turn of fortune could happen to anyone, even Miramax released eight straight unsuccessful films in 1990.

Week 5

The Miramax jaws began to clamp down. With Russell Schwartz in the mix, they explored other crafty moves like ordering in multiple pizzas for the remaining Flint posse members to sustain a final marathon meeting on Friday, September 29, beyond the nine-hour mark. By the time it broke, it was clear that Miramax could not be surpassed by other independents for advance, bonuses, P&A, delivery costs, excluded rights, artistic control, marketing commitment, field office, and charity contribution. It was also telepathically clear between Michael and me that any Miramax agreement must have an escape clause, because we were going back to the studios. Michael looked over at me at one point, asked that everyone else leave the room, then phoned Jim Jacks to reactivate Universal.

It had been exactly four weeks since *Roger & Me* was first shown. Its market value started at exactly the same lousy $50,000 that Goldwyn had offered for *She's Gotta Have It* three years before. But we quickly added the "missing zero," leapfrogging my $200,000 projection along the way. Then the price doubled again. And here we were on September 30 with Miramax sprinting ahead of the pack, adding another 50 percent, reaching the incredulous figure of $1.5 million. The pure Cinderella story was over.

What neither Michael nor I yet knew was that when the first New York Film Festival show ended with a seven-minute standing ovation, two of the people on their feet were Joe Hyams and Susan Dalsimer from Warner. Having seen *Roger & Me* at its absolute apex, Susan leapt into action by calling Lucy Fisher, executive V.P. of worldwide production. She reached Lucy on her car phone and excitedly proclaimed, "I've just seen the film that drives a stake through the heart of Reagan's America, and we should find a way to be involved."

How to Make a Studio Deal

None of the other independent distributors knew that we had reached an agreement in principle with Miramax, *if and only if* we failed to climb up to the studio level. After a one-day respite (including a party for Jim Jarmusch's *Mystery Train*), we reconvened on a Sunday afternoon at our lawyer's apartment to draft the world's most multifaceted deal memo. Richard Heller of Frankfurt, Garbus, Klein & Selz had become Michael's lawyer at my urging: The firm handled Spike, Jarmusch, Errol Morris . . . you get the idea. I organized most of the meeting notes, translating hasty scribbling smeared with pizza sauce into a systematic deal memo. Like the Harvard-trained legal research team in *Reversal of Fortune*, the Flint brigade kept pointing out whatever I'd forgotten.

Later that night, Michael and I went to the New York Film Festival's mid-event directors' party at the Ginger Man. The entire film community was in attendance and the rumor mill was completely out of control. Michael is the Man, and supposedly I'm his scheming Cardinal Richelieu. As we left and walked down 65th Street, I felt the need to make a gesture that would strongly signal that I had internalized the spirit of the movie and had no greedy motivation for pushing the return to Hollywood. In a fit of moral high-mindedness, I told Michael that my fee would be capped at the $1.5 million deal level even if we succeeded in our efforts to get a studio to go double or nothing. I wanted to contribute the difference to some worthy cause in Flint. He seemed moved. I felt proud although in reality we needed the money. It also eliminated the sting of any of my independent friends calling me a sellout. They had already begun doing this in Toronto.

The first completely official offer to come in on *Roger & Me* had been from Bill Banning's San Francisco–based Roxie Releasing. (In 1994 Bill had his biggest success ever with the neo-noir *Red Rock West*.) Roxie has never had much of any working capital. Consequently it was an astronomical stretch for Bill Banning to put a $50,000 deal on the table in the lobby of the Windsor Hotel that first night in Toronto. Undoubtedly it was a bitter disappointment for him when my response contained nary a glimmer of hope. Bill became a gadfly, and stayed that way. I was probably thinking of him when I gave back my percentage.

Two days after the great giveaway, the IFFM 1989 edition got under way with an opening-night screening of *Sidewalk Stories,* my Directors' Fortnight coup. I felt bad for writer-director Charles Lane because it should have been his moment, but everybody there wanted a piece of Mike. Earlier in the day, Harvey sent Trea Hoving in a Miramax limo to the MacDougal Alley gate to secure a copy of our tentative deal memo, which had been polished up. Apparently they found it unsettling that the document was a completely unsigned point-by-point summation of our discussions on which the word Miramax could not be found. At this point, I absolutely could not afford to have any other distributor see evidence of this secret agreement.

One final development of this key day was that the Warners cat was out of the bag. Lucy Fisher wanted to screen *Roger & Me* for everyone there and meet on Friday. We were going on Universal's tab, but "sneaking across the street" (as they say) to check out Bugs Bunny. It seemed only fair since we slipped in Universal on Disney the last time. It had been a week since any major features ran in *The New York Times.* As a going away present, we got an advance of Canby's Sunday Arts and Leisure piece, which was way beyond even his original rave review.

There was some danger in breaking our breathless momentum with the independents to return to Hollywood—even with the shrewd Miramax fallback position. Obviously the fact that we couldn't risk a signed document meant that we had only a verbal agreement. My Zen philos-

JOHN PIERSON **&** ASSOCIATES

Title: ROGER & ME 16mm, color
Territory: The Universe
Media: All media except Channel 4, UK which has a seven year license for three
      showings with a negotiable window
Term: 15 years for all media except syndicated television
      25 years for syndicated television
      Automatically renewable for an identical term if distributor has paid
      overages totalling $500,000.00 or more <u>and</u> the "key man" remains a
      principal in October, 2004.
Advance: $1,300,000.00
Payable: 33% on signing short form agreement
      33% on delivery (see below)
      33% on theatrical opening date, no later than December 15, 1989   *4 Mos*
P & A: $1,000,000.00 in North America within the first ~~six~~ months of release
Bonuses: $100,000.00 upon reaching $4 million North American box office gross
      $100,000.00 upon reaching $5 million North American box office gross
      Both bonuses are payable within 48 hours
Fees (Domestic):
      30% Theatrical
      25% Pay Cable
      30% Pay Per View
      20% Network Television
      35% Syndicated & all other television
      50% Non-Theatrical
      25% Home Video Royalty on wholesale price
Fees (Foreign):
      25% <u>TOTAL</u>, to be divided between North American distributor and
      foreign sales company however the parties see fit
Distribution Costs:
      Direct costs only with the single exception of a 5% overhead on <u>paid</u>
      advertising capped at $50,000.00. No interest charges on the advance.
      It is expressly understood that there shall be no expenses assigned
      to this film that pre-date signing. Distributor agrees to pay for
      the following one-time costs:
      1. <u>Finishing & Lab Costs</u> - including sound remix, title reshoot,
         35mm blow-up (Duart), internegative (Duart), & interpositive (Duart).
      2. <u>Music Clearances</u> - Distributor and producer will jointly seek these
         clearances, license fees and legal costs not to exceed $75,000.00.
      3. <u>"Film Clip" Clearances</u> - Distributor and producer will jointly seek
         these clearances, license fees and legal costs not to exceed _____.
      4. <u>MPAA Rating</u> - if producer and distributor mutually agree to rate
         the film.
      5. <u>Errors & Omissions Insurance</u> - In the effort to secure an insurance
         policy in partnership with distributor, producer agrees to furnish
         a legal opinion from Martin Garbus of Frankfurt,Garbus,Klein & Selz
         that based on the current state of law there appears to be no claim
         that will ultimately prevail with respect to individuals appearing
         within the motion picture. This opinion letter shall be funded by
         the distributor up to $10,000.00. In addition, the legal fees
         incurred in preparing the E&O application and negotiating with the
         E&O underwriter shall also be borne by the distributor. In the
         event of a lawsuit, distributor agrees to finance the defense of
         that suit with Frankfurt, Garbus, Klein & Selz designated as joint

counsel. Distributor will not file a claim against producer and does not require indemnification. In the event that all efforts fail to secure insurance, distributor shall nonetheless release the film theatrically in accordance with the contractual release and marketing requirements.

Accounting:
Monthly through the first six months of theatrical release, quarterly thereafter. Producer reports to be filed and all monies due to be paid within 15 days.

Delivery:
Consists of only two items, specifically excluding E&O insurance
1. Chain of title as it pertains to demonstration of ownership.
2. Access to 16mm negative & already existent picture and sound elements.

EXCLUDED RIGHTS

Publishing:
Producer reserves the rights for all book publishing tie-ins pending review of his contract with Doubleday.

Television series, remakes & sequels:
Producer reserves all rights, but agrees to wait for a period of two years before exploiting these rights.

Foreign Territories:
Distributor and its foreign sales company shall not release the film in South Africa or Israel without producer's consent. Producer is willing to discuss possible compromise solutions to this exclusion.

PBS:
The film shall not be sold to or shown on PBS without producer's consent.

Public Theatre:
The film shall not be shown at Public Theatre without producer's consent.

ARTISTIC CONTROL

Distributor waives all creative involvement and agrees that the title will not be changed, and that the film will not be re-edited in any media in any territory. Producer may choose to exercise various artistic rights including but not limited to:
1. Supervision of video transfer
2. Supervision of subtitling and/or dubbing for foreign language versions
3. Inspection of release prints
4. Taking possession of any imperfect answer prints that are not of release quality.

MARKETING & DISTRIBUTION COMMITMENTS

In addition to the minimum North American P&A commitment of $1,000,000.00, distributor agrees to grant producer full, contractual approval of all marketing decisions and materials including but not limited to: trailer, one-sheet, newspaper ads, tv spots, merchandise, and theater selection. It is explicitly clear that none of these materials shall in any way exploit women or minorities.

"Key Man":
The key man shall remain in place at the distribution company and be available to supervise all aspects of the release of the film on a regular basis.

MARKETING & DISTRIBUTION COMMITMENTS (continued)

Release strategy:
1. Flint, MI – the night before NY/LA openings
2. NY, Lincoln Plaza – December
   LA, AMC Century – December
3. Top 20 markets – January
4. 50 markets – February
   Including the following Michigan cities: Flint, Detroit, Ann Arbor,
   Lansing, Grand Rapids, Saginaw, Muskegan, Kalamazoo/Battle Creek
5. 100 markets – May

Distributor Release Schedule:
  Distributor will open no other films between November 3, 1989 and January 19,
  1990.
Release Prints:
  From Duart, if Duart can match the best price and manufacture the prints
  in a timely fashion.
Merchandise:
  Profits to be divided 50/50 until recoupment of costs, then 100% to producer.
Festivals:
  The domestic commitments that have been made and wil be honored are
  Vancouver, Denver, Chicago, Montreal New Cinema, Virginia, Ft. Lauderdale,
  and SFIFF "Golden Gate" competition. Producer will attempt to hold a
  percentage of the seats in each case for special interest, grass roots
  groups. Foreign commitments are London, Havana, Rio, Leipzig, Florence,
  and Nyons. Future festivals will be by mutual agreement in keeping with
  the release strategy of the film.
Benefits:
  By mutual consent where there is no conflict with theatrical release.
Home Video:
  The availability date must be kept totally flexible in the expectation
  that the film may play for a year or more. BJT NO HV RELEASE WILL THAN
  12 MoS FROM DIST DOMTH. RELEASE
Producer Prints:
  Producer shall have possession of one 16mm and one 35mm release print.
Travel:
  Producer has agreed to make himself available, whenever possible, for a
  period of six months to promote the film. Distributor pays producer per
  diem, hotel, and coach airfare whenever producer requests travel to
  any market. Producer does not cross picket lines, and will not fly
  Continental Airlines. He requires first-class seating only on overnight
  flights.
Publicist:
  Producer has approval over the publicists selected to handle the film.
  Distributor agrees to engage a second publicist to accompany the director
  on the road and coordinate all efforts with distributor's home office.
Field Office:
  Distributor shall pay for a grass-roots field office. The budget for a
  minimum of three months will include an office, telephones, office
  equipment, minivan, materials, and merchandise. There will be a salaried
  staff of approximately five. At the end of three months, producer may
  extend the effort for another three months if he feels the campaign is
  cost-effective.
Academy Campaign:
  Distributor will engage a publicist and consult with producer to formulate

a strategy, draw up an advertising budget, and do "whatever it takes" to secure the nomination and win. Non-theatrical distribution rights will not be sold until the nominations are announced.

Theater Selection & Holdovers:

Distributor and producer agree that it is imperative that the theaters which are booked are secured for the longest possible playoff in each and every market in order to take full advantage of word-of-mouth. Distributor shall exercise good business judgment in keeping prints on screen for maximum exposure, and in <u>no case</u> will the distributor allow any playdate to be shortened or terminated as a result of political pressure from outside parties.

Shared Foreign Expenses:

Producer's willingness to enter into a "world" deal is based on the understanding that foreign distribution costs will be minimized through the sharing of all materials developed by the distributor with the foreign sales company at no cost. As in North America, foreign distribution expenses shall be direct costs only.

THE SPIRIT OF THE AGREEMENT

Charity Contribution:

The first $25,000.00 of distributor profit on the film shall be set aside to buy homes for the five evicted families in the film.

ophy of film sales is that each movie has its perfect moment, and I needed to be confident that *Roger & Me* hadn't yet passed it. (The most notorious example of an opportunity lost forever occurred in 1992 at Sundance. When *In the Soup* won the Grand Jury Prize, the excitement was palpable and the heat scorching. Unfortunately the producers put the independent offers on hold and began the protracted process of going to Los Angeles after the festival and scheduling studio-by-studio screenings. In retrospect this seems like a bit of pigheaded overreaching since studios are not known for acquiring black-and-white features in which Steve Buscemi plays a filmmaker trying to make a film. As time passed, the indie distributors got back home and had a long hiatus to reconsider their degree of interest. In a very sad turn of events, *In the Soup* was eventually "sold" to Triton Pictures for no advance with the producers providing the P&A money—a service deal. Although I didn't yet know it at the time of *Roger & Me*, the sales fraternity now has a shorthand expression for producers who get carried away and miss their moment: "Don't *Soup* It.")

Week 6

This particular L.A. trip was the most confusing one out of three. Michael seemed happiest when staying at an utterly impersonal hotel like the hermetically sealed Registry up the hill from the Black Tower in Universal City. From the higher floors you can watch the surreal, abstract ebb and flow of traffic below on the Hollywood Freeway. Universal's point man Jim Jacks seemed to believe he had an exclusive, proprietary interest in *Roger & Me* since *we called him*! Ultimately this led to some fairly long-lasting bad blood. I can't say that I completely blame him, but his studio did not move with alacrity—or ever offer our target price of $3 million for that matter. For we had now managed to form our own specific, if somewhat arbitrary, concept of the "studio price" for this picture: twice the Miramax deal. Why? Because studios have more money, and money is an excellent way of demonstrating commitment. Otherwise a wise producer might normally conclude that an independent company would do a better job of nurturing a film, although it's not always true.

Universal assembled all their key executives and division heads except distribution prexy Fred Mound. He was an essential figure in our minds and we were vocal about his absence. Without him, it seemed like Universal might just go through the motions on the release of *Roger & Me* in order to be in a position to make more Moore movies.

Two other notes about this rarefied assemblage. Jim certainly did not invite my old friend Sam Kitt, the studio's Director of Acquisitions. Sam had three strikes against him on this film: he never believed that it was the second coming; he passively watched as Mike and Jim locked into a one-on-one relationship; and, most important, Jim had not forgiven him for violating studio hierarchy by failing to cede the lion's share of the credit for bringing in *Do the Right Thing*. It would have been great to see a very familiar face. Instead I was transfixed by the power angle at which Production President Casey Silver held his head.

So here we were witnessing the full-court press of MCA—minus Fred Mound. Although we were not in any way prepared to hear it at the time, chairman Tom Pollock (who by now was very happy with his *Sea of Love* grosses) projected quite accurately that *Roger & Me* should gross $7 million theatrically in North America. Clearly any Universal deal structure was to be predicated on this estimate, which had the effect of putting them at the same level as the independents.

Lucy Fisher at Warners arranged a lunchtime session. It was already daunting to walk past reserved parking spaces for Clint Eastwood and Albert Brooks (!) before entering the hallowed executive dining room with Oscars to the left of us and Oscars to the right. More important, Lucy delivered Dan Fellman to the left of us at the table and D. Barry Reardon to the right (executive vice president and president of distribution, respectively). I was trying not to stare at the DBR monogrammed cuff, which faded away once Barry and Dan started coming on strong about the potential box office for *Roger & Me*, not Michael's future work. Why not $20 million? *Woodstock* here we come! Production head Mark Canton briefly wandered by to give his blessing, but the exceedingly bright, down-to-earth Lucy (her career started at Zoetrope during the Hammett era) was doing just fine on her own. Well, not entirely on her own. Amazingly, she had production exec Lisa Henson and acquisition director Mitch Horwits there with her to do penance. Lisa pointed out that the film was no longer "too small" for Warners. Mitch was a trickier atonement since we had intentionally circumvented him to get higher in the food chain. He had been on the festival beat, especially in Toronto, without quite grasping the degree to which this doc had gripped the popular imagination. When Mitch's turn came to show his newfound enthusiasm, the best he could do was suggest that maybe *Roger & Me* could be blown up to 35mm. Now there's a novel idea. Perhaps Warners could team up with Roxie Releasing and go the whole nine yards.

At the end of our meal, Lucy finally repeated the exact words she heard on her car phone from Susan Dalsimer a week earlier. Suddenly I had a knot in my stomach because everyone was about to split up, with Michael heading off to the Vancouver Film Festival, and we hadn't said one word about "the deal." Although we sensed it was neither the right moment, nor the Warner way, I looked at Michael and sort of blurted out our $3 million asking price, feeling like the child who's pointed out the booger in Aunt Edna's nose. Dan Fellman was left behind to debrief, and I reiterated that we were serious and time was of the essence. Somehow I knew we'd be back before long.

In the meantime, Mike started his next wave of festivals with Vancouver. Before I could bring a stop to it, he had submitted *Roger & Me* to nearly every festival in the world, from Denver to Montreal to Fort Lauderdale to Virginia, Chicago, London, Leipzig—and that was only through November. Coincidentally, the film was also going back to the IFFM one year later. This turned out to be the worst response from any audience, since it was a crowd of envious filmmakers thinking they could do better. The day after those sour grapes, *Roger & Me* hit its first major speed bump.

Harlan Jacobson, editor of *Film Comment*, sat down for a lengthy interview with Mike in the conference room at Frankfurt, Garbus, Klein & Selz. No one was expecting a lawsuit. It was just a convenient location for a much delayed encounter where Harlan had begun to feel like he was pursuing Roger Smith. Although Harlan can be a curmudgeon, there was no particular reason to expect fireworks. Michael called in a fury during a mid-interview break to report a flare-up involving the film's chronology, misrepresentation of the facts, and some weird debate about the workers' revolution and anti-Semitism. I was quite confused, but brushed it off, especially after hearing that the interview resumed and concluded peacefully. My mind was already back in Burbank.

Week 7

The third and last studio session was finally, and rightfully, at Warners' expense with a Sunday arrival. It was World Series time. Thinking that

Mike would appreciate the gesture of staying at the funky, filmmaker-friendly Chateau Marmont, Lucy Fisher had booked us into the seventh floor suite with a commanding terrace view—a great vantage point from which to contemplate a multimillion-dollar future. Despite the vista, by Tuesday no one would be able to take their eyes off the television screen.

Since Disney never really got serious and MGM was in shambles at this point (despite their pickup of *True Love* out of Sundance), the studio endgame was strictly Universal versus Warners. By now they both knew it, but didn't seem to care. Universal didn't have much more to say. In fact at one point business affairs exec Jerry Barton acknowledged that he'd been told to shuffle us around for a while. Of course, no one could fathom how we were there without lawyers. The essence of the Universal offer was a gross corridor participation that depended on the picture's performance. In other words, they would give us the same $1.5 million up front as Miramax; but we'd make out like bandits if it grossed $30 million with the big studio behind it—except they would not guarantee a wide release.

We left the Warners lot on Tuesday afternoon (October 17) after a productive, nondeal meeting with publicity head Rob Friedman, advertising head Joel Wayne, Barry Reardon, Dan Fellman, and the remarkable Joe Hyams. Joe is dean emeritus within distribution and marketing. Specifically, he stays active to take care of two particular Warners filmmakers—Stanley Kubrick and Clint Eastwood. Now add Michael Moore to that list. Joe's friendship with N.Y. Film Festival publicist Joanna Ney was one of the reasons he found himself watching *Roger & Me* three weeks earlier. Friedman wasn't exactly an oppositionist, but he did seem a little bit skeptical, as if he saw through Michael. You could see his reflection in his impeccably manicured nails. This was more intimidating than Barry's monogram. In fact it was scarier than the words "love" and "hate" tattooed on Robert Mitchum's knuckles in *The Night of the Hunter*. How could these guys be so slick and corporate on the one hand, and so personable and independent on the other? There was much talk about the studio's triumphs with other "small" pictures like *Chariots of Fire*. I imagined Michael running to the tune of that insidious theme song. It's easier to think of him in *Roger & Me*'s opening sequence crawling backward until he was two. During this meeting, Team Warner made it clear that Miramax may be fine at their level, but claimed that *sex, lies, and videotape* would have grossed at least $10 to

$15 million more in their hands. I reminded them that they let it slip away, and suggested that they shouldn't let that happen again now.

Warners and Universal are about two miles apart. It had now been seven nonstop weeks since the Telluride debut, and exhaustion was creeping in. Although I'd concluded that Tom Pollock and business affairs head Fred Bernstein were not going to budge, Michael insisted that we drive back over there after the Warners meeting broke up in late afternoon. Always the designated driver, I got lost on the way, partly blinded by the golden sun. I told Mike there was no point going back. He told me to get out of the car if I couldn't take it anymore. I gritted my teeth.

Everything was suddenly different when we got to the Black Tower and headed up to Tom Pollock's office. His big screen television had a scene from Candlestick Park in San Francisco where the World Series was scheduled, but nobody's there. While we were clashing in our Hertz rental, the San Andreas fault had shifted under the Bay Area in a massive earthquake. The southernmost motion actually occurred in Burbank, where the tenth floor curtains in the Black Tower swayed for a few seconds. For a moment I thought this was even better than the *She's Gotta Have It* blackout. Michael is not inhumane, nor is he obtuse when it comes to understanding normal human curiosity. But in this case, he could not fathom why Tom Pollock, Jim Jacks, and the rest of MCA were fixated on televised earthquake coverage and would not focus on *Roger & Me*. Eventually we all got our fill of the disaster and headed down to the parking lot to go home. Tom Pollock had one last chance to personally make a last-ditch attempt to grab the film. He started talking grosses again.

Back at the Chateau Marmont we had a bird's-eye view of an endless procession of planes diverted from Northern California landing at LAX. Warners had sent over some T-shirts. Disaster coverage was on continuously. The time had come to close a deal!

The next morning our two phone lines were busy for hours as we hatched our strategy and consulted with our lawyers, who remained back in New York. Harvey Weinstein called and said that our ex-lover was still waiting and hoping to get married. We told him that today was our last shot in L.A. and, if we could get a plane back in all the mayhem, we'd either come home with a studio agreement and give him his hour to talk us out of it—or get hitched to Miramax once and for all.

Although Warners had not agreed to the price, we all felt that it was crucial to negotiate the myriad of deal points that mattered to Mike. Rather than passing us on to business affairs, Warners hit the perfect note once again by giving Chief Counsel John Schulman the assignment. Richard Heller and Arthur Klein insisted that we *must not* meet Shulman alone. Arthur in particular went on and on about the improved Universal deal that he could get since he had great relationships from Pollock (a former lawyer) on down. It was almost as if they wanted to jinx, delay or undermine Warners. We ignored their advice and left for a meeting with Schulman in Lucy's office. In the space of half an hour, he responded affirmatively to every issue we raised. He had no time to waste because he was in the middle of figuring out how many hundreds of millions of dollars Sony would have to pay for snatching Guber and Peters. It was too easy. On the errors-and-omissions (E&O) insurance question, he stated that Warners would release the film self-insured, if necessary, although he didn't foresee any problems given First Amendment protection and fair use provisions for documentaries. He seemed exceptionally conversant in great detail about *Roger & Me* which struck us a bit odd since they'd had only two screenings. Later we learned how a machine really operates. After one of these screenings, the 16mm print was on the lot for an extra two hours during which a black-and-white dupe print was made. It sort of confirmed what Michael said all along: If you're going to do battle with a giant like General Motors, you need your own giant like Time-Warner.

After John Schulman made virtually every single problem disappear, we proceeded to the co-wizards—Bob Daly and Terry Semel. These visits were pretty brief but memorable. Daly had a fish tank bigger than Sea World, but Semel had Chevy Chase. Chase was still a major Warners box office attraction. He ragged on Semel for forgetting his birthday, then looked at Mike and asked the simple celebrity-to-soon-to-be-celebrity question, "Should I know you?" In later, leaner years Chevy Chase sued Warners for breach of contract, and I often wonder if that forgotten birthday was the start down the slippery slope.

Time was up. We left for the airport. I hated doing it, but I left Richard Heller in charge of receiving the call and accepting the $3 million offer—if it came. The plane was late. The gate area was a postquake zoo. Everyone wanted out of L.A. Michael was confirmed, I was on standby. They called my name and with about two minutes to board I called Heller who told me they just came through with the $3 million. I skipped down the aisle, grabbed Mike and we celebrated until we were somewhere over Kansas—maybe even Hays, Kansas. Maybe I was just hallucinating when I heard the pilot announce that we're over Hays, Kansas, because that was the town that Barry Reardon invoked when he described just how widely he thought *Roger & Me* would play as a Warners release: "We'll take it to places like Hays, Kansas." Michael and I may have been grown men, but we both called our moms with the spectacular news. Mine said, "That's nice."

Week 8

As soon as we got back on our feet in New York, we met with Richard Heller to get to work on the final distribution agreement. I'd handled all of the substantive deal points, but he would need to negotiate every single sentence of a forty-page document—not to mention Warners' option for Mike's next film. More immediately Heller would have to use his powers of persuasion to persuade Britain's Channel 4 to give way on their *first* broadcast rights and wait until a year after SkyChannel aired *Roger & Me*. The 1988 IFFM $35,000 godsend had turned into a major glitch. In a then remarkable, short-lived output deal, Warners received a minimum $1 million license fee for *every* title, including documentaries, that it released theatrically in even *one* city in North America. The studio would not make our deal without this cushion . . . and one other. Domestically Warners had similar guaranteed revenue from HBO. Luckily Channel 4 grasped the unprecedented nature of *Roger & Me*'s conquest and eventually agreed to assume the second television position. A week after our return, the way was clear. Or was it?

Although Warners was ready to pay the advance, make a huge P&A commitment, blow up the film to 35mm, remix the sound, clear the music, release it without errors-and-omissions insurance, set up a roving grassroots field promotion office manned by Mike's friends from Flint, give away tickets to unemployed auto workers, and stage a Flint area premiere on all fourteen screens of the Burton Showcase, Mr. Moore was not happy. Warners had drawn the line on paying for housing for the five families who were depicted being evicted by the relentless Deputy Fred. Michael reminded me that he was always prepared to drive around the Rust Belt showing one 16mm print out of the back of a van if it came to that. And for some mysterious reason he seemed to think that it had come to that right then.

Finally, they agreed to provide $25,000 for housing as a marketing cost—not charity. Harvey took only fifteen minutes of his allotted hour and realized there was nothing left for him to say or do. Michael Moore signed off on Friday, October 27, 1989, exactly eight weeks to the day since the very first audience saw *Roger & Me*. It would open theatrically less than two months later.

THE MORNING AFTER

The explosive impact and daily adventures of *Roger & Me* throughout the fall of 1989 made its theatrical release on the first day of winter almost anticlimactic. And long before then, the first hounds of hell were unleashed and wouldn't stop sniffing around Michael Moore's Cinderella film convinced that it must really be a pumpkin. This is where Michael's all-too-combative personality, without which his entire muckraking career could never exist, began to exacerbate some problems. His worldview is very clear: if you're not with him you're against him. The closing of the deal with the amount of money involved posed the first rite of passage.

As Michael was finally signing on a Friday, a press release was in preparation at Warners for Monday. He wanted to set the right tone by making the announcement from Flint. We live in the era of spin control, but you cannot keep a good reporter down. The *Hollywood Reporter*'s Andrea King, who's now a six-figure screenwriter, was already all over the story. She got to me and wanted to talk *money*. We wanted to stonewall on the big bucks and shift the focus back to Warners' plans for a big release, free tickets for unemployed auto workers, that sort of thing. But King turned out to have an excellent source inside Warners who tipped her on the price. The only problem was that the Warners source leaked a $2 million figure in order to make the studio look more circumspect. I knew I should keep my mouth shut, but my pride was hurt and I told her she couldn't really be that great a journalist because she was a million dollars low.

I wanted to feel celebratory. But later that Friday when I gave Tom Rothman at the Goldwyn Company a courtesy call to inform him about Warners, he confirmed all our worst political fears by calling us hypocrites. Although I wanted to believe that this was mainly sour grapes for making them jump through hoops all the way to New York, I was a little rattled. I immediately defended my honor by pointing out that if I only cared about the money, I wouldn't be giving back half my fee. This action became my sellout safety valve. Michael was oblivious of the suitors he found wanting. Fortunately all the independent distributors got to bitch and moan about us getting in bed with a studio instead of wanting to punish or boycott me for selling the film to one of their competitors. I did a good job of concealing the Miramax "arrangement" for years. And Michael did a phenomenal job of making the Warners announcement exciting, logical, and personal from his Flint home base. He made quite an impression with his unprecedented plan to give away a third of his money to other filmmakers and causes, which turned out to be $100,000 per year. (Leslie Harris later became one recipient.)

Once the news was officially out, there was a sense of stunned disbelief followed by much speculation about Warners' motives. I thought it was clear all along that they expected the film to perform well, had two excellent sources of cable television protection if it didn't, wanted the Oscar for Best Documentary, and believed that Michael's future was valuable. I was also convinced that the parent company was smart enough to understand the image value of this anticorporate polemic/laugh riot in the year of the Time-Warner megamerger. Some insisted on reading more into it. Foreign sales agent Bill Gavin asserted that he knew Warner chairman Steve Ross and Roger Smith had a blood feud dating back to their early days, when Ross had a fleet of GM town cars for his funeral business by day and limo service by night.

We didn't have much time for this sort of juicy speculation. Michael soon started the ultimate promotional tour of one-nighters as the second hardest working man in show business after James Brown. Much of the planning and coordination between Warners, Michael, and the Roger's Rangers field office took place in a mid-November team meeting in Burbank with the entire, reassembled Flint posse.

Warners was working up art and pulling quotes for the campaign. I had been compiling a few of my own favorites, especially a sampling that commented on Mike's appearance. I went back to Toronto for Jay Scott's line describing him as a "beefy individual with a cranium that looks as if a goalie's mask has been permanently affixed to it." Only in Canada would you find such a cruel hockey reference. The ever supportive Carrie Rickey called him a "jumbo-sized guy." Even kingmaker Vincent Canby said "portly, beady-eyed . . . the hefty Mr. Moore shambles through the film." But Alex Patterson in the *Village Voice* really packed a one-two punch in calling Mike "awkwardly large with a face notable mainly for its complete absence of distinguishing features." Whew! I did this in good fun, just like the collection of *She's Gotta Have It* color sequence quotes. Michael was not amused. I recalled my initial attempt to get him on that Thai diet. The pain of these affectionate digs was assuaged by astonishing praise from the likes of Jami Bernard at the *New York Post* who insisted, "Moore deserves one of those genius grants so he can take on any subject of this choosing." I second that.

Warner ad honcho Joel Wayne was also developing a trailer scored with the "William Tell Overture" which required some newly shot Mike footage. The "sell" was comedy, fun, horses jumping off diving boards, great quotes, Everyman taking on the system—but *not* a documentary under any circumstances. For the time being he slugged a black-and-white still photograph into the appropriate spots and recorded a nasal, slightly whiny, midwestern voiceover à la Michael Moore. It sounded suspiciously like a wicked impression from Joel. When Michael eventually shot his bit, it seemed a little forced—unlike Spike's tube socks routine. I know Mike still cringes at his glinting tooth at the end of the trailer when he taunts Roger Smith, "After all, I made you a star." The oversize empty chair in the poster art was also nothing more than adequate. We failed to offer any better ideas because Michael just could not hold still long enough as campaign deadlines came and went.

After festivals in Fort Lauderdale, Chicago, Charlottesville, and London, and trips back and forth between New York, Flint, and Los Angeles, Michael spent Thanksgiving weekend at a documentary festival in Leipzig—still *East* Germany. On the day he returned we got an advance on the new issue of *Film Comment* with Harlan Jacobson's sizzling interview as the cover story: "Michael and Me." The treadmarks across Mike's shirt provided a hint of what was inside. Harlan went to great lengths to make the case that Michael Moore, documentarian, played fast and loose with factual truth, especially chronology, while Michael Moore, human being, was big trouble. I had no moment of doubt on the issue of the truth, although at this point I had not seen Flint with my own eyes. I knew that the film conveyed a sound, fundamental reality about Flint and places like it. The movie was edited to give it a narrative thrust, and consequently an enormous entertainment and market value. It had major league attitude. To quote Vincent Canby's initial review, "Mr. Moore makes no attempt to be fair. Playing fair is for college football. In social criticism, anything goes."

As Michael's close advisor, I failed him for the first time. At first it seemed that *Film Comment's* circulation was so small (and falling all the time) that no one would ever read it, leaving no need of a measured, systematic response—one that finally came a full half-year later in Michael's personal letter to film and video critics prior to the video release. In the meantime all hell broke loose. From December 1989 through February 1990 almost every great development for *Roger & Me* was partly neutralized by bad news. And personality played a determining role. Michael would have liked to ignore the interview and focus on the business at hand. After all, Ebert and Siskel gave big thumbs-up three weeks before the opening and he was ricocheting like a pinball from Flint to Pittsburgh to Washington, D.C., St. Louis, Kansas City, Toronto. But he couldn't help personalizing his counterattack on Harlan, suggesting some weird hidden agenda. Then on December 7 while Mike was passing through New York, Harlan was fired as editor of *Film Comment.* There was some gloating. Joanne Koch at the Film Society of Lincoln Center asserted that the dismissal was a result of falling circulation. With some encouragement from Harlan, the film world believed that he was being unfairly punished for "exposing" Michael, and *everyone* read the piece.

The repercussions were fierce. Although the National Board of Review, L.A. Film Critics Association, and New York Film Critics Circle all named *Roger & Me* Best Documentary in December, none of these groups even remotely considered it for Best Picture. With the Best Documentary Oscar nomination still up in the air, we all realized that any push for a Best Picture nomination was D.O.A. (It remained up to *Hoop Dreams* in 1994 to revive that attempt.) *Roger & Me* wound up on over 100 year-end Ten Best lists, but two extremely influential critics broke ranks. Now I had a dream way back in September that my hero Pauline Kael was going to pan Mike for being patronizing. And she did! However, she used Harlan's "evidence" to go much farther, calling Moore a fraud and a demagogue. *Time* magazine's Richard Schickel added a second loud negative voice to the chorus that same week, proving once again that there were synergies in the Time-Warner merger. Even strong supporters like David Denby felt the need to qualify their praise with asides about "the unwritten law" of documentary sequencing.

I forgot to mention that, in the course of this raging debate, *Roger & Me* actually opened. Michael always wanted a premiere in Flint prior to the glamorous openings in New York and L.A. On Tuesday, December 19, he got his wish. Warners pulled out all the stops, using their clout to arrange for a gala event on *all fourteen* screens of the nearby Burton Showcase (since Flint, as noted at the end of *Roger & Me*, has no remaining theaters). It was free to one and all (popcorn included!) and caused quite a traffic jam as all Michigan turned out to see a native son make good—or at least to see what all the fuss was about.

Janet and I flew into Detroit Tuesday morning and rented a godawful little Geo (a GM car) for the hour-long, snow-showery cruise to Flint. Driving into that town was like entering Oz in reverse. Instead of the magical yellow brick road, the Michigan highways had potholes within potholes from the severe winter weather. The Flint exit off the interstate took us right past a closed auto assembly plant just before we passed the infamous, newly opened prison where, on opening night, wealthy guests paid to sleep in a cell. The *Roger & Me* premiere must have been the biggest event since then.

But the coup de grâce was the city's main drag—Saginaw Avenue. More than half of its storefronts were boarded up in a vivid illustration of total economic devastation. Who cares exactly when Reagan stopped by and bought everyone pizza at the restaurant where the cash register was or wasn't stolen during the lunch or later? As we drove along I thought Harlan Jacobson should have seen this with his own eyes. But what was that ahead? It was the downtown Hyatt with Auto World right across the street. The hotel was in bankruptcy, but in a wonderfully ironic twist of fate, it was open for the *Roger & Me* gala. Even better, we all stayed there. What's more, Auto World may have been shut down, but it was scheduled to reopen for the holidays to counteract the film's negative image. Michael often described his movie with a *Wizard of Oz* analogy: Roger Smith is just like the little man that Toto exposes behind the curtain.

We checked in, then drove on through the north end of town on Saginaw, and, unbelievably, the scene shifted from bad to worse. Michael was speaking at a union meeting. I still can't think of him as Joe Blue Collar, but I don't see how anyone could question his genuine anger or basic sincerity. On the other hand he was now a millionaire, and in the span of that week alone he appeared on *Today, Entertainment Tonight, Prime Time Live* (without Tom Rothman's soundbite), and *David Letterman.* Did I see him carrying a lunch pail on TV?

The enthusiastic, ever so cool Barry Reardon and Joe Hyams were there to fly the Warners flag. Their publicists had produced Roger Smith cutouts to hold one seat for him in each of the fourteen theaters. The local Michigan media had a field day with all this. The audience reception was great, then the reception for the film at the Hyatt found Mike debating Flint's mayor on the air. *ET*'s cameras were rolling. It was your basic three-ring circus.

Relative calm returned the next day with the first three openings in Los Angeles, Toronto, and New York—all exclusive. It felt as if it had taken forever to finally get there. In fact the turnaround time had been remarkably fast. Although expectations were very high, the paying public is notoriously unpredictable. These three initial cities went through the roof. Universal, Miramax, or the other bigger independents would have started the way Warners did, with one significant difference. At the New York Film Critics Awards Dinner at Sardi's in mid-January, the Weinstein brothers pointed out how much they liked the Warners marketing plan in *The New York Times*: a full-page ad followed by another full-page ad followed by a two-page (double-truck) ad followed by another measly full-page ad. (This was beyond their means then, although now, in the Disney era, they buy four-page spreads for Robert Altman.)

The *Roger & Me* release plan was your basic platform with a couple of wrinkles. Warners decided that the all-important key expansion dates would be January 12 and February 9 (the week of the Oscar nominations). The January date had a mixed bag of strategies with very mixed results. Twenty cities opened exclusive runs, and they were quite strong. Five markets opened two or three limited runs, and they were pretty strong. Los Angeles widened to five screens with good results. The New York metropolitan area went on an eighteen-theater break with no better than respectable results. This was the first-ever break for me since the Spike tour. Although *Roger & Me* was on quite a few of the same screens, we didn't make the rounds this time. I did spend a lot of time with Mike at showings in the first three weeks of the Manhattan-only runs. The audience got a real charge when they spotted him in the lobby.

The undeniable bad news from the weekend of January 12 came from the Rust Belt, the heartland, the home state, Michigan. Warners made a bold attempt to test the wider, working-class appeal of the film by going onto twenty-one screens and buying television ads across Michigan. By 8:00 P.M. Friday the jig was up. This was not a general audience "this is your life" theatrical release. Everyone opted to spend their night out at the new Steven Seagal flick. Someone like Michael, or me, would see both. However we don't install rocker panels for a living. Overall the nationwide results were sensational for a documentary: 103 screens with a $6,700 per screen average. But clearly there wasn't going to be any $20 million gross here. Michael pushed ahead as always, but I was a bit disappointed as we headed off to Sardi's Sunday evening. It was both a return to our *New York Times* review victory and a reunion of the class of 1989 courtesy of the New York Film Critics. Winners included *sex, lies, and videotape, My Left Foot, Drugstore Cowboy,* and *Do the Right Thing.*

Michael's promotional schedule throughout these months defies description. Not including the frequently traveled Flint–New York–Los Angeles triangle, he covered thirty-five markets, some more than once. I stayed put for a while and analyzed. The answer was to slow down a little and eliminate a small amount of marketing sloppiness. The *Roger & Me* campaign was review-driven. Warners had a million quotes and Ten Best lists to display, but they didn't always match the critics with the markets. In scanning over a dozen Friday arts sections from around the country, I made one startling discovery. The *other* Warners platform release, *Driving Miss Daisy,* widened on the same Friday and in almost every case its reviews got better placement. Having started in December like *Roger & Me,* it was in the process of becoming that year's *Chariots of Fire.*

And that leads me back to the Oscar race, which was of course a crucial part of the studio's strategy for both films. The documentary committee was scheduled to nominate five titles on January 18. Their standards are perverse and anticommercial. They proudly turned off *The Thin Blue Line* after two reels and declared it *not* a documentary. The "chronology" backlash was whipping all around *Roger & Me,* suggesting the possibility of a similar fate. On the other hand it seemed impossible that the committee could willfully spurn a national treasure over purity. Joe Hyams composed an absolutely brilliant letter to all the committee members to attempt to defuse the controversy. It spanned

M	T	W	TH	F	S	S
NOV. 27 — Linnig 2 FliNt	28 — FliNt	29 — PITTSBuRgh (Film cmmit)	30 — LA (Bios up)	DEC. 1 — LA (Resse)	2 — DC CLOSE 1 12:45 AM SHORT FESTIVAL	3 — (DC FliNt pm
4 — St. wuis	5 — K.C.	6 — TORONTO	7 — N.Y. Harald FiRed !!	8 — N.Y.	9 — DETROIT FliNt	10 — CSchlaTi
11 — DIA! Culver	12 — Boston	13 — SAN FRAN.	14 — L.A.	15 — L.A.	16 — L.A. LA Film crits	17 — M
18 — TODAY SHOW N.Y. NY Film crits — PAGE (9)	19 — FLINT ET	20 — MM in FliNt NY LA Tor ET	21 — CHICAGO Prime Time ET	22 — MiNNEApolis (KSDorHA)	23 — FliNt	24 — FliNt
25 — X FliNt	26 — NY (DETROIT AM) CISEMA 1	27 — NY (Litterman)	28 — ATLANTA ET	29 — CLEVELAND	30 — FliNt & OTHER MichigAN	31 — FliNt / DETROIT MichigAN ★
JAN. 1 — X	2 — SEATTLE KAtzeNBerg	3 — SF #3 (SIEBERT)	4 — MEXICO	5 — DALLAS NOFF?RSSAUSE	6 — CASSIDY FliNt (TODAY) →	7 —
8 — MoNTREAL DC	9 — PittSbuRg DC	10 — SF #2 (SIEBER?)	11 — TODAY SHOW WIDER	12 — WIDER RELEASE	13 — SAN DIEGO (RES)	14 — NY Film CRITICS @ARDIS

15 — MIAMI
16 — CHICAgO
14 — LA Film CRITS

documentary history from the Lumières' train through *Nanook of the North* (a *big* commercial success in its day) to Warner's own *Woodstock*. It also cited support for *Roger & Me* from a long list of Oscar-winning and Oscar-nominated filmmakers. The letter ended up being a response to that day's *L.A. Times* Calendar section story headlined WILL CONTROVERSY COST 'ROGER' AN OSCAR?, in which an anonymous committee member described its chances as slim and none.

Four weeks later, when Valentine's Day rolled around, the nominations were due at 5:30 A.M. I had been in L.A. all month with my pregnant wife and 2 1/2-year-old daughter hanging out on the lot in Burbank whenever possible, getting a taste for life out there. The film was doing decent specialized business having weathered attacks from Ralph Nader (who even supplied documents to his former arch enemy General Motors), op-ed columnists on both coasts, and even the Sundance Festival's managing director, Cinda Holt. I imagined the delight that Roger Smith must have taken in seeing the liberal left and the urbane *New Yorker* go after Michael Moore with a vengeance. GM pulled its ads when *Donahue* did a double *Roger & Me* session at the end of January. Warners jumped up to 265 screens on Oscar watch. The gross was coming up on $5 million.

Now I had my big test when I failed Michael and joined the evil empire. I rushed to the DGA building before dawn only to discover the envelope did not contain his nomination. Joe Hyams' classic letter deserved two separate grades: A+ for composition, and F for effectiveness. When I called Mike in Washington, D.C., to break the news, I wanted to say, "Michael Moore you've just lost your Oscar nomination and wherever you're going, I'm going to Disneyland." But I wimped out. He immediately wanted to start a petition drive of other notable documentarians to expose the ignorance and alleged improprieties of the documentary committee—i.e., three of the five nominated films were distributed by Mitchell Block's Direct Cinema. I was sick of it all, but I told him I'd call back later. Instead we used Barry Reardon's free passes, and we did go to Disneyland for the day.

Michael flew off to the Berlin Festival for the official Warners International launch. In an open press conference, that pesky gadfly Bill Banning was still calling the deal a sellout. Upon Mike's return, Warners sensibly scaled back their advertising expense and stopped funding his nonstop travel. The theatrical playoff faded away over the next five weeks in a predictable manner. Around the time that *Driving Miss Daisy* won Best Picture and multiple other Oscars and Rob Epstein and Jeffrey Friedman's *Common Threads* won Best Documentary, *Roger & Me* had one final burst on 307 screens. Hays, Kansas, was not one of them. Michael went to the Oscars and failed to congratulate Rob Epstein when standing next to him. Tom Pollock's $7 million North American gross box office prediction was precisely on the mark.

Later in 1990, I got back on Michael's good side. After the mania of the winter, many things had taken a turn for the better. First of all, he finally found time to write a hilarious, embellished story for the Sunday *New York Times* about his experiences. This Arts and Leisure piece described a meeting with Spike in L.A. and acknowledged the inspiration of seeing *She's Gotta Have It*. In a surprise to me, he described his four-step program: read Spike's books, use his lab, hire his lawyer, and producer's rep! More important for the home video release, he composed a letter to the press with his considered personal response to the *Film Comment* charges. The only misstep he made was pointing out that no one had complained about the fact that the people who die of AIDS in *Common Threads* do not die in "chronological order." He went on to acknowledge that it's hardly the point because the important issue is government inaction. Between Michael's once-again effective campaigning at the Video Software Dealers Association (the world's largest home video convention, held annually in Las Vegas) and Warner Home Video's exceptional performance, *Roger & Me* shipped 85,000 units. This went a long way toward bringing the studio to break even for their $3 million advance and $6 million (!) P&A expenditure.

Mike still tends to describe worldwide gross revenues as $25 million, which is not quite based in any calculated reality that I know—maybe revenues are half that. The film's ongoing cultural influence is incalculable. Minnesota Senator Paul Wellstone used a direct-steal *Roger & Me* campaign to unseat incumbent Rudy Boschwitz in November 1990. And the list of documentaries that use the "looking for somebody" technique is lengthy. Mike became a larger-than-life national media personality, although not quite as automatically recognizable as he might think. And unlike Spike, he is not defined first and foremost as a *filmmaker*.

Michael and I continued to have our ups and downs. He moved to New York—upstairs from a multiplex. In 1992, I pitched in pro bono to help place his Flint update *Pets or Meat* in the same three September festivals where *Roger & Me* started out, and to secure a distributor, October Films. In the time between the two films, eviction king Deputy Fred had sued Mike (and settled for a modest sum) on the legal theory that he was never told he would be a full-fledged "co-star." It was hilarious to see Fred and the Bunny Lady again. But mainly, it was just plain weird to be repeating everything three years later in a distant echo when Michael Moore had yet to make his next feature, *Canadian Bacon*. Around this time, Mike asked me if I would contribute to the mayoral campaign of a black Democratic candidate in Flint. When I changed the subject he reminded me for the third or fourth time that, aside from him, I made way more money than Wendey Stanzler or anyone else on *Roger & Me*. I suggested that he pay Wendey more of his money.

Pets or Meat was partly funded by PBS and, ironically, aired on PBS with *Roger & Me*. Michael came to my first Cold Spring Film Workshop to preview the short. He was accompanied by John Marchese who was working on a profile for *Esquire*. When his piece appeared in January 1993, I went back in the Dog Eat Dog house. It was basically a hatchet job with people saying things like "Success hasn't changed Mike. He was always an asshole." I wasn't misquoted, but I was only partially quoted when I pointed out, "The pressure is really on Mike. To put it nicely, a lot of people expect him to fail." I did say those exact words, but only after a long explanation of why I believed he had a great sense of story, which should serve him well as a narrative director. Michael's embittered response was to ask me for a list of the people who expect him to fail. I'm the one who feels like a pet one day and meat the next.

When I look back at the whole experience, almost nothing seems that surprising. The debate about documentary "truth" is endless. I came across a Jean-Luc Godard quote that captures my feeling: "In filmmaking you can either start with fiction or documentary. But whichever you start with, you inevitably find the other." Careless *Roger & Me* references still abound. Not long ago I read an *Austin Chronicle* review that weirdly linked Michael to Quentin Tarantino: "Not since Michael Moore was caught playing fast and loose with the timeline of *Roger & Me* has critical attention been so sharply attentive, as certain similarities between

Tarantino's *Reservoir Dogs* and Ringo Lam's *City on Fire* have come to light." What? Perhaps I'm most surprised by one particular personal achievement that simply would not mean much to anyone else. I got the frugal Orion Classics to bid $1 million on a fish that got away. They caught the next one for a lot less.

Role Models

JOHN PIERSON: So you saw *Slacker* on your twenty-first birthday at the Angelika. That theater opened in late 1989. Was that the first time you went there?

KEVIN SMITH: No, the first film I've ever seen outside of New Jersey, unless I'm on vacation with my parents somewhere and then it's still a mainstream film, the film I travel to New York to the Angelika to see is—let me back up a minute.

At this point, my friend Vincent and I are starting to read the *Village Voice* because it's one of the only papers at the Quick Stop that's there all week. The other papers sell out. At the end of the day when there's nothing to read, there's the *Voice*. So we're reading the *Voice*. We're seeing the Angelika. We're starting to read J. Hoberman's reviews. This is a hip thing to us and I'm like, "Vincent let's go see one of these movies, let's go see this one, it sounds really screwy and the poster's kinda weird." That movie was the *The Dark Backward*, with Judd Nelson with an arm coming out of his back, Bill Paxton, Lara Flynn Boyle. The things that send us to this movie are, first the review, it sounded weird, then a piece about the director [Adam Rifkin] in *Film Threat*. Supposedly this new guy director was set to remake *Planet of the Apes.*

We're on the cutting edge, *The Dark Backward*, nobody knows about this and he'll be the one to make *Planet of the Apes*. At the bottom of the *Village Voice* ad, it said come to the midnight screening and receive free pig newtons—which of course were fig newtons with a sticker on them.

The Dark Backward, which was not good at all, was our first independent movie. That was the first thing we ever went to see outside New Jersey, at the Angelika. The first time we see the Angelika we're like "there's an escalator in this movie place. Look at this, it's hip man, you can get coffee", not that we're coffee drinkers, but we buy like a ham croissant sandwich at the café. The lobby's all different from the usual multiplex lobby we go to because they hang up these huge reviews of films and suddenly we feel, "Oh, my God there's a whole different subculture here." We're seeing people who're there. I mean this theater's packed.

And it's like me and Vincent become friends because we're into film. We're just into mainstream movies. We're just into talking about movies. We're both movie brats. And we feel very special when we go to see the *The Dark Backward*, shitty as it is, and I go back to my friends, "Hey I went to see a movie in New York last night" and they're like, "Why!?" and I'm like, "Well it's just not around here" and they're like, "Why can't you just wait for it to come to video?" I'm like, "Well, it's just a totally different experience. You gotta see this theater." And in fact it's years before I get any of them to go to the Angelika. As a matter of fact when *Clerks* screens at the IFFM, it's the first time that any of them go. I try to get them, they just won't go.

The *The Dark Backward* is just a footnote because it gets me out of Jersey to New York. And then I have enough courage to see *Slacker* in New York at a midnight screening.

JP: What attracted you since there were no pig newtons?

KS: The *Voice* review and the image of the Madonna Pap smear girl; it just sounded great. I know it opened in July [1991]. I went on my birthday, August 2nd. And that's the movie that pushed me. It was like "Oh, my God," The whole ride home I'm like "look how simple it is. It's like there's nothing going on, it's dialogue,

I can do this." This is the movie because this is approachable. I can do this.

JP: Technically *Slacker* was not the first thing I did after *Roger & Me*. There's a film in between I don't talk about much called *End of the Night*.

KS: Not to be confused with John Landis's *Into the Night*.

JP: . . . that we took to Cannes in May 1990. It sold very well in Europe but never really happened here. It was by restaurateur-turned-film-maker Keith McNally who, unlike you, was obsessed with European filmmakers, particularly Wim Wenders. But to most people *Slacker* really seemed like my next film. It was an immensely enjoyable experience for two reasons. It was the easiest sale in history because it basically happened in a day because the right person, Michael Barker from Orion Classics, wound up in the right place, in Maine where I was, at the right time in August. Also because I just loved going back to a *film* not a phenomenon. People said, "Oh, now you've done this multimillion dollar deal, you'll never go back." The fact that there was this enormous deal on *Roger & Me* didn't change the basic nature of the material I liked in the first place. So I was really happy to be *back* with *Slacker*. Let's talk about your own personal timing here. *Slacker* was basically made in 1989 and opened in Austin for the first time in 1990. It just took another year for everything to come together for it to finally open in New York. If it had all happened sooner somehow it might not have been your moment?

KS: Yeah, I know, I might have missed the boat. It all falls into place, this is the summer I break up with my girlfriend presumably for good, leaving me lots of free time. She tells me I'm directionless—I'm not pursuing anything, just working in the store. She's going to college, she's on the fast track. I'm like, "Well, I write" but she's, "What're you going to do with it?" I'm realizing I *am* directionless and suddenly we're on the outs and I have nothing to do and I go see *Slacker* and bang! it happens. But, had *Slacker* come out any earlier, maybe nothing would have happened at all. Or maybe it would have happened slower.

JP: Theoretically could it had been something else? It's a silly question but could it have been another film in a different time, like *Laws of Gravity*.

KS: *Laws of Gravity* wouldn't have made me go to New York to see it and I wouldn't have watched the tape in the video store because the box looked cheap. Would there have been a movie somewhere down the line that might have pushed me into filmmaking? It could have been *Trust* but it couldn't have been *Trust* because the first time I see the trailer for *Trust* is in front of *Slacker*.

JP: I would never put *Trust* before *Slacker*.

KS: Hal Hartley to me is still a hero, although I'll laugh if you take jabs at him. When and why did Rick get into film?

JP: When he found out his curveball wasn't good enough.

KS: That's right, he was a jock.

JP: He realized he wasn't heading for the World Series. He's the Burt Reynolds of auteurist directors.

KS: I mean what kind of stretch is that, to go from being like a jock to being like, "Yeah, I'm a filmmaker." Is it as big a stretch as going like, "Yeah, I worked at a convenience store and now I'm a filmmaker." Which is the bigger stretch?

JP: Well, he did the transitional step that people used to do, though. He went from being a jock to kicking around in whatever jobs he had, an oil rig job, a little bit of school, and then he started the Austin Film Society. He took his interest in film and became interested in purveying and conveying that to other people and out of that grew his own sense that he could be someone who made movies.

KS: So he was basically an exhibitor.

JP: Well, yeah, but an exhibitor who had a much bigger cultural influence in his community than a standard operator would because he was providing a unique service. Apparently on the University of Texas campus, film wasn't a big thing, so he was seizing on the available university crowd that was handy. I think he was doing a very traditional American thing. He was creating a community, a support community, that shared his interest, and eventually became the same core group that worked with him to help him realize his vision in a movie. In a way, your experiences were at the Quick Stop, and you didn't have an in-between— no film society, you skipped the oil rig.

KS: I thought about it, but I was like, "It's in the water, it's cold, I don't chew tobacco." Of my leaders, Rick is the most accessible cause he's a guy that was kinda like myself. He made his movie even cheaper than mine. He was young like I am. He was older though. I don't know, maybe it has something to do with that; it's a youth thing.

JP: You're really striking out on new ground here with your second feature *Mallrats*.

KS: The studio tells me, basically you've had your hip, inside movie and it's done really well for you. It's given you a career and the movie itself is doing well. But now imagine opening that up. If you're going to make a film, why not have it be seen by the broadest, widest possible audience, as opposed to just people that are going to be hip and inside? Why have this small joke that only a few people get, like "You hate people, but I love gatherings," when you can open it up and have this big joke that everybody could get. And in terms of thinking about making a studio film, it makes perfect sense. Now this latest draft of *Mallrats* plays to me like an *Animal House*. I don't even have to go back and watch it because how many times have I seen it in my life, a zillion times.

JP: Which moments are like *Animal House*?

KS: You've got Silent Bob swinging through the air at one point. What's funnier than a fat man on a rope? Nothing beats that.

JP: You don't have anybody out of the independent world who's moved out into bigger studio films to use as your perfect role model at this point, right?

KS: Of course Richard is the predecessor. One would almost think I sold my soul to the devil just to get Richard's life. First I want to make my small independent, made for like twenty-seven grand and I'll sell it to a company and they'll distribute it well and it'll do at least a million bucks.

JP: Well, you're past that now. Up to that point it is like a mirror image.

KS: And then I want to make a comedy with Jim Jacks and Sean Daniel at Universal. It's almost the same mirrored existence. But, it begins and ends there. *Dazed and Confused* is really entertaining. But in terms of the execution, what I want to do and what Richard wants to do are really two totally different things. Richard basically is doing what I was intending to do with my first draft. Now it's gotten much bigger than that. The budget does go up a beat, but I mean bigger in terms of scope and who I want this movie to get to. You asked me the other day how I see *Mallrats*. I want this to be like every comedy I saw as a kid and was wowed by. John Landis when he was good, Ivan Reitman when he was really funny.

JP: Now as you get your opportunity to step up to the big time, are Landis and Reitman in a separate solar system or the one you feel you're about to enter?

KS: I don't think I'll ever feel like I'm in that kind of stratosphere. When I told my friend Vincent that I met Landis he's like, "big fucking deal, fuck that guy." I'm like, "Don't you have any respect or any sense of history? This is the man who brought us *Animal House* and *Kentucky Fried Movie*." All he remembers is the recent things. One day, I'm in the Universal commissary with my co-producer Scott Mosier. I was looking across the room—"Holy shit, it's Landis." I wanted to go over there, pull out a dollar bill, start snapping it and say, "What's the last thing that Vic Morrow ever heard? Sounds like a 'copter blade." And then, Don Phillips, who cast both *Animal House* and *Mallrats* waves us over, "Hey, buddy, I want you to meet somebody." Scott's like, "Hey, dude, are you going to pull out your dollar bill?" When I came back Scott said, "Did you pull it out?" I'm like, "Hey, man, no, he's cool." I'll never be in that club, those guys are giants.

JP: Meanwhile Rick's dream is to meet Michelangelo Antonioni. Actually when you backtrack, the mirror distorts a bit right away because *Clerks* was seen by almost three times more people than *Slacker*—although it hasn't added a word to the language.

KS: He didn't add that word to the language. All one has to do is go back and watch *Back to the Future Part II* which pre-dates *Slacker*. When Marty McFly comes back from the future to the past or from the past to the future or whatever, he somehow screwed up the time line and Hill Valley was in a ruins and it was this degenerate town. The principal's on the porch firing his shotgun and when he's firing at the kids over Marty McFly's head he's like, "Eat lead, *slackers*."

JP: No less an authority than *New York Times* language columnist William Safire credits Rick. He analyzed a Clinton speech about American youth being "a generation of seekers, not slackers" by invoking *Slacker*, the movie.

KS: C'mon, giving Richard credit for adding the word to the lexicon. That's like suddenly I'm taking credit for the word *clerks*—which in France they buy, because they don't have that word, but here . . .

JP: You're lucky they didn't call it *Dante Darling* there.

KS: More than just the leap-off point that gets me making movies, *Slacker* also serves as an example of what to do and work beyond even. Of course, you have your icons, the people you look up to. It's not a competitive thing, but you always want to go to where they've been and you want to take it beyond there. Whether it was conscious or subconscious, when you hear things like "You're going to pass *Slacker's* gross" or you read something in the press like, "The obvious comparison is *Slacker* but I like *Clerks* better" it does you a little good. I'm not blowing myself up here, but something I bring up in every interview is Richard's name. You see it in almost every article after my name and my producer's name. And that's because at every point when journalists ask, "Why, why, why?" I say, "Richard Linklater's movie *Slacker*." So I feel like I've done justice by giving credit where credit's due and bringing to the forefront a movie that inspired me, so that maybe people who didn't get a chance to see the movie are going to get a chance to see it now.

JP: Where exactly?

KS: On video.

JP: Yeah, where—given Orion Home Video's disgraceful job?

KS: Well if they've got a laser disk they can just go to Tower Video; they've got nine copies there. Or Big Choice video—which is closed now. The last time I was there, this young girl at the register was telling somebody, "This video store's in that movie *Clerks*." Then I went up and rented porno so I was really hoping that she didn't make the connection. So they can't get a copy around Red Bank, New Jersey, come to think of it.

SLACKING OFF

R ichard Linklater lives and works in Austin, Texas, but he doesn't like to be labeled a regional filmmaker. With three features (and a Super-8mm epic) under his belt, he has acquired a building just off the interstate to house his production company, Detour, and to hang his astonishing collection of Polish movie posters. Detour was named for the memorable Edgar G. Ulmer film noir about a hapless guy who goes spiraling downward in a terrible cosmic twist of fate. In an alternate reality (to cite his own fresh-off-the-bus character who kicks off *Slacker*), Rick might have been that ill-fated character—or else just stayed obscure. But in his reality, Rick's life has been that of a charmed underdog.

Rick shot *Slacker* while Steven Soderbergh was conquering the boomer world in mid-1989. Although it showed as a work-in-progress at that year's Independent Feature Film Market and secured a $35,000 German television sale, it was too soon for overnight success. Rick opened *Slacker* successfully on his own in his hometown a year later, in July, 1990. Austin embraced it, but the rest of America may not have been ready. Austin is an easygoing college town with good food, great music, an excellent alternative weekly, and, especially in the West Campus neighborhood, a ton of talkative twentysomethings with time on their hands. When the national release via Orion Classics followed another full year later in the summer of 1991, the audience was ready to identify with and the media was primed to analyze Generation X. Rick's career was launched in the process. By then he himself was a twentysomething only by the skin of his teeth.

Slacker made Richard Linklater the voice of a generation, but he wasn't really one of them. As the multibrats, like his doppelganger Kevin Smith, were massing at the gates, Rick was the last of the Mohicans. His inspiration came from Ophuls' *La Ronde* and Buñuel's *The Discreet Charm of the Bourgeoisie.* You'll find Antonioni and Fassbinder one-sheets on his walls, and he'd much rather talk about Bresson's *Lancelot du Lac* than either *Jaws* or *The Brady Bunch.* In short, he is a self-trained art-film brat of the highest order—my kind of guy.

The unfinished *Slacker* previewed at the IFFM in the midst of *Roger*-mania. Michael Moore had returned to give his blessing to the next wave of filmmakers. Ironically none of them could get my attention because I was too busy selling Michael's film. One entry was Whit Stillman's beautifully acted, extremely funny *Metropolitan.* My salt-of-the-earth, blue-collar friends insisted I would never go for this sympathetic satire of Park Avenue bluebloods. They were wrong, but it was too late by the time I saw it in Sundance. The able Ira Deutchman had assumed the position as producer's rep. Luckily for me, *Slacker* didn't make Sundance on that go-round and I had another chance at it.

After having nearly missed the *Roger & Me* call the summer before, I went back to Rockport in July 1990, to teach again at the Maine Photographic Workshop. I should probably take a moment to emphasize that I'm not necessarily endorsing the workshop; I do endorse Maine! At one point Kodak was the primary sponsor, but they pulled back. According to local scuttlebutt, the executive director was dumping photographic chemicals that were leeching into the pristine harbor. This second summer in Maine, we had a new addition to the family. Wyatt was two months old. Like his older sister, he arrived on the heels of a hit movie. At least we didn't name him Roger or Flint.

Although I'd made a pact with Michael Moore never to read it again, I threw the new issue of *Film Comment* into the car when we left New

York. I found something interesting in the very back that Robert Horton had filed from the Seattle Film Festival about this plotless movie in which "the people keep moving, like fish swimming blindly upstream." This was *Slacker*, and its writer/director sounded quite articulate. I found out firsthand soon enough because he tracked me down a day later on the phone. I was the one who was slacking off. Rick was well aware of the challenges his work presented. He'd already weathered some festival rejections (Sundance), grudging invitations followed by mediocre reviews (Dallas's U.S.A. Film Festival) and only a modest profile in his best showcase (Seattle). John Hartl's Seattle *Slacker* review had invoked the hippest association of that era by saying "Twin Peaks has got nothing on this place." Better yet, the substantive *Film Comment* piece had reached me and Michael Barker at Orion Classics.

Rick explained that he was in the middle of preparations to open virtually on-campus at Austin's Dobie Theater, but promised to send his tape immediately. Two weeks later and just four days before the opening, he finally sent it along with an apologetic letter. I thought maybe he was a slacker after all. But then I noticed the press clippings he'd included. His $23,000 film was getting more coverage in Texas than that summer's $50 million boondoggle, *Dick Tracy*. Maybe that's because the Warren Beatty film only had Madonna songs while *Slacker* had her (alleged) Pap smear. Rick also enclosed the amazingly well-timed July 16th *Time* magazine eight-page cover story "Twentysomething." The subheading was "Laid-back, Late Blooming or Just Lost?" Clearly there was something going on here, but the film couldn't just work in the abstract. Filmmakers make that mistake all the time. I popped it in the VCR one night with my fingers crossed.

Slacker instantly felt like an engaging twenty-four hour tour across the four corners of a hanging-out college town with an amusing collection of about a hundred losers and schmoozers, conspiracy buffs, angry romantics, vanishing poets, and wacky philosophers. As day turned to night in the film, it might have gotten a little tedious. I might have even shifted into my own dream state. So I watched again the next day. Suddenly I became acutely aware of the absolute brilliance of the structure. The deft filmmaking touch illustrated by the clever links between the three dozen different episodes demanded respect. On top of that, this self-financed, credit-card, family-money, film-stock-in-the-refrigerator feature deployed a crane and a Steadicam in two key early sequences to give it a much bigger scale. It's definitely not just two people in one location.

As *Slacker* opened to its first of many consecutive sellout weeks in Austin, Michael Barker showed up in Maine to help teach my course. Now he *did* know about the film; he'd even sent spies to a Texas cast and crew screening. I knew that Barker and his partner Tom Bernard had both spent significant time in Austin. Michael's wife, Betsy, was from there, and her family still lived there. Although I hadn't yet had a postscreening conversation with Rick, I decided to take a calculated risk and invite the Barker clan over to see the tape after a rich lobster dinner. The plan worked, but not before Betsy and her relatives got bored and dozed off even as the foghorns were sounding on the coast. Michael got into it. The next day I screened it for the class with a result that was to become familiar. The younger students flipped, the older ones found it tedious and indulgent. Of course I felt great falling into the youth camp although I was mid-thirtysomething then.

Ethically, I couldn't go any further with Orion without calling Rick. I got his machine and said, "Call back, something is happening." When he did, I told him I wanted to represent *Slacker*. Then I added that I believed we might have a pending sale. He authorized me to let Barker show the tape to his partners Tom Bernard and Marcie Bloom back in New York (Marcie had replaced Donna Gigliotti ten months earlier). They were ready to buy what was for them, in 1990, a rarity: an American independent film. But they were back to their old lowball tricks. Thinking they had a scoop on a difficult 16mm film, they decided to use their 1985 deal on *My Beautiful Laundrette* as an exact model. That meant a $100,000 advance, no more no less, with another $50,000 or so for 35mm completion costs. The full $150,000 (ultimately it was $160,000) was to be recouped from the producer's share as one total advance.

Rick was thrilled to have a real offer from a top-drawer company, but once he ran the numbers, he concluded that it would be mighty nice to get a little more to cover his deferments. Orion wouldn't budge. Although we were close to an agreement in principle, I suggested that we inform other distributors about the sold-out run at the Dobie and cagily hint that nothing would prevent them from buying a ticket. New Line sent some Dallas staffers, Alison Brantley flew in for Avenue Pictures, and Mark Tusk at Miramax cadged a bootleg tape from either an agent or the actor Steve Buscemi. He's still not telling. Unfortunately, nobody was biting.

Pending an Orion closing, we had submitted *Slacker* to the three September festivals. Telluride and Toronto turned it down without a second thought. The New York Film Festival suggested maybe New Directors would be appropriate. Orion Classics, as was their wont, did not despair, renege, or lose interest. Their operating method was like mine. If they liked it, they figured others would too. But not everyone. Even as the hometown Dobie remained full, a few complaints filtered through. One letter said: "Why are the lives of these unproductive, pretentious, and boring people documented on film? The movie does not mean anything." The documentary description is suggestive. Rick made a scripted movie using the characteristics and contributions of his players. *Slacker* feels real.

We were ready to sign. Rick needed a lawyer. John Sloss, who I couldn't quite remember meeting on the 1978 Wenders tour, had been bugging me to feed him a client since Spike went with the firm of Frankfurt, Garbus. He never quite got the college film society out of his blood as he staged enormously effective benefits for TriBeCa's Collective for Living Cinema until it closed its doors. He was also a well-qualified lawyer, since he'd represented John Sayles for years and had recently added Whit Stillman to his client list. He too had been part of the Maine summer lineup so it felt appropriate. I'm not sure that he was wildly enthusiastic about *Slacker*, but he's certainly served Rick's interests very well over the years. Eventually I steered Kevin Smith and the *Hoop Dreams* filmmakers his way, too. Sloss is a competitor in all aspects of life, save one. I don't think he goes out of his way to beat John Sayles, his original brand-name client, in basketball. One point that John Sloss couldn't win in the Orion Classics license was a reversion-of-rights clause in the event of bankruptcy. You cannot get that kind of language in any contract with a company that isn't already known to be teetering on the edge of failure.

In September, Bernard and Barker were pleased when *The New York Times* ran a "lifestyle" feature describing the contemporary campus café scene as "neo-beatnik." I know this construction always made Rick cringe, but it seemed to provide context for the boomer and older art film crowd. Rick's focus was on *Slacker*'s additional postproduction. Apart from the blowup, he'd found some ingenious ways, involving minimal reshoots, to tighten the feature by about seven minutes and remix it for less than $10,000. This slowed down the process of preparing for Sundance, as did a delayed cash flow from Orion Classics. In fact a 35mm direct-off-the-16mm-negative print was the only way for Irwin Young at DuArt to save the day.

For a while it looked like *Slacker* might get snakebit yet again, even with Orion Classics and me giving it the Sundance push. Competition Director Alberto Garcia simply did not particularly like the film—and he was a mid-twentysomething. He stalled. During the wait, I was also trying to round up support for Rick's future efforts, so I forwarded a tape to Sam Kitt at Universal Pictures. He didn't exactly dismiss it, but he did write a note suggesting "the per capita weirdo quotient in Austin must be mighty high!" Although I'm sure he hated giving me any satisfaction since I was known to satirize his meteoric rise from print shipper to programmer, Alberto finally came through with an invitation for *Slacker*.

The Sundance experience was up and down, or down and then up. The first show was in the best theatre, the Egyptian, at what seemed like a great time, Saturday at 10:00 P.M. For a presumed cult movie, that wasn't late. But after a day's skiing and/or screening, the 10:00 P.M. start posed problems for a ninety-seven-minute talkfest. The audience broke into thirds: one-third loved it, one-third walked out, and one-third fell asleep. Now I'd already developed my theory that nodding off in *Slacker* wasn't necessarily terrible. Nevertheless, the normally unflappable publicist Cara White wasn't too keen on the results. The rest of the week improved with earlier showtimes. Although Rick went home without a prize, juror Gus Van Sant told him that he'd had his vote. Either Gus liked the experimental narrative or he found Rick's Prince Valiant look to be cute. Who didn't?

Beginning with Sundance, *Slacker* was now following in the footsteps of the previous year's *Metropolitan* (although no one could have guessed that John Sloss would eventually forge Castle Rock production deals for both Whit Stillman and Richard Linklater). They'd both had to overcome Alberto Garcia's resistance to get into Sundance, where they'd both thrived. *Metropolitan* had pioneered the strategy of stepping out of that January festival into New Directors/New Films at MOMA two months later as a means of enhancing credibility. This move entailed the complete empowerment of *The New York Times* since the "newspaper of record" printed just about the only serious New Directors reviews. *Slacker* already had Orion Classics as its distributor; the year before, *Metropolitan* had used Vincent Canby's rave to land a deal with New Line.

Unfortunately, this time Canby didn't roar with laughter throughout the film; he roared with laughter throughout the short that preceded *Slacker*, a comedy which mocked some grandmotherly type entrapped by a rocking chair. Once the feature got underway, he settled down and eventually tuned out. When Rick and I made the ritual trip to *The New York Times* lobby for the early review, his excellent cinematographer Lee Daniel came along with a hidden video camera. The paper was twenty minutes late so Lee had time to interview a few New York City slackers, namely the half-dozen oddballs whom I'd seen there waiting for that first edition every single time I went. The review was the definition of the word "mixed." It might have killed distribution prospects. Bernard and Barker have always claimed that they *never* put all their eggs in *The New York Times* basket. Over the years they had overcome some genuinely bad *Times* reviews, most notably for *The Night of the Shooting Stars* and *Wings of Desire*. This review wasn't nearly as bad as those. In fact we were still trying to decide if we could pull the quote, "A 14-course meal composed entirely of desserts." However, Rick wasn't a Taviani Brother or Wim Wenders.

The New Directors audience wolfed down all fourteen desserts. MOMA's Larry Kardish was a big fan of the film. After stumbling over its name in the introduction, he demonstrated why he wasn't part of the commercial marketing world when he told me, "Everything about *Slacker* is great except that terrible title." Michael Moore came to the show and was the first person to actually admit "I slept a little, but it was great." Rick's mom was there. He explained that he'd hit her up for the same amount of money she'd contributed to his sister's wedding, on the theory that he wouldn't be getting married.

One way to dissipate a less than stellar *Times* review is to wait a while before opening the picture. *Slacker* was set to open at New York's Angelika Film Center, the ideal venue, in early July—a full three months later. That spring marked some major changes in my life and some surprising developments for American independent film. The whole concept of the self-distributed, hometown theatrical opening of a film is quite risky. If it doesn't work, distributors will never pick your film up.

And even if it does succeed, they may discount the results as fixed. As some kind of pointless statement a dozen years earlier, *Northern Lights* had first played on the prairie in the Dakotas where it was set and shot. *Slacker* had just made hay in Austin. *Paris Is Burning,* Jennie Livingston's moving documentary about voguing drag queens, came from the downtown Manhattan club scene. As a result of negligible distributor interest, Jennie decided to open in *her* hometown—downtown New York. The film grossed more than $500,000 in its first thirteen weeks at the Film Forum. Ultimately the music rights were cleared, Miramax took over distribution, and the film grossed about $3 million more in a wide national release.

The only comparable splash came from Matty Rich and his highly promotable debut *Straight Out of Brooklyn.* Every single sympathetic review contained the two words "raw power." Matty used Spike to gain some notoriety since *Jungle Fever* was scheduled for a near-simultaneous release. Spike advised Matty to steer clear of his June opening date. Matty turned that into the threat, "I will crush you and keep you out of Cannes." Matty also made the mistake of bragging about his lack of schooling which was an offensive boast in Spike's mind. Spike didn't fail to point out that the obvious lack of film education showed in the work. Goldwyn's strategy was very smart. *Straight Out of Brooklyn* did get out of the gate two weeks before *Jungle Fever* and two months before the mid-summer release of *Boyz N the Hood. Jungle Fever* also caused Spike's rift with Charles Lane to widen. Charles claimed that Spike's interracial movie ripped off an old script of his called *Thou Shalt Not Miscegenate,* which was loosely based on Lane's marriage to a white woman. Within all this fractionalism, Spike and his disciple John Singleton were like two peas in a pod—although it might have hurt Spike's ego a wee bit to be outgrossed two to one by a youngster who'd made the leap directly from film school to a Columbia studio picture.

All these films were ultraurban. I'd lived in New York for seventeen years. That was my beat. Surprisingly I decided to move the family to the woods fifty miles north in the Hudson Valley. What's more, in April 1991, in order to smooth out the economic peaks and valleys of living from film to film, I structured an overall deal with an offshoot of Island Pictures called Island World. My old friend Chris Blackwell took some of the $300 million from the sale of Island Records to PolyGram (negotiated by his partner John Heyman) to restart film production. Heyman was the legendary offshore film financier who had invented the concept of foreign sales, raised tens of millions for studios like Paramount, and produced several Palme d'Or prizewinners. My charter was to provide completion financing several times a year to the low-budget films that I had witnessed run out of postproduction, or even production, money time and time again. My movies were small, so my division was named Islet. The idea of getting into business with me had originated with company co-president Mark Burg, a straight shooter I'd known for years. In the nineties, he unfortunately developed a predilection for making movies (like *The Sandlot*) for and about eleven-year-old boys.

Fortunately I was left to my own devices. The submissions came in at an ever increasing pace as filmmakers embraced the idea of starting production with only a partial budget, often just enough to "get it in the can." There were about 500 films over a three-year period. The first two I tried to finance in mid-1991 were *Just Another Girl on the IRT* and Tom Kalin's *Swoon*. Both deals broke down. (More about that later.)

I felt a tremendous anxiety that I was slacking off, falling out of touch with my constituency as I settled in to my well-financed, comfortable country life. Rick came out to the house once and I couldn't cover up the fact that we even had a pool (then). *Slacker* was gearing up. The delayed release provided time for Clein and White, which had written a fantastic press book, to work all the other press angles, and it also gave Orion Classics more time to perfect the poster and trailer. Although Rick had "meaningful consultation" rights on these materials, he wasn't happy with the less than subtle choices in the trailer. He wrote a series of provocative and thoughtful memos which didn't really bother Bernard and Barker; they just ignored them. Rick's tendency to want to leave a paper trail got him in some hot water later with his second film *Dazed and Confused*. Studios don't like it.

Both the trailer and one-sheet highlighted the film's biggest and possibly cheapest laugh—the Madonna Pap-smear girl. Whether it's slicing an ear off, eating a dog turd, or hearing Bob Eubanks tell a disgusting joke, movies are remembered for their most notorious moments. Now it just so happens that Madonna herself was sitting in the NuArt theater in Los Angeles when the trailer came on screen. As the character tries to market the Pap smear complete with a single pubic hair, she says, "It's like sort of getting down to the real Madonna." Reportedly the entire audience turned to monitor the rock goddess's reaction, but she'd already bolted.

The July 5 New York opening occurred day and date (distribution lingo for simultaneously) with the "official" reopening in Austin. *Slacker* resumed its string of sellouts at the Dobie, and built up a steady following at the Angelika. At that six-screen complex, Todd Haynes' *Poison* opened to a huge $40,000 week, then declined rapidly. Hal Hartley's *Trust* opened slightly better than *Slacker*, but quickly fell back. A year after the Generation X cover story, *Newsweek* called Rick's film "a compelling comedy of zonkitude." *Slacker* held steady for weeks. This was very gratifying because the astute Angelika film buyer Jeffrey Jacobs had balked a little at the booking. L.A. was quite a bit softer after some poor reviews. I got to express my own feelings about the film very clearly in the *L.A. Times*: "There is nothing better than a $20,000 film from nowhere, and *Slacker* was just the most original work I saw last year." As Michael Moore had returned in triumph to the IFFM in 1990, Rick returned in 1991. Amy Taubin wrote in the *Village Voice*: "Richard Linklater was the person most filmmakers wanted to be." Throughout the fall, Orion Classics played off the picture in every possible college market to great effect, and the gross kept rising, eventually reaching $1.2 million. Near the tail end of its theatrical life, just as we were beginning to focus on the home video release, a bombshell hit.

On December 11, 1991, seemingly out of nowhere, Orion Pictures declared Chapter 11 bankruptcy. John Kluge pulled the plug when the company fell half a *billion* dollars in debt even in the year of Kevin Costner's surprise hit *Dances with Wolves*. All those years. All those Oscars. All those losses. Although Orion Classics, with the blessing of Orion cofounder Arthur Krim, operated in an autonomous manner, they certainly didn't have a separate bank account. Bernard, Barker, and Bloom didn't see it coming. Just after their first shock, Tom and Michael received a fax from Ira Deutchman's newly formed Fine Line Features encouraging them to submit their résumés to its Marketing V.P. Yet coincidentally they soon landed on their feet at Sony, taking the Merchant/Ivory smash *Howards End* with them. They got out. We were in for a long-term screwing.

The theatrical release of *Slacker* had been a modest quantifiable success. The cultural impact was much greater; "slacker" became a household word. Rick may not have invented it, but he sure was the popularizer. St. Martin's Press even had a tie-in book that sold more than 20,000 copies. All this setup seemed to augur well for Orion's home video release. Those rights were crucial to the profitability of the film because it had recouped only half of its $160,000 advance theatrically from about $538,000 in gross film rental. Our deal contained an excellent 30-percent video royalty which worked out to about $12.50 per tape. Every multiple of 5,000 units would really make a substantial difference in the producer's share. Even Hal Hartley's *Trust*, a semicomparable film which had done less than one third of *Slacker*'s theatrical business, shipped 12,000 units.

The Orion Home Video division, as personified by the unresponsive V.P. Susan Blodgett, had really gotten set in its ways. Orion Classics foreign-language titles like *Jesus of Montreal* shipped a standard 7,000 units. They saw no evidence that *Slacker* should be treated any differently, especially since the entire company was poised to collapse and they were about to concoct a plan to sell hundreds of thousands of *Dances with Wolves* videos for $5.99 at McDonald's. They were lame ducks in both senses of the word. As I've already admitted, there's no strict or even rational law of supply and demand at the video wholesale or retail level. Susan Blodgett seemed to think that Rick and I were lunatics, as if we were looking for a shipment in excess of 50,000 units. We never asked Orion to match the 45,000 videocassettes that HBO Home Video shipped on Matty Rich's *Straight Out of Brooklyn* or the 35,000 on *The Thin Blue Line* or even the 28,000 that New Line (under) shipped on *Metropolitan*. We just thought that with the right effort, *Slacker* "the video" could fall somewhere between *Slacker* "the book" and Hal Hartley. After all, the American population generally watches more than it reads. Another 10,000 units would have meant another $125,000 to Rick and his cohorts—a very meaningful sum for a $23,000 film. Of course during the Chapter 11 reorganization (from which Orion has now emerged), Detour would just be another creditor in line.

The Classics triumvirate couldn't really help. After ten years of defending Orion's home video operation, they quickly shifted allegiance to Columbia TriStar when they realized how much better their newly adopted division had done with the Pedro Almodovar films after Orion's *Women on the Verge of a Nervous Breakdown*. The other film they had to leave behind at Orion, even prior to its theatrical release, was Atom

Egoyan's *The Adjuster.* It was poorly handled by their successors. I guess we were lucky to be done with *Slacker's* theatrical run.

Rick seemed to get luckier still with his plans for a second feature. Washington, D.C., film critic Gary Arnold had asked him the standard "What's next?" question in late August. For the first time in any interview, Rick told him about a teenage rock 'n' roll movie that would take place on the last day of high school in 1976. Gary told his old friend (and Washington Redskins fan) Jim Jacks at Universal, home of Spike Lee. As the deal developed, Rick quickly had to learn to drop all references to *River's Edge* or *Los Olvidados* and focus on the *Animal House/American Graffiti/Fast Times at Ridgemont High* holy trinity. Of course everyone tried to keep studio chairman Tom Pollock away from *Slacker* for as long as possible. We had Orion Home Video to help with that.

In July 1992, three years after shooting *Slacker,* two years after I saw it, and one year after Orion Classics opened it, Rick went into production in Austin on *Dazed and Confused.* Because of pace-setting directors like Rick, the lag time between first and second feature has decreased every year as the number of opportunities has increased. *Dazed* had more than a few wrinkles along the way, some of which stemmed from his art-film brat personality. On the one hand, Rick reached out to meet the mainstream audience halfway with a teen genre comedy. On the other hand, like *Slacker* (and this must have worried Tom Pollock) his second feature had multiple plots, seventy-eight characters, and an open ending without any particular lesson being learned. The central character Pink had Rick's haircut and, perhaps, his internal conflict about sports; but it was the incoming freshman played by Wiley Wiggens who was Rick's 1976 age—a double surrogate. Being an art/commercial hybrid became the recipe for more than a little disagreement during script rewrites, during production, during postproduction, during the record deal, and finally during Gramercy's half-assed release of the film. Rick did not endear himself to the studio by documenting his strong opinions and feelings, first in a series of written memos and finally in a revealing six-page journal published in the *Austin Chronicle.* At least *Dazed and Confused* has a happy home video ending. Since it never quite got its due theatrically, the videocassette became a smash, with the youth of America actually pulling the soundtrack album up the charts months after its initial release.

Neither the independent *Slacker* nor the studio-backed *Dazed and Confused* had much of any foreign impact; both, in fact, were barely distributed internationally. Consequently it was quite interesting that Rick chose to shoot his next Castle Rock financed, two-character, thinking man's date movie in Vienna. Finally he left Texas, although the screenplay had once been conceived to take place in San Antonio. The time frame of his three features has dropped from twenty-four hours, to eighteen hours, to twelve hours.

Rick and his Generation X Siamese twin Doug Coupland may never fully escape from being co-spokespersons. But if the channel surfing generation boasts, in Rick's words, of "total nonbelief in everything," then he must be in it but not of it. He still writes program notes for his beloved Austin Film Society. On one schedule he called Vincente Minnelli's *Some Came Running* "my favorite film, period." There are still some things worth believing in.

Straight Outta Business

JOHN PIERSON: I'm really just so surprised that earlier in the *Slacker* year you didn't haul off to see *Straight Out of Brooklyn* since Matty Rich is from Red Hook like you.

KEVIN SMITH: I now live in Red Bank, New Jersey, *not* Red Hook, Brooklyn.

JP: I guess this joke isn't funny to anyone but me. I've always gotten stuck on the legend of Matty Rich.

KS: Now there's a story that even I hear about. You know it's like "Oh, the black kid out of nowhere. He's twelve years old when he makes a movie," or something like that.

JP: That's what they say in *My Life's in Turnaround.* He claimed to be nineteen.

KS: *Backstory!* That's the first time it registers.

JP: Matty's the one, right?

KS: Exactly. It's the first movie that I think the hype machine actually spills over to Leonardo and Highlands, and I actually hear about this teenager from the projects, blah, blah, blah, blah . . .

I got my start climbing ladders to change movie marquees, so I know the true meaning of the phrase "marquee value." I was spared that chore on our wedding day. I'm sure other couples have gotten married in a theater; but did they show a film before their vows? We screened Buster Keaton's <u>Seven</u> <u>Chances</u>. <u>Variety</u> reported a solid turnout. That's Janet and me in mid-photo, May 21, 1983.

ROBIN HOLLAND

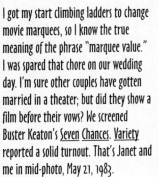

This is the first calendar (1980) from two Clurman Theater rock'n' roll summers. That year we were threatened with injunctions by Bob Dylan, David Bowie, The Beatles, and Allen Klein (on behalf of The Rolling Stones). One night the sell-out audience refused to leave a No Nukes show until we reprised the two Bruce Springsteen songs.

In January, 1979, thousands of people turned out in New York's East Village for an eclectic mix of old, new, borrowed, and blue independent films. American Mavericks was a real novelty in its time. Many of the filmmakers appeared. George Romero was avuncular. Henry Jaglom discoursed for hours. Les Blank cooked up some red beans and rice. And yes, the name Martin "Breast" is misspelled. Entermedia was gigantic, the projection booth was up half a mile of steps, and the projectionist was always asking me to bring him some food.

ENTERMEDIA'S FIRST
FESTIVAL OF INDEPENDENT FILMS
AMERICAN MAVERICKS

ENTERMEDIA
189 Second Ave. (at 12th St.) N.Y.C. 10003
Box Office 212-475-4191   Group Sales 212-533-5715   Chargit 212-239-7177

FESTIVAL CALENDAR

January	7 PM	9:30 PM
January 17, Wednesday	SPECIAL PROGRAM: **The Crazies** GEORGE ROMERO Mr Romero will discuss his work.	**BILLY IN THE LOWLANDS** JAN EGLESON Personal Appearance
January 18, Thursday	RETROSPECTIVE: 20's **The Blot** LOIS WEBER	**ALWAYS FOR PLEASURE** LES BLANK ALSO: **Spend It All** LES BLANK
January 19, Friday	RETROPSECTIVE: 20's **The Salvation Hunters** -JOSEF von STERNBERG	**PROPERTY** PENNY ALLEN Personal Appearance
January 20, Saturday	RETROSPECTIVE: 30's **Our Daily Bread** KING VIDOR	**HOT TOMORROWS** MARTIN BREAST
January 21, Sunday	RETROSPECTIVE: 40's **The Native Land** PAUL STRAND/ LEO HURWITZ	**LEGACY** KAREN ARTHUR
January 22, Monday	RETROSPECTIVE: 50's **Salt of the Earth** HERBERT BIBERMAN	**PLEASANTVILLE** VICKI POLON/ KENNETH LOCKER Personal Appearance
January 23, Tuesday	RETROSPECTIVE: 60's **Nothing But A Man** MIKE ROEMER	**LOOSE ENDS** DAVID MORRIS/ VICTORIA WOZNIAK
January 24, Wednesday	SPECIAL PROGRAMS: Early Shorts by Now Famous Directors	**DARK STAR** JOHN CARPENTER
January 25, Thursday	SPECIAL PROGRAM: **Jive** ROBERT DOWNEY Personal Appearance	**STREET CORNER STORIES** WARRINGTON HUDLIN ALSO: **Pass/Fail** ROY CAMPANELLA, JR.
January 26, Friday	SPECIAL PROGRAM: **Running Fence** MAYSLES BROTHERS/ CHARLOTTE ZWERIN Charlotte Zwerin Albert Maysles will discuss their work.	**THE SCENIC ROUTE** MARK RAPPAPORT Personal Appearance ALSO: **Rapid Eye Movemer.ts** CARPENTER
January 27, Saturday	**NOMADIC LIVES** MARK OBENHAUS Personal Appearance ALSO: **Pilgrims** — PETER HOFFMAN	**TRACKS** HENRY JAGLOM Special Event Mr. Jaglom will discuss his work.

Jan. 28 - 30 **LEGACY** **HOT TOMORROWS**	Jan. 31 - Feb. 2 **BILLY IN THE LOWLANDS** **ALWAYS FOR PLEASURE**	Feb. 3 - Feb. 5 **PROPERTY** **DARK STAR**
Feb. 6 - 8 **PLEASANTVILLE** **LOOSE ENDS**	Feb. 9 - 11 **NOMADIC LIVES** **TRACKS**	Feb. 12 - 14 **STREET CORNER STORIES** **THE SCENIC ROUTE**

See the whole month of programs with a **DISCOVERY PASS;**	$15 — $10 for students. A $66 value!	Tickets & DISCOVERY PASSES on sale at the Entermedia Box Office

bleecker st. cinema

WINTER CALENDAR

JANUARY/FEBRUARY · 1983

SUNDAY	MONDAY	TUESDAY	WEDNESDAY	THURSDAY	FRI. SAT.
2/3 KINGS OF THE ROAD Wim Wenders (W. Ger. 76) Rüdiger Vogler Sun. 1:00, 4:30, 8:00 M. 5:00, 8:30		**4** YOJIMBO Akira Kurosawa (Japan. 61) Toshiro Mifune 3:30, 7:45 THE LOWER DEPTHS Akira Kurosawa (Japan. 57) Toshiro Mifune 5:30, 9:45	**5** FISTS IN THE POCKET Marco Bellocchio (Italy. 66) 4:30, 8:00 BABA (THE FATHER) Yilmaz (YOL (Guney (Turkey 74) 6:15, 9:45	**6** MIDNIGHT COWBOY John Schlesinger (US. 69) Dustin Hoffman, Jon Voight 4:00, 8:00 STRAIGHT TIME Ulu Grosbard (US. 78) Dustin Hoffman 6:00, 10:00	**7/8** NORTH BY NORTHWEST Alfred Hitchcock (US. 59) Cary Grant, Eva Marie Saint 2:00, 6:20, 10:40 NOTORIOUS Alfred Hitchcock (US. 46) Cary Grant, Ingrid Bergman 4:30, 8:50
9/10 THE MAN WHO FELL TO EARTH (UNCUT) Nicolas Roeg (US. 76) David Bowie Sun. 1:30, 4:00, 6:30, 9:00 Mon. 4:00, 6:30, 9:00		**11** THE RIVER KI Noboru Nakamura (Japan 66) 7:00 THE TWILIGHT YEARS Shiro Toyoda (Japan 73) 5:00, 9:45	**12** MONTEREY POP D.A. Pennebaker (US. 68) Hendrix, Who, Janis, Otis, Airplane 5:00, 8:20 THE CONCERT FOR BANGLA DESH Saul Swimmer (US. 72) Dylan, Harrison, Clapton, Ringo 6:30, 9:50	**13** PIXOTE Hector Babenco (Brazil. 81) 3:20, 7:45 XICA DA SILVA Carlos Diegues (Brazil. 82) 5:30, 9:50	**14/15** THE ROAD WARRIOR George Miller (Australia. 82) Mel Gibson in Mad Max 4:15, 7:45, 11:15 THE WARRIORS Walter Hill (US. 79) 2:30, 6:00, 9:30

JANUARY 17-22

The films of Jean-Pierre Melville

The U.S. release of BOB LE FLAMBEUR twenty-seven years after its making has created a "new wave" of interest in director Jean-Pierre Melville, the godfather of the French New Wave. BOB was the fifth of Melville's thirteen features. In conjunction with French Film Week, we are showing six features Jan. 17-22 including his first (LE SILENCE DE LA MER - 1947), his second (Cocteau's LES ENFANTS TERRIBLES - 1949), and his last before succumbing to cancer in 1973 (UN FLIC/DIRTY MONEY - 1972). Melville was always a true professional. His appreciation of American genre films is represented here by BOB and two films from the 60's — LE SAMOURAI and SECOND BREATH. The Tuesday program also includes a special treat: the first and only short that Melville made.

16 PADRE, PADRONE Taviani Brothers (Italy. 77) 2:35, 6:15, 9:55 THE BICYCLE THIEF Vittorio de Sica (Italy. 49) 1:00, 4:40, 8:20	**17** BOB LE FLAMBEUR Jean-Pierre Melville (Fr. 55) 4:40, 8:00 LE SILENCE DE LA MER Jean-Pierre Melville (Fr. 47) 6:25, 9:45	**18** LE SILENCE DE LA MER plus 24 HOURS OF THE LIFE OF A CLOWN Jean-Pierre Melville (Fr. 47) 6:00, 9:40 DIRTY MONEY (UN FLIC) Jean-Pierre Melville (Fr. 72) Alain Delon, Catherine Deneuve 4:20, 8:00	**19** DIRTY MONEY (UN FLIC) 6:15, 10:05 SECOND BREATH Jean-Pierre Melville (Fr. 66) Lino Ventura 4:00, 7:55	**20** SECOND BREATH 6:00, 9:50 LE SAMOURAI Jean-Pierre Melville (Fr. 67) Alain Delon 3:45, 7:55	**21** LE SAMOURAI 3:40, 7:20, 11:00 LES ENFANTS TERRIBLES Jean-Pierre Melville (Fr. 49) Nicole Stéphane 2:00, 5:40, 9:20	**22** LES ENFANTS TERRIBLES 2:30, 5:50, 9:20 BOB LE FLAMBEUR 4:05, 7:30, 11:00
23/24 NEW YORK PREMIERE THE SCARLET LETTER Wim Wenders (W. Ger. 73) Senta Berger, Lou Castel Sun. 1:00, 4:30, 8:05 M. 4:30, 8:05 THE WRONG MOVE Wim Wenders (W. Ger. 76) Hanna Schygulla, Nastassja Kinski Sun. 2:40, 6:15, 9:45 M. 6:15, 9:45		**25** NEW YORK PREMIERE CHUSINGURA Sadaji Matsuda (59) Chiezo Kataoka, Utaemon Ichikawa 5:00, 8:15 Completely different version of the 47 Ronin story	**26** BARBAROSA Fred Schepisi (US/Aus. 82) Willie Nelson, Gary Busey 4:35, 8:00 RAGGEDY MAN Jack Fisk (US. 81) Sissy Spacek, Sam Shepard 6:15, 9:40	**27** SHOOT THE PIANO PLAYER Francois Truffaut (Fr. 60) Charles Aznavour 5:00, 8:00 PICKUP ON SOUTH STREET Sam Fuller (US. 53) Richard Widmark 6:30, 9:30	**28/29** THE MYSTERY OF KASPAR HAUSER Werner Herzog (W. Ger. 75) Bruno S. 3:30, 7:15, 11:00 EVEN DWARFS STARTED SMALL Werner Herzog (W. Ger. 71) 1:45, 5:30, 9:15
30 LILI MARLEEN R.W. Fassbinder (W. Ger. 81) Hanna Schygulla 1:00, 5:10, 9:20 LOLA MONTES Max Ophuls (Fr. 55) Peter Ustinov 3:10, 7:20	**31** ONCE UPON A TIME IN THE WEST Sergio Leone (Italy. 68) Henry Fonda, Charles Bronson 4:15, 6:50, 9:20	**1** ZATOICHI'S FLASHING SWORD Kazuo Ikehiro (Japan. 64) Shintaro Katsu. 3:00, 6:00, 9:00 ADVENTURES OF ZATOICHI Kimiyoshi Yasuda (Japan. 64) 4:30, 7:30, 10:30 Zatoichi tuning up for Yojimbo.	**Feb. 2-8** ZATOICHI MEETS YOJIMBO Kihachi Okamoto (Japan. 70) Shintaro Katsu, Toshiro Mifune W., Th., M., Tu.: 3:30, 5:40, 7:50, 10:00 F., Sat.: 2:10, 4:20, 6:30, 8:40, 10:50 Sun.: 1:00, 3:10, 5:20, 7:30, 9:40		

FIRST SHOWING IN A DECADE!

Zatoichi Meets Yojimbo

Irresistible force meets immovable object in this samurai classic. Although both super swordsmen have seen their share of sequels, with the blind Zatoichi the subject of 24 films, this is their only screen encounter. Who wins the final duel between the invincible Mifune and the invincible Katsu? Our lips are sealed.

bleecker st. cinema
144 Bleecker St. (LaGuardia & Thompson) **SHOWTIMES: 674-2560**

The Bleecker was truly a world-famous rep house cohabited by film buffs, rats, and roaches. I tried to program a little of everything — except Jacques Rivette. Jim Jarmusch, Sara Driver, Spike Lee, Lizzie Borden, and Errol Morris all showed up. This 1983 calendar was heavy on the New German Cinema — especially Wim Wenders.

Jim Jarmusch (left) and Wim Wenders clown around before a fierce <u>Paris, Texas</u> vs. <u>Stranger than Paradise</u> softball game at the 1984 Telluride Film Festival. Wim, who supported the start of Jim's career, showed a good glove for a soccer player.

JANET PIERSON

JANET PIERSON

The winning team. Many are still on the film scene today.
<u>Front row</u> (from left): Sam Kitt, Chris Sievernich (prone), Bingham Ray, Richard Abramowitz, Joachim Cooder, Eamonn Bowles, Maureen McVerry, Dean Stockwell. <u>Second row</u> (from left): Ry Cooder, Mrs. Cooder, Susan Pritchard, Lilyan Sievernich, Peter Moore, Scott Levine, Wim Wenders, Cary Jones. <u>Back row</u> (from left): Georg Alexander (hat in air), Bob Hillman, Tom Prassis, JP, Jane Alsobrook, John Lambert, Anne Cochran, Arnie Sawyer, Claude Chamberlain (behind camera).

DAVID LEE

JANET PIERSON

NO MATTER HOW YOU SAY IT...

'SHE'S HIPPY HOPPY'
— LITTLE BROOKLYN BOY

'THE GIRL'S GOTTA HAVE IT'
— JOURNALIST

'SHE'S GOT A HABIT'
— BICYCLE MESSENGER

'SHE WANTS IT BAD'
— QUEENS SUBWAY RIDER

'SHE'S HE'S SHE'S'
— CONFUSED THEATRE GOER

'THE GIRL'S GONNA GET IT'
— ADVERTISING EXECUTIVE

'SHE'S BETCHA BY GOLLY WOW'
— UPTOWN BANKER

'SHE CAN'T LIVE WITHOUT IT'
— MIDTOWN STOCKBROKER

'SHE'S PLEASE BABY PLEASE'
— TRIBECA PASTE-UP ARTIST

'SHE'S JUST GOTTA'
— JERSEY HAIRDRESSER

'SHE'S GONNA MAKE IT'
— PENN STATION YOGURT SALESMAN

'SHE WANTS TO DO IT'
— BRONX HOUSEWIFE

'SHE'S GOTTA HOTTA'
— VALLEY STREAM GOLFER

...YOU GOTTA SEE IT!

The young Spike Lee surveys his domain from the editing table. The billboard was on Sunset Boulevard, <u>Nola</u> <u>Darling</u> played on the Champs Elysée, <u>Aliens</u> was in Times Square, and of course the Cinema Studio was the very first theater in which <u>She's</u> <u>Gotta</u> <u>Have</u> <u>It</u> opened. When success comes quickly, you can have fun with the ads. Now it's nearly the tenth anniversary, and Spike's made nine features.

JANET PIERSON

JANET PIERSON

SCOTT LEVINE

This is the one and only trade ad I ever ran. It appeared on the back page of <u>Variety</u> on May 27, 1987, after the sale of the first six films. <u>Working Girls</u> was in mid-release. The next three came out later that year. I can't remember whether I expected to drum up more business or simply wanted to show off. Weird people (mainly from L. A.) called. At least it was tax deductible.

The campaign for <u>The Thin Blue Line</u> is a personal favorite —
graphic and cerebral. Both the ads and trailer concealed the fact
that Errol Morris's film was a documentary. Bingham Ray always
called the little running man who looks like a tear "the fugitive
guy." Errol (bottom left) may be a genius, but he's also a dad. We
push our strollers down a Cambridge street in the scorching summer
of 1988.

JANET PIERSON

DOG EAT DOG FILMS

This is your
PARTY TICKET
for
the **WORLD PREMIERE** of

Roger & Me

December 19, 1989
Reception immediately following screening

Hyatt Regency Flint
One Riverfront Center West
Flint, MI 48502

ADMITS TWO

ADMITS TWO

When I asked Michael Moore if he'd be dismayed if I used a photo of him from the early fundraising days without his trademark baseball cap, in a suit and tie no less, he told me he often wears a tie and asked if it was the only picture of him in the book. Then he started to explain how <u>Roger & Me</u> really had grossed a minimum of $25 million worldwide. None of that came from December 19, 1989, the night of the Flint grand opening, because thousands of Michigan residents saw the film for free — with complimentary popcorn.

What a thrilling sight! This was the Warners Burbank Studio "wall of fame" at the end of 1989, year of the Time Warner merger. What could better symbolize the uneasy presence of indies in Hollywood than Roger & Me and Batman side by side (with two palm trees in between.)

Driving into Flint was like entering Oz in reverse. The interstate exit took us right past a closed auto assembly plant just before we passed the infamous, newly opened prison where, on opening night, wealthy guests paid to sleep in a cell. The coup de grace was the city's main drag — Saginaw Avenue. More than half of its storefronts were boarded up.

"NOT TO BE MISSED, this is one of the best American Independents of the year!"
— Seattle International Film Festival

"...captures the tolerant, laid-back atmosphere of almost everyone's favorite Texas city, and fills the screen with agreeable oddball characters from all walks of Austin Life."
— Phillip Wuntch, *Dallas Morning News*

"...drifts down roads not usually taken.... This is a highly promising film."
— Robert Horton, *Film Comment*

"TWIN PEAKS has got nothing on this place!"
— John Hartl, *Seattle Times*

Limited Run
7:15

DETOUR FILMPRODUCTION PRESENTS
SLACKER

writer · producer · director RICHARD LINKLATER   cameraman LEE DANIEL   production manager · casting ANNE WALKER
dolly · gaffer CLARK WALKER   editor SCOTT RHODES   continuity · wardrobe MEG BRENNAN   sound DENISE MONTGOMERY   cast A LOT OF PEOPLE

DOBIE
THEATRE

21st and
Guadalupe
477-1324

SLACKER

The Madonna pap smear girl was always central to the marketing of Slacker, with or without the Orion Classics spirals pattern. The original ad for Rick's self-distributed Austin opening at the Dobie in July, 1990, features festival quotes. Rick Linklater (bottom left) has proven once and for all with his surprising career that nice guys don't finish last.

Rob Weiss (right) leans into the car to direct Michael Artura (his mother's boyfriend) who plays a very bad guy in <u>Amongst Friends</u>. Rob also plays the part of Bobby. Bobby gratuitously shoots a security guard in the buttocks because "it had to be done." The gun in the ad was a first for both me and Fine Line's (then) Ira Deutchman.

"A POWERHOUSE!

A seismic blast of action, humor and emotion... 'AMONGST FRIENDS' puts the overstuffed pretenders of summer to shame. **VIBRANT ENTERTAINMENT!"**
— Peter Travers, ROLLING STONE

"★★★★ **RIVETING!** Powerhouse performances all around. A blunt, shocking portrait of a part of our society that hits all too close to home."
— Mike Cacciopoli, WABC RADIO

"FRESH AND POWERFUL... you can almost feel the torrent of creative energy spilling onto the screen."
— Audrey Farolino, NEW YORK POST

A Film By Rob Weiss

amongst friends

FINE LINE FEATURES In Association With ISLET Presents A LAST OUTLAW FILMS PRODUCTION A ROB WEISS Film "AMONGST FRIENDS"
STEVE PARLAVECCHIO JOSEPH LINDSEY PATRICK McGAW MIRA SORVINO PRODUCTION DESIGNER TERRENCE FOSTER MUSIC WRITTEN AND PRODUCED MICK JONES MUSIC COORDINATOR JEFF STERNHELL
EDITED LEO TROMBETTA EXECUTIVE PRODUCER ROB WEISS DIRECTOR OF PHOTOGRAPHY MICHAEL BONVILLAIN CO-PRODUCER MARK HIRSCH PRODUCER MATTHEW BLUMBERG
[R] Soundtrack available on Atlantic Cassettes and Compact Discs in Association with Tribeca Music FINE LINE FEATURES WRITTEN AND DIRECTED BY ROB WEISS
© 1993 Fine Line Features. All Rights Reserved.

On more than one occasion, I've gotten out of the way as Sony Pictures Classics' Michael Barker (left) and Miramax's Eamonn Bowles (center) debate the fine (and not so fine) points of film distribution and marketing at the Cold Spring Film Workshop.

Murderer's Row. Clockwise (from top): Don Ward, JP, Eric Schaeffer, Christine Vachon, Monty Ross.

Here I am with Lynn O'Donnell, a great friend and producer of <u>Crumb</u> and <u>Living on Tokyo Time</u>.

John tells Kevin Smith (left) not to call his Filmmaker Trophy a "nice piece of glass" at the 1994 Sundance Awards.

WHO SAYS THE CLERKS CAN'T MAKE CHANGE!

THE MOST PROFITABLE MOVIE OF THE YEAR, AND THE MOST PROFITABLE INDEPENDENT FILM **EVER!**

"THE COMEDY EVENT OF THE YEAR!"
-Peter Travers, ROLLING STONE

CLERKS
* COST: $27,000
BOX OFFICE: $3,000,000
PERCENTAGE: 111%

FORREST GUMP
* COST: $55 MIL.
BOX OFFICE: $307 MIL.
PERCENTAGE: 5.5%

SPEED
* COST: $30 MIL.
BOX OFFICE: $121 MIL.
PERCENTAGE: 4.0%

CLeRKS

A Hilarious Look at the Over-the-Counter Culture

* Source: Entertainment Weekly

HIT SOUNDTRACK FEATURING MUSIC BY:
ALICE IN CHAINS • BAD RELIGION • SEAWEED • SOUL ASYLUM • THE JESUS LIZARD

MIRAMAX FILMS

A HOLIDAY SING-A-LONG WITH THE CLERKS!

jingle bells,

the bathroom smells,

the coffee is cold & stale,

we're overworked & underpaid,

but it keeps us out of jail!

"SANTA" CLeRKS

happy holidays from the kids behind the counter!

MIRAMAX FILMS

The original tag lines were "Just because they serve you doesn't mean they like you" and "A hilarious look at the over-the-counter culture" so you know that everyone was looking for a fun sell. The <u>Jingle Clerks</u> arrived about two months into the run, and <u>Speed/Gump</u> about three months later during a last ditch break in San Diego.

Peace. We brought the Floating Cinema to the Hudson River Valley to show <u>Jaws</u> and <u>Aguirre, The Wrath of God</u> under the stars.

So when the film finally does reach video, and I'm into independent film by now, I'm like "Well, I've gotta see *Straight Out of Brooklyn* 'cause this dude made it for like ten bucks, and you know it was sold." My first lesson in realizing how overhyped hype can be is seeing the film and thinking, "My God, they lied. What's the big deal?" Which is exactly what a lot of people said about *Clerks,* like the guy on America Online: "Am I missing something subliminally: What's in this film that I don't get?"

JP: The raw power of a young man from the condos in Red Bank, New Jersey.

KS: I didn't move to the condos until after *Clerks.*

JP: You stayed in the Quick Stop trenches. Matty moved to Park Slope a decade before *Straight Out of Brooklyn,* straight out of Red Hook. Matty's former agent thinks I've been using him unfairly as a negative example for years. I think it was a badly made film that got a sympathy vote that it shouldn't have gotten. So am I surprised that *The Inkwell,* in my view, is equally bad? That in three years of playing in Hollywood this guy learned nothing and made a terrible second feature? Would I ever expect him to make a good film? No, I'm not surprised, and I wouldn't expect him to ever make a good film. But is there something wrong with the system that gives him the opportunity to make *The Inkwell?* No there's nothing wrong with the system. Can you outline everything that let you down about *Straight?*

KS: It sounded terrible. The acting was bad. It looked terrible.

JP: Sounds like that handful of bad *Clerks* reviews.

KS: Ironically the guy who shot *Straight* (John Rosnell) is the first person we consider for director of photography in 35mm on short ends.

JP: I only know the editor [Jack Haigis] because he dragged me to three more films that were even worse, including one by a one-named black filmmaker, Uzo, about an interracial love affair between a red-headed lapsed nun and a blind black artist. When I told Jack that I was no fan of *Straight* in the first place, he asked me to consider what it looked like before his editing job. At that point I gained a whole new respect for him.

KS: I found the DP's name in the back of the *Independent* along with Whit Stillman's DP John Thomas. We talked to them before we decided to use David Klein, who shoots *Clerks* for nothing in 16mm and then outdoes himself on *Mallrats*.

JP: You were thinking at first of going with "experience?"

KS: Yeah, but everything about that film turned me off. I didn't think the story was compelling. By mid-1991 was there a "hood" movie?

JP: Not really. John Singleton opened two months after Matty,

KS: I'm into independent cinema at this point so I know you have to forgive a lot of things. But you can't forgive *Straight Out of Brooklyn* at all. You can't say "Well I'll let the acting slide because the story is moving, or I'll let the story slide because the dialogue's great, or I'll let the dialogue slide because somebody could pull it off visually." There's nothing to fall back on.

JP: You're an unusual exception to the rest of the world. We all love it [loud laughter]. Matty's unbuttoned overalls clothing line didn't last too long either. He was competing with Spike's Joint. When Matty's store closed, Spike called it, "straight outta business." Did you think about opening a boutique for *Clerks*-wear?

KS: *Clerks* grossed $3 million. How much did *She's Gotta Have It* gross—$13 million?

JP: I've never had a movie go over $8 million, and that was it.

KS: The difference between $8 million and $3 million is a boutique. At least with Mars Blackmon you've got a character who can sell some clothes. What am I gonna do? Put Silent Bob on a shirt? Note to myself: if I ever in a future life get a new start as a first-time filmmaker, give me *lines* to be funny with.

THE NEXT SODERBERGH

By the time Richard Linklater started production on *Dazed and Confused* in 1992, his upward mobility had become emblematic; larger scale follow-up features after a first-time indie success were a growth industry. And Sundance was increasingly the catalyst. Whit Stillman (*Barcelona*) and Allison Anders (*Mi Vida Loca*) got underway on their second solo features when Rick did. Steven Soderbergh had already completed, and Miramax had unsuccessfully released, the artsy black-and-white *Kafka*, a film he didn't even write himself. In stark contrast, Warrington and Reggie Hudlin had parlayed *House Party* into a direct jump into the commercial mainstream with Paramount's *Boomerang*, an Eddie Murphy summer picture. New York-based Indian writer/director Mira Nair shifted from the semi-documentary style of *Salaam Bombay* to make a mid-budget feature set in the American south starring Denzel Washington (with his shirt off) called *Mississippi Masala*; Goldwyn released it rather effectively. Looking to overseas financing for the second straight time, Hal Hartley had already cut his *third* feature, *Simple Men* from the same cloth. Hal's European-style auteur career was a variation on the Jarmusch model, only faster. Ira

Deutchman called him "an acquired taste . . . the American Harold Pinter."

Hartley's *Trust* and *Simple Men* were both released with very marginal results in North America by Ira's newest venture, Fine Line Features, the "classics division" of New Line Cinema. Formed in the wake of *Metropolitan* in the first half of 1991, Fine Line picked up where the original version of Cinecom (before the self-destructive rush to production) had left off. Ira had a very strong emphasis on American independent film from both new and established filmmakers. The quality was high, but the bottom-line results were problematic after a booming start. The initial Fine Line success was Gus Van Sant's extremely original road movie *My Own Private Idaho*, with Keanu Reeves and River Phoenix, which grossed over $6 million. Fine Line followed Van Sant's third feature with Jarmusch's fourth *Night on Earth*, a five-taxi-cab-ride anthology film that motored from L.A. to Helsinki. Once again, the performance in North America fell short of *Stranger Than Paradise*, that seminal, first feature that now seemed part of the distant past.

Two key trends were coming to the fore as the independent sector moved into the mid-nineties. The big distributors were getting bigger and in so doing they were finding ways to expand the nonstudio audience for their breakout films. *Kiss of the Spider Woman, Room with a View,* and *sex, lies, and videotape* had been aberrations over a four-year span in the eighties, and none of them could really bust through a $25 million ceiling. In the spring of 1992, two films took off for that finish line. Fine Line released Robert Altman's inside-Hollywood satire *The Player* on more than 400 screens. Sony Pictures Classics rolled out Merchant/Ivory's *Howards End* far slower, and, despite much criticism for their tortoiselike ways, eventually won the race. These were the first of eight independent pictures in the next three years that grossed $20, $40, $60 and finally $100 million in North America alone. The bad news is that not one of the eight was a first feature; and, after *The Player*, only one of the next seven was American—the last in the series, the pièce de résistance *Pulp Fiction*. Notably, four of the eight and three of the top four (*The Piano, Crying Game, Pulp*) were released by Miramax. The fact that these indie megahits now arrived with near regularity had a weird parallel to the audience herd mentality behind studio blockbusters.

The million-dollar question is whether these crossover hits create more opportunities or problems for traditional, smaller debut features. By 1992, the largest independent distributors had increased capacity, ranging from ten to twenty-four pictures per company per year. The centralization of distribution is automatically defined as detrimental by certain grassroots zealots. However, the companies that had competed and failed in the eighties were essentially the companies that either overspent on production and overhead, or simply didn't have a clue how to pick films. As the off-Hollywood infrastructure was becoming more distilled in mid-1992, I picked up the newspaper one Friday (May 15 to be exact) and counted the total number of independent releases playing theatrically in New York City that weekend. There were an astonishing twenty-nine; six from Miramax, five from Fine Line, four from Goldwyn, and four from Sony/Orion Classics. It was a slow season for October Films but they had one too. So the larger independent companies had twenty films in release; the other nine came from eight scattered sources. Some of these distributors are still around, others are gone but they've been replaced. At that moment in May 1992, only nine of the twenty-nine were American. That number would have been higher later in the year, once the crop planted in Sundance in January had been harvested.

The vast majority of the American independents released in 1992 got their pedigrees in Park City. Second features may have been on the rise, and distributors may have been ramping up, but the single most explosive area of expansion was first-time, low-budget production activity. Everyone and his brother was producing a film and submitting it to Sundance: sixty submissions in 1987 had become 300 to 400 five years later. As the pool of films grew larger, the selection process became more unwieldy. The reward was obvious: A higher percentage of each year's Dramatic Competition films wound up in the theatrical marketplace. Attending Sundance became de rigueur after the 1989 *sex, lies, and videotape* sensation. The population influx included several categories of people that I would normally call dead weight. However, in a phenomenon not found in nature, they too have made the wave bigger by riding it. These are the myriad agents, legions of lawyers, and Ford Explorers full of studio production executives and development mavens nearly as young as the filmmakers. Apparently there was enough happening over the next three festivals to keep this crew coming in expanding numbers, even if the next Soderbergh was missing in action.

SUNDANCE 1990

In a perverse protest, I barely made it to the last twenty-four hours of Sundance 1990. I told everyone it was because of my *Roger & Me* duties. Michael Moore had already come and gone with his Flint entourage, complaining in jest that Warner's other filmmaker, Clint Eastwood, had a bigger condo than he did. Cinda Holt, the festival's managing director, took umbrage at Michael's behavior and the controversy spilled over onto the *New York Post*'s infamous gossip column, "Page 6" where I defended Moore. Festival head Tony Safford was leaving to take an acquisitions position at New Line. With Competition Director Alberto Garcia at his side, Tony had pretty much reduced the selection committee to an advisory capacity. My term was up anyway because people like DuArt's Irwin Young worried (incorrectly) that I was selecting my own films. The real-life Steven Soderbergh had actually returned to the scene to serve on the 1990 Dramatic Jury and help champion experimental narrative. He was seen around town in a *Do the Right Thing* sweatshirt.

The lineup that year was strong, with a very intriguing split between the commercial, semi-commercial, and noncommercial. The clearest possible example of this were the three black films. New Line was back (à la 1988's *Hairspray*) with the Hudlin Brothers' entertaining hip-hop comedy *House Party*. It went over remarkably well considering the fact that almost no one in the white middle-class Sundance audience had ever heard of Kid 'n Play or seen the top-rated cable show, *Yo! MTV Raps*. *House Party* seemed like a top contender for the audience prize. Then there was the beautifully made, slightly obscure *To Sleep with Anger* by Charles Burnett. Burnett had struggled over twelve years to make his two previous soul-baring, no-budget films *Killer of Sheep* and *My Brother's Wedding*. His third feature went into production when Danny Glover (coming off *Lethal Weapon*) decided to play the mysterious central character in this unusual folktale where South Central L.A. meets the deep South. Glover's name got the film made, but caused terribly confused expectations when Goldwyn later released it. If his screen partner Mel Gibson had been in it, that probably would have changed the commercial prospects. Goldwyn was roundly thrashed for treating it like an art film, which is exactly what it was. Admittedly their grassroots outreach to the black audience was almost nil.

The person who acted like the biggest star at the festival was Wendell B. Harris, Jr., the writer/director of the third black film. In one of life's stranger coincidences, *Chameleon Street* had been produced in Flint, Michigan, just like *Roger & Me*. In fact, realizing a good opportunity when he saw saw it, Wendell tried to ride the popular Flint bandwagon. His entire family (including his younger brother, a doctor who would later get the film bug and make his own feature) had pitched in to make this disjunctive story about Doug Street. Street, played by Harris, was a con man who would try to pass for anything from a scalpel-wielding surgeon to a foreign exchange student at Yale. Wendell of course just needed people to believe that he was a filmmaker and that *Chameleon Street* was worth $2 million. At least he knocked $1 million off the price paid for that other Flint film. With jaws dropping all over the room, *Chameleon Street* won the Grand Jury Prize—the revenge of Steven Soderbergh. *To Sleep with Anger* was the runner-up.

Jaws dropped further when Wendell arrived at the podium in his dark sunglasses and his Barry White–like basso profundo voice boomed out in the most memorable Sundance incident of egomania run amok. The film never sold. Ironically, Warners monopolized Flint when they acquired the remake rights, but nothing ever came of that. Eventually *Chameleon Street* was given a marginal release by Northern Arts starting at New York's Film Forum. Halfway through the second day of a forty-eight-hour press junket, Wendell abandoned his remaining interviews to go down to City Hall to demand an unscheduled meeting with Mayor David Dinkins. He waited. Dinkins didn't show.

While Wendell Harris was holding court at Sundance, I was sitting at a table with the Hudlins and Sara Risher, New Line president of production since early John Waters days. Like *Hairspray* two years before when there weren't enough prizes to go around, they'd been denied an award that *House Party* could easily survive without. The audience prize went to the American Playhouse production of Norman Rene's moving, if TV-oriented, AIDS film, *Longtime Companion*. After Lindsay Law's long struggle to find a theatrical distributor, Goldwyn's Tom Rothman had taken on the challenge just before Sundance. This award really helped to convey a sense of the film's emotional power instead of just "do-gooder" importance. *Longtime Companion.* went on to gross about $4.6 million while *House Party* clocked about $28 million. Mysteriously these Sundance awards often seem to illustrate the correlation between what you need and what you get as explained by Mick Jagger in "You Can't Always Get What You Want." The Hudlins' only complaint, like many black filmmakers before and after them, was that New Line should have released their film on 800 screens, not 200. Once again, the argument is open-ended, since *House Party* did the vast majority of its business in about 100 key runs. Anyway Paramount gave them everything they wanted two summers later with *Boomerang*.

SUNDANCE 1991

The next year's Sundance started in the very dark shadow of the U.S. bombing of Baghdad. With so many films to watch and debate, it was difficult to worry about the Middle East or anything outside Park City. The edgy and eclectic 1991 lineup demonstrated once and for all that the festival's granola image ("eat it, it's made of all natural ingredients from the farm, it's good for you") was dead. Ironically, this was exactly the moment that Peter Biskind, executive editor of *Premiere*, wrote a blistering exposé of all the Sundance Institute's financial ills and internal conflicts. Because I was unimpressed with the diversity of projects selected for the script-driven June Directors Workshop, I added to his assaultive article by saying, "They wouldn't know what to make of *Roger & Me* or *She's Gotta Have It* if they tripped over it." At any rate, the festival itself was casting a really wide net. And the Sundance braintrust decided they would do without *Premiere*'s $10,000 sponsorship from that year forward. (This was a stroke of luck for *Entertainment Weekly* which was waiting in the wings.) That year's alumni, all of which went into theatrical release, included *Slacker, Poison, Trust, Straight Out of Brooklyn, Paris Is Burning, Daughters of the Dust*, and *Hangin' with the Homeboys*.

The contrast between the response to the latter two films at Sundance and later in the outside world is pretty revealing. *Homeboys* was a $2 million New Line production written and directed by Joseph Vasquez—a coming of age story set in the Bronx, presumably with black and Hispanic audience appeal. It was the screen debut for the talented John Leguizamo. *Homeboys* was generically recognizable and smarter than average, so it played fairly well at Sundance. It turned out to be a hopeless in-betweener in the marketplace, a fact that New Line must have discovered in research seminars because they really let it die on the vine. When the filmmaker was asked who the audience for the film might be, he said that the four characters each represented one aspect of his own personality. Even with these multiple niche audiences, it grossed only a small percentage of its budget. Now *Daughters of the Dust* may have won a token, if well-deserved, cinematography prize, but it stiffed at Sundance. It stiffed because its future target audience was nowhere to be found in the state of Utah. Unsurprisingly, this set the film's distribution prospects way back for over a year. Julie Dash never lost faith that she would find a way to prove that her unknown audience existed, an audience of black women who read Toni Morrison's novels. She prevailed when Karen Cooper provided an opening at the Film Forum where business was standing room only.

It was Todd Haynes' homoerotic, three-part *Poison* that won the Grand Jury Prize and successfully took full advantage of that credential when released by the tiny Zeitgeist Pictures. Todd's vast talent had been obvious to me a few years before when he used Barbies to act out the brilliant, strangely poignant *Superstar: The Karen Carpenter Story.* (Richard Carpenter has made it nearly impossible to see this masterpiece since it contains many Carpenters songs.) *Poison* was much tougher going. I remember walking out into the Angelika lobby during a 1990 IFFM screening where everyone was standing around discussing Todd's genius. All the distributors were outside talking instead of inside watching because they'd walked out in disgust over the Genet-inspired scene where an expectorating squad fired gobs of spit into a guy's mouth. The Reverend Donald Wildmon turned out not to be too keen on this NEA-sponsored scene either.

The 1991 Sundance audience award went to a sappy, cliché-ridden minor league baseball film called *One Cup of Coffee.* I felt a lot of sympathy for the daring program of new Festival Programming Director Geoff Gilmore until he told me that this trite film made the tears well up in his eyes. Miramax bought it, changed the title to *Pastime*, released it regionally, then gave up as it disappeared without a trace. Another disappearing act was my own biggest black sheep, *End of the Night.* This Keith McNally film starred underground film legend Eric Mitchell as a soon-to-be father who cracks. Gorgeously shot by Tom DiCillo, it had been to the Directors' Fortnight nine months earlier but remained unsold in North America. I couldn't resist describing the film's plight to Aljean Harmetz of *The New York Times,* and I suppose I didn't exactly endear myself to Keith when she quoted me as saying, "It's the end of the line for *End of the Night.*" Unfortunately, it was.

SUNDANCE 1992

By Sundance 1992, the festival felt like it had been filled to the brim for three years, yet stable, mature, and manageable. Maybe everyone was beginning to forget about finding the next Soderbergh. Once again there was a diverse and pungent lineup that would spawn more than half of the twenty-eight American independents that opened theatrically in 1992, and in most cases fared none too well. Repeating their 1990 maneuver, Goldwyn managed to acquire the title that won the Audience Prize, *The Waterdance* by Neal Jimenez and Michael Steinberg, just before the festival. Based on Neal's own experience, it featured a strong cast led by Eric Stoltz and Wesley Snipes and even had an uplifting ending. Since Goldwyn could never fully overcome the paraplegic subject matter, even with their feel-good heavenly clouds on the one-sheet, *The Waterdance* grossed only $1.5 million. Other disappointments in release included Bill Plympton's animated feature *The Tune* (which I sold to October), Tom DiCillo's *Johnny Suede* (Miramax), Alex Rockwell's Grand Jury Prize winner *In the Soup* (Triton), Anthony Drazen's *Zebrahead* (Triumph), and Tom Kalin's *Swoon* (Fine Line). Despite their commercial stumbles, several of these films showed it was a good year for actors. Seymour Cassel entered every scene laughing and played off Steve Buscemi beautifully in *In the Soup*. Michael Rapaport and N'Bushe Wright had a powerful awkwardness as an interracial high school couple in *Zebrahead*. And last but not least, Brad Pitt played his first leading role like a low IQ Jim Jarmusch in *Johnny Suede*—a performance, despite many denials, that seemingly became fodder for Tom DiCillo's second feature, *Living in Oblivion*.

Now *Swoon*, a fractured, homoerotic version of the Leopold/Loeb case, was a film for which I'd expected to provide completion financing for its producer Christine Vachon. She'd produced the previous year's *Poison*. As we were moving toward a deal, we got hung up on the issue of who would sell the foreign rights, and for what fee. Although Amy Taubin's *Village Voice* column had already announced *Swoon* as Islet's first investment, American Playhouse and Fine Line swooped down at the behest of newly designated executive producer James Schamus and snatched it away. James and his partner Ted Hope have gone on to great success with their company Good Machine, in particular with Ang Lee's *The Wedding Banquet* and *Eat Drink Man Woman*. *New York* magazine even named Schamus one of the "100 smartest people in New York." I felt a little burned by this deal, especially when Schamus later described Islet's deal terms by using the analogy of "being on the top floor of a burning building with only one possible ladder down." Somehow I didn't mind having been used as a stalking horse when I saw the completed film in Sundance. I thought Playhouse and Fine Line really had their work cut out for them.

I saw Gregg Araki's HIV-positive-lovers-on-the-run *The Living End* immediately afterward and found it to be far more effective, energetic, promotable, and, ultimately, likely to succeed. October's Bingham Ray and Jeff Lipsky felt the same way. They worked that film all the way to a $1 million gross, making it one of the Sundance success stories. The IRS release of Allison Anders' *Gas, Food, Lodging* was another. She benefited from a great welfare mother backstory, and gained well-deserved sympathy for being an all-too-rare, gifted female director. Wim Wenders' surprising influence on American indies struck again with Anders. After sending him many letters, she had gotten her first film job as a production assistant on *Paris, Texas*.

Distributor Seth Willenson also caught a major break with the critics, especially Ebert and Siskel, on another IRS title that had been rejected by Sundance and every other festival. Carl Franklin's *One False Move* had to weather far more vitriolic dismissal than *Slacker* ever did, partly due to violence, partly due to genre. But in the end, almost accidentally, the film followed a roundabout out-of-town release pattern from Seattle to Chicago to New York where the critics just exploded. Carl Franklin's approach didn't exactly reveal his cartoonish *A-Team* roots. If Geoff Gilmore had seen his way clear to invite *One False Move* to Sundance in January 1992, it would have been extremely interesting to see if Franklin's straightforward, horrifying visualization of the reality of violence would have stolen any of the thunder from the bravura stylized violence in another dramatic entry.

On the festival's first Saturday around 10:30 PM at the Holiday Village Cinemas, the lights went down and a bunch of guys started talking about Madonna and tipping. Then they got down to business with their guns and one memorable razor. *Reservoir Dogs* blew everyone away. At least it blew everyone away who didn't go dashing out of the theater in complete disgust. Although it could not have been more different in tone, *Dogs* was produced on the *sex, lies, and videotape* model: a similar budget financed by a home video company, a recognizable cast, and an L.A. writer/director who was already in the loop. Three years later, the circus was finally back in town. Ladies and gentlemen, I give you at long last, the next Steven Soderbergh. His name is Quentin Tarantino and he wants to make movies for a *large* audience!

From here on out, Sundance would be bursting at the seams. It's often been said that life's what happens while we're making other plans. While everyone is looking for the next Quentin, they should think about all the other notable filmmakers that emerged from or were boosted by Sundance between Soderbergh in 1989 and Tarantino in 1992: Reggie Hudlin, Maggie Greenwald, Norman Rene, Whit Stillman, Hal Hartley, Julie Dash, Todd Haynes, Richard Linklater, Matty Rich, Jennie Livingston, Allison Anders, Alexandre Rockwell, Tom DiCillo, Gregg Araki, Tom Kalin, Neal Jimenez, Anthony Drazen, Joe Berlinger, and Bruce Sinofsky.

Dogs

JOHN PIERSON: We've talked about Quentin Tarantino probably a thousand times this year, before you saw *Pulp Fiction* in Cannes and virtually every day since. What has he meant to you? Let's just dig right into that.

KEVIN SMITH: Flavor of the decade. You can't help but feel a tinge of, I don't know if it's jealousy or animosity, towards a guy that people hail universally for something which is a good movie but which is by no means a cure for cancer. But then again, you can't blame him; you have to blame the press. You can only blame him if he starts to buy into it. Since I don't deal with him on a daily basis I don't know if he has. But he serves as a great example. A great example of how not to believe the press. *Pulp Fiction* is a great film but does it warrant every article that's been written? Does it warrant the hyperbolic description of the film? If you ask me, *Reservoir Dogs* works better as a structured film—more so than *Pulp Fiction*. *Pulp Fiction* has great moments. The great moments in *Pulp Fiction*, let's say you take five great moments, are probably better than all the moments in *Reservoir Dogs*, but *Reservoir Dogs* is a better, more linear film. It's a tough call. I'm not comparing Quentin to Jesus Christ but ignore the man; just listen to the message (or the movie) and the message is he's a great filmmaker.

JP: I was at Sundance the year of *Reservoir Dogs* . . . of course, I'm always at Sundance; it's my tenth anniversary year coming up. I'm at that infamous first screening in Park City where all of us non-Hollywood, independent types were just blown away. It had been a major concern of Geoff Gilmore's to show a film with that kind of implied level of violence. It was a pretty earth-shattering moment.

KS: The first time I ever hear or see anything about the Q, it's a trailer on *Total Recall* from Live Home Video, the company that actually financed *Reservoir Dogs*. When the film first came out via Miramax it was weird because we remembered it as Live before that—the same trailer. And we didn't know what Miramax's involvement was at that point. So me and Vincent trek into the city to see *Reservoir Dogs* at the Loews East Village. It was new and exciting. And man, the dialogue crackles. It's unlike any movie we've seen before. It's like every movie you ever want to see. It's like the movies you wish they were making more of. Dialogue, good-looking violence, great characterization, good actors, we're like whew! This is the independent film that is gonna make a zillion bucks. As we all know it winds up making 2.5 million.

JP: A little less than 2.5 and never comes to Red Bank.

KS: So we're telling our friends about the film, "There's a scene where he cuts off this dude's ear, he's doing a little dance, it's got a great soundtrack." I found one of the only soundtracks available in Jersey at this mall in Toms River. You can't explain this movie to friends enough. But luckily we don't have to because two weeks later, we're at a comic book show in NYC and there's a bootleg of *Reservoir Dogs*, among bootlegs of whatever the major releases were there at the time. So I buy it for about $15. It's a great bootleg—pristine, right from the Miramax library. So I take the bootleg home and show it around to all the friends. Everybody's into it. And soon there's a small pocket in Monmouth County, New Jersey, of Quentinites. By the time *Pulp Fiction* comes around, *Reservoir Dogs* has come out on tape so there's a lot more Quentin legions. But part of the downfall of *Pulp Fiction* is that while it's great for Miramax—Miramax makes a lot of money and makes Quentin a household name—it just doesn't feel as cool anymore to be a Quentin fan. Once you knew you were in a small clique where very few people knew who he was. Now everyone knows who he is. Who's that guy who directed *Aguirre, the Wrath of God?*

JP: Werner Herzog.

KS: Right, now it feels kinda cool somewhere inside to know Werner . . . say the name?

JP: Werner Herzog.

KS: Right and be part of an exclusive part of that clique that knows him and likes his work. But he's got no mainstream appeal, he's definitely not a household name?

JP: Well there was no such thing in the seventies. You had all this marginal and specialized art product, both English and foreign language, which was of great importance to a very small elite group of people. Part of the appeal was their elite knowingness, but another part was that it just wasn't designed to be marketable to any particularly broader niche. The nineties are quite different. *Reservoir Dogs*, theatrically at least, is one of these amazingly interesting cases because it appears that it can be pushed over into a larger audience that's used to this normal fare with a twist. But there were impediments to its wider success until video, where everyone seemed to catch up with it.

KS: Of course, it was a new release, good-looking box and word-of-mouth on it was great. You go to the video store, we're behind the counter recommending it. "What's good?" "Oh this . . . it's got a lot of violence but hey—"

JP: You're not inspired by Quentin to the point of telling people to check out Eric Rohmer instead?

KS: No, once again, I don't know about the plagiarism allegations at this point.

JP: No believe me, this is not someone he could have lifted anything from. Eric Rohmer is a French director who makes very elegant talky movies that are not filled with snappy repartee. He's just someone whose reputation Quentin claims to have made at the Manhattan Beach video store.

KS: Maybe up until the point Quentin decided to be a filmmaker he thought his lot in life was to make these directors really famous in that video store, but I never felt that compulsion. I'm out for number one. I want to make me more known than Eric Rohmer or whatever.

JP: For better or worse, you are!

KS: Boil it down, isn't that what you do? You take something you find that you're really into like *Clerks* and take it to the people. So in essence you're a very selective, very finicky, video clerk.

JP: I have a college degree, unlike either of you guys.

KS: And you have a high school degree, which beats Quentin right there. But that's why the downside to *Pulp Fiction* was that now everybody knows the guy and you don't have that special feeling, "I know Quentin's work." God knows, with $100 million in box office you gotta say even in Peoria. So there was a brief pocket where maybe this guy could be influential. Now he's influencing many others besides myself and my friends.

JP: Quentin's image is that he was influenced by "all films." He clearly wanted to avoid the Scorsese typecasting, so Scorsese's a director he rarely talks about—and then its *Taxi Driver*, not *Mean Streets*. Did you ever hear him?

KS: No, he never mentions him, never credits him. Has he used any of his actors?

JP: Only the godhead himself, Harvey Keitel. He clearly didn't want to be painted into that corner.

KS: You've gotta credit him for being an idiot savant. He downplayed the Scorsese connection and, because of that, no one has really compared him. And now Quentin's his own screwy entity.

JP: Well that's not really true because critics have thrown *Reservoir Dogs* time and again into the category I call Sons of *Mean Streets.*

KS: He comes off as an utter goon in interviews and other movie appearances like *Sleep with Me* and *Destiny Turns on the Radio,* but he's talented and prolific.

JP: Point blank question then: Since you thank Jarmusch, Spike, Rick, and Hal Hartley . . .

KS: When we were at the Munich Film Festival after Cannes, Quentin finally saw *Clerks* and said, "Well you mention those four, you don't even mention me."

JP: He said that?

KS: He said that. It's a Quentin quote. And I said "Well, there is an homage in there to you with the car trunk in the opening montage." And he goes, "Right, right, right, right—that's what was cool about it."

JP: I actually thought that shot was out of Aldrich's *Kiss Me Deadly.*

KS: Like the glowing briefcase in *Pulp Fiction.* Some people say my dialogue is very Quentin-like.

JP: Some people? Like your distributor for example! Was it part of your more exclusive instinct to thank the people who meant something to you who were still cool, so that you could feel like you were part of an elite group? And if you put Quentin in?

KS: Right, right, right. It never occurred to me as such. I like to give credit where credit is due. I just never thought he was such a big influence because once again *Reservoir Dogs* is an example of a film that I can never do. It's glossy, looks great, has stars. I can never do that. Plus it's like a genre . . .

JP: Does it have dick jokes?

KS: It has dick references. Take a look at this.

JP: I remember this. Tarantino profile, *New York Times Sunday Magazine*, December '92, he says:

> If you say "I'm going to make a movie about disenfranchised youth or minimum wage kids" then it becomes obvious. To say you want to make a movie about being twenty-nine years old and working at a minimum wage job, that's a heavy burden to start off with. That's like saying "I'm going to do an anti-war movie." Why bother? Why not just say "I don't like war" and be done with it?

KS: Do you know how traumatic it is when someone whose work you eagerly admire basically says your idea is no good? This quote did what all my detractors never could: it cast a seed of doubt.

Sons of Mean Streets

In 1992, monologist Spalding Gray was the funniest awards ceremony moderator Sundance ever had. Quentin Tarantino wasn't
laughing because *Reservoir Dogs* did not win any prizes. He only hit
the jackpot. Harvey Keitel was the obvious direct link to the work of
Martin Scorsese—specifically his hugely influential *Mean Streets*. As
Scorsese looked to John Cassavetes, nineties filmmakers like Quentin,
Nick Gomez, Rob Weiss, and Michael Corrente looked to Scorsese.
Tarantino grew up in various parts of the L.A. basin and his whole world
was Southern California, where, strangely enough, Scorsese shot most
of *Mean Streets* for budgetary reasons. That put Tarantino, his producer
Lawrence Bender, and his financier Live Home Video, in a completely
different orbit from mine. I had to make do with the East Coast boys.

Laws of Gravity is reportedly the one feature by an acolyte that most
disturbs Martin Scorsese. Its first waking up shot, its two central male
characters and their relationship, the fact that the crazy one is actually
named Jon (like De Niro), and the violent inevitability of the ending
do come quite directly out of *Mean Streets*. But this story of loyalty and
honor among low life petty thieves on the streets of Greenpoint, Brook-

lyn, still has a tremendous lifeblood and visual identity all its own. As a result of Jean de Segonzac's stunning handheld camera work, the correlation between form and content makes for the best art. (Woody Allen had Carlo Di Palma try the same thing in *Husbands and Wives* and viewers just got nauseated.)

Laws of Gravity was produced for only $38,000 cash in the fall of 1991 by a filmmaking collective called the Shooting Gallery. The principals were Nick Gomez and producer Bob Gosse, both out of the SUNY/Purchase film program, along with lacrosse-playing executive producer Larry Meistrich. They had taken over an entire floor of a loft building on Lower Broadway that had once been occupied by Civil War photographer Mathew Brady. It was a down-and-dirty, low rent operation located four blocks across Franklin Street from the overpriced, upscale TriBeCa Film Center. Not only would you not ride with Robert De Niro or Harvey Weinstein in their elevator; you were lucky if their elevator was working. The film was submitted in rough form to Sundance. Geoff Gilmore thought it wouldn't be ready in time. Nick was a former editor who had cut SUNY/Purchase classmate Hal Hartley's *Trust*. Nick's own film was practically edited in his mind while he was shooting it, so it was quickly finished and ready for MOMA's New Directors/New Films.

I saw *Laws of Gravity* a few weeks after returning to New York from the *Reservoir Dogs* Sundance and quickly signed on for representation just as it was being officially invited to New Directors. At the same time Richard Abramowitz, former Cinecom distribution head, had gotten involved with the newly reactivated RKO Pictures, a trademark now owned by multi-millionaire film dilettante Ted Hartley. Abramowitz stayed in constant pursuit of the film. Neither he nor I could shake the intensity and authenticity of the performances, especially the lead, Peter Greene. Much of the rest of the cast (Edie Falco, Adam Trese, Paul Schulze) had all come out of the SUNY/Purchase acting program. Having Falco and Arabella Field play two strong female characters in the film helped to ameliorate the "boys with guns" posturing.

It was the era of rising testosterone. The Shooting Gallery team was macho, but savvy. When Nick shaved his head, focused his intense glare, and played up his tough street-guy background, it felt like an act. It felt like an act because he was bright, well read, and really acute. He also had the self-awareness to recognize that he wasn't really a writer. But what a visceral director!

As a feature in search of a distributor, *Laws of Gravity* faced a serious choice in the weeks leading up to its New Directors premiere on Saturday, March 21. To wait or not to wait. To push hard for a distributor in advance, or confidently expect a rave in *The New York Times*. Despite my experience, I didn't have a definitive answer beyond strongly encouraging all distributors from New York and Los Angeles to attend the one and only advance press screening on March 10. Ira Deutchman seemed like a likely prospect so I begged, cajoled, and threatened him in an attempt to circumvent the pro forma advance scouts. The description on the schedule had immediately invoked Scorsese with a reference to "Brooklyn's mean streets."

Basically the film was starting at ground zero as an untouted discovery. Since 75 percent of the titles in New Directors each year are never heard from again, especially if reviewed badly or blandly by a *New York Times* third-string critic, I resolved to do something for the first time ever. After consulting with festival publicist Joanna Ney, I wrote to Vincent Canby urging him to review *Laws of Gravity*. In the letter, I placed Nick's debut in the tradition of "a number of American independent filmmakers whose work you've championed though the years"—Spike, Errol Morris, Michael Moore, and Richard Linklater. Then I added, "All right, you really didn't go for *Slacker*, but it was the hit of New Directors/New Films last year. *Laws of Gravity* holds its own against these smashing debuts."

Canby showed up for the screening. Ira Deutchman didn't. Most of the rest of the New York distributors were there, but no one flew in from the Coast. Olivier Jahan and Pierre-Henri Deleau from the Directors' Fortnight grudgingly left the safety of the Magno Screening Room where they were making their Cannes picks. J. Hoberman, Amy Taubin, and Manohla Dargis were all there from the *Village Voice*. Dargis was another SUNY/Purchase alumnus and was overheard expressing her amazement on the way out since Nick had been "a real asshole" in school. Her subsequent overheated review contained the words "throbs," "pulses," "bristles," "macho," and "ballsy."

In March 1992, my Islet division was nearly a year old. Chris Blackwell and John Heyman had recently named former Geffen Company business affairs head Eric Eisner to run the parent company, Island

World. Eisner had walked away with tens of millions of dollars when MCA acquired Geffen Records the previous year. Before then, his claim to fame had been coming up with the idea of suing Neil Young for delivering noncommercial material to Geffen Records (at least according to David Geffen in *Rolling Stone*). Eisner had now gotten the movie bug, and unfortunately Islet didn't fall below his radar. He heard about Nick Gomez from his production co-president Chris Zarpas, had a strong notion that Blackwell would be excited about his work, and insisted that I circulate copies of the videotape. Eisner's instinct was prescient; his follow-up was abysmal.

By the day of the press screening, Blackwell was in hot pursuit of *Laws of Gravity* as an Island Pictures presentation, Nick Gomez as a filmmaker, and the Shooting Gallery as a production facility. Chris had the wonderful, easygoing ability to impress everyone by having a car pick us up outside MOMA to drive us all to Philadelphia to go backstage for the second date of the U2 "Zoo TV" U.S. tour. We never met U2's Bono or The Edge in Philly; but Eisner and Blackwell came downtown to the Shooting Gallery for further talks about future projects two days later. I was in a terrible bind. Islet was funded by Island World, but I had a moral imperative to get my filmmaker clients the best possible deal. Once again, Island Pictures had ceased any and all direct distribution activities after *Sidewalk Stories*, the film that had squared my accounts with Chris Blackwell. Any domestic *Laws of Gravity* release would have to be sublicensed through an active distributor.

Disappointingly, those distributors were holding back or, even worse, passing on the film. In the week before the public showing, Ira Deutchman finally saw it and found it "too small for Fine Line." Harvey Weinstein and his troops also screened it at TriBeCa. Harvey immediately realized that *Laws of Gravity* was in direct competition with *Reservoir Dogs*, and he passed. We resolved to get Nick's debut on screen before Quentin's. Even the Directors' Fortnight, which normally eats up gritty, streetwise, New York City films, passed on this one; Jahan liked it, but his boss Deleau had no interest.

The Canby review didn't alter the landscape. Although he referred to the film time and again (even in his *Reservoir Dogs* review) for the rest of 1992, Canby's original judgment seemed tempered and unquotable. He accurately described Jean de Segonzac's "remarkably sensitive handheld camera" as "the star" of the movie. I think distributors picked up more on his description of the narrative as "bleak." Even worse, the headline writer came up with a major turnoff: SHABBY LIVES IN BROOKLYN, WITH CAMERA LOOKING ON. Jeffrey Jacobs at the Angelika Theater and Jonathan Dana at Triton Pictures both called this a negative review.

Jonathan Dana had escaped from Atlantic Releasing and started Triton Pictures with then fashionable Japanese financing in 1990. Although he discounted *The New York Times* review, he still joined the pursuit of *Laws of Gravity*. Triton had set up shop with a prestigious 9000 Sunset Boulevard address—Island's former digs. Acquisitions V.P. Bobby Rock had thrown in his lot with Dana after Atlantic collapsed. The week after the New Directors premiere, we screened for all the L.A.-based distributors with poor results. I'm sure the inferior 16mm screening circumstances didn't help our cause, especially after the print got a huge emulsion scratch through an entire forty-minute reel sometime after October Films saw it and passed. When Goldwyn passed, their longtime acquisition maven Howard Cohen made a revealing admission that may have been a key to understanding the film's problems: "Sam Goldwyn, Jr., doesn't like lowlifes." It looked like the new Triton and even newer RKO Pictures were the only bidders . . . the only *low* bidders. And their futures turned out to be very uncertain.

I painted a much rosier picture as I reported back to Blackwell and Eisner. To them, the deal was more about the future than the present. I often found it impossible to render judgments about careers. In this case, I loved the do-it-yourself theory of the Shooting Gallery and Nick's kinetic direction, but I had more trepidation about his screenwriting. They sent me a copy of the prospective second feature called *Animals*. It was *Laws of Gravity* redux with car thieves in the Somerville section of Boston, Nick's hometown. In fact, he'd cannibalized the *Animals* script to write *Laws*. I was dismayed and over a barrel. The original $38,000 film had generated only modest distribution offers, and the follow-up script was awfully similar with a $2.5 million budget. Because my heart was with my filmmakers, I convinced myself that the *Laws of Gravity* deal would improve. However in good conscience, I had to tell my energized parent company that *Animals* was a bad idea. Nobody listened. Chris Blackwell paid an advance of $400,000 plus $50,000 in additional delivery costs for a $38,000 first feature and two option pictures. The bizarre internal mechanics meant that my division, Islet, got a $30,000 fee (7.5 percent) on the deal.

The formula for disaster was in place. Blackwell is a man of many homes, time zones, phone numbers, and pet projects. He agreed to the Gomez deal on a cellular phone while walking down the main drag in Kingston, Jamaica, with music blasting out of storefronts in the background. He knows how to enjoy life. He can also disappear for days on end. He left Eric Eisner in charge of closing the production deal on the next picture. Eisner wanted to play the Hollywood game while feigning interest in edgier independents. He came across as acutely intelligent in conversation even when he was trying to persuade Nick Gomez to direct a psychodrama starring Elizabeth Taylor as a kind of *Who's Afraid of Mean Streets?*

Nick, Larry, and Bob were in love with their own bad-ass attitude. Just as I was beginning to get enough distance to realize this myself, indie producer James Schamus walked into the New Directors directors' party with *Swoon*'s Tom Kalin, took one look at an extended table with a dozen people in the *Laws of Gravity* contingent and said, "There they are—the big dick swingers." Negotiations on the Island option were a nightmare. The parties even fought over what day *Animals* was officially submitted, thus starting the ticking thirty-day clock. (Island asked for a grace period as a result of the L.A. riots.) The budget was a major hurdle unless some marquee names joined the cast. Eisner pushed for Marky Mark Wahlberg after Nick brought the name up in joking frustration one day. The Shooting Gallery concept of a name was the virtually unknown John Leguizamo. (Blackwell loved his one-man stage shows and had financed the filming of one of them). But his designated negotiator Eric Eisner was unconvinced. The combination of personalities was gruesome. The agendas were in utter conflict. I felt embarrassed but constrained, since *Animals* seemed likely to generate critical complaints of being a "carbon copy" as had Jim Jarmusch's second (Island) feature *Down by Law*.

I tried to keep an arm's length away from this imbroglio by focusing solely on the release of *Laws of Gravity*. One day, Jonathan Dana and Bobby Rock of Triton Pictures were in New York and made their pilgrimage way downtown to the Shooting Gallery. Afterwards they took me aside in a restaurant next door, and I thought they were now excited enough for me to get them to raise their offer. I desperately tried to keep my whole body from drooping when they told me the true purpose of our tête-à-tête. Their Japanese financier Kadakawa had pulled the plug.

They still wanted the film, but couldn't even pay a $100,000 advance. I stumbled out. RKO Pictures was the last resort.

Blackwell recouped only $150,000 from the RKO deal. His foreign sales head Ann Dubinet, who had come over from a very successful stint at Goldwyn and saved the day in Island World's first year with astronomical international sales on the teen action/adventure movie *Toy Soldiers*, scared off the buyers who offered modest advances on this small film by quoting high prices. As Eisner squelched the *Animals* deal, all hopes were riding on the theatrical release of *Laws of Gravity* in North America.

RKO's Richard Abramowitz was saddling up for the first time since getting bucked by Cinecom. He worked hard, but his booking leverage was circumscribed. We made his job that much harder by imposing a contractual condition that Nick's movie open by the end of August. The reasoning was simple: Beat *Reservoir Dogs* to the punch. We were under the impression that Miramax would take the Tarantino film to the New York Film Festival, then open in October, so a six-week head start seemed right. When Jeffrey Jacobs couldn't commit the Angelika until October, Abramowitz had to resort to the Waverly Theater in New York's West Village. This venue had been an art hot spot in olden times, but it had become a boring, commercial circuit theater with absolutely no identity. The *Gravity* boys liked the idea because the Waverly was across the street from some notorious, twenty-four hour a day basketball courts, and they seemed to be under the misapprehension that this was their audience. Executive producer Larry Meistrich kept insisting that he could deliver sellout audiences all week long no matter where the film played.

The New York reviews were great across the board. *New York* magazine's David Denby called it "extraordinary, exhilarating . . . it cost the hilarious sum of $38,000. All it takes is talent." Business at the Waverly started off at a mediocre level and then tailed off. Los Angeles fizzled. The film triumphed at the Toronto Film Festival, where it almost hadn't been invited, but stiffed when it opened there. It closed out the Boston Film Festival, received rave reviews everywhere (especially the *Boston Globe*), was featured on the cover of the *Boston Phoenix* (since Nick was a hometown boy) and opened at the ideal theater—the Nickelodeon. It grossed a mere $1,800 for its first weekend. Its total theatrical box office nationwide was only $200,000—about 35,000 tickets.

Rushing into the Waverly was obviously a blunder. RKO's graphic campaign with its dominant tabloid-style title treatment was no great shakes, but the *degree* of failure was remarkable. There were two consolations, one positive, one negative. *Laws of Gravity* may not have been seen by a lot of people but a disproportionate number were filmmakers. It was an insiders' favorite for its camerawork and performances. It's one of the least successful theatrical titles I've represented, yet filmmakers *always* ask about it, both newcomers and established figures like Atom Egoyan and Spike Lee. That took some of the sting out. The other consolation was that *Johnny Suede* before it and *Swoon, Simple Men, My New Gun,* and *In the Soup,* all in the month right after it, fared no better.

Laws of Gravity may have gotten the most raves in this oversaturated batch of underperforming releases, but it had the toughest subject matter. A year later at the Edinburgh Film Festival in Scotland, just prior to the film's U.K. release, Larry Meistrich was still claiming that *Laws* had strong blue collar appeal and would have thrived in communities like Asbury Park, New Jersey. I don't buy that argument for a second, but the home video release did get into a wider cross section of homes when it shipped 17,000 cassettes. The Triboro Home Video box clearly helped. It had a cheesy new photo of the cast with guns and lusty prose in the descriptive blurb: "These are the people who steal the radios from your cars . . . who live on the fringe, right near the edge. One push and they're gone." Maybe one of them broke into Sam Goldwyn, Jr.'s Mercedes.

Peter Greene gained as much as anyone from *Laws of Gravity.* He gained a little more from the video box photo shoot than anyone else. Since he was the only member of the cast who had left New York for L.A., he had to be flown back and put up at the Paramount Hotel. When he checked out of his room, the VCR did too. Peter had a huge 1994, with his villainous appearances in *Pulp Fiction* and opposite Jim Carrey in *The Mask.* In between his debut and those features, he acted in a number of very quirky low-budget films. In the most notorious and daring performance, he played a clinically dead-on schizophrenic gouging out his fingernail in Lodge Kerrigan's *Clean Shaven.* Lodge is a gifted and pure cineaste who came to me quite early with that film, long before it made people faint at Sundance in 1994. Peter Greene had told me very insistently that it was his best role. While I respected the work, I never considered financing it for a second. When I saw Peter in Sundance and congratulated him on his performance, he said, "I told you to invest in *Clean Shaven.*" I told him what a relief it was not to have one nickel invested. He started to look angry. Since I'd just seen him led off in handcuffs after an altercation at a Los Lobos concert the night before, I quickly left.

Although not that many people saw *Laws of Gravity* at the Waverly, Barry Brown, Spike Lee's editor, was one of them. Then he took Spike. Then Spike went again. Afterward Spike called me very excited about the film and Nick Gomez, but very dubious about the $38,000 budget. His $175,000 on *She's Gotta Have It* had included all deferments, insurance, legal fees, blowup to 35mm, sound mix. I explained that Nick's film had been shown at MOMA and sold as a 16mm $38,000 film, while acknowledging that it had climbed up to his budget level once it was ready for full-fledged 35mm release. Spike was very keen on talking to Nick about doing another feature sponsored by 40 Acres and a Mule through his Universal deal. Nick and the boys already had a big fan in Spike's Universal production executive Sam Kitt. Sam's studio career had been a challenge from the start, but he always fought the good fight for new talent. Once Spike heard about *Animals*, he wanted Nick to find something new. He told Nick flat out that the Jim Jarmusch school of "minor variations on the same theme" was not the answer to developing a career. For the first time, Nick Gomez listened to an outside voice and realized that it was pointless to keep up the defensive pretense that *Animals* was "completely different" from *Laws.* Eventually everyone pulled together, shifted a little sideways, and came up with *New Jersey Drive.* (Ironically, *New Jersey Drive* opened the same week in 1995 as the Island production of *The Basketball Diaries* co-starring Marky Mark himself, who received excellent notices.)

In the meantime, *Reservoir Dogs* finally hit theatrical screens in October 1992 without the benefit of the New York Film Festival. It was controversial and much acclaimed, two factors that normally assure success in the specialized world. Miramax gave it a major launch, perhaps anticipating the beginning of a dynasty, but a funny thing happened on the way to the bank. *Dogs* was too violent for many members, especially women, of the specialized audience. But it had too much talk and not nearly enough real action for the commercial action crowd. It certainly wasn't hurt in any way whatsoever coming out after *Laws of Gravity.* Interestingly, Tarantino has said more than once that he wrote *Reservoir Dogs* to be made in 16mm for $30,000 like *Laws of Gravity*, essentially in one warehouse location. (It's a little known fact that he had tried this ultra-low route with an earlier, incomplete feature.) The only major difference afforded by his $1.5 million budget was that he got Keitel, Roth, Madsen, et al., as his cast. But the dearth of large-scale action is still inherent in the script and finished movie. Miramax may have felt some frustration for a moment, but the Weinsteins had cemented their relationship with the flavor of the decade. And they had simultaneously released a Neil Jordan movie with a "secret" which was on its way to a $60 million gross through their inspired marketing. *The Crying Game* gave Miramax an enormous lift just as the company was becoming a bit strapped for cash in its ever expanding realm of activity.

In its initial theatrical release, the legendary Tarantino debut grossed about $2.4 million, the same amount as Rose Troche and Guin Turner's *Go Fish* two years later. Of course, absolutely everyone on the planet has seen it now on videocassette. It's a subject of endless fascination to wonder about the $30,000 version of *Reservoir Dogs* that could exist somewhere in a parallel low-budget universe.

$26,685

JOHN PIERSON: *Clerks* had a $27,000 or under, depending upon which accounting you use, budget. In general terms how do you feel about this raging debate, that seems to be taking the form of internecine warfare in the independent community, about whether these low budgets are for real or not. Obviously they've been promotable, but people get a little pissy about whether there is such a thing as a $27,000 releasable film or $7,000 releasable film.

KEVIN SMITH: Is there? Didn't Strand Releasing do that? I mean they used to release 16mm? So, at that point, yeah there is. But when you start to go into a wider release?

JP: A small distributor like Strand does release 16mm. They take their chances on the E&O insurance, or maybe they have films with no rights problems so they slide on that as well. So there you go. But maybe the film still has deferments that are paid because when Strand releases the film you actually make some money. So even then the budget's no longer what it was in the first place.

KS: True. But can it be done? Ah, let's say that Strand had bought *Clerks* and decided to release it in 16mm and since we had no deferments, that's it.

JP: Strand's Marcus Hu said, "You know it's competitive out there when Miramax is buying a film like *Clerks* and giving it 'the treatment.'"

KS: That's why it was a rude awakening to find out about *El Mariachi*. To hear the rumblings early on that this was not a $7,000 movie, and then to get the real story later on, what the cost breakdown is, and realize we've been duped. And it's not so much that we've been duped, but the public has it fixed in its mind that you can make a $7,000 film. While that's good to a point because that's inspiring and it's like if that guy can do it I can do it, it's also bad in general for the independent arena because then we can't use that as leverage. We never thought the $27,000 was a big deal at all because the $7,000 movie had already been done. So we thought if anything people would say "for its money, *Clerks* is fine." Since the lowest of the lowest had been announced, we never thought it was any kind of marketing tool. So we never thought to write that anywhere or to sell it that way. Then you find out that it still is. No matter what it is if it's under a certain amount the general public is still going to be excited, like "Wow, an underdog made it."

JP: You started with a budget or you just spent as you went along?

KS: We never had a budget. We used the Peter Broderick article from *Filmmaker Magazine* from the year before that had the breakdown from *Laws of Gravity*, *El Mariachi*, which was completely useless; and *The Living End*. We ended up using the *Laws of Gravity* budget. What was that, $23,000?

JP: No, *Laws* was $38,000

KS: We wanted to come in lower. We never prebudgeted, we never said we're going to need this, this and this. We had the credit cards of course. We had the limit to the point that if it ever hit $20,000 to $25,000 we'd have to start worrying. But we figure it's going to cost in this neighborhood. So when the film was done and completed, then I added up everything and found out what the exact number was. The only reason I added everything up was that Peter Broderick was doing the new *Filmmaker* article for the next year—a follow-up. But nobody except us in Sundance 1994 submitted their budget that year. That was weird because the three films that were featured the previous time, everybody did their budget. There was a budget-breakdown column.

JP: The first one was during Sundance, but the films had all come out or been sold beforehand. So it was safe. The second time, no one but you wanted to spill it until after the sale or release of the film. But later on, lips tend to loosen.

KS: If you think about it, nobody even mentioned their budgets at Sundance in 1994.

JP: That's a really key point. You were defined as *lowest* which is the only advantage that one could have. It probably wasn't true because *River of Grass* looks like it was made with trading stamps.

KS: And I think that's a direct result of the *Filmmaker* article. Were it not for that article, I wouldn't have totaled up what the film cost at that point. I think I would have waited as long as I could. I had all the receipts, I just never wanted to sit down and do the math.

JP: So your budget was just an adding machine tape after the fact.

KS: And the bottom line was $26,685.

JP: So it's not like you have some big moral code about it? You benefited from the advantages of the low-budget story, therefore it would be unseemly for you to attack anybody else for using it. You just seem pretty casual about it.

KS: At the 1994 IFFM orientation, somebody asked, "My budget is lower than *Clerks*. Should I use that as an advertising thing?" On the one hand that's kind of flattering, but I don't think it should be about the budget necessarily. I mean we had a low budget, but we also had a film to back it up that some people seem to like. Even . . .

JP: Even Costa Zeher didn't say that his film cost less than *Clerks*, he just said that his film was so much funnier [laughter]. In fact, it cost a few bucks more if I remember. Somebody on America Online complained, "C'mon already with this $27,000 budget."

KS: The one who said, "I saw these guys at the IFFM and it really cost 1.5 million."

JP: Yeah, exactly. He posted: "Miramax has now poured in $1.5 million."

KS: That kind of irritated me because he didn't hear us correctly. We were careful to say in every interview, whenever people said this was a $27,000 movie, that we made it for $27,000 and that's what they bought, and it was a completed film in 16mm. Now we have to, of course, blow it up to 35mm and the price becomes a little more, and we have to remix and the price becomes a little more. While it was a $27,000 movie, it certainly didn't stay a $27,000 movie. We were real clear about that point. Where this guy came up with this $1.5 million number . . . that's just beyond me.

JP: He was way off the mark before the film opened. But when you total the $200,000 in completion costs, the million in print advertising and $700,000 in electronic media over the half-year of the run . . . not to mention other promotional expenses like your high international profile in Cannes, the Alan Dershowitz appeal of the NC-17 rating, the guy winds up being a prophet. Miramax easily spent a couple of million bucks on the release, even more than the Columbia Pictures expenditure on *El Mariachi*.

KS: The lesson taken away by any firsttime or would-be filmmaker is definitely the debunking of the myth—costs $7,000 "makes" $2 million.

JP: So the second bottom line becomes profitability. Being from the old school, I like the idea of being efficient and only spending money that's money well spent. But then you go to your grave never really being sure what more might have been out there. On *Clerks*, I kept saying you're not going to get an 18-year-old in to see this no matter what you do. Nothing's going to change anything. I was also the one who said *Hoop Dreams* wouldn't gross much more than $1 million, and it went over $7.5 million. I like being a reverse jinx. I wish it had worked better on *Clerks* too. I wish every high school kid in the country had gone off to see it. Miramax gave it the shot, Sony soundtrack and all, and should earn about $1 million in fees.

KS: So summing up Harvey should be happy, especially if there's a TV series, because *Clerks* is profitable for Miramax. We're happy because it made us high-profile, if not quite a Spike Lee household name because Spike's much louder than we are in general, but it made us notable— not just a footnote in the history of independent film. For one full year we got to ride the press wagon—January to December—the entire time. It's not the most profitable indie film in history like they claimed in those San Diego ads.

JP: *Lion King . . . Gump . . . Clerks* !

KS: Were we more profitable than *El Mariachi*?

JP: The answer is yes, especially with your 60,000 video cassettes and his under 20,000. I mean that was break-even at best. Mark those words, it's not defamation because it's true!

KS: Were we more profitable than *Amongst Friends? Slacker? Reservoir Dogs?*

JP: The respective answers are yes, yes, and yes theatrically. But *Dogs* beats you in video.

KS: So I make out because in the end we never expected this to be a hugely profitable movie anyway. And the money we made at the front end was great enough for us, for me. It paid my bills. I got to pay everyone involved. Although I never had formal deferments to pay, people got paid anyway. It got me a car, and it went toward financing a place to live. We refer to the condo as "the house that Dante built." But what it did more than anything financially was to put me into the next inning of the ball game. Okay here we go, now we're going to make a bigger movie.

JP: Tom Bernard just told me, "Tell Kevin that Sony Classics would not have been able to do what Miramax did for *Clerks*." He flat out said it. They would have spent less.

KS: In the end Charlie Brown, what have we learned? We should all be pleased. From the top, the people that bought it, Miramax, all the way down to the people who were in the film who never would have been in a movie were it not for *Clerks*. Nobody should be disappointed. We just wish they'd spent a little less money.

How Low Can a Budget Go?

lacker and *Laws of Gravity* were back-to-back releases for me. One cost $23,000, the other $38,000 to complete in 16mm, show at festivals, and sell. This was a far cry from the prototypical, still intimidating $200,000 to $300,000 budget from the second half of the eighties. A politically cranky, experimental filmmaker like Jon Jost might have made over a dozen features for under $20,000, but almost nobody looked to him as a mentor. One of the few who did was Gregg Araki who made two features for pennies before Jost loaned him some equipment, which enabled him to upgrade to *Slacker* budget level for his 1992 feature, *The Living End*. Once Linklater, Gomez, and Araki came along and *Filmmaker* magazine published their line budgets in a very influential article by Peter Broderick, the inspirational miracle of the ultralow budget feature caught on like wildfire.

The distance between a $2.5 million budget, which almost no one can raise privately, and $250,000 is vast. However the gap between that mid-level and the ultra-low $25,000 is deceptive. Spike Lee expended about $80,000 in cash to get to the *She's Gotta Have It* print that we showed at (and sold just after) the San Francisco Film Festival. Robert

Townsend charged less than $100,000 on his credit cards to film the *Hollywood Shuffle* skit material that he screened for Goldwyn after which they provided the rest. Spike's cash expenses weren't that far out of line with *Laws of Gravity,* which was shot in conventional 16mm and didn't require a blowup before screening. The *Hollywood Shuffle* budget, on the other hand, took an enormous quantitative leap not unlike the one that Robert Rodriguez's *El Mariachi* would take at the hands of Columbia Pictures.

Everyone in the industry assumed that I would take great exception to the "alleged" $7,000 low-as-you-could-possibly-go budget for Rodriguez. For many years I've been a seller of films. If a distributor assumes all the costs after buying a film, I believe that the cash cost of the commodity sold is a valid figure. But so is the full, all-in cost of production fronted by the distributor, especially when calculating "alleged" profits. So I don't call the Rodriguez budget "alleged"; he sold a $7,000 movie cut on video and didn't personally spend another cent on it. Once Columbia assumed control and spent a million completing and releasing the film, the profit or loss became their problem. It failed to outperform *Laws of Gravity* in home video since *El Mariachi* was subtitled.

Throughout the years I've concluded that you simply cannot blow up a feature from 16mm to 35mm, remix sound, and secure insurance without it costing at least $60,000. On average, music rights, deferments, and other lab deliverables (like the costly and obscure foreign sound dubbing element known as the music-and-effects, or M&E, mix) will bring just about every film's total up to $100,000. When music and deferments are pricey, add another $50,000 for a total of $150,000. So when you see an ultralow budget, it's not a bad idea to do a little quick mental addition. Now if a film has been picked up by a distributor who is bearing this cost, the battle has been won. If the film eventually earns an overage, it will come only after these costs and a number of others have been recouped. Does that mean there's some advantage in raising more of the money yourself in the first place? Certainly not, if it slows you down for years or completely defeats your attempt to start production.

It's become a world of piecemeal, ad hoc, stop-and-start financing. More low-budget features are started with partial budgets intended to get it in the can, or maybe only shoot sample scenes, than full ones. Companies like mine have encouraged and implicitly endorsed this rash behavior. The key personality elements in most cases are a writer/director who is almost overconfident and a core support group that feeds the wonderful delusion that come hell or high water the film will be made! Spike, Mike, Slackers, Dykes—every single film I've described, and a few more to come, fit the bill.

The composite prototype low-budget production would observe the following guidelines:

1. The script is written to fit the budget, keeping in mind an inventory of available assets.
2. There is an organized rehearsal period with the cast and director of photography that may be longer than the compressed shoot itself, whether principal photography is twelve straight days or twelve days on weekends over six months.
3. Sets and locations are cheap or free.
4. No one in the small cast and crew gets paid a salary, and even the deferred salaries are modest.
5. Since film stock and processing are unavoidable expenses, the shooting ratio is very low after using a Kodak student discount and getting DuArt to defer half its lab fee.
6. You have to feed people decently and pay the caterer.
7. Postproduction consists of a low-rent Steenbeck in your apartment or after-hours access to an AVID video editing system.

Amazingly if not advisedly, Rick Linklater, Gregg Araki, and Kevin Smith all claim they never really had a budget. They just had the knowledge that they could raise about $25,000. With credit cards and a family member or two with a modicum of disposable income, the universe of potential filmmakers suddenly expands. (It's obviously easier to get credit now than when I was twenty-two.) My credo has always been "style, not production value." I get very nervous when someone calls and immediately starts telling me how their film looks like a million bucks (or some other multiple of its actual budget). In 1994, I even changed the name of the company to Grainy Pictures. Somewhat unfairly, this phrase has come up repeatedly in reviews to describe my favorite movies.

It's almost an encoded, insider consumer warning. I celebrate the word and have no use for those who use it scornfully.

There are certainly repercussions from using a low budget for publicity purposes. First of all, distributors may turn the knowledge of that minimal cost against a producer when negotiating a deal. If there are many wealthy bidders, as in the case of *Roger & Me*, you can laugh in their face. *Laws of Gravity*, on the other hand, was victimized. I still fondly recall the fact that I didn't have a clue what *Living on Tokyo Time* cost until after the sale.

The only reason to promote a low budget, especially one that was raised via original means, is to get more press coverage and perhaps a sympathy vote. Even as it becomes a big yawn, the press often embrace the story almost as a crutch when there's no other angle. The impact at the consumer level is highly debatable. One viewer might cut you some slack, while three others go to see a James Cameron film instead. My favorite financing story of the moment is a feature called *Joint Adventure* that's selling $15 baseball caps that say "Admit One" on the back. This guarantees admission to any theater where it's playing if and when it ever opens.

And this brings us back to the lowest of the low, the film that flung the gauntlet, *El Mariachi*. Even my dentist asked me about "that $7,000 movie." If everybody who was aware of "EL $7,000," and the fact that Robert sold his body to medical science to finance it, had gone to see it, the gross would have been $50 million, not $2 million. Rodriguez had a great rap partly scripted by his clever handlers at ICM, who brilliantly brokered his deal with Columbia Pictures. Agent Robert Newman once told me that ICM wrote the line about the Columbia statue logo costing more than the entire movie. I love Robert's turtle, and his whole big family whom he's been using in his videos since he was eleven. But in the end, his film was nothing more or less than your basic career-starter. If he established a franchise in the process, it's not exactly *Rocky*.

When *El Mariachi* played at Sundance in 1993, Robert Rodriguez spoke eloquently on the Twenty Somethings filmmaker seminar that I moderated. He described the fifty $1 million features he'd make if a studio gave him $50 million. Rob Weiss was Bachelor Number One that day and he blathered on and on. His film *Amongst Friends* lost the audience prize to *El Mariachi* by a fraction of a point. The innocent mariachi had to learn to kill to defend himself and survive. Rob Weiss wasn't saying whether he had or hadn't killed anybody before making his movie. There's no confusion on one subject; *Amongst Friends* did *not* have an ultra-low budget.

Shannen

JOHN PIERSON: One of the underlying mysteries of the entire experience of living this life and writing this book is that so many things that you might never expect to connect up, dot to dot, wind up all forming this one huge ten-year picture. I never in a million years thought there would come an occasion where there was some link between Rob Weiss's world and your world.

KEVIN SMITH: It's funny, when Shannen was cast in *Mallrats* the first question out of people's mouths was not, "Isn't she going out with Rob Weiss?" That would of course be from the film end; but everyone else in all the world is like, "Oh, is she really a bitch?" When my friend Brian first got back from the shoot, the first question everybody asked was, "Did you go with her?" He's like, "What do you mean? Why would Shannen Doherty go with me?" And he said he got asked that question five times. Really bizarre.

JP: When did you get the idea? When did you get fixated on wanting to have her in the movie?

KS: It was a bizarre, gradual process. The first place that it came up was with mad Malcolm from *Film Threat*. One of the first times we ever met, he said, "You're doing a *mall* movie! You gotta cast Doherty." I was like,

"Are you insane, why?" He said, "Because she's the good load." I'm like, "She'd never do it." So that was then. It never came up again except from Malcolm's lips to God's ears. When we were in casting, maybe in the last two weeks, Don Phillips said, "Hey, Shannen Doherty's people called, she wants to audition." We're like, "What? You're kidding?" She was about the highest profile person to come in. We had a lot of people, including an *Amongst Friends*er, and another *Amongst Friends*er who were both real bitter guys.

JP: You still have trouble figuring out which one was which.

KS: One was that guy who carried a gun, and the other was the other guy who carried a gun.

JP: Wimpy Andy, bad Billy, or soulful Trevor who rode the bike. The critic Manohla Dargis once described the film as, "I shoot therefore I am."

KS: It wasn't Trevor, it was the other two. When I heard Shannen wanted to come in we were all wondering, "Will she bring Weiss? Will she bring Weiss?" She didn't live up to her reputation at all. She was nice as hell—and funny. I immediately jibed her and she was taking it, and giving some back. She was great. And after seeing her read for the first time, she was a TV actress yet not a TV actress. She knew how to play the emotions but she added a little more depth to it than just your standard TV actress. She wasn't just playing to the camera. She wasn't using what she refers to as, "looks 1, 2, and 3" from *Beverly Hills 90210*. And the best thing about her is that she has this rapid-fire delivery that really fits the dialogue.

JP: Did you expect that? Did you have any signs that she would have that rapid-fire delivery?

KS: She was kind of fast in *Heathers*, a cult fave of course. It was before she even auditioned, when I was just talking to her, that she was just whipping out the words. So when she finally came out to read the René part, hands down she got it. Which was also a boon for us, because the studio was like "Ooh, you've got Shannen Doherty to do the movie?" I would have thought that would have been a liability because there's so much enmity towards her. I would have thought the studio would have been like, "no way" but the studio was all for her. And she didn't bring Rob, but she did mention that her boyfriend was a director at which point all I flash on is that *TV Guide* interview where she said "Rob—my mentor, my shaman, my lover . . ."

JP: The Liz Smith interview. Shannen said ". . . a teacher, a friend, an inspiration."

KS: You say something like that, you got to figure that this is the romance of the century—like Wallis Simpson and the King of England or something. But one time during production, she's all upset over this nasty argument she had with him. I felt like I was in high school again, and here she was with what seemed like one of those really bizarre, sick boyfriend relationships, where he's like "I'm going out to (the name of some club) and I'm going to fuck everything there."

JP: He said that?

KS: That's what she told me. And it made her really upset, and she was about to shoot a scene. He's a director; he should know better. I mean, here she is about to do a scene in a comedy—a comedy, for God's sake—and her boyfriend's telling her he's going to some club to fuck everything there.

JP: I'm glad I wasn't at that club. He threatened to punch me once.

KS: And this whole thing bugs the shit out of me —not just because I'm the director—but because this girl is something special. I mean, yeah, she's got this reputation. But any kid who grows up with the media scrutinizing their every move would get a reputation. In reality, she's such a sweetheart; such a great person. And here's this guy—her boyfriend for Christ's sake—who's supposed to love her and every-thing, and he says things like that, and tells her she shouldn't try for fea-tures—she's just a TV actress. I was so pissed.

JP: Sounds like someone had a crush. Why doesn't she go for the easy retaliatory comment regarding his career?

KS: You mean because *Amongst Friends* made like three bucks.

JP: But it did have that big, big, big, big, bigger than big look.

KS: And you'd think that after the movie came out and did nothing, that people'd be like "Rob Who?" But my boy Ben Affleck, who's in *'Rats* and was in *Dazed and Confused* told me that when he and his friend Matt were taking their spec script on the rounds before making their Miramax deal, not just one, but three studios said "We've got to get a young director to do this, someone with style—like Rob Weiss." Hot young director Rob Weiss. They always refer to him as "hot young di-rector." How many years is this after *Amongst Friends?* And Shannen's right there with the studios. She calls him a genius.

JP: There's something sweet about the fact that she believes in him.

KS: And she does, big time. The first time she referred to him as "ge-nius filmmaker" I really had to choke it back. I saw *Amongst Friends* and while I didn't think it was horrible like my friends did, I also didn't think it was the second coming. I say technically, he's a much better filmmaker than me. He knows how to move that camera around better.

JP: You have to make two leaps of faith here. First, you have to be-lieve that he's primarily responsible as the driving force behind each and every element of filmmaking from script to performance to look to camera movement. That's a debatable point based on what every-body else who worked on the movie says. But you have to discount that too, because people who work on movies are always taking more credit than they should.

KS: That's true.

JP: But the stories from the set indicate that while he may have set the tone . . .

KS: One always has to assume that these things should be taken with a grain of salt too. Catch someone on the wrong day and they'd say, "Oh Kev?! The look of *Mallrats* belongs to Dave." And I'll say, yeah. David Klein deserves a huge amount of credit. I really took the title, Director of Photography seriously, That's basically what he did. Does that hold true for Weiss? Is it true that Weiss fell asleep on the set?

JP: They filmed him in 35mm since of course *Amongst Friends* is one of my three 35mm *real* movies.

KS: What were the other ones?

JP: *Sidewalk Stories*, a silent film, because since there was no sound they could afford to splurge on 35mm. And *Sleepwalk* of all things.

KS: Wow that was 35mm because of Otto Grokenberger. That's too funny. That's three of the least successful films. First timers: "Stay in 16mm. Here's your warning."

JP: Yeah they filmed him asleep on set not between shots, but *during* a shot.

KS: What'd they just turn the camera around?

JP: Yeah. Obviously it wasn't during a shot unless it was a dolly shot off of Trevor's bloody body rising up from the swamp.

KS: "Wait, there's another body in the ground . . . oh, that's Weiss."

JP: Even if you do give him 100 percent credit for everything that's in that film, you have to figure out exactly what that means. Is it just one "big" savvy manipulative pastiche of elements that make you look like a hot young director who can handle "youth themes" and who can handle . . . I refer to it all the time as a film which is brilliant in its deployment of smoke and mirrors to make it appear that there's something there when there's essentially nothing there. It's all surfaces. But attractive ones, for some people anyway.

KS: Well, definitely for the studios if they're saying, "We've got to attach someone young and hot like Rob Weiss." So maybe he achieved what he set out to do, because apparently Shannen maintains that he is a *writer*-director. I remember asking her one time, point blank, "Do you think he's better as a writer than a director or vice versa?" She said, "I think he's equally great at both." I was thinking, "You are snowed." Of course I didn't say that. She sees this guy through love's eyes. Where I'll give this guy any points is the technical craft of filmmaking. But as a writer? How many times have we heard this *Amongst Friends* story? And how believable is that dialogue? And how believable is the whole scenario? I'm not saying every movie has to be believable . . . but there's nothing in that movie that seems very plausible. Including didn't he not wear a helmet when he was riding that motorcycle? I mean where can you not wear a helmet riding a motorcycle?

JP: I'll tell you one thing, he certainly demonstrated how much pride he took in his writing after months of struggle trying to write the voiceover for that opening flashback scene. It has approximately 250 percent more words than can be fit into the available amount of screentime. The issue came up of "Maybe you could cut this back a little bit?" Once he'd written it, no way. Every word was going in the movie.

KS: It's funny, when you watch that trailer you think it's going to be a fast-talking film, which it's not. You can tell they savor each line. You told me your theory on the "We can't get out of here movies," which is just hysterical because it's like, "What, nobody's got a car?" I said that to Shannen once and she got defensive. She said, "Like guys stuck at a convenience store *is* believable?" Uh, Shannen, you got me there [*laughter*]. So, yeah she's in love.

JP: Your characters got as far as the funeral home. They could have kept going when they're being chased out of there.

KS: That's like every movie going back to *Mean Streets*. "Yeah, we can't get out." Nobody's got a car. Nobody can cross the bridge. And I pointed that out, and I listed every movie where they can't get out, and she's going, "When you're in a situation like that, you can't just pick up and leave." I said, "Hey man, if I was in a situation where my one friend was killing my other friend, I'm outta there. I don't want to get mixed up in that." And she says, "Oh if one of your friends killed one of your friends you wouldn't try to kill him?" I said, "*No!*"

JP: She said that?

KS: I swear to God. I mean you have to understand this is Shannen. That's why to a certain degree she calls Rob her perfect match, which is kind of true because he talks the talk. I don't know if he walks the walk. She definitely talks the talk *and* walks the walk. I mean this girl would definitely kick my ass and have a more than fighting chance of doing it too, because she's just such a bruiser. And, yeah, I imagine if someone did try to kill her friend, she would try to quote/unquote whack her other friend. That's why they get along.

JP: Maybe he could direct an outside screenplay. I mean there was an existing *American Psycho* script, he didn't write that, right? That was just a directorial assignment.

KS: She said he got offered a lot of projects that he turned down. And she said that the things he turned in to Universal where he had his deal, the studio didn't want to make. Jacks was there for that conversation and he said, "Well maybe none of the subject matter was commercial enough."

JP: How do you feel, no matter what Shannen Doherty would say to defend him, about a situation where the team that made a movie was so much at each other's throats, and where they hate each other, and nobody can get their stories straight because everybody is so totally unhappy with having worked together both during and in the entire aftermath of the process?

KS: How do I feel about it? I betcha if the movie had been a success all would have been forgiven. I mean, if you read stuff about *Jaws*, when they made it, everyone was at each other's throats, and when they made *Neighbors* everyone was at each other's throats and *Neighbors* tanked and they're still at each other's throats. *Jaws* was successful and everything was forgiven. If *Amongst Friends* had made a ton of money, everybody would have been like, "Hey, what's Rob's doing next? Let's all make a movie with Rob." But since it didn't do well, of course you do get a lot of sour grapes and finger pointing. "Yeah, if we'd all stayed true to this vision, which was mine, then we could have succeeded, or, if he'd followed his vision, which was his, then we would have failed even worse." It goes back to the old Jack Haigis *Straight Out of Brooklyn* thing, "Think about how bad it was before I edited it."

JP: I don't think anybody ever came to grips with what the film really was, or who the film might really be for.

KS: Rob Weiss, man.

JP: That's clear—before, during, and after.

KS: So they thought they were making something largely commercial?

JP: They thought they had a film that could make the rest of my piddling lineup look like the low-level art product that it was. They thought they had a film that could take all those grosses combined and quadruple them. There might have been one moment of doubt. Otherwise there was always some sense of "it's got to be dealt with as big." That means you pay for our apartment to live in and our phone and every single other thing.

KS: That's the pride goeth before the fall. They thought they were making the next big thing and because of that they were entitled to what comes with big things. Even while we were making *Mallrats*, even after the Tom Pollock congratulatory call, even after things were looking really sweet and Universal's really high on it, we still take it with a grain of salt. It's not like we're going to start asking for our own limo or better digs. You can never really tell until the movie's out there, until it's proved itself. As far as asking to be put up while you're making your "low-budget," movie, that's really unfair.

JP: Any further words of wisdom on this subject.

KS: It's a bizarre case. Based on all you've told me and everything I've read about him, I think Rob Weiss typifies everything you don't want to be as a first time filmmaker.

JP: It's almost three years later. I don't know if you're speaking from a moral position or a practical one, because you can't necessarily say this didn't work for him, as you were just pointing out before.

KS: In the end it worked, and it's one of those things where it's kind of unfair that it did work. But the bad attitude gets rewarded—*Milk Bar* is scheduled to shoot late in 1995. [It didn't. Savoy Pictures went under.]

JP: Yeah, I didn't meet Shannen on your set. It's probably just as well.

KS: She was always saying that he was going to be there—that he was going to show up at some point. But then they had that whole fight. I asked, "Well, is he ever going to come out here?" She said, "I don't want him to. He's unsafe."

JP: Really? At any speed?

KS: Second time she came in to audition I said, "Did you bring Weiss with you?" She said, "No, he'd just talk your ear off." So next time around I said, "Is he coming out here or what?" And she's like, "No, he'd just demand a part in the movie."

JP: One obnoxious young filmmaker around here is quite enough.

KS: So you've got Rob Weiss—Pierson's take, Rob Weiss—Shannen's take, Rob Weiss—genius, hot young filmmaker; Rob Weiss —nasty boyfriend and esteem wrecker. Will the real Rob Weiss please stand up?

JP: You'll probably get "whacked" for saying that.

KS: One thing is clear—when you're with Rob Weiss, you are not amongst friends.

JP: There's a tag line.

Amongst Jerks:
Rob Weiss and the Dark Side
of Overnight Success

Toll Money

When I first laid eyes on Rob Weiss he was practically rubbing heads
with the actor Paul Sorvino. It was after a screening of about fifteen minutes of dailies from the first two weeks of production on his suburban
bad-boy epic *Amongst Friends*. I couldn't imagine why the level of intensity between them was so high because I hadn't yet realized that Paul's
daughter Mira played the female lead. Matt Blumberg and Mark Hirsch,
Rob's hapless producers du jour, had invited me to see the in-progress
footage so I chatted with them. Soon enough Sorvino threw in $10,000,
which he may have never gotten back, to keep the production going.
Two weeks later my company Islet wound up committing $263,000,
then $336,000, and ultimately over $600,000 to complete and deliver
Amongst Friends over two years later. By then Rob Weiss had made a
three-picture deal with Universal and a side deal with TriStar with absolutely no end result. In 1994 he started dating Shannen Doherty and
his name was attached to the Ed Pressman production of the outra-
geously violent Bret Easton Ellis novel *American Psycho*. Again nothing
happened. Rob Weiss is no psychotic; he's just crazy like a fox. While

lying in his bed interviewing himself in his father's house in Woodmere, Long Island, he figured out how to beat the system. Unfortunately I became his accomplice, at first blindly, and then because of financial imperatives. I regret it, but therein lies the tale of the dark side of overnight success.

When the actor Tim Roth talked about the experience of working with Quentin Tarantino on *Reservoir Dogs* he told the *Village Voice* that he didn't consider Quentin to be a first timer because "he's been rehearsing all his life." The implication is that he was preparing to be a *filmmaker*, not an instant celebrity; that just came naturally with the territory. For the far more calculating Rob Weiss, the order was reversed. He too had been preparing all his life, but *Amongst Friends*, his first film, was just a means to an end. Rob did write it and even started shooting it before he, or any of the rest of us on the East Coast, had heard anything about *Reservoir Dogs*. His inspiration was a hybrid: Martin Scorsese "the director" crossed with the small-time gangsters in Scorsese's films.

Rob's life seemed to be an audition for a bit part in *GoodFellas*. His upbringing in the posh Five Towns area on the south shore of Long Island, just beyond the wastelands surrounding JFK Airport that *GoodFellas* captures so well, seemed to contain some small hint of danger and excitement. His father, Carl, ran a casino junket business that might have dealt with a few characters on the distant fringes of criminal activity. Carl did have a helper named "Chubby" to take care of problems. Rob wrote the *Amongst Friends* screenplay right around the time that *Straight Out of Brooklyn* was released. Having paid close attention to the backstory legend of Matty Rich, he began shaping his own persona based on the power of suggestion and convenient memory lapses. Rob had been a club promoter at places like Manhattan's Milk Bar; this may have put him in contact with unsavory elements. He briefly studied design at Parsons; he can't remember whether he quit or was asked to leave. Then he studied film at the New School, which he remembers definitely asked him to leave. The only issue is whether he did or didn't strangle a classmate with a mike cord in an acting exercise just prior to his departure. The whole "did he or didn't he" biographical element suggesting danger is best summarized in an ambiguous quote he later gave *Premiere* about whether he had or hadn't killed anybody.

So here we have a genre film, a posturing director, and a relatively slick production. How and why did I get involved? The amazing thing about film deals, even my own, is that they sometimes get made for unexpected and inexplicable reasons. Why would Samuel Goldwyn offer $1.1 million for Michael Almereyda's black-and-white, pixilated vampire film *Nadja* at the 1994 Toronto Film Festival? Is it simply because there was nothing else to buy? Were they desperate knowing that Miramax would grab *Priest*? Did their relationship with David Lynch on *Wild at Heart* play a part since he financed *Nadja*? (Ultimately October Films released this film) I was vulnerable on *Amongst Friends* because I was on the rebound. Islet had tried and failed in its first half year to do deals on *Just Another Girl on the IRT* and *Swoon*. Islet had just been left at the altar on *Swoon* a week before I saw my first footage from Rob Weiss's film.

During the 1991 Independent Feature Film Market two very young "producers" were handing out screening invitations to see dailies at the TVC Film Lab for a new feature that was described as *Metropolitan* meets *GoodFellas*. It was pretty nervy to sneak into the market to promote their film while it was shooting. I soon found out they'd had no choice. Having started with $70,000 raised by Carl Weiss from his casino junket buddies, and the belief that they could get *Amongst Friends* in the can for that amount, the money was all spent two weeks into a scheduled six-week shoot. Many first-timers start production without their full budget in hand; very few budget so ineffectually that the well starts to run dry one third of the way through. Rob's original producer had jumped ship for L.A. after failing to raise $30,000. He soon got an offer to play a bit part on *Beverly Hills 90210*. Somehow a rookie unit production manager named Matt Blumberg and a production assistant named Mark Hirsch were available to step up into the roles of producer and associate producer. They were both intelligent, analytical, and Ivy League-educated; but Matt and Mark were complete film novices. Matt was a Yale anthropology major; Mark had actually gone to the prestigious Wharton Business School. Obviously they were *not* from Rob's world. It was strictly a marriage of convenience. Despite my pit stop at Yale, they also turned out to be way too deluded to be from my world either.

Matt introduced the screening in his very soft-spoken, almost word-swallowing voice as consisting of fifteen minutes of "randomly selected dailies," half with sync sound, the other half silent (MOS). Dailies are the raw material from which you build a finished film in the editing room—the actual, unedited camera takes from production. These turned out to be not so randomly selected. The material with sound focused exclusively on the two chubby, jogging-suit-clad hustlers named Vic and Eddie pitching a drug deal in extreme close-up to the unseen protagonist. They might as well have been selling the movie to the screening-room audience. I was hooked immediately. The balance of the footage was silent and showed scenes of the three central male characters, upper middle class pretty boys, who wind up on the wrong side of the law. Matt immediately started talking about the scale of the movie, how big it looked, what crossover commercial potential it had. Mark piped up with the implied competitive threat of an offer from TriStar Pictures. Since they believed they needed $150,000 to finish, I decided I should read the script to fill in the blanks even if it meant losing out to TriStar in the meantime, a possibility I found highly doubtful. That was the day that Rob Weiss talked Paul Sorvino into writing a check. Sorvino's money, in conjunction with investments from Matt, Mark, and Rob's close friend Jeff Sternhell, prevented production from shutting down.

I went off and mulled. The screenplay was just one cliché piled on top of another in a flat stack. On the other hand, the milieu was different and the direction appeared to be quite energetic. I asked to see more dailies, not just the crowd-pleasing Vic and Eddie. The additional material was unrevealing except for seeing the female lead and figuring out the Paul/Mira Sorvino connection. Finally I spent some time with the auteur himself. Rob Weiss was an overconfident blowhard from day one—which is not to say that there wasn't an underlying charm and uncanny shrewdness to his braggadocio. If I'd had another picture at the time, I would have backed off. I took the plunge.

The production was in desperate straits, but Matt, Mark, and Rob (collectively Last Outlaw Films) tried to pretend that they had some negotiating leverage in the situation. Their act was laughable. I never insisted on more than 50 percent of the equity, nor did I gouge them on sales fees. During week four of their shoot, we moved toward a closing. The major impediment was that the amount of cash they needed increased every other day, rising from $150,000 to $263,000 by the time the deal was sealed—about 70 percent of the cash budget. Late on the afternoon of Friday, October 25, we signed and the Island Records New York office came through with $5,000 in cash (at last I was a bagman) to get through the weekend and pay the one and only unavoidable bill—catering! Ironically, Rob had spent precious production time that week right across the Hudson River from my house around West Point trying to get the perfect mountain roadside motorcycle shot. This shot never wound up in the film and isn't missed. However the ill-advised reach for bigger scale perfection that the motorcycle quest illustrated had rapid consequences.

Once Islet committed funds to *Amongst Friends*, I was the one who temporarily lost any leverage. Because there's never been a fully audited production budget, the explanations are elusive. One fact is crystal clear: The movie went $70,000 over budget in its final two weeks, and the opening flashback sequence wasn't shot. There are check journal entries like $10,000 in petty cash, or $5,000 for tolls. There were added scenes both good and bad for which Matt, Mark, director of photography Mike Bonvillain, or the lead actors took partial authorial credit. At one point, Bonvillain, the unsung hero of *Amongst Friends*, turned the camera around and filmed Rob Weiss asleep on set in his director's chair. Low-budget filmmaking is tough, even when it's not so low-budget; but somebody's got to stay awake.

The other part of the Islet/Last Outlaw deal structure that had complicated the original negotiation involved the deferments. Islet and Last Outlaw had to recoup their investments before any cast and crew deferred salaries could be paid. That was a given. But nobody got into net profits until after those deferments, so the total pool was important. I thought I'd seen it all through the years, but I was totally unprepared when Matt handed me his computer printout with a bottom line of $506,550. It turned out that even the guy who ate a cannoli in one scene without speaking a line got a deferred salary. There were over fifty names, some like Rob himself in multiple categories. There would be no profits until the producer's share of all revenue surpassed $1 million. The Last Outlaw brain trust always assumed that a $2 million minimum sale was probable. Rob seemed to be under the misinformed impression that he could get that from cable television alone, although that prospect made him miserable as an artist. Maybe he just had a premonition that *The New York Times* television listings would call his film "a panting, thin suburban echo of *Mean Streets*. Much noisy posturing."

According to Rob, my problem was that I kept thinking small since my background was "art" pictures like *Slacker*. During pre-production and principal photography *Amongst Friends* had certainly broken all the tenets of low-budget cost cutting. Now it was about to waste a quick $20,000 at the outset of postproduction. While Rob stood by passively in a soon-to-be recurrent syndrome, Matt went to Magno Sound and hired a sound editor who had never before cut a picture. He assembled the narrative very conventionally, and it had absolutely no punch. Rob always said, "You can learn everything technical you need to know about filmmaking in three days . . . Welles said it, or Hitchcock—one of those guys." The first editor was fired and Last Outlaw was now $90,000 over budget. As we moved into the dead of winter and I prepared to leave for Sundance (where I would see *Reservoir Dogs*), I laid down the law: From now on, a low-salary editor working in a low-cost editing suite.

The answers were Leo Trombetta and Troma Films. Leo was another sound editor looking for an opportunity to get out of that box. He turned out to be very talented but a little thin-skinned. Rob got to play the role of bully while masquerading as an artistic perfectionist. First he would instruct Leo to find imaginary takes that didn't actually exist, then he would disappear for days on end, until finally he would pop up with threats that Leo better change certain sequences "or else." This psychodrama was enacted on the unheated top floor of a building on Eighth Avenue, which was the headquarters for cheesy horror schlockmeisters Troma. They must have been between sequels of *The Toxic Avenger* since the postproduction floor was empty. The building was a walk-up and it was inspiring to walk past posters for films like *Surf Nazis Must Die* in the stairwells. Although we missed the original target Cannes deadline by a mile, *Amongst Friends* slowly began to round into shape. I was well practiced by now in the art of watching rough cuts, but this one horrified me. There was no there there. When Rob told me he aspired to make a film like Michael Mann's *Thief* or Phil Joanou's *State of Grace*, I began to realize that we were dealing in surfaces, surfaces that would hide the absence of content or meaning; but how could a modestly budgeted film pull that off?

Since Matt, Mark, and Rob were always acting cocky, I offered them their first chance to buy back 100 percent of their movie at cost at the end of February, 1992. They'd finally managed to film some pickup shots and the material for a boyhood flashback opening sequence just before then. Rob was disgruntled because I'd told him to forget the ultimate motorcycle sunrise (or was it sunset?) shot. I was disgruntled for three reasons: no one, not the director, producers, editor, or double-duty DP, had a clue how to cut together the prologue; the kids didn't really look like their grown-up counterparts, who were difficult to tell apart for starters; and Rob was blocked on writing the voiceover to stitch everything together. Voiceovers after the fact are frequently a sign of trouble, a BandAid over a hemorrhage. In rare cases—like the super 8mm footage narrated by Matt Dillon in *Drugstore Cowboy*—this strategy can work in an artistically seamless way to save the day. I had my fingers crossed.

Other early rough cut screenings were fairly disastrous—except for the Vic and Eddie scenes that had hooked me in the first place. I had other filmmakers like Nick Gomez and Bob Gosse of *Laws of Gravity* in to take a look and they were pretty critical of the unmodulated, "pedal to the metal" pace. Rob explained to me that other directors are a terrible sample group because they're jealous and competitive. I thought he was describing himself, although in this great American land of opportunity he would wind up having the last laugh. I wasn't laughing. I was looking for a way out of a financial quagmire. Although I had never done it for other filmmakers, Islet was even paying rent and phone bills for Matt and Mark on the theory that their apartment was the production office. Essentially they forced my hand by claiming that they would otherwise have to stop supervising postproduction to take other jobs, thus leaving Rob in charge. Rob came at no cost, since he was still living at home in the Five Towns. Occasionally the production had to pay for a parking lot when someone drove him into Manhattan for a friendly visit to Leo Trombetta's Troma editing room.

Eight months into postproduction, we hit a wall. I had given Last Outlaw a second chance to buy me out with money they theorized could be raised on Wall Street. Unsurprisingly nothing happened. Islet's $263,000 had been spent for an unmixed, double system version that was at least another $75,000 away from completion. The one encouraging sign was that a lot of scratch music had been laid into the crude soundtrack to drive the movie forward and give it some added emotional weight, and it was working. In a real coup, Rob and his producers had persuaded Mick Jones of Big Audio Dynamite (formerly of the Clash) to give them the plaintive song "Innocent Child" for the prologue. Mike Bonvillain suggested the idea. Jones didn't stop there; he volunteered to score the entire movie for studio cost only. Of course only about three minutes of his three hours of material appeared in the finished film, but the gesture was much appreciated.

We had to team up to face Eric Eisner of Island World when we screened the picture for him in early July. Eric was a little slow off the mark when he returned from a July 4 white-water rafting trip. The days came and went as Rob and Matt cooled their heels for an entire week in Los Angeles waiting for him. Eisner already had enough indie distraction because this was also the peak of the Nick Gomez/Marky Mark casting brouhaha and he was working on rewrites of Michael Moore's *Canadian Bacon*. When he finally managed to cross Sunset Boulevard for a double system *Amongst Friends* screening, a splice broke about twenty minutes into the film. He walked out impatiently. By doing so he gave Rob, Matt, Mark, and me something we hadn't really had since signing our deal: a sense of solidarity. Ann Dubinet, Island World's foreign sales head, put the icing on the cake by showing complete disinterest. After telling me that I'd be throwing good money after bad since *Amongst Friends* had none of the brash originality of *Laws of Gravity*, Eric Eisner told me it was my decision to make on whether to put in the additional $75,000.

Finally I shared the Last Outlaw feeling of embattlement because my neck was on the line. I had a two-step strategy. We spent another $12,000 to create an all-new improved scratch mix containing a wish list of potentially costly music such as the Red Hot Chili Peppers combined with then unknown new bands such as the Stone Temple Pilots, whose first record had just been released. I remember getting carried away and telling Rob he could even use a Guns 'N Roses track if he wanted, which he didn't. Then we started the distributor screening rounds with the fine picture cut minus opticals, two intertitles to mark the passage of time, and credits. It was almost *exactly* the version of *Amongst Friends* that brought Rob fame and fortune five months later. Fine Line Features saw it first in New York; acquisitions V.P. Bob Aaronson found it wildly implausible. Miramax was next; once again they already had *Reservoir Dogs,* which awaited release. Then Marcie Bloom from Sony Pictures Classics found it unworthy of their highbrow standards. West Coast screenings covered Goldwyn, Universal Pictures, then Universal's newly formed joint venture with PolyGram called Gramercy Pictures. Zanne Devine was Universal's liaison to the new division, which was headed up by Russell Schwartz after his stints at Island and Miramax. No one rejected *Amongst Friends* out of hand, but no one came close to biting either. Screening an unfinished first feature is almost always a pointless exercise. In this particular case, it may not be coincidental that four of those companies would later compete fiercely over Rob Weiss once the "Sundance factor" kicked in.

The final double system showing of *Amongst Friends* that would ever take place was a Sundance screening for Geoff Gilmore and his associate programmer, Cathy Schulman, in the first week of October. They invited the movie pretty much on the spot, which was a good thing since the ambitious Rob Weiss had already relocated to Los Angeles by then and was lurking about in the projection booth. Rob had quickly secured an agent, United Talent Agency's John Lesher, and a manager who were quick to accept credit for the Sundance selection. I had to laugh. No one was closer to that process through the years than me. But Geoff and Cathy simply loved the film. He thought of it as this year's equivalent to *Reservoir Dogs*, while she wrote a program note that gushed, "a film so pure in style it appears spontaneous. Weiss captures the beat of a generation . . . intense and frighteningly real."

Even I started to get excited again as the saga of *Amongst Friends* entered year two.

HITCHCOCK: WHO NEEDS HIM?

Geoff Gilmore invited *Amongst Friends* to Sundance exactly one year to the day from the original dailies screening. Although the festival was more than three months away and the film still needed to be mixed and completed, I began to obsess on the deal. Both film submissions and attendance at Sundance went up by 30 percent, to 225 features and 5,000 people respectively. It seemed like festival fever would soar to an all-time high for the hot films. I wanted to make sure that I didn't miss a beat. One sales strategy that came to mind was the ticking clock premise of making a deal *during* Sundance just before the awards were announced. I even wrote a memo to Island World's chief financial officer on December 3 which said, "The goal from here is to make a deal by January 31, 1993—the final day of the Sundance Film Festival." My research showed that films had certainly been sold in the weeks before and the weeks after, but none during the actual ten days of the event. In fact no one had even made a phony on-site announcement of a previously struck deal.

I also wanted *Amongst Friends* to be linked with and epitomize any common festival theme. Well this was certainly a terrifying illustration of the proverbial warning, "Be careful what you wish for, because it may come true." Rob Weiss became the walking and talking embodiment of that year's defining image: the "twentysomething filmmaker." When Geoff and Cathy asked, I heedlessly agreed to moderate a panel including more than half a dozen of the sizable twentysomething contingent. I had no bias about wisdom or discipline coming with life experience, but it did strike me as truly remarkable that the median first-time filmmaker age had plummeted from mid-thirties to mid-twenties in less than ten years. Rob was fretting throughout the prefestival wait that he would have absolutely nothing to say on this panel, that he would sit there like a statue. I didn't worry about that for a second.

I did have to worry about his picture's final cut and mix. Rob had caught optical fever; the first reel of *Amongst Friends* had over two dozen dissolves. Since dissolves are a fuzzy aesthetic replacement for a hard cut and all opticals are costly, I didn't savor this approach. Rob wouldn't listen to any of us. I asked Barry Brown, editor par excellence, to come in for one last stint as an editorial consultant. After all the picture had only been in the cutting room for an entire year. Why not three more days with a fresh set of experienced eyes? Knowing of his frequent collaboration with Spike, the troops were shocked when Barry walked in because they expected him to be black. I was happy to authorize his fee because he saved the production an equivalent amount in discarded dissolves. Barry would say "that would be a great straight cut" and Rob would go "check!" In truth Leo Trombetta had done an excellent job (even while receiving death-threat notes), and nothing else really changed.

Sound work was more complicated. Once Rob had written the opening voiceover and declared it done, lead actor Steve Parlavecchio simply had to figure out how to speak at "Weiss-speed" (which is two steps beyond warp speed.) If viewers couldn't decipher it all, that would simply add to the mystery. Director Maggie Greenwald had her post-production office for *The Ballad of Little Jo* down the hall at Todd-AO; she claimed she'd never heard young boys cuss, scream, and fight so much about everything. I explained that it's always painful giving birth to a masterpiece.

Part of the film's punch was inevitably going to be supplied by its wall-to-wall music. Matt and Mark had gone to Kathy Malta at Sony Music Licensing and made a festival deal for about ten songs, ranging from Tony Bennett to the Beastie Boys, with a preset amount for the theatrical upgrade. Sony and other labels were just beginning to get very aggressive about music licensing for independent film soundtracks. They'd just hit big with Cameron Crowe's Seattle-grunge compilation for *Singles*. On its own the Sony sum wasn't out of whack, but *Amongst Friends* also had about that many songs again from Warner Special Products. One in particular, "I Could Have Lied" by the Red Hot Chili Peppers, we didn't even list in the press book knowing that there would be big rights problems. Matt and Mark were generally evasive when I asked them where the music money was supposed to come from. I said no when they asked for a break in getting Island's "Low Spark of High-Heeled Boys" by Traffic. Otherwise I put on blinders, crossed my fingers, and figured that we'd let the chips fall where they might after Sundance. Of course they'd led me to believe that those "chips" would never total more than $75,000 to $100,000, far less with a soundtrack record deal.

The first finished print of *Amongst Friends* was ready about twenty-four hours before its first Saturday night Sundance show. This last-second rush was becoming pretty standard. What was *not* typical at the festival was something that I highlighted in the press notes: "Nineteen people who were involved in making this film, most in their mid-twenties, will be attending Sundance." The total actually reached twenty-three. They came by plane, train, and automobile; "Vic and Eddie" drove from New York in their Cadillac. This conveyed a real sense of camaraderie, which should have been taken with a grain of salt, like the film's ironic title.

When much of this group assembled for breakfast the morning after the premiere, their future looked very bright—so bright in fact that Rob was wearing sunglasses inside. He had been close to self-immolation just before his 10 P.M. show (the *Reservoir Dogs* memorial slot) started the night before. Now he'd mellowed out. Although he couldn't eat, his chain smoking was less frantic and he managed to sip a little orange juice. After many postscreening accolades, he had instantly taken the Hollywood crown as "hot young director" of Sundance 1993. I was eating like a horse, confidently knowing, after fifteen long months, that *Amongst Friends* would be sold for a tidy sum.

The feeding frenzy around Rob and his actors left the producers out in the cold. Quentin Tarantino and Lawrence Bender have remained a very tight director/producer duo over time. Rob Weiss had no use whatsoever for Matt Blumberg and Mark Hirsch. He wouldn't even acknowledge Matt and Mark publicly at Sundance until I tried to force the issue. After threatening to punch me out, I thought he agreed to thank them before each show after they thanked me. When he failed to do it, he said he forgot. Matt and Mark had a very hard time grasping the simple, if unfair, notion that each independent film has only *one* "auteur" as far as the industry and journalists are concerned. I repeatedly tried and failed to drive this point home. Even if Rob had been more generous, they still would have been buried.

Rob didn't need to sort through offers from dozens of agents since he already had John Lesher in place. He didn't have to worry about whether to stay near his roots or move to L.A.; he'd already moved out. He was fond of pointing out that he lived in a black and Latino neighborhood from which he would regularly jog through South Central. (There's a line in his film about "sixteen-year-old Jewish kids thinkin' and acting' like they're Flavor Flav.") Although the announcement was held for the festival, Lesher had already made Rob's first Hollywood deal. Cary Woods of Fried/Woods Films, a production company associated with TriStar Pictures, signed Rob to write and develop a hit-man movie called *Murder, Inc.* Cary, a former William Morris agent who had represented cutting-edge indie talents like Gus Van Sant, was impressed by the energy in an early screening of *Amongst Friends.* He also had some discretionary funds burning a hole in his pocket, so he took a flyer. Knowing how long it had taken Rob to write the voiceover for his own film, I figured Cary would be waiting for a while. I didn't guess that Fried/Woods would be totally disbanded with Cary at Miramax/Disney and Rob Fried heading production at Savoy Pictures without Rob Weiss having written a single word of *Murder, Inc.* for them. One day over lunch, I asked Cary Woods what Rob had delivered; he held up a plain, white, blank napkin.

The slick surface, attractive actors, and Five Towns milieu of *Amongst Friends* made Rob a very appealing figure to a number of male studio executives. By the time the festival ended, Universal Pictures had the inside track. Shortly thereafter they announced a three-picture deal with Rob Weiss. None of this action would profit me; Rob's future was his own, thank God. I tried to see him less and less as Sundance zoomed along. The lowest point was the infamous Twenty Somethings: The New Generation panel, where he had predicted he would become catatonic.

Whatever skills I have as a moderator were useless that day. I'd acquitted myself pretty well on several previous occasions in Sundance and all around the United States, but this callow youth theme was a lost cause. With Rob there, almost nobody else but his new friend Jennifer Lynch could get a word in edgewise. Although she's the daughter of David Lynch and made the intentionally perverse, unintentionally derivative *Boxing Helena* for several million dollars, Jennifer managed to explain how "five years of lawn mowing and beading bracelets" had gotten her film done. Robert Rodriguez explained that the only way to hear his production story was to attend an *El Mariachi* screening with his formally scripted twelve-minute prescreening presentation. When I opened with a quote by L.M. Kit Carson from that day's *New York Times* about these young filmmakers being the "television generation," several panelists countered with an ad hominem attack, denied watching television, then proceeded to cite *The Brady Bunch* or some other seminal seventies tripe over the next two hours. Knowing Kit's credits, Bryan Singer supplied the tersest quip: "Has anyone ever seen the remake of *Breathless?*"

And then there was Rob. I asked about influences after briefly explaining my theory that aspiring to greatness results in different work than just believing that you can make better films than most of the studio crap that's out there. Rob explained that his sense of film history went "all the way back to the early seventies" and that he'd seen essential movies like *The Wanderers* twenty times (or was it twenty-something?) In a postscript he added, "Hitchcock? Who cares about him?" Rob's single most supportive critic, Peter Travers of *Rolling Stone*, apparently got a big kick out of all this because he later reported, "Such Generation X candor raised a few hackles. A voice yelled, 'Will somebody shut him up?' To Weiss's credit, nobody could."

I felt miserable about this panel for months afterward. The only saving grace was that it was sponsored by the Gap, and I got the first jean jacket I'd ever had in my life. Months later I was wearing it one day when I finally got up the nerve to watch the videotape and relive the pain. I found myself probing the subtext, and suddenly I realized it wasn't so bad . . . and it certainly wasn't my fault. One really obvious good point was the panel's diversity. There were two women; one, Leslie Harris, was

African-American. (Even if she was actually over 30, she was 29 when she started *Just Another Girl on the IRT.*) Robert Rodriguez was Hispanic. Tony Chan was Asian American. Although Rob might have been an extreme case, they were all desperate to make it and they had all tailored their stories accordingly. Tony Chan made *Combination Platter* in his father's Queens restaurant and still waited tables there. Jennifer Lynch talked about everything except her father—beads, Kim Basinger, knocking down doors. Leslie did the struggling black-woman filmmaker routine. Robert Rodriguez, old *El 7,000* himself, mastered the art of aggressive humility. There was media mastery across the board, and at one key juncture I asked a direct question about it. At the time I'd been very frustrated with the nonanswers. The videotape showed the reality. The way that each participant sidestepped or put their own spin on the response proved how media savvy they really were—the children of Matty Rich.

After all this wheel spinning on *Amongst Friends* I was willing to embroider on Rob Weiss's spin until the cows came home—or the awards presentation at least. The fourth and final screening had been a mob scene of press and distributors. Goldwyn, Gramercy, and October had been in the hunt all week. Finally Fine Line's Ira Deutchman set aside his staff's mixed reports from earlier screenings, saw the film, and joined the race. We took a frigid walk outside as I explained the ticking-clock deal concept. Ira immediately got it and grasped the added promotional value. The other distributors had been slow on the uptake. Goldwyn's pitch that year was to emphasize their success at promoting first timers from Jim Jarmusch to Kenneth Branagh, Matty Rich, and Mira Nair! Apparently they forgot that Mira made *Salaam Bombay* (not to mention several feature documentaries) before *Mississippi Masala*. October was splitting their vote between *Amongst Friends* and Victor Nunez's third feature in thirteen years, *Ruby in Paradise*. Gramercy, via PolyGram, was being unusually frugal. PolyGram's Robert Jones eventually would acquire most of our Western European rights for $380,000. I shouldn't have been selling those rights myself, but Island World's Ann Dubinet was nowhere in sight at Sundance.

The hours before the awards were frantic. I really hoped that Fine Line or Goldwyn would jump way up to $1 million for North American rights because I knew that nothing less would begin to satisfy Matt, Mark, and Rob. I had already gleaned that feature writers loved Rob's story, but a number of critics found *Amongst Friends* to be bogus. Poly-Gram's head Michael Kuhn refused to budge on the Gramercy offer despite the possibility that Rob was heading to Universal, the joint venture partner. Two hours before showtime, Fine Line went as far as anyone would—$750,000 for North America. A novice producer once told me that this size advance was "the standard deal" as if you could just fall out of bed in the morning, pick up the phone, and say, "send over the check." He found out the hard way when he produced an unreleasable feature called *Fall Time* which was not entirely unlike *Amongst Friends*. The Fine Line offer and Ira's appreciation of seizing the moment meant a lot. Matt and Mark spurned it. Although I was under no obligation to heed their opinion, I told Ira no.

We were fully expecting to win the Audience Award, and believed that it would take the film to the next level. With two dozen cast and crew members in Park City, we figured that we'd gotten out the vote (if you know what I mean). The people behind the Dramatic Competition entry *Inside Monkey Zetterland* had been seen casting many ballots. The agents from ICM and the executives from Columbia Pictures had been working hard for Robert Rodriguez. We just put "Vic and Eddie" outside each screening hustling voters as they walked past the ballot box. Unfortunately everyone had been so nervous, and I'd been so distracted, that we'd failed to work the very first screening. And that's undoubtedly why we lost by a "fraction of a point" (according to Geoff Gilmore), to *El Mariachi*. In a bizarre split, *Ruby in Paradise* and Bryan Singer's semicoherent *Public Access* shared the Grand Jury Prize—clearly a prize that *Amongst Friends* was never going to come close to winning. The irony is that Singer had just as much flash and just as little thought as Weiss. Despite his dismissive comment about L. M. Kit Carson, he was a much nicer person. Yet *Public Access* was never released in North America and I was stunned later when PolyGram and Spelling International financed Bryan's second feature, *The Usual Suspects*. The old days of needing a first-time theatrical success before landing a follow-up opportunity were long gone; now you didn't even need a theatrical release! The ultimate irony is that Bryan Singer's second feature was terrific—full of engaging directorial flourishes with an airtight script by his screenwriting partner.

Rob proceeded to prepare to set up shop in his Universal bungalow while Matt and Mark drove the print around L.A., taking a few meet-

ings on the side. Rob made fun of them for not knowing how to bluster their way through. Mark outdid Rob's hubris by claiming that he
wanted to attach Tom Cruise to one of his projects. Why not be optimistic? They once explained their four-step procedure: "Set out to do
something—begin—discover unanticipated difficulties —overcome." I
stayed back in the office allowing only ten days of follow-up screenings
prior to the sale of the film.

The studios took a look as production executives got excited. Then
distribution heads like Barry London at Paramount or Barry Reardon
at Warners would take one follow-up look and pass in thirty seconds.
October Films threw its lot in with *Ruby in Paradise*, which was available for about $500,000. PolyGram focused on the foreign side. Skouras
Pictures tried to join the bidding late with the support of an Island executive who also sat on their board; I found them wanting in the area
of theatrical distribution. Their primary financing now came from a
Paramount Home Video output deal so they had to wait until Paramount passed. Lloyd Levin at Largo Entertainment kept making noises
about getting involved "somehow," but clarification was never forth-
coming. He seemed offended at Sundance when I had the nerve to ask
how Largo, which was *not* a distributor, might release the film. John
Lesher gave me a look like I'd just belched in the guy's face. Maybe
Lesher was still upset that I'd expressed skepticism when his United Talent Agency bosses assured me that they could get Michael Kuhn to double or triple the Gramercy offer. I never really minded the onslaught of
Hollywood types in the Sundance indie film axis except when they
presumptuously (and ineffectually) stuck their noses into my business.
Predictably the final bidding boiled down to two of the major independents—Goldwyn versus Fine Line. Not wanting to "soup" the deal,
I brought the issue to a head on February 10. Ever since *She's Gotta Have
It*, my Goldwyn relationship had been slightly strained. Then *Roger &
Me* greatly exacerbated the situation. Tom Rothman was sometimes
quick to call me money-grubbing. In this case, the Goldwyn offer for
world rights (minus Germany, where we expected a big deal) was nearly
identical to the sum of the Fine Line offer plus the PolyGram European
package. However, they were nervous about the unresolved music
issues.

I went with Ira at Fine Line; it was our first distribution reunion since
Parting Glances at Cinecom in 1985. Rothman complained that I

hadn't even been interested in talking about the Goldwyn release strategy. In a way, he was correct. Ira had already expressed both the pros and cons of handling *Amongst Friends* without any prompting from me. He was the master of media manipulation and press angles. He had also reduced the advance to $650,000, since our magic moment in the Utah snow had come and gone. I thanked Matt and Mark for settling me down when I'd wanted to make the sale on the spot. Between the $100,000 lost on the advance and the $150,000 that they soon informed me the music was going to cost, Last Outlaw had actually managed to create a scenario in which a $1,030,000 total in sales revenue was disappointing to them. I was jubilant. The back end of the Fine Line deal was fairly creative skewing in our favor in home video and in their favor on cable television. Little did I then know that net profit deal points would be just about as meaningful as Monopoly money.

MURDER INK

In the press release announcing the deal in the trades, Ira Deutchman said that while he expected good results, he knew that it was not "one hundred percent certain that it would be universal across the board, because the film is not what people normally expect from an independent film." His prediction came true with a vengeance. In the months of soft magazine feature coverage leading up to the release of *Amongst Friends* on July 23, the response was 100 percent encouraging and entertaining. In the one and only month of the theatrical release of the film, the actual hard reviews were nearly 100 percent critical.

Not only was Ira an unflappable gentleman in the face of these changing fortunes, he was also a good sport about numerous song changes and an endless wait for the myriad music licenses and elusive soundtrack deal. In fact at one point I heard him state publicly that the real test of a producer's relationship with a distributor wasn't a mutual success but a flat-out disaster. I wondered if he was looking at me and making a prophecy. I also knew that the increasingly successful and dominant Weinsteins would never be caught dead talking like that.

Potential hints of disaster peeked through right away. Although I had my own shorthand description of *Amongst Friends* as "YoungFellas," I wasn't happy when other people started those Scorsese riffs. Coming out of Sundance, the *Village Voice* called it "GoodFellas Lite" while the *L.A. Weekly* went with "GoodFella Jr." *Premiere* dubbed it "Boyz in the

Chutzpah" while *Details* resorted to "Weiss Guy." "Cocky" quickly became the adjective of choice to describe Weiss; but as long as Bruce Weber was photographing all the pretty boys in the cast for *Vogue,* all was well with the world. Maybe Rob was right about me and my small pictures. I'd never had a movie with a four-page spread in *Vogue,* or a full page in *Sassy,* or a jeans layout in *GQ.*

Then *Premiere* returned to the scene in July 1993 with a longer story, also headlined "Weiss Guys," just as Rob was twitching over having bought $4,000 worth of new furniture. He complimented himself at the end of the story by saying "Man, is this great dialogue or what?" However the single most telling moment, and perhaps the beginning of the end, was a pull quote at the top of the page which read, "I'm not going to say I killed anybody. I didn't kill anybody—but I'm not gonna say I didn't. You know what I'm sayin'?"

I called Ira and publicist Mary Lugo at Clein and White and asked them what they thought. They tried to reassure me that Rob made good copy. I even sent him a note encouraging him to keep plugging away with his promotional work because it made a big difference. Unofficially I showed the *Premiere* piece to ten innocent bystanders; nine said "asshole." In case there was any doubt, headlines soon turned into "Vanilla Weiss" and "Mean Tree-Lined Streets."

Somewhere around the "I did/I didn't" controversy, Matt and Mark described their concept for the film's release. Matt asked me if I'd seen the ads for *The Crush,* a large-budget Morgan Creek production being released by Warners with at least $12 million in P&A support. I told him that I had and asked if there was something about that campaign that appealed to him graphically. He said no; he just liked the size of the newspaper ads and frequency of the television spots. When I told him I didn't understand, he proceeded to suggest that Fine Line should release *Amongst Friends* the same way. I explained that their initial P&A commitment was about 4 percent of that amount and hung up the phone having realized that a Yale degree in anthropology does not preclude massive delusions about the film business.

Matt and Mark had other bigger worries. I'd pulled the plug on their free rent, and Con Ed sent them a disconnect notice, which they forwarded to me. If the film had been delivered with cleared music, they might have had some cash on hand—assuming, of course, that Rob hadn't snatched it. Although Rob was telling people that he'd gotten a

AMONGST FRIENDS MUSIC LICENSE SUMMARY

All the Young Dudes	$3750.00	Chysalis	8/13/94	$10,000.00	Sony	9/1/93
	$11250.00	EMI	8/16/94			
Brass Monkey	$7500.00	Polygram	6/23/94	$15,000.00	Sony	9/1/93
	$7500.00	Def Jam	10/17/9			
Brooklyn	$4000.00	First P	11/1/93	$3,500.00	WSP	7/17/93
Confusion	$0.00		8/1/93	$0.00		
Crawl	$2,500.00	Sweet Water	8/19/93	$3,000.00	WSP	7/17/93
I Could Have Lied	$15,000.00	Moeb.	5/25/93	$15,000.00	WSP	7/17/93
I Shall Be Released	$15,000.00	Dwarf	8/1/93	$7,000.00	CEMA	9/2/93
Intro	$5,000.00	EMI	8/16/93	$2,000.00	WSP	7/17/93
It's a shame Ray	$2,400.00	Bug Music	6/23/93	$4,000.00	WSP	7/17/93
	$1,600.00	PolyGram	6/23/93			
Jesus	$5,025.00	Warner/Cha	5/18/93	$7,000.00	WSP	7/17/93
	$2,512.50	LBM	8/26/93			
Kid's Alright	$2,000.00	Matador	12/1/93	$4,000.00	Bette S	11/16/93
	$2,000.00	4AD	8/1/93			
Love Scene	$5,000.00	Harry Fox	8/16/93	$15,000.00	Sony	9/1/93
Never				$5,000.00	Sony	9/1/93
Passing me by	$15,000.00	EMI	8/16/93	$4,000.00	WSP	9/1/93
Piece of Pie	$3,000.00	Floated	9/15/93	$3,000.00	WSP	7/17/93
Skydreamer	$7,500.00	Harry Fox	6/23/93	$10,000.00	Sony	7/17/93
Train Going Backwa	$4,000.00	Harry Fox	5/21/93	$4,000.00	WSP	9/1/93
Vertical Interlude	$4,000.00	Warner/Cha	5/21/93	$5,000.00	WSP	7/17/93
Wild Child	$3,000.00	HTH	8/1/93	$3,000.00	WSP	7/17/93
Wild Thing	$5,000.00	Varry White	6/22/93	$6,000.00	WSP	7/17/93
Yankees	$500.00					7/17/93
Score	$2,156.57	Voice of London		$2,156.57	Jones	
ST	$136,194.07			$127,656.57		
synch	$136,194.07					
master	$127,656.57					
Total	$263,850.64					

special deal from the Red Hot Chili Peppers because he knew Flea, the only special deal that Last Outlaw had made was a $30,000 license with a penalty clause if the song was used in any advertising, including the trailer, or even listed in the press book. Mott the Hoople's "All The Young Dudes," and the Beastie Boys' "Brass Monkey" also cost $30,000 each. The Band's version of Dylan's "I Shall Be Released" was a steal at $22,000. A rap track by Pharcyde called "Passing Me By" had already been licensed for Universal's *CB4* for less than $5,000. The act was on Atlantic Records, our eventual soundtrack label. So for Matt, Mark, and Rob the special price was only $19,000.

In addition to the Pharcyde track, a series of eight other switchovers to WEA/Atlantic soundtrack titles necessitated another Todd-AO sound remix. Since this was meant to be an opportunity to rerecord the opening voiceover and make some other improvements throughout the film, Rob flew in for the occasion as did his buffer, Mike Bonvillain. Matt insisted that I should pay airfare for both of them. I had a hard time swallowing even one ticket for Mr. Three-Picture Weiss, and categorically refused to front the money for a director of photography to go to a sound mix. Then John Lesher called to demand that I rent a car for Rob during his New York stay. I blew my stack. Lesher's response was, "Why are you so confrontational? It's not as if Rob's asking to be paid for his time." Rob's name was on a contract obliging him and Last Outlaw to complete and deliver a film to Islet so that we could deliver to Fine Line and our foreign buyers and get paid, and he was looking for perks. I told Lesher we didn't need him at the mix. Then Rob called himself to make his case with the implied threat that his promotional efforts might flag. Fine Line didn't need him in New York right then. I was stumped and livid. I never told him to move to L.A. I just couldn't fight with him anymore. I told him that on principle my company refused to pay, but that I would personally if he was strapped. I thought that he would refuse the offer. Obviously I still hadn't grasped Rob's piggish nature.

This run-in occurred at a key moment in the financial history of *Amongst Friends*. Even with the soaring music costs, Islet was guaranteed to recoup its fees and investment. Two years into the deal, bank interest had eaten up just about all the profit. Rob's car, had it been a production expense, would have come out of Last Outlaw's deferment pool. Rob and his producers were simply not examining the chain of consequences. Playing the part of numbers cruncher, I wrote, "Given our *known* revenue expectations of $1,030,000, any dollar spent now reduces the deferment pool below 25 cents on the dollar." Then I put on my prophet hat and added, "In the worst case scenario where the film's performance is marginal, we may never make up the difference. Rob, what are you going to tell all those people? You're not going to blame me!" Oh I forgot to mention the fact that except for the replacement songs, Rob refused to change anything else during the $18,000 remix. He claimed it might jinx his film's charmed life. Two months later, delivery costs crested around $350,000 above and beyond Islet's $336,000 investment. On paper, the pro rata deferment payout dropped to 8 cents on the dollar.

In the interim, *Amongst Friends* was released. It was jinxed, and it was marginal. Fine Line's initial exclusive runs were, in many cases, nearly invisible, so the film never reached a wider platform. The critics were quite harsh, sometimes hilariously so. Matt Zoller Seitz wrote the single most insightful critique in the *Dallas Observer:* "It's a wonder Weiss is still alive. Sounds like the epidemic of teenage drug killings in wealthy Long Island neighborhoods might be the biggest missed story of the eighties . . . In many ways, Weiss, despite his moronic bluster, deserves sympathy . . . Even if his timing had been better, *Amongst Friends* would still feel metallic, hollow, and lifeless."

In general, two things struck me as unfair in the reviews. One was the Scorsese complaint. Admittedly the *Mean Streets* cycle was utterly exhausted and Rob compounded the boys-with-guns clichés by shooting himself in the foot repeatedly with his arrogant behavior. Rob took the heat, yet the critics couldn't have known that he started *Amongst Friends* way back around the same time as *Reservoir Dogs* and before Nick Gomez. Two years of postproduction made the film marketable but only to an audience that had already moved on. The second fallacy was the frequent claim in negative reviews that *Amongst Friends* had been embraced by many critics. Aside from Peter Travers, the good pile is a short stack. Owen Gleiberman in *Entertainment Weekly* theorized, "Could it be that people are now so eager to find the Next Big Thing that they can't resist trying to create it?" Apparently Rob was being penalized for his transparent ambition because this comment perfectly describes film trends in the nineties.

The release was basically history by Labor Day. The attempt to come

Vanilla Weiss

The director of *Amongst Friends* on his style, his critics, and growing up white and dangerous on the mean streets of Long Island

By Matt Zoller Seitz

"At film schools, you have all these kids from the suburbs who are writing gangster films that take place in the city. And that's so far removed from them. It's just empty formal posturing. They should be writing stories about sitting on their couch watching gangster films."

—Independent Long Island filmmaker
Hal Hartley

"You gotta be kidding!" Rob Weiss, director of *Amongst Friends*, hollers to his pal Rick, who's hanging with him in Room 1071 of Manhattan's posh Mayflower Hotel during the movie's press tour.

"Hey, get this," Weiss tells the reporter on the other end of the phone. "We ordered up some room service, some juice. Turns out these things are like 15 fuckin' dollars apiece. Damn! Fifteen dollars apiece! Enjoy it, I guess. We got 30 bucks worth of fresh fuckin' juice right here in front of us. I'm glad I'm not paying for this. Whoever is is getting murdered on this thing."

Spoken like a true Horatio Alger—a tough-as-nails street kid who grew up underprivileged, made a splashy directorial debut that got Hollywood's attention, and is at last enjoying the fruits (and fruit juices) so long denied him.

Problem is, Weiss isn't Horatio Alger. He grew up wealthy in the Five Towns section of Long Island; his father, an importer, gave him the $20,000 nut to begin financing *Amongst Friends*. Weiss raised $70,000 more by hitting up friends and relatives in the area.

Amongst Friends—a flashy, violent melo-

> ## Weiss dollies his camera, tilts it, does the handheld hokey-pokey with it, but never for any discernible reason.

drama about three rich Jewish kids from Long Island who get sucked into the brutal world of small-time gangsterism and discover, too late, that they cannot escape—grabbed heavy press attention at the Sundance Film Festival this year. Now Weiss is being courted by the big boys in Hollywood. For the past week, Weiss has been doing 10 to 12 print and broadcast interviews a day. Clearly, he's tired of certain recurring questions and answers them in a surly, impatient honk—a hybrid accent

that's Long Island sneer plus MTV faux-gangsta rapper.

Ask him, for instance, about *Amongst Friends'* position in the canon of violent films by twentysomething directors—a subgenre that includes *State of Grace, Boyz N the Hood, Menace II Society, GunCrazy, My New Gun, Laws of Gravity, The Living End, Straight out of Brooklyn,* and *Reservoir Dogs*—and Weiss becomes almost livid.

"My movie is not a *gangster movie*," he says. "I gotta tell you, I'm gettin' real tired of hearing that all the time. Every time I pick up a newspaper I see some critic saying my movie is yet another Martin Scorsese knock-off, that the camera moves and everything are stolen from *GoodFellas. GoodFellas* this, *GoodFellas* that, Scorsese and *GoodFellas*. They've called it *Good-Fellas Lite* and *Mean Streets 90210* and other shit. All I can say to that is 'Fuck you.' That's a shortcut in thinking. They're taking the easy way out, taking the cheap shot, because they don't actually want to sit down and really *think* about my movie and what it's saying, so they slap a label on it, call it *GoodFellas 90210*. What the fuck is *that* all about?"

Critics say *Amongst Friends* reveals more about the gangster movies Weiss worshiped as a kid than the psyche of Weiss' generation? Well, for their information, Weiss' film is *autobiographical,* dammit.

"I mean, some of the camera moves are similar to some of what Scorsese did, moving the camera a lot, and of course I respect his films, but I didn't *copy* him," Weiss maintains. "This is *my* style. This is how I make movies. I mean, from the technical aspect, yeah, there's a voice-over by the narrator, and there's a voice-over in *GoodFellas,* too, but so fuckin' what? Those are cinematic devices. You gotta look at the story and the characters, look at what the film is saying. These guys are the kind of guys I *ran* with growing up."

Well, then, autobiographical or not, aren't the three main characters in *Amongst Friends*—Trevor (Patrick MacGaw), the sensitive friend who just wants to get by; Bobby (Joseph Lindsey), the crazy, dangerous, ambitious friend; and Andy (Steve Parlavecchio), the conflicted narrator who must somehow navigate these two poles of behavior and come out alive—just a tad familiar? Aren't they even *vaguely* reminiscent of the characters in *Mean Streets* or, for that matter, such Scorsese-influenced films as *Menace II Society* and *State of Grace?*

"The guys my film is about, and a lot of the guys who are *in* the film, are guys who came from my neighborhood," Weiss says. "People say they can't believe there are guys like Bobby in Five Towns, hoods and criminals and guys who are crazy and just don't give a fuck, but I *knew* these characters. I mean, I knew guys who make the

Faux-B-boy hoods (Frank Medrano and Lovis Lombardi) glower at the hero of Rob Weiss' inane *Amongst Friends.*

guys in this movie look like *nothing*. I knew guys who were a lot worse than Bobby. I knew guys who were *50* times crazier and more violent than Bobby."

Fifty times more violent?

Really?

It's a wonder Weiss is still alive. Sounds like the epidemic of teenage drug killings in wealthy Long Island neighborhoods might be the biggest missed story of the '80s, right behind the S&L scandal and Iraq-gate.

In many ways, Weiss, despite his moronic bluster, deserves sympathy.

He's in an unfortunate position. The recent rise of the twentysomething gangster film (and make no mistake—that's exactly what *Amongst Friends* is, whether Weiss will admit it or not) has given American moviegoers a whole new mountain range of cinematic experiences, from the peak of Quentin Tarantino's *Reservoir Dogs* to the valley of Phil Jouanou's awesomely boring and derivative *State of Grace.* And before that, audiences have had four decades' worth of gangster pictures to fondly recall, from the jaunty urban swagger of Cagney and Bogart and the Dead End Kids to the postwar pessimism of Stanley Kubrick's *The Killing* to the affectionate '70s revisionism of *Farewell My Lovely* and *The Long Goodbye.* If *Amongst Friends* had come at the beginning of this current wave—which owes its first and most passionate allegiance to Martin Scorsese—instead of arriving late in the game, who knows what the critics might have said?

Probably not much, I'd wager. Weiss dollies his camera, tilts it, does the handheld hokey-pokey with it, but never for any discernible reason—just to screw around and play MTV. In the new Hollywood, however, this is called "stylish," and it's enough to get you noticed. Even if Weiss' timing had been better, *Amongst Friends* would

still feel metallic, hollow, and lifeless—as devoid of real feeling as Irwin Winkler's 1992 remake of *Night and the City,* which, like *Amongst Friends,* re-creates the camera moves and wiseguy arrogance of Scorsese's films without capturing one iota of their gut-crunching immediacy.

Don't get me wrong: I'm not saying *Amongst Friends* is bad because Weiss didn't grow up poor and/or black. Weiss' film is bad because it's a vacuous exercise in style, crammed to the gills with ridiculously clichéd visual tics, like the 360-degree whirling camera used to convey disorientation; crushingly familiar characters and situations, like the scene where the cigar-chewing, elderly crime boss reassures one of the boyz not to quit his crew because, whether he knows it or not, he's *amongst friends*; and a half-assed sociopolitical awareness which, rather than making the film seem hip and self-critical, only makes it seem more clueless.

For instance, when a friend of Trevor's bitches about how Trevor and his friends are irrationally obsessed with black culture but don't really understand it, the film temporarily threatens to investigate its own complex origins. But because it's only alluded to in the rest of the film, never really explored, this theme ultimately seems more an excuse for white B-boy posturing than an explanation for it.

"Kids today are very influenced by urban culture," Weiss says. "Everybody wants to believe they had to struggle to make it. The guys in my movie are like that. There are tons of kids in Long Island like that. A lot of my brother's friends are like that—into rap, talking all this shit about Scotty Pippen, and here they are driving around in a Jeep Cherokee."

Good point. Too bad it's never directly confronted in Weiss' movie. When Weiss talks about how his characters are brain-

Continued on next page

Vanilla Weiss

Continued from last page

washed, how they're conditioned by society to "feel like they have only one choice," he's onto something; from the womb to the tomb, American consumer culture trains both wealthy white kids and poor black kids to think that getting rich at all costs—whether to escape the 'hood or please Daddy Megabucks—is the way to go. But by failing to truly explore this idea—by letting it serve as a crutch on which to support a bunch of boringly glitzy bad-boy set pieces—Weiss drops the ball. In that sense, *Amongst Friends* is a lot like its director: both mistakenly believe they're a lot smarter than they really are.

Maybe the real problem—of which *Amongst Friends* is but a symptom—is that, with few exceptions, the independent film industry in this country isn't independent anymore, either in financing or in choice of subject matter. Count the number of times you've heard supposed indie filmmakers eagerly confess to interviewers that they made their first film to "get a foot in the door" in Hollywood, and you'll be counting all day. Rather than nurturing the next John Cassavetes or Melvin Van Peebles or Stan Brakhage—iconoclasts whose determination to experiment drove them to independent filmmaking because it was the only option they could live with—the industry has become a farm team for Hollywood.

In this dysfunctional world, Quentin Tarantino somehow stitches together bits of Peckinpah, Scorsese, Kubrick, and Fuller into one spectacular heist script; makes *Reservoir Dogs*, a bloody, intelligent, weirdly original gangster flick; then uses that film's success as a springboard to write bastardized versions of the same material for Tony Scott (*True Romance*) and Oliver Stone (*Natural Born Killers*). Tarantino doesn't seem to care that the ferocious commitment to an independent, cutting-edge vision that made *Reservoir Dogs* so terrific is almost impossible to sustain in Hollywood. Why should he? When you're hanging with Christian Slater, who has time to think about it?

Ultimately, Tarantino—and Weiss, who shares many of his sensibilities—aren't making gangster films as a vehicle to comment on America, or their generation, or even their generation's affection for Hollywood B movies and cheesy cop shows. First and foremost, they're making gangster films because they love gangster films, period—and because gangster films are part of a rigidly defined genre, with plenty of potential for splashy sex and violence, and are thus easier to use as a Hollywood calling card than something like *Slacker* or *Just Another Girl on the IRT*.

With these maxims in place, the key question for young filmmakers who dream of having their buddies don expensive suits, tote handguns, and whack people changes from "Is a gangster movie really the best way to say what I want to say?" to "What can I do to make my gangster film marginally different from other gangster films and thus justify having made it?"

Gangster pictures can have artistic value or political importance: look at *GoodFellas*,

which used the genre to turn Reagan-style laissez-faire capitalism inside out; or *Menace II Society*, which used gangster (and gangsta) hyperbole to investigate the hypocritical posturings of white liberals and the black middle class; or *Reservoir Dogs*, which compensated for being derivative and emotionally shallow by mercilessly critiquing both American pop culture and itself.

But what's irksome about *Amongst Friends* is that it gets the relationship between form and content backwards; rather than, say, using the gangster-film genre to comment on the disillusioning moral climate in which today's youth were raised, the film uses prattle about disillusioned youth as a pretext to make yet another gangster film. *Amongst Friends* is gangsterism for gangsterism's sake. Again, there's nothing inherently wrong with that credo; but when you see film after film after film embracing it, you begin to wonder whether some talented (and artistically relevant) new voices aren't getting drowned out by gunshots and jukebox oldies.

In that respect, Hal Hartley was

Director Rob Weiss on his detractors: "They don't really want to sit down and think about my movie."

absolutely right; his films are hit and miss, but in his own idiosyncratic way at least he's investigating how grown-ups in his native Long Island live, love, and die, rather than using blather about autobiographical influence and the corruption of Generation X to justify making a nonmusical version of *Bugsy Malone*.

All that stuff doesn't bother Weiss. He already has his foot in the door. Pretty soon he'll be helming a Bruce Willis cop flick or a direct-to-video psychosexual thriller starring Marc Singer and Sally Kirkland. Or something. Anyway, when your room service is comped, who cares?

"OK, listen," says Weiss. "What I really wanted to do with *Amongst Friends* was...RIIIICK!" he bellows. "Yo, yo, yo, yo, yo, Rick, Rick, Rick! *Rick!* Put it *up!* Put up the *volume!*

"Hold on a second!" Weiss yells into the phone. "Listen to this! The trailer for my movie is on TV! It's on TV! Rick, put it up!"

There is a brief pause, during which the faint sound of televised synth music and gunshots can be heard over the howling of Weiss and his friend Rick.

"How d'ya like *that?*" he asks, getting back on the phone. "Know what? You just lucked out, man. You just witnessed a piece of *history.*" 00

Amongst Friends tag lines

You don't have to come from the streets
to be a gangster

When betrayal is a way of life
You don't know if you're amongst enemies or . . .
AMONGST FRIENDS

From trust to betrayal.
From jealousy to violence.
From ambition to murder.

AMONGST FRIENDS

When you grow up rich and privileged,
The respect you earn on the street
Isn't something you can buy
It's something you've got to pay for
AMONGST FRIENDS

Andy, Trevor & Billy
Three guys who found trouble, and
Then found out they were amongst friends.

Until your life is on the line,
You never know if you're truly . . .
AMONGST FRIENDS

They always knew what they wanted,
Now, all that stands in the way of their ambition . . .
Is each other.

AMONGST FRIENDS

It was always the three of us
Until what we wanted the most
Destroyed all we had

Money.
It was the beginning of the friendship.
And the end of it.

In a suburb where gangsters
Live next to dentists
Next to lawyers
Three kids grow up seeing
What makes their world go round.
Money.

Three kids growing up
In a suburban world of privilege
Where money makes the rules
And power makes the money.

They grew up
In a suburban world of big houses,
Nice cars and rich fathers.
They wanted something
Money couldn't buy.

Danger. (Respect?)

My grandfather was a bookie
His money sent my dad to law school.
My dad did everything
So I could grow up to be whatever I wanted.
All I ever wanted was to be like my grandfather.

Three rich kids from a good neighborhood.
They don't need to break the law.
But they like the challenge.

Three rich kids from the suburbs.

Some people break the law because they have to.
They do it because they like to.

Three kids from a rich suburb
Where living was easy.
But crime made them feel alive.

They grew up rich.
But they wanted something more.
Respect. Power. Danger.

Power. Money. Privilege.
Three rich kids who didn't have to earn it.
So they stole it.
In a suburb of privilege and prestige
Three kids who want the only life
Their fathers' money can't buy.
A life of crime.

They came from the right neighborhood
But they chose to live on the wrong side of the law.

Three rich kids
Sharing a dream.
To make it big in the world of crime.
When their dreams came true
So did the nightmare.

In their neighborhood,
Kids grow up to be doctors, lawyers, and stockbrokers.
But these three friends had different ambitions.
And chose a life on the other side of the law.

Three friends.
Power came between them.
Money divided them.
And betrayal destroyed them.

Best friends.
They grew up rich.
They grew up privileged.
And they didn't need college for their chosen career.
Mobster.

Three rich kids from a good neighborhood.
They were given everything.
But deciced to take what they wanted.
At the point of a gun.

Rich kids.
Their parents' money let them choose any future.
Instead, they chose a life on the wrong side of the
law.

The lure of danger.
The seduction of money.
The price of ambition.

Sometimes crime makes you pay

Three rich kids from a sheltered suburb,
Who always knew what they wanted to be . . .
Mobsters.

AMONGST FRIENDS
Some childhood dreams do come true.

Rich kids from a suburban world of privilege.
They could have been anything they wanted.
But all they wanted was respect.

Trevor. Billy. Andy.
Suburban rich kids who wanted
Something different out of life.

The thrill of crime.
The respect of the streets.
The power of the mob.

The lure of money.
The seduction of power.
The price of betrayal.
AMONGST FRIENDS

They didn't realize what they had.
Until it was gone.

They thought they were privileged.
They thought they were powerful.
They thought they were . . .
AMONGST FRIENDS.

Trevor, Billy, Andy
Power. danger. respect.
When you're amongst friends
You'd better worry.

Never underestimate the power of money.

They never had to earn anything . . .
Except respect.

Money can't buy respect.

Respect.
It's something money can't buy.

Trevor, Billy, Andy
Played bad guys since they were kids
Then the game got dangerous
Don't worry you're . . .
AMONGST FRIENDS

They longed for the hustling, petty gangsters day of
their grandfathers
But the rules had changed.

Billy, Andy, and Trevor played bad guys since they
were kids
But then the game got dangerous.

Billy, Andy, and Trevor played bad guys since they
were kids
Then the rules changed.

Suburban kids playing bad guys
Until the game got tough

Billy, Andy, and Trevor played bad guys since they
were kids
Until the game got serious (dangerous?)

Billy, Andy, and Trevor played bad guys since they
were kids
Until the rules changed

Playing tough guys was fun until it became a reality

Playing gangsters was a gas until you got caught

Billy, Andy, and Trevor played bad guys since they
were kids
Then they got caught

Nobody knew that the bulge in their pockets were
guns.

Is that a banana in your pocket or are you . . .
AMONGST FRIENDS

Trevor, Billy, and Andy do like girls . . . really!!

They had everything . . . so they stole.

They were born with everything but they wanted
more.

They were born with everything but that still wasn't
enough

They played for power, would the game tear them
apart.

It was only a game . . . but the game got rough.

It was only a game . . . but the game got dangerous

They were born with everything they'd ever need
except respect

They had everything they would ever need. So they
stole.

They had money, power and the respect of their
neighborhood
They thought they had everything
They thought they were . . .

AMONGST FRIENDS

Born with everything, they wanted more.

Life is about making money. Or is it?

Some things money can't buy.

Money comes and money goes. Some say friendships
are the same.

You do it once, you can do it everyday.

Anybody can get whacked. Anybody.

It ain't just happenin' over there. It's happenin' over
here.

There are some things it may take your whole life to
understand.

The choices a man must make are not always easy.

Your best friend is sometimes your worst enemy.
Always watch your back.

Some rocks are better left unturned.

The world can seem a harsh place unless you are
AMONGST FRIENDS.

Friendships are *supposed* to last forever.

Isn't friendship supposed to last forever?

What could sever the bonds of childhood?

Who can you trust if not your best friend?

Some lessons can't be taught in school.

From the playground to the streets.

Good doesn't always triumph over evil . . .
AMONGST FRIENDS.

When it comes down to it . . . who can you trust?

up with a perfect tag line had lasted longer. There were over eighty suggestions. We started in Sundance with "They had everything . . . So they stole." Eventually it became "Lifelong friends. Born with everything, they wanted even more. The only thing that stood in their way was each other." Along the way we considered "They never had to earn anything . . . except respect," "Playing tough guys was fun until it became a reality," and "Anybody can get whacked. Anybody." In a lighter moment, Rob's music supervisor, Jeff Sternhell, came up with "Nobody knew that the bulges in their pockets were guns." Maybe it should have been "The rotten apple doesn't fall far from the tree."

Carl Weiss was featured in the Long Island edition of *The New York Times* as a result of his son's film. I learned that his alias had been Tony Fanelli because his boss felt Jewish guys "don't make good collectors." I also learned that Chubby, his henchman, had once required the fire department to remove his 460 pounds from a collapsed chair. Carl suggested that he had Rodney Dangerfield attached to his script "The Junketeer." I felt sympatico with Rob's dad because we were the two who'd funded his kid.

Unlike Matt and Mark, Carl Weiss had bigger worries than his utilities bills as the months went by. Other than small signing advances, which had been applied toward delivery, Islet had still received and distributed no money. At one point, Carl offered to send Chubby to Sony to help collect the music licenses. His gambler friends (with names like Nick G. and Chuck S. according to my investor list) were getting tired of waiting. Hell, a normal, everyday, well-capitalized corporation like Island World was getting tired of waiting. I was between a rock-headed producer and a hard place.

Essentially I had my last direct contact with Matt and Mark in late September1993, when I sent them a letter that is excerpted below:

Islet and Carl Weiss are the primary reasons that *Amongst Friends* exists, since there are no movies made without money and no one else ever gave you any. During their fifteen minutes of fame, filmmakers often convince themselves that they would have found the financing somewhere else because of some inevitable fate. I find that notion patently absurd.

Having provided the opportunity of a lifetime, Islet gets nothing else from this film but its sales fees and its totally just, contractual, first position return on investment. (Given my internal 10 percent per annum in-

Investor List / Money Spent To Date
20 October 1991

Mr. Weiss	$52,500
Paul Sorvino	$10,000
Hunter Adams	$10,000
Hayley Guzman	$1,000
John Novack	$2,500
Nick G.	$2,500
Chuck S.	$2,500
Mike	$2,500
Tom Maseko	$2,500
Grandma Weiss	$5,000
Phil Weissman	$2,500
Mike Rappaport	$2,000
Mark Hirsch	$2,500
Matt Blumberg	$5,000
Jeff Sternhell	$10,000

=========

$113,000   ~ raised

$103,000 ~ spent

terest rate, my return is wiped out anyway.) We don't get three-picture first-look deals at Universal Pictures. Neither do you! But that's because you allowed yourselves to become passive/aggressive victims in a situation that benefited your employer Rob Weiss, his pretty-boy actors, and even his father. It's Rob Weiss whose interests you work for, not me. After nearly two years, you still fail to grasp the nature of our relationship. Islet is not a producer; John Pierson is not a producer. Islet is an investor, copyright co-owner, and sales agent. You, on behalf of signatory Rob Weiss, are struggling to fulfill the legal obligations of Last Outlaw Films to Islet.

Throughout the last year, you've threatened on more than one occasion to get other jobs—as if that would have derailed completion and delivery. If only you had made good on that threat and I had hired a professional postproduction supervisor, everyone would have been spared much bumbling, battling, and brinksmanship—not to mention saving some bucks.

Your reference to me as the "voice of experience" seemed a little sarcastic. I don't need to blow my own horn. I'll let the entire movie industry and nineteen other filmmakers pass judgment on my skills in the "first-time filmmaker business." The problem is that until *Amongst Friends*, I'd never been involved with your particular combination of pigheadedness, blind optimism, woeful ignorance (remember *The Crush?*), vague answers, and championship whining. You always imagined *Amongst Friends* as bigger than all my other films as if that should increase your sense of entitlement. As a result, you generally refused to hear or acknowledge the relevance of any other poverty-stricken producer tales of the past. Nobody on my roster has ever had a postproduction office once they left the editing room. Several edited in their bedrooms! Well, now that your movie is demonstrably not bigger than say *Slacker*, I could regale you with current stories about the two young women from Chicago who are finishing *Go Fish* in New York while sleeping on the floor. Or I could mention that the *My Life's in Turnaround* team seems to be able to keep up with the film's demands out of their homes without pestering me to pay either one of their rents or phone bills.

Would my attitude be different if *Amongst Friends* had been a success? Very possibly—but it's not. And I'll fill you in on the way the film's failure is playing with all the other distributors out there. No one would suggest that Fine Line did a good job, but the degree of the catastrophe leads to two conclusions: 1. An enormous sense of relief over not being stuck with a hopeless film and 2. a belief that "yours truly" performed another magic act in his ongoing history of remarkable deals.

I feel terrible that you think I couldn't "trust" you. I never said so. Did you not lead everyone at Island World to believe that the music license money was a very short-term cash flow? Have you not told Tim Craig at Frankfurt, Garbus for over a month that the Sony master license agreement would be faxed the next day? Did you not have Island World set aside $59,500 (accruing interest) on August 25 for Warner Special Products and then not pay them? [They did three months later.] Can you not understand why someone in my extremely exposed position might find it difficult to trust you?

Don't call me. Don't write me. Especially, whatever you do, don't fax me since I wouldn't want to see another $11.65 charge for fax paper on your next expense report. Actually I strongly urge you to send all your expense reports, phone bills and rent bills to the commander-in-chief of Last Outlaw Films, Rob Weiss—or of course his trusty agent John Lesher. They'll be your co-stars in the *Amongst Friends* chapter of the book.

Your pal,
John Pierson

The music licenses and film were finally delivered in December. By then, the U.K. opening had made the U.S. release look like a smash hit. *Reservoir Dogs* had been a bigger hit there than here; that fact inspired the original acquisition. I received a producer statement from Poly-Gram with a bottom line so minuscule that I asked for a list of the names of all the people who had seen the film. I had spent hour upon hour for the entire year trying to execute the foreign deals and make good on delivery. Lesher had been unable to persuade Rob to travel overseas to promote *Amongst Friends*. It was probably just as well.

Rob wasn't anywhere close to having a "go picture" although he'd been hanging with Oliver Stone. To fill the gap, he quickly agreed to act in the film *Jimmy Hollywood* when director Barry Levinson asked him. The day I learned this news, Doris Toumarkine of the *Hollywood Reporter* called to see if I had any news tidbits. Now Doris wasn't always the world's best reporter. She once called Islet "fallow" ground for indie filmmakers. I asked her what she meant, and she proceeded to explain that she'd never mastered the difference between the words "fallow" and "fertile." Anyway studio friends of mine had seen the Levinson script and told me that Rob's part would be that of the "obnoxious young film-maker." I told Doris that Rob was going to be in Barry Levinson's new Paramount film about Hollywood, playing the "obnoxious" young film-maker. She followed up with Paramount in order to file an item, after which she left me a message saying that I'd been "mostly correct:" Barry Levinson was making a film about Hollywood at Paramount in which Rob would appear. However the studio pointed out that he wasn't play-ing the "obnoxious" young filmmaker; he was playing the "passionate" young filmmaker. And therein lies the tale of Rob Weiss. In his one brief scene in the finished film, neither word comes to mind. He's actually (gulp) appealing.

Many people called *Amongst Friends* "GoodFellas 90210". Well, Rob's original producer, who left for a bit part on that show, never made it as a regular. Rob was able to direct his passion toward Shannen Do-herty, and she toward him.

Islet made its money back. My hair turned gray around the ears. Ira Deutchman no longer runs Fine Line, although this fiasco had little to do with his demise. The 23,000-unit video release made up for about half their loss. Rob freaked out when New Line Home Video mentioned Scorsese's name on the box. I like seeing it on my shelf because the genre description on the spine says Gangster/Crime. Carl Weiss was arraigned on Long Island in January 1995, on charges of grand larceny and fraud. Maybe Chubby could help.

THE ODD COUPLE: SUNDANCE 1994

ou Reed and the Velvet Underground asserted that one's life could
be "saved by rock 'n' roll." Well, mine was redeemed by dykes 'n'
dicks. The despair I felt throughout my relationship with Rob
Weiss and his producers tainted my overall attitude towards
younger filmmakers as a group. Fortunately at the very beginning of
1993, just before the *Amongst Friends* Sundance, I saw twelve minutes
of footage from Rose Troche and Guin Turner that would become
Go Fish. As their feature was rounding into shape much later that
year, I saw a very long version of Kevin Smith's convenience store epic
Clerks. Now I'm not a lesbian, and I've never had a slave wage job—
with or without under-the-counter oral-sex discourse. But I was simply
thrilled to get involved with two films that I loved, both made with a
lot of heart.

I had adopted a simple, new, three-part test for getting on board with
any film post-Weiss.

1. Do I love the movie?
2. Do I think there's a theatrical market for the movie?

3. Do I have a good feeling about being partners with the film production team?

Only a 100 percent score constituted a passing grade. Two out of three wasn't good enough. I vowed that I would never again choose a movie that I didn't personally embrace, even if it seemed like it might be highly marketable to distributors. And I would never even be tempted by a terrific movie with a great hook made by a prima donna careerist. I read both Kevin and Rose the riot act on this point. With the full knowledge that rules are made to be broken, and that the independent film world was changing every day, I tried to start anew with this three-part mantra. *Go Fish* and *Clerks* fit the bill individually; it was an extra added bonus that the "go-go Girls" and the "clerky boys" bonded.

Go Fish started its charmed life as *Ely and Max* in Chicago in the spring of 1992. Chicago is a city with a burgeoning indie film scene. I've tried to show my support in every possible way with frequent appearances and contributions to the excellent local *Chicago Film Letter* (now defunct). Around the time I read about a local lesbian feature called *Ely and Max* New York producer Christine Vachon called to tell me about it. Rose and Guin had just approached her and her partner Tom Kalin, a Chicagoan, for help. Since I was on my way out there, I planned on meeting them and seeing as much of their material, from the 60 percent of the film that was shot, as they could show. No one filled me in on the interpersonal data that Rose and Guin had been a couple when the movie started, but had subsequently split up.

When they walked into my hotel room, I guess no one had told them what to expect of me either. They seemed a bit nervous and self-conscious, while I just curled up in my stocking feet on my bed to watch their extremely raw black-and-white footage. Many of us in the biz were on the lookout for the right lesbian audience feature. As Christine later said, "the so-called community was looking for this kind of movie." The sample scenes from *Ely and Max* had charm and spunk, but they were crudely assembled and filled with awkward cutaways to close-ups of tapping feet. Guin played a glamorous lead role while her co-star V. S. Brodie felt like a real person. I read Guin's script which contained some very elegant writing but an extremely thin story line. This caused a moment's doubt about expanding to a feature-length film. Christine, the experienced professional, reassured me, then Rose, the articulate, hilarious and enthusiastic director, described her spinning top/visual strategies. For the meager sum of $53,000, it was impossible to say anything but "yes," especially after I learned they hadn't wanted to take any money from a man. One could argue that it might have been better business to provide $70,000 on the condition that they start over from the beginning in color.

I didn't see Rose and Guin again until mid-May. I returned to Chicago for an all-day summit at the MacArthur Foundation to pry loose some additional funds for *Hoop Dreams*. Afterward I saw a few reels of their rough-cut scenes. Rose and Guin still had a long way to go and were already behind schedule, especially if we were going to Toronto in September. But the spirit of the film felt perfect. I knew that I could count on Christine to ride shotgun on the physical side of postproduction. Once Christine and Tom Kalin brought Rose and Guin to New York over the summer, progress on the film was slow but steady. Rose was doing her own painstakingly beautiful optical printing for the experimental transitional sequences in the film. Kay Armatage of the Toronto Festival saw only about fifteen minutes of the movie and instantly invited it; I guess it fit the right profile.

I was looking for a better title than *Ely and Max*. I have a personal bias against film titles with two names in them (except *Thelma and Louise*). These two particular names also sounded male or unisexual. When I suggested considering a title change to something a bit livelier, there was some initial resistance. Christine acted as emissary. When she called me one day with some potential new titles, she told me there were three in ascending order of preference. The first was *Leave It to Beaver*. I told her to stop busting my chops just because I wanted to make it easier to sell the film. The second was *Once Upon My Girl*; I apologized for being a straight man (in both senses) and told her to spare me the last one. But she kept going with *Go Fish*. I said, "I don't know if they're serious, but that's a great title."

The first draft of the *Clerks* script was called *Inconvenience* and Kevin even had his own tag line: "A Story of Bads and Goods." By the time Kevin Smith was shooting his film on the overnight shift in the spring of 1993 at the Leonardo, New Jersey, Quick Stop where he worked all day, it was called *Clerks*. A year later Miramax would coin the real tag: "Just because they serve you doesn't mean they like you." *Go Fish* actually didn't seem to have enough screenplay for a full feature, *Clerks* had enough dialogue for one and a half—not to mention its violent, highly dramatic ending. Kevin rehearsed his cast intensively to deliver his rapid-fire lines, then shot the film in twenty-one straight days. Unlike Guin, he didn't have to work on his own lines for the character that he plays since Silent Bob is literally that. Guin and Rose shot off and on over a full year. Consequently Guin's performance in her own film required amazing consistency.

As fall began, and the *Amongst Friends* soundtrack hit the cut-out bins, *Clerks* and *Go Fish* both came to the attention of Sundance. I arranged a private screening of *Go Fish* for Geoff Gilmore and Cathy Schulman on Friday, October 1. Coincidentally, David O. Russell's *Spanking the Monkey* screened directly in front of us. I'd known its producer, Dean Silvers, and executive producer Janet Grillo, for years, and they'd asked me to finance postproduction. I couldn't get past my qualms over the incest scenes, but I was impressed that New Line's Grillo had scored left-over *House Party 3* raw stock for her husband David's feature debut. It ran forty minutes over, pushed us back, and resulted in Gilmore's leaving our show before the final twenty-minute reel. Without speculating too much about all the whys and wherefores of the six week delay in inviting *Go Fish*, or whether we really needed to recruit seminal lesbian critic B. Ruby Rich as we did to advance our cause, *Go Fish* eventually made the festival line-up. So did *Spanking the Monkey* and half a dozen other very low-budget titles—including *Clerks*.

Clerks had to travel a far more serendipitous route. Kevin reached the dubious conclusion, after reading a *Slacker* feature by Amy Taubin in the *Village Voice*, that his great hope was the Independent Feature Film Market. When the market staff assigned *Clerks* an 11 A.M. screening slot on the final Sunday (October 3), Market Director Rachael Shapiro assured him that it was great positioning because he could work the crowd for an entire week beforehand. Screening attendance was almost nonexistent, and Kevin must have thought his print was headed to the meat locker at the Quick Stop. There was some impostor wearing Ira Deutchman's Fine Line badge, and a crazy woman ranting about neo-Nazis in New Jersey. In a near miraculous twist of fate, a guy who failed to identify himself on the way out started a long-lasting domino effect.

Bob Hawk found *Clerks* to be both hilarious and haunting, or as he eventually wrote in his Sundance program note, "a wail of ennui." As a member of the festival's advisory committee, he pushed the film un-

	CARD LIMIT	CASH ADVANCE	INT.
DISCOVER —	4000.00	4000.00	19.8%
PRUDENTIAL VISA —			9.9%
BANK-AMERICARD VISA —	1800.00	1800.00	19.8
CITIBANK VISA —	2600.00	2600.00	19.8%
CITIBANK MASTERCARD —	2600.00	2600.00	18.8%
FLEET VISA —	3000.00	3000.00	14.4%
AT&T MASTERCARD —	2000.00	2000.00	15.9%

JAN FILM LAB

10¢ PER FOOT — NEG
13¢ PER FOOT WORKPRINT

$$
\begin{array}{ccc}
400 & 400 & 400 \\
\times .23 & \times .10 & \times .13 \\
\hline
1200 & 000 & 20\,00 \\
8000 & 4\,000 & 4000 \\
\hline
92.00 & 92.00 & 60.00 \\
\end{array}
$$

$$
\begin{array}{c}
92.00 \\
\times 8 \\
\hline
736.00 \\
\end{array}
$$

tiringly and effectively. He was responsible for bringing it to the attention of writers Peter Broderick and Amy Taubin. Amy tracked down a skeptical Kevin to request a tape, then featured their phone conversation and the movie in her *Voice* column; it was the first press coverage outside of Monmouth County, New Jersey. Everyone started peppering me with calls, imploring me to check out the film. At the time, I was trying to convince myself that I was out of the repping (without financing) business; I also already had two potential Sundance entries. When *My Life's in Turnaround* was rejected, I was ready to contact Kevin. But he beat me to the punch.

His journal entry picks up the story:

> The first time I heard John Pierson's name was in a conversation I'd had with Bob Hawk. He was described as a miracle maker, a treasure hunter.
>
> "If John Pierson likes your movie," Bob promised, "you'll get distribution."
>
> It was the first time I'd heard that particular sentiment, but certainly not the last. And while it's in no textbook (yet) the Pierson Promise—as it's known—still finds circulation, traditionally from one filmmaker in the know to one up-and-comer.
>
> Others echoed Bob's words over the next few weeks: Amy Taubin, Peter Broderick, and more. The anticipation had reached a fever pitch by the time I finally spoke to the man himself.
>
> It was a Friday night. After waiting—like a schoolgirl, hoping to be asked to the Prom—for his call, I took the initiative and called Pierson myself. It was about six at night, so I figured I'd hear back on Monday, if I was lucky. And one hour later, while I'm on my way out to see *The Nightmare Before Christmas*, the phone rings.
>
> It was the man.
>
> I could scarcely believe it. This player was calling me on a Friday night, mere minutes after I called his office, no less! And from his home, for God's sake! But that's what's so cool about John Pierson: He makes you feel important; so important that you warrant a call on a Friday night from his home. So important that he gets back to you right away.
>
> We talked. I sent him a tape. A week later, I heard back from him. He loved the movie, thought it was hysterical, but wouldn't know how to sell it. "If you're ever in town . . ."

And that was where I believed my connection with John Pierson ended. And it did . . . for about a week.

Seven days later, I get another call from the man, who admits to having watched the film a few more times. He has an idea to vastly improve its chances of getting picked up.

More calls followed. Each time he broke down a little more. On one occasion he actually said: "Sooner or later, we're going to wind up doing this officially."

And we did.

The crucial missing link in Kevin's story is what happened when his tape arrived. I was out of town, so Janet watched first. When I returned, she told me very simply, "If you're not repping films anymore, you better not watch *Clerks*." This was our equivalent of the line in the Uncle Remus Tar Baby story, "Whatever you do, don't throw me in the briar patch." Obviously, like *Working Girls* and *Laws of Gravity* in earlier years, she loved it and acted as an catalyst. Once I watched, my resistance broke down.

We sat down to make a plan. Kevin kept calling me Mr. Pierson and refused to change until he'd proven himself. He quickly agreed to cut Dante's murder at the end of his Quick Stop shift, the ending originally inspired by *Do the Right Thing*—a "real movie." Since the Sundance invitation had come in, we had to figure out what strategy to follow before the festival. Audiences always improve comedies; but I'd laughed myself sick at the *Clerks* tape and I concluded that its true fans (or likely buyers) would do the same. Kevin's deal expectations were very modest —a $75,000 advance prior to Sundance would have been a keeper, especially from his preferred distributor, Miramax. Since he'd already sent Mark Tusk, their acquisitions V.P., a video copy, it seemed like the right approach to make the film available to the other major independents —Sony Classics, Fine Line, October, and Goldwyn.

Although I was systematically withholding *Go Fish* from every distributor, Goldwyn had an inside line on both films due to strange circumstances. In a case of extraordinarily bad timing suggesting egregious conflict of interest, Sundance Associate Programmer Cathy Schulman accepted an acquisitions position at Goldwyn during the festival selection process. She filled her new company in on *Go Fish*, although she was looking for a more glamorous lesbian film, and charted a course away from *Clerks*, a film that made Sundance over her objections. When Goldwyn's competitors later complained about them having an unfair advantage, Triton's Jonathan Dana pointed out that all those whiners "should have hired her."

Although I wasn't a recent staff deserter, I also had an insider's knowledge of the 1994 lineup. Twelve of the seventeen features in the Dramatic Competition had approached Islet for completion financing and/or representation throughout 1993. This was logical, since it turned out to be the year when the ultra low-budget aesthetic was totally dominant. I didn't feel the need to celebrate an across-the-board philosophical victory. I just wanted to position my two dramatic features and help *Hoop Dreams* in any way possible. I persuaded Christine Spines to write about all three in the *Premiere* Sundance preview. Selling seemed like it might be harder this time because the previous festival's releases had failed pretty abysmally. All of the Twentysomething panel films had lost money along with films by grown-ups like Jefery Levy's *Inside Monkey Zetterland*, Keva Rosenfeld's *Twenty Bucks*, Michael Steinberg's *Bodies, Rest, and Motion*, John Turturro's *Mac*, and Martin Bell's *American Heart*. October Films managed to eke out a small profit on *Ruby in Paradise* through very hard work.

I felt unabashed. The *Go Fish* hook was a warning to distributors to see it or weep on the first Friday of the 1994 Festival. There were two pieces of bait: *Claire of the Moon* and *She's Gotta Have It*. *Claire* represented the lesbian "floor" and Spike (an obvious artistic inspiration) the breakout potential. As the direct link to Spike's debut, I felt particularly comfortable writing to distributors that *Go Fish* "just might become for the lesbian audience what *She's Gotta Have It* was for the black audience." I had a twinge of guilt about exploiting *Claire of the Moon* until I remembered sitting through it. With dreadful reviews and minimal P&A support, Nicole Conn's dyke odd couple had grossed $900,000 from its vastly underserviced audience—this despite the director's honest admission that it was "not particularly that good."

The only sales hook I could come up with on *Clerks* was a return to Kevin's inspiration, *Slacker*. On that occasion distributors Tom Bernard and Michael Barker were both intimately familiar with Austin, Texas. This time around, Bernard lived within two miles of Kevin's location, the Leonardo Quick Stop. He'd even been in buying Gatorade while the staff (presumably including Mr. Smith) was watching *Jeopardy*. Tom refused to go by the store to pick up a tape we set aside for him. He later explained his theory that local filmmakers would be nothing but trouble. While Sony Classics was shuffling around, Mark Tusk fell hard for *Clerks* and organized a 16mm screening for Harvey Weinstein and the entire Miramax staff. Although I completely misinterpreted Mark's postscreening message in early December as putting us "in play," it turned out to be more of a good news/bad news scenario. The good news was that all the young staffers were excited by *Clerks*. The bad news was that Harvey hadn't lasted fifteen minutes. This notorious chain smoker got bogged down in the antismoking sequence and didn't even make it to the thirty-seven dicks. Tusk slowly fanned a flame back to life. Other distributors copped a skeptical wait-and-see-at-Sundance attitude. In a break with my standard skepticism about agents, I introduced Kevin to the Creative Artists Agency's Tory Metzger and he signed on with her. They both struck me as extremely decent, no-nonsense people who could make a good team.

Rose, Guin, Kevin, and Scott Mosier all met for the first time, a little warily it seemed, in the *Postcards from America* editing room, where the *Clerks* bloodbath ending was cut in December. I was just getting to know the completely unflappable Scott, and beginning to realize the crucial role he'd played in the production. As the "outsider" (from Canada no less), he'd catalyzed Kevin and his New Jersey slacker buddies into action, then organized the production to ensure that it would be completed. They were very tight—the antithesis of my recent experience. The *Go Fish* promotional nail clippers had just been conceived that day—the ultimate giveaway. There seemed to be a little jostling for position. I certainly didn't see the signs of the beginning of a beautiful friendship. The next time we all met was around the baggage carousel at the Salt Lake City airport on Sundance opening day. I needed their respective press books to overnight to *The New York Times*. Once again I sensed some competitive edge as I drove Rose and Guin up the mountain, and left Scott and Kevin back at the festival shuttle.

Go Fish was set up to open the festival with a bang on the first Friday afternoon at the Egyptian Theatre. I'd learned the value of an onsite sale by failing to pull it off with *Amongst Friends*. Ideally *Go Fish* would go fast. *Clerks*, on the other hand, was going to need a slow build, a slow burn. The Sundance schedule suited this strategy since the first three shows were in a small theater while the key fourth and final screening would be at the Egyptian on the second Friday, exactly one week after *Go Fish*. I went through the drill with Kevin.

The opening lines in Kevin's Sundance journal were: "It begins. We get into Park City after a van ride in with a British director looking to make films in the U.S. (Aren't we all.)" At the opening-night party, the *Clerks* and *Go Fish* posses started getting along and Janet helped grease the wheels. "She's cool," Kevin assessed. But in a paranoiac mood he wrote, "Mr. Pierson seemed to dote on R&G, but it's to be expected—he's got a year and a huge investment with *Go Fish*. With us it's a few months and some Fed Ex bills. We've been relegated to the sidelines. In retrospect, I wonder if he would rep us, if he could choose to do it again."

Of course I would. But in the meantime, the *Go Fish* ploy had worked like a charm with an instant overwhelming response. Kevin described it as "funny, sweet, and spicy—just like the girls." Once again *Spanking the Monkey* affected our fate; it screened simultaneously at another theatre. Miramax's Trea Hoving opted for the competition because she had a close friendship with Janet Grillo and, as it turned out, a small investment in Grillo's feature. I didn't mean to punish Trea, or other distributors, but Goldwyn had come to buy *Go Fish*. Moments after the Egyptian premiere ended, negotiations with them began at a pizza parlor next door. At one point Tom Rothman decided to pursue world rights: "There are lesbians everywhere."

Technically I held them at bay until after the second screening on Saturday evening, but I knew Tom Rothman would acquire the picture. He had come to Utah for the weekend leaving his earthquake-shaken family behind in jumpy Los Angeles. He may have called me a "hypocrite" after *Roger & Me* and "greedy" during *Amongst Friends*. Goldwyn may have still been trying to figure out where the missing zero went on *She's Gotta Have It*. But our star-crossed history was about to turn. Miramax, Sony, and Fine Line were all there, but they moved too slow. We closed the deal at an out-of-the-way rib joint with ten people around the table: only I ate red meat. Twenty-eight hours after its world premiere, *Go Fish* was the first film sold at Sundance that year. In fact it was the first film ever sold during the festival.

There were two big problems. I missed most of the first *Clerks* screening picking ribs out of my teeth. Up until now I hadn't felt neglectful towards Kevin and Scott (I saw the journal a year later). But missing his

ISLET/GOLDWYN   1/22/94   PROPOSAL/DISTRIBUTION

— GO FISH —

1. WE ARE IN A PERIOD OF EXCLUSIVE NEGOTIATION UNTIL 6:30 PM TONIGHT

20 NETWORK
40 NT
20% FEC *VIDEO*
30 TV/AM SYN
2. BASICALLY I WOULD PREFER TO HAVE GOLDWYN ACQUIRE WORLD RIGHTS/ALL MEDIA/FULLY CROSS-COLLATERALIZED.

35 SYNDI *ALLIANCE*
3. ISLET DELIVERY SHALL CONSIST OF THE FILM ELEMENTS <u>AS THEY EXIST NOW</u>, CHAIN-OF-TITLE, MUSIC LICENSES AND OTHER NECESSARY DOCUMENTATION.

20 YEARS
4. THE TERM CANNOT BE PERPETUITY, BUT LONG ENOUGH TO MAKE YOU COMFORTABLE

5. ANY ADVANCE GUARANTEE THAT WE PROPOSE BELOW SHOULD BE MATCHED BY AN IDENTICAL AMOUNT P+A COMMITMENT. *OK*

10 30/30
30
(6 MOS)
6. ANY PAYMENT SCHEDULE SHOULD INCLUDE A MODEST AMOUNT ON SIGNING AND NO STAGGERED PAYMENT LATER THAN SIX MONTHS AFTER RELEASE.

25-90 FM
7. IF YOU ACCEPT MY TERMS, I'LL SWALLOW YOUR STANDARD √35% THEATRICAL FEE WITHOUT GRIPING.

8. IF YOU ACCEPT MY TERMS, I'M WILLING TO AGREE TO A DEAL BEFORE TONIGHT'S SCREENING WITH ONE CONTINGENCY. WE SHOULD HAVE DINNER IMMEDIATELY AFTERWARDS (8:15 PM) WITH ROSE, GUIN, VALERIE, AND TOM KALIN

So that you can make your eloquent Goldwyn presentation.

9. So here we go with the real nitty gritty. In order to make a deal right now (acknowledging that Goldwyn would be a great distributor for this film) on a preemptive basis, I'm using a domestic gross box office performance of between $1,500,000 and $2,000,000. No matter what sort of gross participations you can propose, the domestic component of the advance guarantee I'm asking for is $250,000. The rest of the world I define as being worth at least $150,000 making the total advance. To close this out $400,000. If this figure seems out of line, I thank you for your aggressive interest. Just remember two things. I did put a figure on the table (at Odeals on 57th & 6th) in NYC for "Roger and me". You balked. And to go all the way back to my start with Goldwyn, this deal is exactly what Island paid for "She's gotta have it" (foreign + domestic weren't crossed film)!

Best regards,
JP

— Cap of 50¢ on Delivery —

premiere was a mortal sin, even for a $450,000 deal. Kevin found it understandable, but he wrote "Mr. Pierson breaks my heart." Janet got there and saved the day. I made it later. The audience laughed and laughed and "gushed" afterward. Kevin felt so great that he claimed, "Even if we never get picked up the $27,000 was worth it for this alone." It was an excellent start although the screening was short on distributors.

The second problem stemmed from wounded pride. My longtime friends at Sony Pictures Classics had decided to announce a deal on the documentary *Martha and Ethel* on the festival's first weekend. They'd seen this film long before and had an agreement in principle to distribute it since the last week of December. How do I know? The producers kept calling me for hours of free advice on negotiating tactics and deal points. Now they were stepping on my *Go Fish* toes, and I was angry. I've cheated on deal announcements; the Cannes hoopla for *She's Gotta Have It* is a prime example. Nevertheless I have a professional code that Sony violated when Marcie Bloom claimed that she saw *Martha and Ethel* for the first time at Sundance and bought it immediately. *Variety* printed the story, and unfortunately the *L.A. Times'* astute Ken Turan repeated it. Caryn James at *The New York Times* wasn't fooled, especially since Sony's publicist had been talking to her about the movie before Sundance ever started. Caryn did focus in on the skillful orchestration of the *Go Fish* sale.

I felt vindicated, but Rose and Guin may have had the impression that everything happened too quickly. I thought we maxed out unless someone decided that an experimental, black-and-white, lesbian feature had enormous crossover potential. The other distributors were hopping mad, but no one suggested *Go Fish* was worth any more than Goldwyn paid. I also knew that Goldwyn under the savvy guidance of (recent) distribution head Eamonn Bowles, was in a perfect position to release the film in June—gay pride month. Despite wide acclaim and the added bonus of the filmmakers' vivacious personalities, *Go Fish* had some vulnerable points. Caryn James began to paint it into a corner when she wrote, "Sometimes witty, sometimes amateurish and didactic, it is more notable for its subject than its uneven result." With this mixed message in mind, Tom Rothman and I agreed that New Directors/New Films was not a necessary stop on the *Go Fish* road to release.

In the meantime *Clerks* had another screening, this one in the early

For Sundance, Struggle to Survive Success

Islit Inc.

Among the movies at the Sundance Film Festival this year are "Go Fish," top, with Anastasia Sharp, and "Four Weddings and a Funeral," with Andie MacDowell and Hugh Grant.

By CARYN JAMES

Special to The New York Times

PARK CITY, Utah, Jan. 24—"Success is a tricky mistress," Robert Redford said. "It's nice to have, but it's a tricky thing to embrace." He ought to know. Though he was talking about the Sundance Film Festival, the festival's problems are the kinds that usually nag at movie stars: How to survive the pressures of fame? How to avoid being typecast?

Sponsored by Mr. Redford's Sundance Institute and devoted to independent films, this is the pop icon among American festivals. Every January, film makers—and the agents and distributors who lust after them—must show up here, or the industry will wonder what's wrong with their careers.

But the Sundance myth of small films exploding into the marketplace has always been more illusion than reality. This year the people behind the scenes and those who are arriving in this tiny ski-resort town recognize that fact, sometimes for minutes or even hours at a stretch.

The truth is that this year's festival is fraught with paradoxes. It opened on Thursday night with the premiere of "Four Weddings and a Funeral," a mainstream romantic comedy by Mike Newell (the director of "Enchanted April"), starring Andie MacDowell and Hugh Grant. Between now and the awards ceremony next Saturday, viewers will see everything from a first feature called "Clerks," made for just over $27,000, to "The Hudsucker Proxy," starring Paul Newman and released by Warner Brothers.

•

Distributors arrived with lower expectations than usual. After all, there hasn't been a moneymaking hit from Sundance since the now-canonized "Sex, Lies and Videotape" in 1989. But two days into this festival, the Samuel Goldwyn Company bought a low-budget black-and-white lesbian movie called "Go Fish" and created a frenzied sense of competition. All bets about not falling for the Sundance movie du jour were suddenly off.

And then there is the often-forgotten detail that the Sundance Film Festival does not take place at Sundance, the Redford resort, styled in Southwestern chic. Most of the festival is held in un-chic Park City, about 45 minutes away, with some screenings at Sundance and in Salt Lake City. Anyone who has tried to park a car on narrow Main Street in Park City, or strained to hear the sound in a makeshift theater in a local school auditorium, can see that the festival has outgrown this place. Yet it is committed to staying.

Sundance itself, where Mr. Redford was host at a lunch for film makers on Saturday, seems like Shangri-la by

comparison. Never mind that Sundance is south of Park City and lower in altitude; going there conveys the sense of trekking up the mountain to find some cinematic shaman.

Sitting in his small office at Sundance on Sunday—the Indian pillows resemble the kind that appear in the Sundance sales catalogue, the blue plaid shirt and jeans make him look as everyday as Robert Redford can look—he mulled over the festival's future. "The success is there, but now what do you do with it?" he said. "Are we just going to sit there, embrace it, dance with it? Or are we going to move ahead? My role here is to keep stating the purpose. I want to keep this festival belonging to the film makers, and make sure it doesn't get co-opted or overpowered by outside forces."

Those forces are lined up. There has been an influx of films from major studios, which are increasingly using Sundance's out-of-competition sections to begin marketing campaigns. "The Hudsucker Proxy" is made by Joel and Ethan Coen, whose 1983 film "Blood Simple" was also

A film festival tries to maintain its focus and avoid being typecast.

shown at Sundance. Universal will bring "Reality Bites," a glossy take on the "Slacker" generation, directed by the comedian and actor Ben Stiller.

But the 16 films in the dramatic competition and the 17 in the documentary category suggest a return to the festival's low-budget grass roots. About half of the dramatic-competition films were made for less than $100,000, lunch money in Hollywood. "It's not like I'm trying to become Cannes West here," said Geoffrey Gilmore, the festival's program director. "To some degree the distinction between studios and independent films is becoming more and more gray, and we're reflecting that."

The festival's opening-night films have always been more mainstream than most at Sundance, and often too sincere for their own good. Films like "Stanley and Iris," "Once Around" and last year's "Into the West" (also directed by Mr. Newell) went on to become box-office flops, suggesting something like a Sundance first-night curse. "Four Weddings and a Funeral" may be able to break that pattern. It is a light comedy about a young Englishman, played by Hugh Grant, who keeps running into a woman, played by Andie MacDowell, at weddings. Their romance is as thwarted and inevitable as in any old-style Hollywood movie.

Russell Schwartz, the president of Gramercy Pictures, said that bringing "Four Weddings" to Sundance allowed the company "to see if we've got to do any tweaking with our campaign." A few days after the premiere, he said: "The question was whether it would be perceived as a British comedy, but we haven't been getting that response. I guess if this picture plays in Salt Lake, we're in good shape."

Though Ms. MacDowell and Mr. Grant were hits in Salt Lake, Cannes's reputation as the glitziest of festivals is safe. Sundance is still about making discoveries, many of which become dangerously overhyped. Last year's prize for drama was split between "Ruby in Paradise," which went on to the New York Film Festival and then to lackluster business, and "Public Access," a film that never found a distributor.

Ira Deutchman, the president of Fine Line Features, defined his expectations in terms that echoed what other distributors said: "I don't think anybody going to Sundance now believes that there has to be some breakthrough movie every year. It took a few years of disappointments for people to realize that."

These days, there aren't even many surprises for buyers. Of the films up for grabs in the dramatic competition—about a dozen—almost all had already been screened for distributors, who come to catch the audience reaction.

"Go Fish" was the calculated exception. It proved that while two days is too short a time for the clichéd Sundance "buzz" about hot films to start on its own, it is entirely possible to orchestrate a buzz. John Pierson of Islet Productions, who was selling "Go Fish," kept the film under wraps until the festival. He told all the potential buyers to be there for the first screening on Friday afternoon and to be prepared to make a fast offer.

At the second screening on Saturday evening, all the usual suspects showed up. People from Fine Line, Goldwyn, Miramax and Sony Pictures Classics were there, some for

Balancing small independents and big studios: the line is blurring.

the second time, and with varying degrees of interest. That night, Goldwyn bought the world rights to the film. Tom Rothman, Goldwyn's president of production, said: "We now have eight days at the festival with all of our staff already here, because we have three other films being shown. They can immediately begin the work of positioning the film."

Their work might be harder outside Sundance than it is here, where diversity is the ultimate buzzword. "Go Fish," a first feature directed by Rose Troche, is a happy-go-lucky lesbian movie about a group of friends who try to fix up a woman named Max with a woman named Ely. Sometimes witty, sometimes amateurish and didactic, it is more notable for its subject than its uneven result. But it was so cheap to make (it's one of those lunch-money movies) that no one seems too worried about whether it will cross over to straight audiences. "I think every lesbian who goes to movies in the world will see it, and it has crossover potential," Mr. Rothman said. But if it doesn't appeal to heterosexual audiences, he said, Goldwyn is "still going to do very well."

Mr. Rothman knows as well as anyone what companies like his are doing at Sundance. He summed it up by looking at his watch and saying: "Maybe I should check my messages, because maybe Steven Spielberg called while I was out, but I doubt it. We're in the new talent business."

morning, that went through the roof. The very first review broke courtesy of Dave Kehr in the *New York Daily News* who called *Clerks* "a blend of Howard Stern and David Mamet." Momentum started to build. So did the relationship between the New Jersey boys and Chicago lesbians. When Kevin introduced his show, he plugged *Go Fish* and described it as "the only film at Sundance in which you see the producer's bare ass."

Although Kevin told *Entertainment Weekly*'s Anne Thompson, "There are no lesbians where I come from," he was getting a crash course. I kept driving to the Salt Lake City airport and Amtrak station to pick up even more members of the Chicago/Wicker Park lesbian contingent—eight in all. They were all staying in my two-bedroom condo where our only supply was a gallon-size bottle of Scotch. One afternoon I came home for a nap and found my bed already occupied. Kevin's gang was holed up across town with economy-size boxes of Trix and Fruit Loops. When not promoting her backside, Kevin described Guinevere poignantly: "Such a pretty name for such a pretty girl. It is cool that she's gay because you can play with her, talk smack, and not get crossed wires. Good fences make good neighbors." Rose, who at twenty-nine was six years older, had referred to him as a "wunderkind." As their very curious peer, he learned far more about Rose and Guin's affair than I ever would. I did know that Guin had grown up where I now live in the Hudson Valley countryside near West Point where, she told me, she felt completely out of place. She called Kevin a "big fucking romantic," and he decided, "She's probably the first female friend I've had that won't end badly."

It was a love fest, and I was having a blast selling two films I embraced. Harvey Weinstein arrived at the festival for the first time in a few years and survived an attack from a disgruntled screenwriter at an overcrowded Miramax party. He berated me for the premature Goldwyn deal, and warned that I better just plan on selling *Clerks* to them as well. Amid the banter, I tried to explain that Eamonn Bowles was one of the keys to the deal. He threatened to hire him away; a year later he did! The mid-week shows of both *Clerks* and *Go Fish* were the worst as a result of low energy and technical problems that gave the sound an underwater quality. For *Clerks* this could have been devastating because Fine Line's Ira Deutchman and Sony's Michael Barker were both in attendance. Fortunately, the press that resulted from earlier screenings was appearing every day. Kevin and Scott had their best opportunity yet to observe the exact whereabouts of the dead spots in the 103- minute version, and they had already delineated 10 minutes of cuts. No one had yet asked about the weird point-of-view shot that now ended the film so abruptly, or noticed the "pop" on the soundtrack.

Although *Clerks* delivered on its own merits, Kevin's modest "I worked in that convenience store and plan to be back there for my shift next Monday" backstory certainly didn't hurt. The *L.A. Times, Variety,* and *The New York Times* all picked up on this angle in excellent coverage. Caryn James expressed skepticism over Kevin's return to the Quick Stop and added, "If you want to buy milk from Kevin Smith you better move fast." I did not hire a publicist at Sundance for either *Clerks* or *Go Fish,* although "unofficially" Clein and White were extremely generous about helping on the latter film.

By Friday morning as we counted down to the final *Clerks* show, the media attention had reached a crescendo. The second trade review in the *Hollywood Reporter* was as good as *Variety* while *Newsday* and the *New York Post* also chimed in. At the screening introduction, Kevin even produced a review he claimed was from *Convenience Store Weekly.* That afternoon would be the ideal moment to strike. Mark Tusk, with help from Trea Hoving, assured us that he'd brought Harvey Weinstein back into the fold and promised to deliver him to the screening. Now one of the reasons Harvey returned to Sundance in 1994 was that his wife, Eve Chilton, had co-produced a film for the Disney Channel that was having its premiere in the festival: *Tommy: The Amazing Journey* (coincidentally, Barry Brown was the director). Beyond showing support for Eve, Harvey was undoubtedly trying to show Miramax's ongoing commitment to independent film in the aftermath of the Disney acquisition and mega-success of *The Piano* and *The Crying Game.* That multimillion-dollar deal and its potential repercussions still had everybody talking. Becoming involved with a triumphant, underdog, pipsqueak, foulmouthed, $27,000 comedy certainly couldn't hurt their indie street credibility.

The table was set. Geoff Gilmore introduced the show by saying, "If Kevin Smith didn't exist, we'd have to invent him." It felt like all eyes were on Harvey. I know mine were. He was sitting between Tusk and producer Cary Woods. The crowd went nuts from the opening credit sequence. Around the twenty-minute "thirty-seven dicks" mark (which would soon become the fifteen-minute mark), I began to hear Harvey's laugh; it was loud and it was frequent. *Clerks* had peaked at precisely the right moment, and I knew that Miramax would buy it within an hour of the show's conclusion. On the way to a summit at a restaurant called The Eating Establishment, I passed by the October Films retinue of Bingham Ray, Jeff Lipsky, and acquisitions director Marcia Kirkley and asked them if they were prepared to speak now or forever hold their peace. They weren't ready, and frankly other distributors had remained a bit tepid over how to market the film. I walked on.

Kevin's journal picks up the story:

At the Eating Establishment, John is in mid-discussion with Mark (peculiarly quiet), a Miramax exec, another quiet guy, and the king of all impresarios—the modern day P.T. Barnum himself—Harvey Weinstein. There are potato skins on the table and the topic of conversation is *Clerks*. Harvey is big—he talks big, he thinks big, he is big. He says he wants *Clerks*, and he wants to release it big: big soundtrack, big book (I'm in heaven), big push with marketing, something he knows well. Mark looks like a child, quiet and sullen like a geisha during Harvey's pitch. Occasionally, he makes eye contact and smiles. Scott and I chuckle maniacally. It is the most unbelievable moment in my life. Then things get really cool as John slips into his dealmaking mode. He rejects their first offer, explaining that it would have been a great pre-Sundance figure, but with four screenings, the film has proven it's not "a pig in a poke." We adjourn to the side and discuss a viable figure, agreeing that asking for a lot of money was never our first concern—being at the 'Max was. We go back, John lays down the acceptable figures, and Harvey explains that his new philosophy in business is to "make people happy by giving them what they want." He agrees to everything, shakes our hands, I thank him profusely, and he's off with his assistant (Jon Gordon). That leaves me, Scott, John, Mark, and David Linde (the exec) to hammer out the contract on yellow legal paper. John argues over the perpetuity arrangement, and David Linde looks on like a bookish jock. When the deal is set, I sign on the line that is dotted, and we head out, off to the Miramax condo for celebratory drinks. Tusk unearths my letter to him that accompanied the tape he had requested many moons ago. We drink, smoke, and all is right with the world.

I concur with that sentiment. However, Kevin added, "What seemed almost impossible actually came to pass: Miramax bought *Clerks*." And in an unprecedented deal point for me, Harvey guaranteed opening all fifty of the top fifty markets. I truly felt confident all along. Otherwise I never would have agreed to let a writer from the *Chicago Tribune* tag along with me throughout the week charting the course of the deal. It would have been too embarrassing if the film had fizzled. Instead it was a hoot to be able to read quotes about the movie from other acquisitions mavens like Sony's Marcie Bloom: "I'm afraid it's been done." I now had the first and second on-site distribution deals in the history of Sundance.

Having greased the wheels, I was happy to see one more of that year's films join the "sold" ranks at the next night's Awards Ceremony. Audience-winner *Spanking the Monkey* closed with Fine Line exactly when we'd tried and failed to lock up *Amongst Friends* the year before. I thought Kevin was likely to win a bigger prize, so I didn't advise him to speak his piece when he shared the Filmmaker's Trophy with Boaz Yakin's *Fresh*. He stood on stage and said it was a "nice piece of glass." Disappointingly, *Go Fish* was shut out. I know that actor Matthew Modine, my former New York City neighbor, and filmmaker Allison Anders excitedly cast their votes for Tom Noonan's stage-acting exercise *What Happened Was* to give it the Dramatic Grand Jury Prize. I've never understood the meaning or value of prizes, but I suppose that's my own blind spot. Filmmakers love to receive them, and the press can't resist writing about them. It seems to give some sort of structure to life. At the party afterward, Kevin actually won a much bigger reward when he met Jim Jacks, the man who would produce his second feature, *Mallrats*.

Both *Clerks* and *Go Fish* built beautifully over the next half year. Rose and Guin went to Berlin with Goldwyn's backing, and foreign sales stacked up quite nicely. Kevin and Scott made thirteen minutes of cuts (the last three with "input" from Miramax) to prepare *Clerks* for New Directors/New Films, where it became the dominant title. Janet Maslin perfectly captured the way I feel about my very favorite low-budget films when she called it "a classic example of how to spin straw into gold." Both films needed to be blown up to 35mm and remixed with similar deadlines: *Clerks* had been invited to the International Critics Week Section of Cannes in mid-May, while *Go Fish* was scheduled to open in New

York on June 10. In 1994, June wasn't merely Gay Pride Month in New York City. It was also the twenty-fifth anniversary of Stonewall and the Gay Games were scheduled to bring thousands of lesbians to town. As the tag line suggested—"The girl is out there."

The entire front half of the summer release schedule was exceedingly light for the independent distributors, presumably out of fear and respect for the annual Hollywood juggernaut. Goldwyn's Eamonn Bowles saw a great opportunity for niche-market counterprogramming with *Go Fish*, on the Fourth of July weekend no less. Building on the groundwork of three weeks of high grosses in New York and a sensational, emotionally charged opening night slot at San Francisco's Gay and Lesbian Festival, Eamonn took *Go Fish* out on fifty screens in all the top markets over the holiday. (A good indication of its effectiveness is that Fine Line copied the plan chapter and verse for its release of *The Incredibly True Adventure of 2 Girls in Love* a year later.) The picture had a $550,000 weekend and went on to gross $2.4 million—more than *Reservoir Dogs* in its initial theatrical release. Many of these successful runs were booked by Bert Manzari in the Goldwyn-owned Landmark Theatres circuit. There is no more valuable outlet for off-Hollywood films. As Tom Rothman had predicted back in Sundance, "Even if it doesn't appeal to heterosexual audiences, it's still going to do very well." Well it didn't, and it did.

I never believed *Clerks* would cross over to the foreign audience. The quietly confident David Linde of Miramax International, had guaranteed that he would be able to sell the film. If I'd believed him and had faith in the film's translation (both literal and psychological), I would have negotiated a lower foreign-sales fee. I thought we were giving up 30 percent of very little revenue. Cannes proved David right and me dead wrong. Foreign advances topped $500,000 (eventually overseas revenue doubled that). Not only did Kevin bring home two awards, he got to meet Duran Duran's Simon LeBon on a yacht next to the Miramax yacht. When Kevin called to tell me excitedly about winning the Prix de la Jeunesse, I thoughtlessly let all the air out of his balloon by labeling it the "booby prize" —Spike's words when he realized it meant no Camera d'Or.

By the time *Clerks* opened theatrically in mid-October, *Go Fish* was long-gone from America's movie screens. The *Clerks* delay stemmed from a Sony soundtrack deal featuring Soul Asylum and Alice in Chains, further remixing, a threatened NC-17 rating, and finally a desire to capitalize on the wide release of the enormously acclaimed *Pulp Fiction*. Miramax actually sent out over 800 *Clerks* trailers on *Pulp* prints.

Rose pretty much went off her own way. Guin has stayed close with the boys. After the thrilling Sundance roller coaster we shared, we all got together for the last time on my fortieth birthday. Rose and Guin gave me some beauty-care treatments to help keep my face young. I laughed hard; but when I thought about it later, I realized that it was Rose and Guin and Kevin and Scott who had made me feel young again. Their good fortune was my redemption.

In Hock and Staying There

I s it quality or is it luck? A very insistent filmmaker needed to know
the answer to that question about my successful films. Obviously, it's
both. However, Branch Rickey, the legendary baseball executive who
brought Jackie Robinson to the majors, pointed out, "Luck is a fact,
but should not be a factor. Luck is the residue of design."

No one has more respect for the enormous challenge of making an
independent, low-budget film than I do. When the challenge is well met,
a triumphant first feature may result. However, since I screen upwards
of 400 works-in-progress year round, I'm no stranger to failure. It's so
easy to pick on Hollywood's out-of-control wastefulness on *Waterworld*
or *Ishtar* or, in the old days, *Cleopatra*. But at least studios are like
banks; the loss is a bit abstract. Starting with the filmmakers themselves,
the private investors who, more often than not, lose all their money on
an indie movie actually feel the pinch in their wallets. The cumulative
loss really mounts up over several hundred titles, and as the volume of
production increases the situation worsens.

When given an opportunity by *The New York Times* to describe the
hundreds of homeless movies on display at the 1992 edition of the In-

dependent Feature Film Market, I came up with the image of the base of a pyramid, a vast cross section showing the width and breadth of independent filmmaking, warts and all. Over time only about one in ten rises close to the tip of the pyramid, and only one in a hundred makes money. Then in an article-ending quote, much to the chagrin of the market's organizers, I added quite bluntly: "Looked at collectively, it's a nightmare. There is a certain desperation because most of these filmmakers are in hock and they're probably going to stay there."

Unsurprisingly the *Times* story had a far more optimistic headline: TRADING A CAN OF FILM FOR A DREAM COME TRUE, just as *Clerks* did the very next year.

This chapter is dedicated to those dreamers who have tried and fallen short. Many have written to me describing their goals and aspirations. Then I watch the results. I can only hope that others may learn from their miscalculations, and that my obituary won't match that of a former Berlin Film Festival programmer: "He watched them until he dropped."

I'll reprint one letter in its entirety, then deconstruct it.

To John Peerson,

My name is Costa Zeher. I'm a filmmaker from New Jersey, around roughly the same area as Kevin Smith, who mentioned you in two articles in the local papers. I tried to get in contact with him for advice, but he hasn't returned my call, the jerk. Anyway, I saw his movie, and I thought that if you didn't mind being involved in his piece of garbage, you'd love to throw in with my film, *Mae Day*.

Mae Day is about a group of filmmakers who fight over the concept of a film they're trying to make. It's a comedy—the people who've watched it around here (although not Kevin Smith, the jerk) say it's the funniest movie they've ever seen—way funnier than *Clerks*—and that our film looks a hundred times better. We've had a prospectus drawn up on the box office potential for our film, and I'd be happy to show it to you upon request. Our budget was thirty-two thousand, and if everything goes right, we should gross eighteen million theatrically.

Anyway, watch it and give me a call. My business card is enclosed. I'd like to get to work on whatever contracts we have to sign with you immediately.

If he wants a contract, he should probably learn how to spell my name. Usually the comparisons to other successful movies are more positive. The barebones *Clerks* sometimes brings out the worst in competitive filmmakers. One truly clueless individual told me, "The best thing about it is just that they got it done." Otherwise this project falls into five standard traps.

1. It jumps on the local bandwagon.
2. It emphasizes production value ("looks a hundred times better").
3. It promotes the low budget indiscriminately.
4. It has a gigantic box office pseudoprojection.
5. It's a movie about a movie.

The final point is the ultimate kiss of death. In fact I recently saw a work-in-progress where a character said, "That's like the only kind of movie they make anymore." More about that later.

The basic point learned from Costa Zeher is how "easy" it is to project a profit. Where *sex, lies, and videotape* used to be the example of choice, the recent role models have been far more numerous, varied, and sophisticated. Yet the analysis is still utter sophistry. One gay film was described as far less difficult and demanding than *The Living End* and *Swoon*.

Thus, it is only logical to forecast a better financial performance for *film x*

THE LIVING END

Domestic Gross	1 Million
Budget	$30,000

SWOON

Domestic Gross	$500,000
Budget	$80,000

Both films have also been generating a substantial amount of revenue through foreign distribution and recent video release.

FILM X

Domestic Gross	$2,000,000 (forecasted)
Prod. Budget (thus far)	$20,000

Beware those parentheses.

Sometimes you just let your numbers do the talking abstractly. Here's the old screen-by-screen pyramid scheme that might seem logical line-by-line until you reach the mind-boggling bottom:

> I developed the screenplay which is based on my own experiences growing up as a child of an alcoholic . . . You will find a full business plan regarding this project attached.

U.S. THEATRICAL RELEASE

$ 6.00	Average per ticket
x 50	Seats per theater
$ 300.00	Total per screening
$ 300.00	Per screening
x 22	Screenings per week
$ 6,600.00	Total per week/per theater
$ 6,600.00	Per week/per theater
x 75	Theatres
$ 495,000.00	Total dollar figure per week
$ 495,000.00	Total dollar figure per week
x 8	Weeks in release
$3,690,000.00	Total dollar figure in US

Just remember, that's *only* 50 seats per show.

Theatrical gross predictions aside, guaranteed ancillary income is often described with the utter certainty that my experience has contradicted over and over again. Here's a composite:

> Video distribution for the rental market is 10,000 units. With the filmmaker seeing $15 per unit this brings in a minimum of $150,000. A filmmaker can see a minimum of $100,000 for cable rights to a feature. Some low-budget films have received ten times that. The "floor effect" of the low estimates, which are paid for pictures with bad releases and bad reviews, practically *eliminates* downside risk. For "art" films like ours, the advance is usually somewhere between $100,000 and $300,000.

So every film makes a minimum of $350,000.

But the letters that predict profits in the end are not nearly so common as the ones that ever so enthusiastically describe the horribly misconceived birth of a feature. Two examples:

> It's a comedy. It is also the true story of how I discovered my mother's incestuous childhood. It seemed as though I annoyed you on the phone or perhaps you are used to persistent filmmakers. Be assured that I don't bother people for money. If you don't think my film is worthy, all I ask is that you come to the theater and give me your $7.50 when it's released.
>
> Why This Movie Must Be Made:
>
> Everyday over 2,500 children witness the divorce or separation of their parents.
>
> 50 to 70% of marriages disrupt. [sic]
>
> Number of TV sets . . .
>
> in 1947: 170,000
>
> in 1991: 750 million

Flattering yourself may be an even better way to get my attention.

> If you were fortunate enough to know martial arts, you would recognize that one of the box office attractions is Ho-Sung Pak. Out on the video market is the game Mortal Kombat, which features our leading man. . . . This is already much more than a good idea.

Those producers raised $3,000 out of a $3 million budget, or was it $4,000 out of $4 million? Of the other half-dozen martial arts films that have reached my desk, the only one that struck a chord described itself as "John Woo meets John Waters."

Confidence is important. Shrinking violets are rare in the movie world. But some folks go too far:

> I am a thirty-two-year old, writer-director that is destined for greatness . . . I have created an idea that reveals the depth and range of my talent that can also be brought to fruition cheaply without compromising its entertainment value.

If you're trying to sound like an expert who can raise millions, you shouldn't write about your plan to shoot in "Panna Vision." And it probably doesn't make sense to proudly announce, "To date we have raised enough money to hire an attorney."

Sometimes the generic soft sell is the way to go: "We have 92 minutes that looks, sounds, and acts like a movie." When all else fails, you can always try to pack in the maximum number of references to other films in the minimum number of sentences.

> My screenplay is an ensemble comedy along the lines of *Naked in New York, Go Fish, Clerks*, etc.: an art-house work with commercial viability. It has been compared to the writings of Woody Allen, Henry Jaglom, David Mamet, and Barry Levinson, among others, and is kind of like *Diner* meets *Annie Hall* meets *Sexual Perversity* . . . with a little *Slacker* thrown in. I also produced the low budget feature *The Life and Tales of Tony D.* (remember the finger?).

How could I ever forget "the finger." It was the best surprise that ever arrived in the mail. A Chicago Italian-American with a successful public-access cable TV show turned it into a feature film. To put me in the right mood, he also sent homemade vino and cheese. His note said,

> You may have noticed another little item included in the package. This particular item once belonged to the last producer's rep I showed my film to . . . he didn't like it.

And there it was wrapped in a bloody tissue: a very lifelike severed ring finger—with the ring!

That was an excellent fake, but the next fund-raising letters were for real.

> Having suffered from a near fatal accident in 1986 in which he lost his right leg, the winter of 1992 found the director inadvertently coming upon the financial resources needed to produce the Christmastime drama. "Some films cost an arm and a leg to produce . . . mine just cost a leg," he often jokes. In retrospect however, the out-of-court settlement afforded the director the opportunity to set out . . .

On July 14, he was diagnosed with colon-rectal cancer. He made sure to capture his entire ordeal on video. While cancer has given him some new ideas about life at thirty-three years old, he was quoted in the local newspapers that he "will have to find a way to market the cancer."

One director insisted on a face-to-face meeting so that he could drop a bombshell. He described his movie about an HIV-positive detective in the meat district. When I sounded cool, he told me he had a great marketing hook; he too was HIV-positive. His salesmanship disgusted me, so I retaliated. He was crestfallen when I told him he was too late—the French director of *Savage Nights* had already died of AIDS on the eve of its debut. At least the director who killed himself on camera was only making a fake documentary, not an art snuff film.

In addition to the "Admit One" hat that I mentioned earlier, two other funding ideas top the chart. A woman tired of her Pizza Hut delivery job wrote:

> I have even thought of donating three of my eggs for $3,000 a piece, but I'd feel awful funny having some kid walking around with my genetic code.

Or then there's the basic public television approach.

> For donations of $100 or more you will receive a VHS tape of the film when it is completed. For donations of $200 or more you will be noted in the film's credits.

If you can make it cheap enough, your profits can soar.

> I just directed a very, very, very low budget documentary title. It was filmed with my buddy's camcorder on a VHS cassette. I've already made over $75 selling it to my friends and cronies (a 700 percent return on investment).

Then there's always the pitch based on surefire demographics. When stand-up comedy crested in the early nineties, I received a half-dozen films involving stand-up comics, each with a packet explaining that seven million people attended comedy clubs every week. In an extraordinary coincidence, I saw four separate Elvis-imitator movies in a one-month period in 1991, long before the postage stamp. In all cases, the unstated assumption was that The King had a following. One of the four threw in Elvis Costello to cover all the bases. More recently, I've seen a shift to a sports angle.

> Golfers (25 million) love movies about golf and none have been produced since *Caddyshack*. We know that the golf angle will provide a ready audience for a video release.
>
> The film is set in the world of a soccer team. Soccer sells. It's the fastest growing sport in America with total participation of 16.3 million.

Golf, soccer . . . bowling? Yes, there was even a bowling noir although I forget how many millions of Americans, I was told, hit the lanes every weekend.

So how can I possibly respond to all these supplicants? Never with a form letter. I learned that lesson first-hand when, at the filmmaker's behest, I forwarded a tape to a distributor who thought I was the producer. The rejection slip said, "We want you to know that our decision is not a reflection on the quality of your production." Of course not; they're obviously looking for lower quality. And what exactly am I looking for aside from originality? One producer described a Pierson film in the third person:

> We are currently producing the kind of film that John Pierson has made a career of championing—unconventional storyline, complex characters, topical subject matter, artful cinematography—the kind of film that you can have a good argument about afterwards over coffee.

Unfortunately it remains unfinished.

I'm willing to screen films more than once as they change and get closer to completion. It's not unusual for the title to change along the way. Two films called *Loser* probably should have sought alternatives. A rap film changed from *Let's Get Busy* to *Let's Get Bizzee* to gain street credibility. A film called *Nobody's Sweetheart* became *My Favorite Sweetheart* after Jeff Lipsky passed through the producer's city with the half-serious advice that "My" titles usually fared well. (Eventually it wound up as *Season of Change*.) I don't usually volunteer to see a movie again that's left me utterly cold. Once I told a relentless, self-promoting filmmaker, step-by-step, what I hadn't liked about her sample work. First I didn't like the visual look. She assured me she was changing to a new cinematographer. Second I didn't like the performances. She was recasting. Finally I didn't care for the screenplay. She was rewriting. She was so quick to agree with my criticisms that I asked her how she would have responded if I'd told her I loved the look, acting, and writing. There was silence on the line.

Just like Hollywood, indies have been big on movies about vampires, serial killers, hostages and hit men. At least, the first category has yielded amusing titles like *Blood 'N' Donuts* and *Jugular Wine*. Indies have learned that sex often sells. Even more often it doesn't – especially if it's between a sock puppet and a crisply uniformed nurse. The only minor blessing about those genres is that they come out and say what they are. There's a film called *blessing* whose director, Paul Zehrer, had to spend much of his time and energy denying that it was a "farm movie."

Even when you escape from the unwashed masses, trouble awaits. *Blessing's* filmmaker Paul Zehrer missed his window of opportunity with the Goldwyn Company between his IFFM buzz and Sundance fizzle. It seemed to leave him somewhat embittered. Although set on a Wisconsin dairy farm, it was much more than that in its emotional portrayal of a family. But if I had a nickel for every time Paul said "not a farm movie," I could have paid down his debts. You should never describe what your film isn't. *Blessing* had a snakebit companion film in the 1994 Sundance called *River of Grass* by Kelly Reichardt, which provided the ideal, self-destructive self-description: "What's left is a love story without the love, a murder mystery without the murder, and a road movie that never gets on the road." In other words, an antimovie. *Blessing* finally opened in New York for one week via self-distribution.

Paul and Kelly were two of the 1994 Sundance crop who came to me beforehand. What are producers looking for from me? At the outset, they want a boost. I once saw a cannibal musical that was like the *Rocky Horror Oklahoma Picture Show*. The producer went to Sundance guerrilla-style, finagled his way onto MTV, pointed me out across a crowded room and said on air, "That's John Pierson over there; if he were to like our film, we'd be doing really well for ourselves." We never got to test that syllogism although the Fox Network was interested. When all hope is lost, they want another chance.

A year or so ago you viewed a rough cut of my film. You were quite complimentary regarding my talent, but you assessed that there was no market for the film. You were right. I read recently that Microsoft likes to hire people who have tried to start a business and failed, because these people have learned lessons that Microsoft could never teach them. Knowing what I learned during my project, and feeling the sureness of my confidence now, I could not agree more with that philosophy.

It's been said that if things don't go very right for a film, they go very wrong. I've been fortunate to wind up in the very right column most of the time. However I too am in hock and (apparently) staying there on one recent movie, *My Life's in Turnaround.* Around the time of the Elvis binge, I also swore off movies about movies. There are lots of great ones spanning film history; and Altman pulled out all the stops in *The Player.* But I really believe young filmmakers should find something from real life as their subject. This doesn't mean that everybody should make a film or that everyone has an interesting real life. I could not disagree more with the Writers Boot Camp philosophy that "in our hearts and minds, everyone has a screenplay." (Not to mention an inherent understanding of grammar.)

Quadruple hyphenates Don Ward and Eric Schaeffer asked me to play the role of a producer in *My Life's in Turnaround.* I said "no." They invited me to a rough cut. I watched it and said no. They made more cuts and invited me again just after I returned from selling *Amongst Friends* at Sundance 1992. I was ready for a new movie, the boys were charming, I said yes. Just like Paul Zehrer's denial, I immediately started telling people it wasn't really a movie movie, it was a romantic comedy featuring a very funny new comedy team with wonderful supporting roles for Martha Plimpton, Phoebe Cates, and John Sayles. Nobody really bought that argument. It also took an entire year to get a marginal distributor to buy this film.

Don and Eric got launched as writers, directors, producers, and actors. They opportunistically abandoned a loyal William Morris agent for the greener pastures of Creative Artists Agency. They had a near green light with TriStar, a deal with New Line, a series called *Too Something* for Fox Television, and an Eric solo feature for Motion Picture Corporation of America/TriStar. I wasn't so lucky. After a triumph on opening night at my ultimate good luck film festival in San Francisco, where we jokingly claimed the film had a $6,999.99 budget, I tried and failed to get *Turnaround* invited to key festivals like Cannes, Telluride, Toronto, London, New York, Sundance, and New Directors/New Films. On the day after the premiere in San Francisco, I had a $250,000 offer from Roxie Releasing—about $200,000 more than Bill Banning pulled together for *Roger & Me*. This offer was easy for Bill to make since he reneged a week later. Sony Pictures Classics' Marcie Bloom had been interested before I got on board; then she saw it again and her enthusiasm flagged. Piers Handling at the Toronto Festival declared that the film was "just not funny" after his entire staff gave it a big thumbs-down. I cajoled him by bringing up past slights and near oversights on *Slacker* and *Laws of Gravity* to no avail. That was perhaps the bitterest defeat.

After a successful showcase at the meaningless Hamptons Film Festival, a Russian gem importer/exporter made a mysterious distribution proposal. As soon as I tried to clarify and quantify it, the offer evaporated. Arrow Releasing became the distributor of last resort. I should have known there was trouble ahead when I signed the no guarantee deal on Martin Luther King day in an ice storm, went outside, and promptly fell flat on my back. It was all downhill from there. Essentially I had to book the film into the Angelika Film Center myself. Jeff Jacobs was extremely cooperative. It actually opened decently with good reviews, and business increased each week. I loved seeing Arrow's tacky American Film Market-style poster outside

Since the attention-craving Eric Schaeffer wasn't about to miss an opportunity to meet his public, he practically moved into the theatre. One day former mayor turned film critic Ed Koch came out of a *Turnaround* show and Eric made a beeline toward him to find out what he thought. Koch muttered "piece of shit" under his breath and then pushed on to the bathroom. He explained himself later in his review in the *Manhattan Spirit*:

I've mentioned in earlier columns that I have a benign prostate condition so when the movie ended I quickly got up to go to the bathroom. A guy chased after me and said "I'd be remiss if I didn't ask what you thought of the movie, Mayor Koch." I instantly replied, my mind on my prostate, "It's a piece of shit." He responded, "Oh that's good to know." When I returned to my friends, one said "That guy who stopped you looked like one of the stars." Come to think of it, he did. And if it was he, and he happens to read this review, I want him to know I didn't intend to be rude.

The New York run got bumped after six weeks because Arrow had no clout to battle Miramax, Fine Line, and Goldwyn at the Angelika. By the time *Turnaround* opened around the country in late summer, there was heavy specialized competition and it died. Arrow's in-house home video division eventually shipped a near invisible 3,000 videocassettes, which did coincidentally, pay off their distribution fees and modest expenses. My $116,900 investment was lost, as was the $37,000 in limited partnership monies that Don Ward and Eric Schaeffer raised. Their careers may be thriving. At the very least, their feet are in the door. I don't participate in their future earnings—unless of course the Fox Network show is deemed to have characters based on their roles in *My Life's in Turnaround* since I own half of the TV spin-off rights. There have been a slew of additional movies about movies ("the only kind they make anymore") in the last year. I've made it a point to not even see them.

For many other aspiring filmmakers, it's worth the risk of going into hock in order to turn things around and attain the life of Don and Eric or their peers. Returning to this chapter's first letter, Costa Zeher has no worries because he was created by Kevin Smith as a diabolical ruse after he sampled my mail. Kevin worked *Mae Day* out of his system in his one semester of film school and moved on to a real-life movie at the Quick Stop.

Jay Westby, a Portland filmmaker, summed up the career aspirations best in an article about Budget Lite ("no budget" being too "negative") production:

> I fear my generation of filmmakers will come to be known as the "credit card kids." These films are working as springboards to successful careers. The filmmakers to whom this has happened are big jerks. Spoiled brats. They think they're on top of the world, what with their film festivals and three-picture deals. And oh, how we all want to be just like them.

Go Fiscal:
Anatomy of a Back End

So once you're out of hock crossing over into the promised land, how much money can you expect to pocket?

When Rose Troche and Guin Turner showed me their grainy fifteen-minute videotape of crudely assembled scenes from *Go Fish* in a Chicago hotel room in January 1993, I just knew that my company Islet (now Grainy Pictures) would provide the investment to finish that film. That's exactly what happened through a triangular arrangement between me, Kalin Vachon Productions, Inc. (KVPI) and Can I Watch Pictures (Rose/Guin). Islet contributed all the cash and sales expertise. KVPI supervised the balance of production and all of postproduction, bringing technical experience, efficiency, and warm hugs to the process. Rose directed, edited, and even did her own optical printing (Guin designed the shimmying, shimmering credits) for a film that wound up exceeding all my artistic expectations. I always believed that *Go Fish* would be a surefire draw for the lesbian audience, but I was simply knocked out by its visual panache.

Several years have passed since I first saw a fraction of the film. In the year after its world premiere, Rose Troche made a string of half-joking public statements about how everyone was making money from her movie except her. I managed to laugh this off as grandstanding because Rose is a live wire with a cutting sense of humor. That's one of the things I love about her. I also have a little experience with half-informed first-time filmmakers going off half-cocked after a little success. Anyway, Rose never said anything in my presence.

It's time for a group therapy session on "misunderstandings about money" because of an outrageous statement that Steve McLean, the British writer/director of a fractured narrative based on the writings of gay artist David Wojnarowicz called *Postcards from America*, made in the 1995 Sundance issue of *Filmmaker* magazine. First he grandly stated: "It seems to me that part of the success of no-budget filmmaking is also its failure. Why should the studios give people money if the films get made so cheaply with no initial financial investment and can then be picked up for no money. Huge profits can be made this way. Of course, these profits are never going to go back to those people who sweated and toiled over these films." These are basically the mildly irritating musings of a naive cinema socialist. It would have been fine if he'd stopped there, but he didn't.

Having spent time with Rose when she was strapped for cash, he felt foolishly entitled to add a far more specific complaint: "And while you must celebrate that a film like *Go Fish* can be made very cheaply and then bought by Goldwyn, you wonder who's making the money. And you actually don't really have to wonder because you know who is."

It's human nature to be suspicious. It's a low blow to express that suspicion through innuendo. I take enormous pride in being fair, standing up for my producers, and having my company profit equitably. That's why I've gone to war alongside two dozen first-time filmmakers. But they aren't the only people taking risks. Distributors and investors play a crucial role too. The only thing worse than misinformation is disinformation. So let's trace every last dollar on the *Go Fish* distribution deal.

Goldwyn agreed to pay a $400,000 advance, with up to another $50,000 to complete and deliver the film in 35mm. Delivery involves a very long list of sound and picture elements, documents, insurance, video master, continuity, photographs, and on and on. The $50,000, which should have been plenty, was treated as a distribution cost against any future producer's share of profit. In other words, Goldwyn would have been out $450,000 if *Go Fish* had flopped—plus the release costs.

The other basic facts, which we'll return to later, are that the film had a North American box office gross of $2,400,000, and foreign sales totaling about $400,000.

Islet signed a contract with KVPI, which in turn had a separate agreement with Can I Watch Pictures. As in my standard agreement at the time, Islet took a 50 percent equity interest in net producer profits in return for its $53,000 investment. Did I sweat or bleed? No. On the other hand, KVPI found no other investors and Rose and Guin had raised only about $10,000 on their own, with which they'd shot the initial portion of *Go Fish* on weekends. Simple arithmetic reveals that Islet actually accounted for 84 percent of the cash. I never sought more than half the profits.

Aside from the equity split, Islet's deal had several advantageous points for me and two key givebacks for the producers. When Islet invested, I got a 15 percent fee as sales agent—in this case $60,000. Obviously, after years of low fees, I had to swallow hard before jumping to that level. But when you put cash on the barrelhead, it seems fair to charge as much as many agents who take no financial risk at all—especially since some people believe that I'm pretty good at my job. I try. Having no money at risk in *Clerks* or *Crumb*, I didn't know what to charge. So I took no fee for those sales.

As a balance to my *Go Fish* sales fee, the producers received $15,000 in deferred salaries. I also granted a $20,000 production cost recoupment, about $10,000 above their actual dollar amount. This helps to balance Islet's 20 percent interest factor on the money, or $10,600 in this case on the $53,000. Since Islet's money came from an interest-charging source and was not repaid for about eighteen months, it shouldn't exactly count as profit.

The very first hard cost that is deducted off the top of any of my deals is an amount for sales and marketing costs. After getting everyone to Sundance and having a crash condo for a passel of wonderful lesbians from Chicago for a full ten days, Islet spent about $6,500. Since postproduction ran over the $53,000 budget, I allowed KVPI to throw about $7,900 of that overrun into my sales and marketing column. This shift forgives a producer obligation and reduces the cost to KVPI by half. In this case, coming in over budget was hardly a crime, especially since Rose as a director is an absolute perfectionist through force of will.

That concludes the recoupments before the 50/50 net profit split. To summarize, Islet's $53,000 plus the producers' $10,000 resulted in a $63,000 budget, with another $14,400 in sales and marketing costs for a total of $77,400. Islet received a $60,000 fee (15 percent of $400,000) plus $10,600 in interest (an arguable "profit") for another $70,600, while the producers received $15,000 in salaries and $10,000 as a production cost surplus for a total of $25,000.

After all of the above deductions, the balance from the $400,000 advance is $227,000—or $113,500 to each side. Now Islet pays KVPI and has no direct legal involvement in the KVPI/Can I Watch deal. However during the chain-of-title documentation for *Go Fish*, I received a copy of that underlying agreement and found it quite intriguing to learn that KVPI kept 30 percent of their half with the other 70 percent going to Rose and Guin. Assuming that KVPI paid out the aforementioned $25,000 deduction to Rose and Guin in addition to their $79,450 (70 percent of $113,500), they would receive $104,450 while KVPI would keep $34,050 (30 percent of 113,500). Although Tom Kalin in particular was invaluable throughout the completion and delivery process, neither he nor Vachon ever risked any money on *Go Fish*. Admittedly Islet, my old company, came out as king of the hill since it earned a profit of either $173,500 or $184,100, depending on whether you count the interest.

A large part of Rose and Guin's frustration may relate to timing. Almost every substantial distribution guarantee is meted out on a three- or four-part payment schedule. There is a built-in conflict between every producer wanting money sooner and every distributor wanting to delay payment until later. I meticulously crafted a deal memo with Goldwyn, which should have resulted in $280,000 being paid by the *Go Fish* opening date (June 10, 1994) with the balance six months later. My best laid plans were upended when final delivery of *Go Fish* was several months late—primarily as a result of unlicensable music and minor picture changes in the final reel. Islet passed through Goldwyn's payments to KVPI very quickly, including 100 percent of the initial $40,000 check on signing. The next $240,000 was not received until more than two months after the opening. These transitional moments before cash actually gets into your bank account are very hard on any young filmmaker who has been living hand-to-mouth prior to being discovered and doesn't want to stay that way for one extra minute. If Rose felt Goldwyn or Islet dragged their feet, she should have looked in the mirror or called her executive producer, Tom Kalin. The simple truth is that KVPI and Can I Watch Pictures could not deliver the picture in a timely fashion.

Incidentally the final $120,000 payment (six months after delivery) finally occurred in January 1995. I found myself wishing that Goldwyn had bent more on timing, but they stick to the strict terms of their contracts. Perhaps if the film had been in "profit" on the distributor's balance sheet, it would have made a difference.

That word "profit" leads to a quick analysis of the film's performance and revenue stream. The eventual collected gross film rental for *Go Fish* in North America was about $900,000. Both box office gross and gross film rental would have been higher if the film had penetrated beyond the highly motivated lesbian niche audience. Most reviews unfairly ghettoized the picture, and as a result it opened explosively (over $500,000 on 50 screens over the Fourth of July weekend) but faded fast. That pattern recurred in the U.K., site of the first foreign opening, and other territories. Goldwyn took a 35 percent fee on theatrical distribution leaving a balance of about $585,000. On the $400,000 in foreign sales, their 25 percent fee left a balance of $300,000. The combined revenue total was $885,000.

The distributor of course has very substantial costs for prints, advertising, promotion, shipping—not any overhead, just the direct out-of-pocket costs on this particular title. In the case of *Go Fish*, those distribution costs totaled slightly more than $1 million. There are no huge surprises here. Advertising was half the total, while prints and lab elements added another $200,000. Rose and Guin did a ton of excellent promo work all over the country and around the globe from Madrid to Jerusalem to Tokyo. Filmmakers are certainly entitled to savor the sweetness of a first success. I always get a contact high myself. First-class travel can push the publicity budget up to a couple of hundred thousand dollars; it did. Partly as a result of Goldwyn ordering a worthless, rushed 35mm blowup for last February's American Film Market after *Go Fish* had already taken Berlin by storm (in 16mm), the $50,000 delivery amount also soared way past the mark. Simply put, the money that Rose suggests she didn't get is also the money that *Islet lost out on*! Higher expenses delayed recoupment for everyone. At least I didn't have to go to Japan.

Between their costs and the advance, Goldwyn had to recoup a lit-

GRAINY PICTURES, Inc.

44 Market Street, Cold Spring, NY 10516 (914) 265-2241 FAX: (914) 265-2543

GO FISH
Samuel Goldwyn Company / World Rights

[code: **KVPI** (Kalin/Vachon Productions) / **CIWP** (Can I Watch Pictures)]

Advance		$400,000
Deductions		
Islet invest recoup	53,000	
CIWP production recoup	10,000	
Islet Sales/Mktg. cost	6,500	
KVPI Budget overage	7,900	
Islet 20% Interest	10,600	
CIWP deferred salary	25,000	
Islet 15% sales fee	60,000	
		$173,000
50/50 Split		$227,000
Islet/50%	113,500	
CIWP/35%	79,450	
KVPI/15%	34,050	

Back end Recap

Gross Film Rental/Domestic	$900,000		
Less Goldwyn 35% Fee	315,000		
		$585,000	
Foreign Advance	$400,000		
Less Goldwyn 25% Fee	100,000		
		$300,000	
Revenue Total			$885,000

Distribution Costs			
Advertising	$500,000		
Delivery/prints/lab	300,000		
Publicity/Promotion	190,000		
Shipping	50,000		
		$1,040,000	
Advance		400,000	
Interest (accrued)		10,000	
Total costs			$1,450,000
Less Revenues			885,000
Current Goldwyn Deficit			(565,000)

tle more than $1.4 million leaving them a theatrical deficit of about $500,000 (part of their 1995/first quarter $20 million corporate debt). On paper, they had taken distribution fees totaling $415,000, so you might conclude they were doing just fine with video, television, and foreign overages still to come. Eventually Goldwyn's fees will surely surpass $500,000. In the old days IFP founder Sandra Schulberg used to say that it was morally wrong for distributors to make any fees off of a film before the original investors were repaid. Well she wasn't living on planet Earth because distributors are in the business of distributing movies for fees in order to make money. And anyway, in this case the investors were in profit on the basis of a quarter of the advance.

So the critical question concerning future, back-end profits revolved around the remaining ancillary rights. *Go Fish* had two strikes against it. It was black-and-white with lesbian content. On pay cable, the Cinemax Vanguard series showed it only after 11 P.M. The home-video campaign should have been labor intensive. Some gung ho distributor might have lobbied long and hard to push 25,000 units on a timely release. Unfortunately Goldwyn was nearly a year behind schedule, delayed by the protracted negotiation of a multimillion dollar video output deal with Hallmark involving an extensive package of Goldwyn titles. This deal did not augur well for the highly specialized *Go Fish* since Hallmark's biggest past success had been the ultra-mainstream *Lonesome Dove*. Wholesalers dismissed the film and the major retailers did not realize street level lesbian demand. End result: 10,000 *Fish* units.

The projected bottom line on back end looks bad. Even if *Go Fish* eventually generates another $50,000 foreign (less 25% fee) and $125,000 payable (less 30% fee), it would have needed to ship about 30,000 videocassettes to earn any further producer overage. Despite the fact that *Go Fish* doubled *Slacker*'s disastrous home-video performance, the only possible reaction is deep frustration.

What's the moral of this story? If you want more profit as a producer, you should preserve more of your equity. That's easier said than done. *She's Gotta Have It* was an artistic inspiration for *Go Fish*, but Rose and Guin couldn't emulate Spike Lee's equity. Both by design and happenstance, he owned two thirds of the profits in his breakthrough film. This put big bucks in *his* pocket. Then again his film grossed about three times more than *Go Fish*. My $10,000 investment for 10 percent of his film also resulted in a better return for me.

Go Fish is a feel-good movie that left some people feeling bad. I don't understand, and I don't plan to change my behavior much at all. Everyone made some money on a lesbian, black-and-white, experimental film from Chicago with loads of voiceover, some uneven performances, and many enigmatic shots of spinning tops. I do fault myself for failing to push Goldwyn to give us a performance "bump" at the $2 million box office mark, adding another $50,000 to the advance. In the competitive buying environment at Sundance, they probably would have gone that extra step.

I wish Rose the best. She's a strong new voice. Her name's been attached to several upcoming, larger budget projects. Yet so far she's in the limbo in which women directors get stuck too often. I have no idea if she'd still be sitting in Wicker Park with half a film if I hadn't come along.

As for Steve McLean, and his plan to redistribute the wealth, Islet would be pleased to accept the first $200,000. That's the amount we put at risk in *Postcards from America*. We invested out of loyalty to producer Christine Vachon in anticipation of future profits for everyone on *Go Fish*, a full six months before *Go Fish* went to Sundance. Rose Troche's film worked; Steve McLean's will never recoup more than a minute percentage of its budget. He should be entitled to enjoy the loss from his own sweat and toil on his first feature. In July 1996 we finally received a royalty of exactly $238. If Steve will match that sum, I propose buying $576 worth of lottery tickets.

A Doc in the House

People always want to know, "Do you ever get involved with docs?" Often they ask this question after we've already discussed *Roger & Me* or *The Thin Blue Line*. After an entertaining, story-driven documentary becomes a milestone, one tends to put it in a whole different category than say *Stone Masons of the Newfoundland Plateau*. When you watch hundreds of titles, documentaries are far more interesting than dramatic indie features; yet they almost never secure private equity financing. I can really enjoy watching feature-length docs about bluegrass music, female motorcyclists, theremins, soup kitchens, UFOs, animal rights, or Orson Welles without remotely being tempted to put cash into them. The odds of theatrical success are long in the first place, and docs often have fairly large budgets to recoup before profits. The secret of micro-budgeting is a short, well-planned shoot. Nonfiction films, more often than not, have to follow a subject over time, then search for structure in the editing room over more time. Both cost money.

This consideration held me back when I was presented with investment opportunities in a Chicago basketball epic and a portrait of a comic book genius and his bizarre family. Terry Zwigoff's *Crumb* was produced by my good friend (and *Living on Tokyo Time* producer) Lynn O'Donnell for about $300,000. It started in the mid-eighties, but my first limited partnership memorandum is dated May 15, 1991. Almost exactly two years later on May 17, 1993, I met the creative team behind *Hoop Dreams* for the first time at a day-long "think tank" in Chicago at the MacArthur Foundation. They were five years, and $500,000, into their landmark achievement. I was selling *Crumb* to Sony Pictures Classics just as *Hoops* was launching its six-month theatrical release via Fine Line in the fall of 1994. On the one hand, both films might seem dwarfed by the simultaneous mega-success of *Pulp Fiction*. But review for review, they held their own in the best film of the year sweepstakes.

Beginning with *The Thin Blue Line* in 1988 and gaining huge momentum with *Roger & Me* the next year, the theatrical documentary has shored up its niche in the marketplace. As underdogs, documentaries get an extra added proactive push from the film press, which is trying to even the playing field. But it's never level for general audiences. *Roger & Me* and *Hoop Dreams* were great high-profile triumphs which each drew about 1.2 million ticket buyers to theatres. The vast majority were neither blue-collar workers nor inner city (read "black") youth. So, is the elite, review-reading audience for docs expanding rapidly? I think not. In the same way that 20 million "show-me-something-mister" viewers are waiting for the next *Pulp Fiction*, about one-twentieth of that number is waiting for the next *Hoop Dreams*.

My policy has become: Don't invest; don't predict boffo box office; but do absolutely everything possible to support great nonfiction work. (I even dream of running a foundation to give money away one day.) Of course not every high-impact documentary has an impact on me. My personal favorite between *Roger* and *Hoops* was Barbara Kopple's wonderfully ambiguous view of the Hormel strike, *American Dream*. It cost over $1 million, a reasonable amount when you consider the five-year off-and-on 16mm shoot in Austin, Minnesota. Her director of photography was Peter Gilbert, who even then was shooting his own five year feature *Hoop Dreams*—but with Sony Betacam! *American Dream* is bathed in shades of gray. It fared poorly in theatrical release, via the short-lived Prestige division of Miramax, because it was hard, if not impossible, to tell the bad guys from the good guys. That hadn't been a problem on Kopple's earlier landmark *Harlan County, U.S.A.*, an influential film from 1976 whose actual mediocre performance has been mythologized through the years. Barbara won Oscars for both films, the second in 1991, a year when *Hearts of Darkness, Paris Is Burning,* and *Truth or Dare* were not nominated.

I drew a blank on three major 1991 documentary releases. *Paris Is Burning,* a $450,000 film, was on the festival circuit at the same time as *Roger & Me,* and I failed to grasp its appeal. *Truth or Dare:* Who wants to know more about Madonna, and then not learn much of anything anyway? Barry Brown did a phenomenal job cutting that film with very limited participation from the director Alek Keshishian. Although I liked *Hearts of Darkness* as much as Les Blank's fantastic portrait of Werner Herzog in *Burden of Dreams,* I was quite surprised that Triton scored with the film after it had played on Showtime. Seeing Coppola making *Apocalypse Now* makes the feature itself even greater.

Triton struck again (their last gasp) with the documentary hit of 1992, Errol's *A Brief History of Time.* When I claim that doc costs add up, here's "Exhibit 1." After Errol edged over the $1 million budget barrier on *The Thin Blue Line,* he kept going as the Hawking feature sucked up $3 million like a black hole. (Warners actually took the cake when they sucked up to producer extraordinaire Quincy Jones and spent even more on the vanity production *Listen Up.*) At Sundance 1992, *A Brief History of Time* succeeded *American Dream* as Grand Jury Prize winner in the Documentary Competition.

The Audience Prize winner that year was *Brother's Keeper* by Joe Berlinger and Bruce Sinofsky, the story of an upstate New York murder trial involving three low-IQ dairy-farmer brothers. Although Joe and Bruce had worked for Maysles Films, their major artistic influence was Errol Morris. More important, their industry view was totally warped by the long shadow of *Roger & Me* and its $3-million-dollar-deal. Joe's a great promoter. He primed the Sundance pump by sending out a multiple mailing of hilarious oversize postcards featuring his subjects, the grizzly, toothless Ward brothers. Once the festival started, they came (with their $450,000 American Playhouse–sponsored film), they saw (that they were the top doc), and they conquered (but only in their own minds). The filmmakers made a fatal error with distributors by mentioning a $250,000 to $500,000 price tag for their film. Since it was a crowd favorite, they may have built up to that level over time. But their insistence struck many as arrogance and made it easy to say no—especially since the "working" version of *Brother's Keeper* was clearly fifteen minutes too long. Distributors passed. Many documentarians secretly covet a *Roger & Me* deal. On several panels, Barbara Kopple has asked me to tell the whole story for inspirational purposes. Unfortunately Joe and Bruce let their inflated expectations slip out.

Fortunately, the Berlinger and Sinofsky story has a second act. With additional support from American Playhouse, they self-distributed—normally a desperate move. Joe is so relentless that it made sense for him to devote himself full-time for a full year to selling the film (no regular distribution company would have dropped everything else). His innovative ideas included the "homecoming" engagement. The two directors between them had grown up or lived in about half a dozen cities, not to mention the film's actual location of Muncie, New York. All of these play dates got an extra boost with that native-son-makes-good angle. With total release expenses of under $200,000, *Brother's Keeper* had a domestic gross of over $1.4 million. Collecting some of the film rental proved difficult without the leverage of follow-up product, but the boys showed everyone. Despite their success, one of the things they proved was that their film wasn't worth a $500,000 advance for North America in the first place—especially with only 7,000 home video units.

Around the time that the Ward Brothers opened in New York in the fall of 1992, I took a documentary from Hoboken, New Jersey, to the New York Film Festival. *Delivered Vacant* was a longitudinal study in novelistic depth by the talented and obsessed Nora Jacobson. It charted Hoboken's housing boom and bust over an eight-year period. I gave Nora $68,000 to finish this great chronicle on the one condition that she cut it down from three and a half hours to less than two. She came in at 118 minutes, and couldn't cut a frame more. It never quite caught on theatrically, and the running time made domestic and foreign television a near impossibility. I treasure the scope of Nora's achievement; but by the time she was willing to consider a 90-minute television version, Ellen Schneider at PBS's excellent, high-paying documentary series *P.O.V.* had withdrawn an offer to buy it. I get excited by almost any longitudinal study (*35 Up*, which Peter Gilbert also shot, comes to mind), but I was paying a price over length.

It was in this state of mind early in 1993 that I traveled to Chicago to speak at the IFP/Midwest and meet with Rose Troche and Guin

Turner for the first time. I had a message from one Fred Marx, a man who would later claim to have a thirty-six-inch vertical leap, at my hotel about a project called *Hoop Dreams*. As he explained the four-years-in-three-hours trajectory of the documentary to me, I couldn't wait to see it. He promised it would only be a couple of weeks. Two months later, when I still hadn't seen any sign of it, the MacArthur Foundation called to ask me to attend a day-long social issue documentary panel in mid-May where *Hoop Dreams* would be the major case study. After Gordon Quinn at Chicago's Kartemquin Educational Films and KTCA, the Minneapolis PBS affiliate, had gotten the ball rolling, MacArthur got over their traditional stumbling block and poured $250,000 into an *individual work*. Usually they practiced the umbrella approach of backing entire institutional programs—like *P.O.V.*

The morning the *Hoops* tape finally arrived, May 7th, I happily set aside my *Amongst Friends* work, and watched. I was the first outsider to have this privilege. Three hours and seven minutes later (with one interruption to change tapes), I felt I'd seen the best film of the decade. That first time I cried through half of it, finding the story overwhelmingly emotional. Janet came in to the office at lunchtime, and I told her she had to watch right away. I didn't plan to, but I also watched straight through again. This time there was less tearing up, more amazement over the better-than-fiction content—not to mention being awestruck over how the filmmakers captured everything and then found a compelling structure.

I called Fred at Kartemquin. He wasn't there. His fellow filmmaker, Steve James, got on the line. I gushed. I asked if there was a four-hour version. At the time, I had no idea that Steve had been living on soup throughout much of the production with three small children at home and a tireless wife working overtime. Two years later, he described the impact of my call: "It put me on Pluto. This is no lie. It was the first time I permitted myself to think that we actually had a great film." By then, I'd been to his modest house in the Oak Park suburb of Chicago and realized that his kids had an immense collection of sugary cereals that would have made Kevin Smith proud. I'd also seen his sweet, left-handed jump shot.

I went to the MacArthur meeting with two goals. I wanted everyone there to know I thought it would be criminal to cut *Hoop Dreams* down to two hours, which was the PBS-contract length. I also said it absolutely had to be transferred from video to film for the New York Film Festival and/or Sundance and "limited theatrical playoff" in the brief window that existed before its scheduled 1994 NCAA Final Four airdate.

The rest is history, although my contribution was behind the scenes. Not too many people were thinking at the MacArthur think tank. There were PBS people, there were Corporation for Public Broadcasting people, there was a sports psychologist, there was a minority ad agency guy, even a high school basketball coach. Astonishingly the two- versus three-hour version debate went on for months, as did the plea for another $70,000 to transfer to film for festivals. I had the wrong idea about how quickly the wheels might turn. Just because the foundation had $3 billion didn't mean they'd whip out a roll of hundreds. Of course, they did come through in the clutch. I thought I contributed one more good promotional idea that day. In order to play up the "Sweet Home Chicago" (as bluesman Jimmy Reed sings) angle, I advised getting a tape to Roger Ebert ahead of time.

I helped approach Richard Pena at the New York Film Festival. When the film was invited, Richard told me the filmmakers had backed out. They weren't ready. I screamed at Fred, but what can you say to people who've spent 20 percent of their lives working on a masterpiece. Anyway Sundance was the next logical choice. I forwarded a tape to Geoff Gilmore with a personal plea not to add it to a huge stack. Barbara Kopple called too. Someone on staff said it was "too long." Geoff eventually saw the light.

Once invited, I plugged *Hoop Dreams* in *Premiere*, then encouraged Steve, Peter and Fred to hook up with local Chicago sales agents Dave Sikich and John Iltis for representation. I already had a full plate with *Go Fish* and *Clerks*. If I'd known everything that would happen to *Hoop Dreams* over the next year, would I have acted any differently? Unfortunately, I simply couldn't have done the job in Sundance with the wall-to-wall action with Kevin Smith and Rose Troche. I was a *Hoops* cheerleader, a sub proud to be drawing pine at the end of the bench. The eventual $7.5 million domestic gross was about seven times greater than my high-end *Thin Blue Line*-level prediction.

There are a few misconceptions about the ascendancy of *Hoops* that require correction. Roger Ebert and Gene Siskel were instrumental in making others acknowledge the greatness of *Hoop Dreams* as an enormously important, transcendent *film*, not just a documentary about basketball. However they didn't *make* the film. When they broke all protocol by reviewing it before it had an opening date, before it even had a distributor, before it had even played its first show in Sundance, they did something very special. But the audiences, industry mavens, and other critics who saw the four shows in Park City that same week were responding directly to the work.

In retrospect, some dilettantes have also suggested that somehow the $400,000 advance on the Fine Line distribution deal should have been better—again the *Roger & Me* fallacy. Despite Tom Bernard's hyperbolic comment that the film could gross $25 million, Sony Pictures Classics never bid on it. Aside from Ira Deutchman's offer, the other bidders (Goldwyn and Orion) were in the same ballpark. Orion was the likeliest to go higher up the ladder (as they did later on *Crumb*), but they were essentially a stalking horse. After all, when you've come out of a bankruptcy and several key players on your roster have the title "consultant" it's hard to be taken seriously. Ira and Liz Manne of Fine Line made an impressive pitch for *Hoop Dreams* at the eleventh hour on a Sunday in Chicago. They emphasized audience outreach (translation: inner-city youth) via extensive tie-ins with their new parent company Turner Entertainment and the NBA. (During the 1995 NBA Playoffs Turner advertised: "thirty games in thirty nights. Now that's a *Hoop Dream*.") It landed them the prize.

So what did they do with it? Once a film has attained a certain destiny, there's a tendency to look back admiringly at every well-planned step. In actuality, *Hoop Dreams* probably was a success that could not be denied despite the fact that the first ten weeks were very rocky. The brilliant maneuver of having *Hoops* at the New York Film Festival (one year later) as closing night was truly inspired. However, opening day and date against *Pulp Fiction* in New York and Los Angeles later that week was nearly suicidal. The numbers were bad. The producers and their "stars" also weren't happy with the rearview arms-raised-over-the-skyline ad campaign. Arthur Agee took one look at the player on the poster and said, "Who's the white lard ass?" The critics poured on the superlatives, but *Hoops* hit the post-Thanksgiving doldrums and had dropped to a measly dozen screens during Christmas week. The year-end accolades kicked in, but the single run at the Piper's Alley in Chicago couldn't accommodate the overflow crowds for a three-hour picture with very few daily shows. Once the year turned, Fine Line started adding screens, then blew it all the way out to 250 runs the week of the Oscar (non) nominations in early February 1995. Ira Deutchman's tenure had ended in between, but his legacy on *Hoop Dreams* endured.

During the early winter lull, I went too far in playing the part of perpetual skeptic when I told Steve James it was all over. I never should have spoken that cruelly since Steve had often kindly described me as the film's "patron saint." My prediction was no longer a double whammy reverse jinx; I thought the film was dying on the vine. Ira took a longer view. He also used the lull for one of his ultimate acts of spin control. For the first time since we floated the idea on *Roger & Me*, he planted the concept of nominating *Hoop Dreams* for Best Picture. In a very well-crafted letter, he solicited the press to beat the drum for this idea. Once again Ebert and Siskel led the charge as they had all along on this film. (They'd tried briefly in 1989 for Michael Moore before the backlash got too strong.) One article after another mentioned the dark horse candidate for Best Picture, *Hoop Dreams*. Certain very foolish writers mentioned the nomination as a real possibility in the same paragraph where they suggested *Pulp Fiction* could be in trouble because of its violence. Lose the battle, win the war. We'll never know whether this documentary was number six or number twenty-six in the secret balloting. Given the fact that *actors* make up the largest group of voters, it would be more than a miracle if a doc ever made the top five. In the meantime the press got very charged up on the proactive trail.

As zealous missionaries, they were practically gunning for the much derided documentary committee. There'd been a scandal nearly every year since 1988. The ever-enterprising Joe Berlinger was the filmmaker who actually got *The New York Times* to write an editorial questioning the exclusion of *Brother's Keeper*. I figured *Hoops* was sunk when they made the hopeless play for Best Picture. I'm not a conspiracist, but I could just imagine committee members thinking, "Who do they think they are? We'll nominate *D-Day Remembered* instead." *Crumb* hadn't even made it past the half-hour mark with that crowd. The exclusion of *Hoop Dreams* resulted in one of the most massive press barrages I can remember. It also propelled the movie beyond even *Roger & Me*, and created an enormous recognition which fueled a record-setting home video shipment of 140,000 units. Some of this revenue will flow back to the three filmmakers, co-stars Arthur Agee and William Gates and their families, Kartemquin, Iltis/Sikich, the two high schools, and forty-one secondary profit participants. KTCA-TV gets the largest share; the MacArthur Foundation gets the glory. As I told Steve, their masterwork "surpassed *Roger & Me* in all categories except one—producer profit!" Losing the Academy nomination was clearly a short-term good. However, the three passionate filmmakers won't have that Oscar for the rest of their lives.

This final scandal resulted in some basic changes in documentary committee rules. The committee was split between New York and L.A., with each body seeing half the eligible films *in their entirety*! The eligibility requirement was changed to a minimum seven consecutive day theatrical run. Unfortunately, this reform is a mixed blessing for two reasons. Producers with more money can and will buy a four-wall run. More important, the tried-and-true distribution strategy of waiting for a nomination or the Documentary Oscar itself *before* opening theatrically has been eliminated.

At any rate, it was too little, too late for Terry Zwigoff and *Crumb*. His struggle to complete the creepily intimate portrait of the always sketching Robert Crumb and his distinctly dysfunctional family actually took longer than any of these other titles. Ultimately *Hoops* is very much a feel-good movie, especially if you don't dig too deep. Its performance reflects that fact. *Crumb* gets under your skin. The only possible way you can feel good is by recognizing that you're much better off than the Crumbs. Once again the critics have tried to outdo one another in the number of superlatives per sentence. Producer Lynn O'Donnell's advance description of the project in the 1991 prospectus was shockingly prescient in laying out the exact critical context in which *Crumb* would be discussed. Her financial forecast may turn out to be as prophetic since she audaciously projected "moderate and very realistic" producer revenues of $470,000–$700,000.

By February 1995, *Crumb* had already been called "one of the years' ten best" or even "the year's best film," repeatedly. It didn't exactly start that way. Once Terry and Lynn shook loose some money from people like Matt Groening, got a presentation credit from David Lynch, and steered a course for the Toronto and New York Film Festivals in the fall of 1994, the end was in sight. Crumb left the United States for France in 1991. By 1993, they'd dropped the idea of filming him there for lack of funds. It might have spoiled the movie, since his departure at the end creates a very particular feeling.

Terry Zwigoff is as cranky and whiny as his long-time friend Robert Crumb. As he had shown in his previous featurette *Louie Bluie*, he's also an extremely talented documentarian. Terry's physical being might seem fragile, but he has an iron will. I hedged on making any investment in *Crumb* for years. Finally Lynn put my feet to the fire, and I agreed to sell it—although I still thought I was out of the repping business. At first I also believed *Crumb* was too long at a full two hours, until I heard what festival co-director Tom Luddy had said when he rejected it for Telluride. With the film still running in the background, he informed Terry that these little biopics should only be an hour long.

Off we went to the world premiere in Toronto with one critical trade/press screening before the two public showings. The distributors were *there* in force, even the Turner-deal $100 million man, New Line's Bob Shaye. Except for October Films' Bingham Ray and Jeff Lipsky, they were all gone before the end—many at the ninety minute mark. Terry looked ashen. A couple of lesser critics voiced their approval afterward, but I felt no great optimism. Even October thought it could use trims.

The next morning, the critics had slept on it, and it seemed to have gotten under their skin. *Newsday's* John Anderson and both Jami Bernard and Dave Kehr at the *Daily News* filed the first favorable reviews. The turnaround started. The public went for it. The distributors came back and started to get in line. It took the New York Film Festival to canonize *Crumb*. At the press screening, no one walked out. In fact you could have heard a pin drop. Terry almost looked happy.

Sony Classics, October, Orion, Zeitgeist, Kino—anyone could have done an able job. However the last two have little capital, and October demanded fifteen minutes of cuts. After long sacrifice, money was important to *Crumb's* producers and they couldn't grasp exactly why it wasn't more free-flowing. Orion offered substantially more than Sony, but everyone there was still a consultant. Case closed. At least I thought it was until an extra month went by with no final agreement and much empty posturing. Sony stood by their $195,000 advance, no more and no less, out of which the film had to be completed in 35mm and delivered. I felt we'd plucked a film from the edge of the abyss and brought it to the verge of a solid deal. Lynn, Terry, and the other producers were disgruntled. Terry actually collapsed in bed for weeks. I knew Sony Pictures Classics would net out as much revenue as they possibly could on the theatrical release.

As for their Columbia TriStar video release, no one could tell if it would perform more like *Brother's Keeper* or *Hoop Dreams*. (It was 2 1/2 times the former, or 1/7 the latter.) Robert Crumb certainly wasn't going to be around to go and gladhand wholesalers from Blockbuster at the Video Software Dealers Association convention. Fortunately the original version of the film received an R rating so it can go to Blockbuster. Apparently the MPAA wasn't looking too closely at the very graphic artwork. Or maybe they shut if off like the Academy documentary committee.

The next time someone asks, "Do you ever get involved with docs?" I'm just going to answer, "No, but they always seem to get involved with me."

The Clerky Boys

JOHN PIERSON: Finally, after all these sessions we have to talk about *Clerks.*

KEVIN SMITH: Didn't I just tell you the other day that I can't even talk about it anymore?

Epilogue: It's a Wonderful Life, July 4, 1995

Kevin Smith may have run out of words, but I still have to wrap it up. As he would say, "What have we learned, Charlie Brown?" At least I managed to get this far by showing independence instead of telling what it is.

If I had Jimmy Stewart's guardian angel and floated over the independent film scene (my Pottersville) without having lived through the last ten years, would anything be different? Would Rick Linklater be unknown outside Austin? Would Kevin still work at the Quick Stop? Would Eric Schaeffer still be driving a cab in Manhattan? Would Michael Moore have a show on Flint Public Access instead of the Fox Network? Would Rob Weiss be playing gin rummy with Chubby? Who knows? It is an enterprising group, and I'm just a conduit. One thing I do believe with all my heart is that Spike's exemplary career would be exactly the same. And since I haven't even met Quentin Tarantino, he would still be king.

Ebert and Siskel devoted an entire show to the meaning of Quentin. Ultimately they advised him to stop acting. But along the way they used the buzzwords "watershed," "one man new wave," "the Tarantino generation," "director as rock 'n' roll star," and "the church of Tarantino" (okay, the last was just an internet update). But two unironic statements really struck me. In describing *Pulp*, Siskel said, "As *all* great films, it criticizes other movies." All? Later Ebert discussed Quentin's inspirations, then added, "*You* can be influenced by the same films that influenced Tarantino." If only I could start life all over again.

In sharp contrast, the curmudgeonly liberal humanist Rob Nilsson went on cable television in the Bay Area to deliver an acerbically funny thirty-minute diatribe about Tarantino as the culmination of a terrible fifteen-year cycle where movies have been about "just about anything except everything that matters." He labels him the "master blaster of irony" who portrays "civilization as comic strip," where the worst crime is to be unhip. Nilsson entered filmmaking as a Cassavetes disciple. As co-director of *Northern Lights* at the end of the seventies (coincidentally about fifteen years ago), he has not been well-served by my book or the viewing public. His complaints might sound like sour grapes as his forgotten or overlooked work has shifted from overt social consciousness to video experimentation. But his search for emotional honesty and his plea to stop measuring everything with a box office ruler does not fall deaf on my ears. In one amazing, breathless sentence he calls Tarantino "a synthesizing, syncretizing, synergistic fool pooling art, commerce, friendly public relations, and a 'what me worry' smile for all those industry hacks who have felt left out of the hallowed hallways of high art for so long." My translation would be: movie brat, art-film brat, and multi-brat all rolled into one—for the first time.

I like *Pulp Fiction* the movie, yet distrust *Pulp Fiction* the phenomenon. It is the determining off-Hollywood event of the last year, and probably the last ten years. Yet there are a few problems in using it as a bookend for this entire independent decade. If a film like *Stranger Than Paradise* empowered new filmmakers, *Pulp* has almost the opposite effect. And it certainly doesn't suggest a further evolution. Even worse, you have to bend over backward and jump through hoops to define *Pulp Fiction* as independent. Begin with the fact that it stars John Travolta and Bruce Willis. Even without their profit participations, it cost $8 million dollars. It was originally set up at TriStar and, eventually had a 1,200-print release by Miramax, a division of Disney. If Kevin's friend Walter was right that independent means a film that average people never hear about, then *Pulp* obviously doesn't qualify.

And if *Pulp* is independent, why isn't a Miramax Woody Allen release or a New Line Jim Carrey romp? Like the landmark Supreme Court pornography case, you may just have to know it when you see it. New Line honcho Bob Shaye is scheduled to receive the IFP Gotham Award for Lifetime Achievement in supporting independent film. His company recently announced a new feature that will unite Freddy Krueger and hockey-mask Jason for the first time. Like *Wes Craven's New Nightmare*, it could qualify for an Independent Spirit Award. One thing is clear: The definition of "independent" now is much more elusive than a decade ago. Could that be a dictionary in Travolta's glowing briefcase?

To take a stand, I rechristened my company Grainy Pictures, inspired by a string of Janet Maslin reviews in *The New York Times*. First she noted that *Clerks'* "fuzzy, grainy production values place it at the garage-band level." Then she warned that *Turnaround* was "grainy enough to look at times as if it's been shot through a tea bag." On *Go Fish*, she switched over to a remark about "muddy sound." (Muddy Pictures just doesn't have the same ring to it.) These were all *positive* reviews.

Yet some say I'm no longer independent myself since Grainy made a two-year first-look deal with the Miramax juggernaut. I defused criticism by declaring that I'd joined the "evil empire." Goldwyn's Tom Rothman left me a chuckling message saying I had "sold out to the fat boys." Shortly thereafter he jumped to a studio, Fox, to run their specialized Searchlight Pictures division, then became overall head of production. One of Tom's first productions was Spike's ninth feature in ten years, *Girl 6*. Spike's Universal deal ended with *Clockers* after five films in six years.

Recently I finally watched the deluxe laser disk of his debut, *She's Gotta Have It*, and it felt like a slap in the face. I knew that there had been conflicts through the years with the film's actors, and that Spike had talked about being embarrassed by their performances. But I was taken aback when he nearly disavowed the movie on the audio commentary at the end of the disk: "But personally you know, I just don't . . . It's not a big favorite of mine." That struck me as far more serious than John Lurie telling me he can't stand his acting in *Stranger Than Paradise* anymore. Both films excite me as much now as they did then.

Through the years, I think I've enjoyed my life in and out of the movies as much as anyone I know. But is there something about this decade that suggests innocence lost? Has the world become a meaner place? It may be inevitable when filmmakers start their careers not by aspiring to greatness, but by despising all the crap that's out and concluding that it would be easy to do better. Everyone certainly has to be more calculating now. At the same time, I *almost* feel more innocent than ever. The thing I lost after *Roger & Me* was not my innocence, but my lust for the deal. There might have been a small moral crisis, but mainly I didn't really believe that deal would ever be topped. I downsized to *Slacker*. The enormity of *Pulp* reinforces my resolve to think niche. I do worry about independent film being judged by deal terms and box-office results, as studio films have been ever since the consumer press started printing the weekend grosses. On a certain level this book endorses that measuring stick, but only in an attempt to portray, in a realistic fashion, the truth about profitability.

So what gains are the studios reaping from the new talent pool? I don't know exactly (modest budgets might be one answer), but activity is burgeoning. Since I started writing in Fall 1994, Gus Van Sant, Jim Jarmusch, Kevin Smith, Nick Gomez, Todd Haynes, Michael Moore (finally), Tom DiCillo, Gregory Nava, Richard Linklater, Gregg Araki, Bryan Singer, Rusty Cundieff, the Hughes Brothers, and Carl Franklin have all completed new films—half of them for studios. David O. Russell, Eric Schaeffer, Allison Anders, Hal Hartley, the Hudlins, Michael Corrente, Joel and Ethan Coen, and John Sayles have all commenced new films. Robert Rodriguez and Steven Soderbergh did both. After the release of Steven's second studio picture, *The Underneath*, he began work on his own micro-budget feature, the pathologically revealing *Schizopolis*.

As Soderbergh returns to his roots, Tom Bernard and Michael Barker enthusiastically continue to run Sony Pictures Classics as old dogs who don't believe in any of the new tricks—except for the fact that they're releasing six American indies in 1995 alone, as opposed to the three they distributed between 1987 and 1993. They bash Miramax's profligacy at every opportunity; Michael even used to do it at our Miramax-sponsored Cold Spring Film Workshop. Lynn Hirschberg wrote a Miramax profile in *New York Magazine* that read like a mash note to Harvey Weinstein. Although I believe we're all linked by a love of films, she made an unbelievably astute mid-article parenthetical aside: "the indie world is a spiteful, fractious place." Bernard and Barker have hunkered down for the long haul. Just because Atom Egoyan's Miramax release *Exotica* (successfully?) played on 440 screens didn't mean Sony was even remotely tempted to release Hal Hartley's fourth feature *Amateur* with more than forty prints, despite some producer grumbling. When their super efficient, old school model works, a film like *Crumb*, with its built-in audience, can gross more than *Clerks* with a cool $2 million less in distribution costs. Of course Terry Zwigoff's career may not receive quite the same boost.

For years, the filmmakers have come and gone. Finally, even the permanent government is breaking up. Tom and Michael's closest peers, Jeff Lipsky and Ira Deutchman, are out. When the *Pulp Fiction* $100 million express arrived, these two distribution pioneers departed after twenty years. They finally got the filmmaking bug. Jeff is planning to write and direct his own privately financed first feature. Ira hopes to produce a film for the persistent Alan Rudolph as Alan enters the third decade of his offbeat directing career. Since any revolution comes from the young, the best thing that could happen would be if a couple of kids fresh out of film school saw those vacant positions and resolved to try to fill them one day with their upstart ideas.

But first the audience has to be retrained, or in the case of these under-twenties, trained for the first time. Millions of consumers under twenty are turned on by a wide array of fairly obscure music on independent record labels. Yet few ever go to a review-driven, nonstudio movie—almost none without television advertising. As for the twentysomethings, the aging boomers, and the aging boomers who still want to act like they're twentysomethings (like me), the chains of laziness must be broken. We don't mind thinking about a movie we've seen, but we show less and less of an inclination to want to think too hard about *what* to see. As Hollywood attempts to prove H. L. Mencken's adage that no one ever went broke by underestimating the intelligence of the American public, the indies have to carefully coax and direct whatever intelligence is left. There's no lack of effort. In mid-May 1992, twenty-nine off-Hollywood features from thirteen distributors were on screen in New York. Exactly three years later, there were twenty-eight from thirteen.

And here's the irony: Everyone sees *The Piano*, yet *Ruby in Paradise* drops dead the day Jane Campion's film opens. *Pulp Fiction* nearly wipes out *Hoop Dreams* in New York on their competitive first weekend. When Harvey Weinstein says that the success of a terrific film like *The Piano* is good for everybody, he's not examining the statistics. It's certainly good for Miramax. Indie blockbusters expand the audience for the next indie blockbuster. Exceptional marketing causes a small handful of titles to become "satisfaction guaranteed" must-sees while the rank and file often go begging. The first half of 1995 has been congested, with very spotty results. 1994 wasn't bad; a number of films (ranging from *Clerks* to *Go Fish* to *Hoops* to *Spanking the Monkey* to John Dahl's *The Last Seduction* to Ang Lee and Whit Stillman's second features, *Eat Drink Man Woman* and *Barcelona*) found a degree of success—like water seeking its own level. On the other hand fewer viewers have seen *Laws of Gravity*, or *Swoon*, or Tom Noonan's *What Happened Was...* in theaters than saw Werner Herzog's masterpieces in the seventies. The comparative intellectual impact of these films on the cultural elite is also a pale shadow.

However their impact on other filmmakers is enormous. They're taking inspiration where they find it. As ever, Sundance 1995 shone a spotlight on the next batch of "filmmakers to watch" although there was no next Sodertino or Quentinbergh. The guy with the bowling noir is no longer in hock and staying there; he now has a $3.5 million picture. The festival itself has entered the sardine phase of overcrowding. 1989 was the last year that you could get a free drink; in 1995 you couldn't even get into the party to get to the cash bar. Sundance announced its own Viacom sponsored cable channel—one of 500?

So what do I make of new technologies in the decade to come? Late in 1984, repertory theatres appeared to be in the pink of health, yet video had plowed them under within two years. When I ran the Bleecker Street Cinema, I reported to its owner, Sid Geffen. Sid was a devilishly clever, some would say crooked, rogue and he loved to gamble. Although I had almost no money then, he preferred to make $100 bets. Over the course of a year I won several hundred dollars from him. One day he proposed a wager and I refused to take it because, as I told him, "I'm just not sure." He became furious and said, "Is that how you've been beating me—by betting only when you're sure? I'll never make another bet with you." Sid died in the late eighties, an unchanged man, and the Bleecker houses a video store and bar. And I'm still hesitant to bet on a future that seems so changeable even as certain trends keep recycling. Yet even the most insulated computer nerd knows that you have to depend on the creators of the software before anything else.

One final thought about technology, perhaps the one and only occasion when independent film and cryogenics come together. I read a story about the Kodak Pro-Tek film preservation vaults in Hollywood. Normally you might think of this facility as a place to store the *Gone With the Wind* negative. But no! Some indie producers who utterly failed to make a dent in seeking theatrical distribution for their first feature wouldn't give up. They just went into suspended animation by opting to archive the film "until a later time, perhaps years later, when a change in the theatrical environment would make the time right for the feature to gain wider exposure." Hope springs eternal. On cinema's second centennial, maybe this frozen film will have found its audience and *Pulp Fiction* will have been forgotten. Maybe not.

THE LAST WORD

JOHN PIERSON: The number-one question that anybody would have—could you get your career started now with a film like *Clerks?*

KEVIN SMITH: Impossible. I don't think so. Particularly not at Miramax. Particularly not the career that I have at this moment.

JP: It's a Miramax world now.

KS: I've said it a zillion times, and I'll continue to say it until I hit the grave, we were more lucky than talented. Particularly on the first movie. I love *Clerks*, and it still stands up.

JP: Agreed.

KS: We said the right thing at the exact right time. And I always said a year earlier, a year later, nothing would have happened. That has never been more true than now.

JP: It's ten years later. Would you be making a digital feature?

KS: I know me. I wouldn't have done a video film. I would have gone for 16mm, because the filmmakers that I read about, the people that I was weaned on, the people that inspired me, the Jarmuschs, the Spike Lees, the Richard Linklaters—even the Hal Hartleys, although years later he would break my heart(laughter)—they shot in 16mm.

JP: Just like I said in the original book, *Stranger Than Paradise* was actually 35mm. What's the Hartley heartbreak?

KS: He was once asked how he felt about being a mentor to young film-makers, a la Kevin Smith thanking him in the credits of *Clerks*.

JP: Uh . . . Oh, I remember now. It wasn't exactly a quote.

KS: I'll closely paraphrase the writer. "So exhausted was he after giving his vitriolic response that he had to go lay down." Apparently not a fan. So right then and there I took down my framed *Trust* poster off the wall and used the frame for something else.

JP: Nobody's heard from Hal in a while. Is the era of the rarified, European-style filmmaker officially over?

KS: For a filmmaker it's a viable approach, but I don't think it makes much economic sense. Once he said he had to lay down after bitching about me so hard core, I lost interest.

JP: In your imagination could you have made something else that would have worked in the contemporary climate?

KS: John, you're assuming that I have imagination to begin with (laughter). Many critics will tell you that you're absolutely wrong in that assumption. I can't go out on a limb and imagine me making any other movie. If I were to make *Clerks* today, there would be no impact, because even network TV has become more racy than it was ten years ago. Now, granted, they don't employ all the colorful dialogue that we do, but even sitcoms on the WB and UPN are getting there. I remember reading Owen Gleiberman's *Clerks* review in *Entertainment Weekly*, and he said something along the lines of, "This is what a sitcom will look like in ten years." And he was not that far from the truth. You know, shy of talking about butt-fucking or sucking your own dick they're almost there.

JP: I should watch more TV.

KS: I don't know that if I made *Clerks* today that anyone would give a shit. Because I don't know that we would have been saying anything or doing anything that would have been that extraordinary. That being said, I still get people today, who come up to me and have just seen *Clerks,* and still think it's funny as hell and it hits them in a certain way—not just people who are like, "Hey I saw that movie and it made me want to be a filmmaker." So I don't know who's right, me or them.

JP: *Clerks* and *The Brothers McMullen,* the movies that launched a thousand filmmaking ships.

KS: Cinema on the whole has progressed in ten years. It's taken massive jumps, which means you're competing for people's attention even more. And the independent field has just become so clogged and muddled at the same time, and co-opted. There are more independent films coming out on a weekly basis, as you pointed out, than you could shake a stick at.

JP: On average in New York, four per weekend—eight in the fall.

KS: We'd get lost. We'd get completely lost.

JP: And you can't imagine trying to avoid getting lost by having the name-cast version of *Clerks?*

KS: I don't think that movie ever would have worked with a name cast.

JP: Personally, I think it would have been ridiculous, but I still enjoyed tossing it around in my mind for a few minutes.

KS: We came close when Miramax wanted us to make *Chasing Amy* with David Schwimmer, Jon Stewart and Drew Barrymore. The movie wouldn't have been nearly as effective. It helped that there were actors in that movie with whom audiences weren't overly familiar. Now granted, since then, some of them have become incredibly overly familiar, and much maligned in the press as of late [hi Ben], but that movie worked largely for audiences because it didn't have anybody they knew, so you could believe the dialogue and situation. And you weren't taken out of the movie by it being some actor you'd seen before.

JP: Unless you'd seen *Mallrats*. But it's a good point.

KS: Same thing for *Clerks*, probably more so with *Clerks*. I mean, you joke about Ruffalo and Macaulay Caulkin. Nobody could get past that. People would be like, "Hey, it's the *Home Alone* kid saying, 'jizz-mopper.'"

JP: Yeah, and wondering whether he did it before or after *Party Monster*.

KS: Exactly. I think you can never point to a better case of timing than our movie. I mean, yeah, there are certainly movies where timing was impeccable, like *Blair Witch*, which was far more successful. But in terms of not just launching a single movie but an entire career? I was insanely, insanely lucky.

JP: Talent breeds luck.

KS: Everything was right in the industry at that point. I'm not saying everything in the industry is wrong now, but the same variables aren't in play anymore. The playing field is completely different. The soil has been mined completely. I'm mixing metaphors (laughter), but I don't know that you can plant the seeds anymore, because the soil has been demineralized.

JP: I'll leave that one to spell-check. What's the last thing you can remember seeing that was a first-time feature with no names in it? And I admit up front, I would have to struggle to answer that question myself. I mean, that was such a trademark for this book's era.

KS: This summer I saw *American Splendor*, but that had Paul Giamatti . . .

JP: And Hope Davis. That doesn't count.

KS: I did see the aforementioned *Party Monster,* and that had Seth Green and Macaulay Culkin, among others. I don't know, I can't think of a movie that I've seen recently that had a cast that I'd never heard of before. I came close the other night on cable, this Canadian movie *Way-downtown,* but I didn't watch it because I didn't know anybody in the cast! (laughter)

JP: I find it fascinating that Sundance still thinks they're fighting the good fight, and they bend over backwards to try and prove that they're still the home of first-time directors. But again, it just ain't the same thing.

KS: In my old warrior stance, I'd want to claim that our year was the last year before it was co-opted; but no, it had been co-opted by Hollywood before that.

JP: Forget about that. Afterwards you still have an unknown Neil LaBute introducing an unknown actor like Aaron Eckhart, or Darren Aronofsky with a completely unknown cast in *Pi* or, of course, the missing filmmakers in *The Blair Witch Project.*

KS: And there's the obvious—Ed Burns came after us.

JP: Burns was the year after, but it kept going for a while. It's great when new directorial talent introduces new onscreen talent. The two things do in fact play off one another, or at least they have traditionally. Bill Sherwood introduces Steve Buscemi. Even Tom DiCillo with Brad Pitt.

KS: And Burns introduces Burns. You raised a great question. How did studios find filmmakers prior to this? It's something you don't usually think about. Who decided that Scorsese should get a budget?

JP: Roger Corman. Scorsese, Coppola, Bogdanovich, Demme, Dante, Jim Cameron, even Ron Howard.

KS: Does that make him the Harvey, or Sundance, of his day?

JP: Way cheaper than Harvey, but nobody seemed to mind. You also have to wonder who's lost their jobs to the youngbloods. I used to joke that it was old-school guys like Dick Donner, but he [*Timeline*] and Richard Linklater [*School of Rock*] both have Paramount films out right now. Rick's got the hit.

KS: Never was I happier for a fellow filmmaker. Perfect example of a director using the actor properly.

JP: Could you summarize the different areas in which your View Askew empire has expanded?

KS: More than I imagined we'd ever do if we ever got in. Obviously we have a lot of merchandise that we make. And it's all kind of . . .

JP: In contradiction of your famous quote on page 201. Look it up.

KS: What was the exact quote? Who's going to buy a shirt with Silent Bob's face on it?

JP: Yeah. Note to myself. (laughter) If I ever in a future life get a new start as a first-time filmmaker, give me lines to be funny with. Presumably lines that could be put on t-shirts.

KS: There are easily 30 shirts with Silent Bob's face on them, and four different action figures of Silent Bob—not to mention Jay, of course. We just keep making stuff. Recently I got into a back and forth on our Web site about how much "we" charge for the DVDs, as if I name the price point on the movies. When it comes to the movie, I get to make it and that's about it. What I do have call over is the little action figures, and I've had a blast making those.

JP: Do you feel like you've been part of something bigger than just your own work?

KS: Yeah, in terms of independent film?

JP: I'm not going to throw the phrase out there. Whatever...

KS: I'm a guy who they still refer to as "independent filmmaker." Some more-savvy journalists have started calling me "cult filmmaker," but years after our first movie they kept calling me "independent filmmaker"—even after Universal gave us six million to make *Mallrats*, which was pretty far from an independent film.

JP: Right, but this is a really loaded question, because after three *Spy Kids*, they're also still saying that about Robert Rodriguez.

KS: I think they kind of tag you with it based on your first movie. But is anybody calling Bryan Singer "independent filmmaker Bryan Singer"? I mean the dude's made two *X-Men*.

JP: That's true.

KS: Those flicks made hundreds of millions of bucks worldwide. Robert would be the weird exception to that rule, because he has made movies that made over a hundred million bucks and people still insist upon referring to him as an independent.

JP: I think the idea is they're kind of homemade. But my argument is, so is—

KS: George Lucas—

JP: *Phantom Menace*, and so is *Apocalypse Now*.

KS: Maybe it's just time to redefine the term "independent." It doesn't mean low-budget anymore. It means, I guess, a film with a a voice, a very distinctive voice. In that instance I guess I am still an independent filmmaker because regardless of what people have said about the movies we've made, they each have a very . . . You know who they came from. Some people would argue that's a bad thing: "Ugh, all the characters sound like Kevin Smith." But they have a very distinctive voice and distinctive point of view and we've been able to maintain that for ten years. I feel pretty good about that.

JP: On a cultural level do you feel like you've been a part of something bigger than a guy making his own movies with a distinctive voice?

KS: That's a very loaded question, and it's one that I don't know if I can answer without seeming arrogant or egotistical on some level. I would wager that there are more people who know my name than know the names of even the four directors who inspired me to some degree . . . maybe not Spike. I don't think I've quite beat out Spike Lee . . . because you know, they named a network after him.

JP: He couldn't block it. If I get IFC to rechristen itself Smith TV, will you hire Johnnie Cochran to sue?

KS: The fear for me over the last two years looking back over the decade is that I think I became more noticeable than the movies to some degree. I had a conversation with Jon Gordon of Miramax about whether I'm a director or just a really good self-promoter—and that's a kind of sobering thought from time to time. I think I've been able to balance the two by doing the movies but also being a quote-endquote "personality," for lack of a better description. There's the Panasonic commercials, Roadside Attractions on *The Tonight Show*...

JP: You've been personally responsible for lowering the Jay Leno demographic by five years.

KS: Yeah, at least. And the ratings are always strong on my pieces, which is kind of cool.

JP: Well deserved, although he does bring you out right after the monologue. That must be a good leg up.

KS: Then there's the college gigs. There was a whole *Evening with Kevin Smith* DVD, with me just talking to college kids for four hours. At a certain point I'm thinking, "Wow, people know me as much if not more than they know the movies." There's times when that bothers me and times when I feel like we're coexisting kind of peacefully, me and my film career. So yeah, I've kind of become part of the pop cultural landscape. A bit. I don't know if that's a good thing.

JP: Michael Moore is a persona on the political cultural landscape more than a filmmaker or writer.

KS: Right. I watched *Bowling for Columbine*. It was deftly handled and entertaining to watch. But at the end of the day, I felt like the film did the same thing that he was accusing the media of doing, which was scaring people. Michael's an interesting cat, definitely more personality than filmmaker. I wonder if he would agree with that.

JP: He would deny it with his dying breath. He would deny that he's just selling himself. He'd say the work has its own—

KS: But it's a slippery slope because the two are so insanely connected. He is the work. It would be interesting to see if he could make a documentary that maybe had his voice, but in which he wasn't the central figure. But that's not what he does, so why should he try? Apparently what he does is working quite well for him, particularly when there's a Republican in the White House.

JP: Do you feel like you're part of a movement or a group that has changed the culture? Do you feel like it's really made a difference?

KS: I think so. I feel so. I'm part of the larger film family, my name is right there in Halliwell with Steven Spielberg. But I derive more satisfaction from being part of a smaller family, from being part of the Miramax mafia (laughter), rubbing elbows, if you will, or being mentioned in the same breath in articles with the likes of Quentin, or Anthony Minghella, or Robert Rodriguez. It gives you a familial sense, like I am one of those guys. I'm a Miramax guy. And that's my identity. There've been moments where I didn't know if I would always be a Miramax guy, or moments where I'd have to decide if I would be a Miramax guy any longer. And I've always come down on the Miramax side. I hope Miramax doesn't go anywhere, because I'm fucked!

JP: (laughter) A lot of filmmakers, not to mention the studios and their indiewood competitors wish they'd go to hell. Why is that you and your siblings have made it work, where so many others have not chosen to extend the relationship?

KS: With Miramax? That's a good question. You have to be made of a certain type of mettle, I think, to work under those conditions. For us, thankfully, we haven't gotten the full-blown Weinstein treatment as much as others have. I've only seen the classic Harvey that Ken Auletta wrote about in *The New Yorker* one or two times, maybe three max, whereas other people have seen him on a regular basis.

JP: The classic bad Harvey?

KS: Classic big bad Harvey. Generally our relationship (me and my producer Scott Mosier) with Harvey has been pretty low key, pretty amicable. I mean we've gotten away with making movies that I'm not sure anyone else would have let us make. In fact, I know that nobody else would have let us make them. That dude let us make 'em—from picking up our first film which, you know as well as I, had no other buyers at Sundance, all the way up to *Jersey Girl*. With that cast, I'm sure somebody else would have put up the money. At least that's what Affleck always contends. Let's stop at *Jay and Silent Bob Strike Back*. Who on earth would have made that movie except Miramax?

JP: At first I wasn't feeling very grateful about their support for that film. But I know what it meant to you as a gesture to your fans. Scratch that. It made me heave with laughter the other day.

KS: The fights have been very few and very far between—which is odd considering we've never made a movie that made more than thirty million bucks. Like we've never done *Pulp Fiction* business. You know you always hear Harvey saying, "Miramax is the house that Quentin built," and then people wonder why Quentin can take one movie and split it into two. It's because Harvey feels like Quentin can do whatever he wants because of *Pulp Fiction*. He put them on the map in such a major way. We've never had that kind of commercial success. For whatever reason, the dude has always made money off of us and genuinely seems to like us.

JP: Didn't you say Quentin returned the favor at some charity event recently?

KS: We went to Tom Sherak's MS Dinner of Champions benefit where the Weinsteins were being honored for all their charitable work. We're sitting in a room in the middle of Hollywood, in an audience full of people that you really felt just didn't like Harvey and Bob.

JP: And you're there because?

KS: They'd asked me to write a tongue-in-cheek animated short about the history of Miramax. I write a scene where the brothers are sitting at their kitchen table trying to come up with a name for their film company. Harvey's throwing out names, Bob's making fun. October—it'll never last. Dreamworks—that sounds like a gay bar. It gets kicked back to me because they don't want to make waves, wind up on Page Six, start a holy war with Jeffrey Katzenberg. So, on the eve of the *Kill Bill* release, they choose Quentin to introduce them. Well if my little joke would have caused a ripple, Quentin created this vast chasm between the honorees and their audience: "None of you fucks know what you're doing. These are the only two guys with any balls in this business. Ladies and gentleman—Harvey and Bob Weinstein."

JP: In the spirit of charity.

KS: I have a more bizarre paternal relationship with Harvey, and to a lesser degree Bob, than I did with my own father. My father I never really got into fights with. He was just my dad and that was that. He was a very soft-spoken man. Harvey is kind of the archetype paternal figure. He loves you but wants to tell you what to do at certain points in your life because he knows better. You're young and you don't. But he's always rooting for you at the end of the day.

JP: Always?

KS: Except when he's trying to convince Ben to do *Shakespeare in Love* and NOT *Dogma*. You know, various incidents like that.

JP: And Affleck managed to do both—for the glory of Miramax.

KS: I can definitely point to times in my life when I was mad as shit at Harvey Weinstein. I'm sitting in one of those moments right now. But at the end of the day it'll pass. I'm just not like one of those filmmakers that throws his hands up in the air and says I'll never work at Miramax again.

JP: Like Merchant/Ivory or Spike Lee.

KS: Why? Why would you do that? Why would you cut yourself off from the option? Particularly when they've done so many films that I respect, including my own?

JP: Yeah, but what if he's a parent who wants to take your money and give it to his favorite charity?

KS: What if he was that parent? Take my money and give it to his favorite charity? Would his favorite charity be him? Takes him a while sometimes to cut you a check, but he cuts you a check. There are times when I look at what I'm actually paid to do, and I'm kind of astounded that they give me what they give me in terms of salary or even a budget for the movies. *Jersey Girl* is a thirty-five-million-dollar movie, and granted, a large portion of it went to the cast—Ben got ten, Jennifer got four, so right there you're looking at fourteen, so you're down to twenty-one. But I got paid handsomely to make that movie. Although I never bring it up to them, you could probably pay me a lot less.

JP: You're not in Red Bank or Red Hook or Leonardo or Highlands anymore. You're in Hollywood now. Knowing you, I'm sure you're in it but not of it. But it's fun, right?

KS: We went to see *Return of the King* the other night, the premiere in Westwood. That's the first *Lord of the Rings* I've seen in a theater, the other two I watched on my screeners. Since I'm not getting DVD screeners this year, I'm going to see a lot more films in the theater because I can't handle VHS anymore. Looks too bad. Peter Jackson, along with Orlando Bloom and some other actors, had a photo gallery from the premiere up on AOL. Fucking the third photo is me and Mewes. The dude took a picture of me and Mewes at the premiere. The caption was "Jackson sees fellow director Kevin Smith and Jason Mewes of *Jay and Silent Bob* fame at the theater." I tell you, it was a weird kind of "ohmigod that's kinda cool."

JP: I'm telling you, you and Peter Jackson are physically connected. And you should definitely start the clothing line together.

KS: No, no, it's true. He's another Mr. Longshorts.

JP: We were standing around watching him direct at his Wellington, New Zealand studio during the final reshoots in May. We're going, "They definitely need to do the clothing thing together."

KS: Burly dude with a beard, wears long shorts and also spends an inordinate amount of time on the Web.

JP: Separated at birth. Older than you, but younger than you think.

KS: And he also did come from the same background. His early movies are very indie. Very, very hard core. *Heavenly Creatures* is my favorite.

JP: Newsweek reported that Jackson and Miramax, the original home of *Lord of the Rings*, are teaming up to audit New Line. Now that's ironic.

KS: Harvey was there at the premiere too. He was kind of cute because he was carrying around a poster under his arm. And we asked "What's that for?" He kinda sighed, "You know who Orlando Bloom is?" I say, "I don't know him, but I know who he is." And he goes, "I gotta get his autograph." I said, "Why?" He said, "My daughter told me to get his autograph." So he went, sat through the movie, didn't get any thanks at the beginning, then went to the party afterwards. I guess he got there before us. So me and Gordon and Mosier and Mewes were heading into the party and Harvey was on his way out, poster still under his arm, going, "I got it signed, I'm going home." It was a really human moment for a dude who's often been called an inhuman monster. (laughter)

JP: Any other humanizing moments with Hollywood's movers and shakers?

KS: Here's my latest—my only, actually—Jerry Bruckheimer story. I went to the DVD Exclusive Awards show to present an award to Stan Lee the other night.

JP: Oh yeah, I forgot to bring up all the comics you've been writing or your retail store, Jay and Silent Bob's Secret Stash. Do I get paid now?

KS: Anyway, as I'm trying to leave the building, they're insisting that I've got to take a gift bag. I feel like I don't need the gift bag because a) I don't need whatever's in there, and b) I can afford to buy whatever's in there myself. So I don't want to take the free shit. But they shove it in my hands and make me embarrassed to not take it. So I'm outside and who walks past but Jerry Bruckheimer. He kind of nods at me and keeps walking. Then he stops and turns back and does a, "Kevin. How are you?" But the funny fucking part of the story is that even Jerry Bruckheimer is carrying home a fucking gift basket.

JP: You're more up to speed on family entertainment with a daughter now right?

KS: Oh God, yes. And I can tell you what works and what doesn't. I was always marveling at your ability to call the movies that would be hits based on the enthusiasm your kids had to see 'em. And now I can kind of do that myself. Although I gotta say, the kid was one for two between *School of Rock* and *Elf. School of Rock* she insisted on seeing twice in theaters. She loved that movie!

JP: And Elf?

KS: She could take or leave. When we left the theater she said she liked it, but she was a little bored. She liked the Santa stuff, of course. And, thankfully, the movie ends with the Santa stuff, so she woke up again for that. But *School of Rock*—man, her eyes didn't leave the screen, and then she was dancing in the aisles as they were performing at the end. That's the power of cinema right there.

JP: (laughter) Fiji style. Wait a second . . . How old is Harley now?

KS: Four and a half. I remember leaving movies as a kid and wanting to be, you know, Han Solo. I don't walk out of movies now going, "Holy shit, I want to take on Mordor or battle the Orcs." A movie's just a movie to me, I mean the last time a movie inspired me was *Slacker*.

JP: Are you still inspirable at your age? You were twenty-one when you saw *Slacker*.

KS: Can I still be inspired? When I read your intro, it just made me want to go write. Sometimes you forget and all it takes is one powerful piece like that to snap you back into place and you go ohmigod yes, I want to be a storyteller. That's what I do. And I wanted to be part of that fraternity twelve years ago. And now I am a part of it. And I have a responsibility to do something with that. To not just be the guy that's mad because Harvey wants to cut more of his movie than he feels comfortable cutting out. Or upset because we had to move our *Jersey Girl* release date from November 7 to March 19. Or worried that all the backlash against Ben and Jen is going to affect the box office of the movie. That's all scenery and smoke and mirrors and you can fixate on that and forget about what's at the heart of it. Why I'm even sitting in this position right now on this particular movie is because I really wanted to tell that story. And I did. I should be happy with that and concentrating on that and not the details, the shitty little details that come along with the job—with accepting someone else's money to make a movie— that come along with the climate, the media climate, when you start casting people who are not unknowns in your movie—who are the exact opposite of unknowns.

JP: Thanks for a great first decade. You started off today grumbling about naysayers on your message board. I'm here to tell you, get off the Net and start writing. And if you really can't ignore those jerks, send Jay and Silent Bob to their houses to beat them up.

APPENDIX I

AMERICAN "INDEPENDENT" THEATRICAL RELEASES

The following is a sequential log for a decade-plus of American independent cinema. No studio productions are included, yet studio acquisitions qualify. With a larger independent like New Line, we felt free to pick and choose those films with a higher quality pedigree. By the end of 1995, the proliferation of productions from companies like Miramax and PolyGram caused a selection meltdown. Even so the annual release total jumped over forty for the first time, having been stuck at thirty per year from 1988 through 1994. (AP) denotes films receiving funding from PBS's American Playhouse. [S] denotes films that were featured at Sundance, a percentage that increases every year. For two bonus points find the "ringers" that were shot in Brazil and Taiwan.

Fall '84 through 1985

TITLE	DIRECTOR	DISTRIBUTOR
Stranger Than Paradise	Jim Jarmusch	Goldwyn
The Brother from Another Planet	John Sayles	Cinecom
Stop Making Sense *(doc.)*	Jonathan Demme	Cinecom
Paris, Texas	Wim Wenders	Fox Classics
Choose Me	Alan Rudolph	Island
Blood Simple	Joel Coen	Circle
Variety	Bette Gordon	Horizon

TITLE	DIRECTOR	DISTRIBUTOR
Streetwise *(doc.)*	Martin Bell	Angelika
Enormous Changes at the Last Minute	Mirra Bank/ Ellen Hovde	First Run
1918	Ken Harrison	Cinecom (AP)
Pumping Iron 2 *(doc.)*	George Butler	Cinecom
Almost You	Adam Brooks	Fox Classics
Secret Honor	Robert Altman	Cinecom
A Flash of Green	Victor Nunez	Spectrafilm (AP)
Kiss of the Spider Woman	Hector Babenco	Island
Dim Sum	Wayne Wang	Orion Classics (AP)
Crossover Dreams	Leon Ichaso	Miramax
Mixed Blood	Paul Morrissey	Cinevista
Buddies	Arthur J. Bressan, Jr.	New Line
Gringo	Lech Kowalski	self
The Trip to Bountiful	Peter Masterson	Island

Key Foreign Films: The Gods Must Be Crazy, Ran, Shoah, Dance with a Stranger

1986

TITLE	DIRECTOR	DISTRIBUTOR
Always	Henry Jaglom	Goldwyn
Parting Glances	Bill Sherwood	Cinecom [S]
Smooth Talk	Joyce Chopra	Spectrafilm (AP) [S]
Trouble in Mind	Alan Rudolph	Alive [S]
Desert Hearts	Donna Deitch	Goldwyn [S]
On Valentine's Day	Ken Harrison	Angelika (AP) [S]
Home of the Brave *(doc.)*	Laurie Anderson	Cinecom
Hard Choices	Rick King	Corinth
On the Edge	Rob Nilsson	Skouras
The Great Wall	Peter Wang	Orion Classics [S]
Mala Noche	Gus Van Sant	self/Frameline

TITLE	DIRECTOR	DISTRIBUTOR
Signal 7	Rob Nilsson	self
Belizaire the Cajun	Glen Pitre	Skouras (AP) [S]
She's Gotta Have It	Spike Lee	Island
Hard Traveling	Dan Bessie	New World [S]
Sherman's March (doc.)	Ross McElwee	First Run [S]
Down by Law	Jim Jarmusch	Island
True Stories	David Byrne	Warners
Nobody's Fool	Evelyn Purcell	Island
Native Son	Jerrold Freedman	Cinecom (AP)

Key Foreign Films: A Room with a View, My Beautiful Laundrette, Mona Lisa, Three Men and a Cradle, Sid & Nancy

1987

TITLE	DIRECTOR	DISTRIBUTOR
Square Dance	Daniel Petrie	Island [S]
Billy Galvin	John Gray	Vestron (AP)
Working Girls	Lizzie Borden	Miramax [S]
Waiting for the Moon	Jill Godmilow	Skouras (AP) [S]
Swimming to Cambodia	Jonathan Demme	Cinecom
Hollywood Shuffle	Robert Townsend	Goldwyn
Heaven (doc.)	Diane Keaton	Island
Sweet Lorraine	Steve Gomer	Angelika
River's Edge	Tim Hunter	Island [S]
Sleepwalk	Sara Driver	First Run [S]
Living on Tokyo Time	Steven Okazaki	Skouras [S]
Dirty Dancing	Emile Ardolino	Vestron
Matewan	John Sayles	Cinecom
China Girl	Abel Ferrara	Vestron
The Whales of August	Lindsay Anderson	Alive
The Glass Menagerie	Paul Newman	Cineplex
Positive I.D.	Andy Anderson	Universal [S]
Anna	Yurek Bogayevicz	Vestron

TITLE	DIRECTOR	DISTRIBUTOR
Slamdance	Wayne Wang	Island
Sign o' the Times *(doc.)*	Prince	Cineplex
The Dead	John Huston	Vestron

Key Foreign Films: My Life as a Dog, Jean de Florette, Maurice, Prick Up Your Ears, Wish You Were Here, Dark Eyes, Tampopo

1988

TITLE	DIRECTOR	DISTRIBUTOR
Patti Rocks	David Burton Morris	Film Dallas [S]
Five Corners	Tony Bill	Cineplex
Promised Land	Michael Hoffman	Vestron [S]
Hairspray	John Waters	New Line [S]
End of the Line	Jay Russell	Orion Classics
Stand and Deliver	Ramon Menendez	Warners (AP)
The Moderns	Alan Rudolph	Alive
Tokyo Pop	Fran Kuzui	Spectrafilm
Mondo New York	Harvey Keith	Island
Someone to Love	Henry Jaglom	Castle Hill
Unholy	Camilo Vila	Vestron
Da	Matt Clark	Film Dallas
Beirut: The Last Home Movie *(doc.)*	Jennifer Fox	Circle [S]
In a Shallow Grave	Kenneth Bowser	Skouras (AP)
Sticky Fingers	Catlin Adams	Spectrafilm
Midnight Crossing	Roger Holzberg	Vestron
Call Me	Sollace Mitchell	Vestron
Suicide Club	James Bruce	Angelika
South of Reno	Mark Rezyka	Castle Hill [S]
The Beat	Paul Mones	Vestron
Candy Mountain	Robert Frank	IFEX
Decline of Western Civilization II: The Metal Years *(doc.)*	Penelope Spheeris	New Line
Mr. North	Danny Huston	Goldwyn

TITLE	DIRECTOR	DISTRIBUTOR
The Wash	M. Toshiyuki Uno	Skouras (AP)
The Thin Blue Line *(doc.)*	Errol Morris	Miramax (AP)
The Wizard of Loneliness	Jenny Bowen	Skouras (AP)
Miles from Home	Gary Sinise	Cinecom
The Prince of Pennsylvania	Ron Nyswaner	New Line
Patty Hearst	Paul Schrader	Atlantic
Mystic Pizza	Donald Petrie	Goldwyn
Big Time *(doc.)*	Tom Waits	Island

Key Foreign Films: Au Revoir les Enfants, Babette's Feast, Wings of Desire, Salaam Bombay, Women on the Verge of a Nervous Breakdown

1989

TITLE	DIRECTOR	DISTRIBUTOR
Parents	Bob Balaban	Vestron
The Chocolate War	Keith Gordon	MCEG
Sarafina *(doc.)*	Nigel Nobel	New Yorker
Rachel River	Sandy Smolan	Taurus (AP) [S]
Heathers	Michael Lehmann	New World [S]
Dream a Little Dream	Marc Rocco	Vestron
Tapeheads	Bill Fishman	Avenue [S]
84 Charlie Mopic	Patrick Duncan	New Century Vista [S]
Powwow Highway	Jonathan Wacks	Warners [S]
Heat and Sunlight	Rob Nilsson	self [S]
Signs of Life	John Coles	Avenue (AP)
Earth Girls Are Easy	Julien Temple	Vestron
Cold Feet	Robert Dornhelm	Avenue
Vampire's Kiss	Robert Bierman	Hemdale
Scenes from the Class Struggle in Beverly Hills	Paul Bartel	Cinecom

TITLE	DIRECTOR	DISTRIBUTOR
Ice House	Eagle Pennell	self
Valentino Returns	Peter Hoffman	Skouras
sex, lies and videotape	Steven Soderbergh	Miramax [S]
Heavy Petting *(doc.)*	Obie Benz	Skouras [S]
Drugstore Cowboy	Gus Van Sant	Avenue
Breaking In	Bill Forsyth	Goldwyn
Apartment Zero	Martin Donovan	Skouras [S]
True Love	Nancy Savoca	MGM [S]
Sidewalk Stories	Charles Lane	Island
Gingerale Afternoon	Rafal Zielinski	Skouras [S]
Mystery Train	Jim Jarmusch	Orion Classics
Let's Get Lost *(doc.)*	Bruce Weber	Zeitgeist [S]
Roger & Me *(doc.)*	Michael Moore	Warners

Key Foreign Films: High Hopes, Henry V, My Left Foot, Camille Claudel, Scandal

1990

TITLE	DIRECTOR	DISTRIBUTOR
The Plot Against Harry	Michael Roemer	New Yorker [S]
New Year's Day	Henry Jaglom	self/Rainbow
Driving Me Crazy *(doc.)*	Nick Broomfield	First Run
Laserman	Peter Wang	Original Cinema [S]
House Party	Reggie Hudlin	New Line [S]
For All Mankind *(doc.)*	Al Reinert	Self [S]
Henry: Portrait of a Serial Killer	John McNaughton	Greycat
In the Spirit	Sandra Seacat	Castle Hill
Bail Jumper	Christian Faber	Angelika
In the Blood *(doc.)*	George Butler	self
Longtime Companion	Norman Rene	Goldwyn (AP) [S]
Big Bang *(doc.)*	James Toback	Triton
Big Dis	Gordon Eriksen	First Run [S]

TITLE	DIRECTOR	DISTRIBUTOR
The Unbelievable Truth	Hal Hartley	Miramax [S]
Metropolitan	Whit Stillman	New Line [S]
Wild at Heart	David Lynch	Goldwyn
After Dark My Sweet	James Foley	Avenue
Berkeley in the Sixties (doc.)	Mark Kitchell	Tara [S]
Pump Up the Volume	Alan Moyle	New Line
Life Is Cheap	Wayne Wang	self/Spotlight
The Lemon Sisters	Joyce Chopra	Miramax
King of New York	Abel Ferrara	New Line
To Sleep with Anger	Charles Burnett	Goldwyn [S]
The Kill-Off	Maggie Greenwald	Cabriolet [S]
Vincent & Theo	Robert Altman	Hemdale
The Handmaid's Tale	Volker Schlöndorff	Cinecom
Tune in Tomorrow	Jon Amiel	Cinecom
Last Exit to Brooklyn	Uli Edel	Cinecom

Key Foreign Films: Sweetie; Cinema Paradiso; The Cook, The Thief, His Wife and Her Lover; Cyrano de Bergerac

1991

TITLE	DIRECTOR	DISTRIBUTOR
The Grifters	Stephen Frears	Miramax
The Long Walk Home	Richard Pearce	Miramax
Book of Love	Bob Shaye	New Line
Meet the Applegates	Michael Lehmann	Triton
Alligator Eyes	John Feldman	Castle Hill
Iron & Silk	Shirley Sun	Prestige/ Miramax [S]
Superstar: Andy Warhol (doc.)	Chuck Workman	Aries
Paris Is Burning (doc.)	Jennie Livingston	self/Miramax [S]
Poison	Todd Haynes	Zeitgeist [S]
Chameleon Street	Wendell B. Harris, Jr.	Northern Arts [S]
The Object of Beauty	Michael Lindsay-Hogg	Avenue

TITLE	DIRECTOR	DISTRIBUTOR
Never Leave Nevada	Stephen H. Swartz	Cabriolet [S]
A Rage in Harlem	Bill Duke	Miramax
Eating	Henry Jaglom	self/Rainbow
Truth or Dare *(doc.)*	Alek Keshishian	Miramax
Hangin' with the Homeboys	Joe Vasquez	New Line [S]
Straight Out of Brooklyn	Matty Rich	Goldwyn (AP) [S]
The Hours and Times	Christopher Munch	Good Machine [S]
The Dark Backward	Adam Rifkin	Greycat
Slacker	Richard Linklater	Orion Classics [S]
Trust	Hal Hartley	Fine Line [S]
Pastime/One Cup of Coffee	Robin Armstrong	Miramax [S]
Twenty-One	Don Boyd	Triton [S]
My Own Private Idaho	Gus Van Sant	Fine Line
The Rapture	Michael Tolkin	Fine Line
1000 Pieces of Gold	Nancy Kelly	Greycat (AP)
The Comfort of Strangers	Paul Schrader	Skouras
City of Hope	John Sayles	Goldwyn [S]
Resident Alien *(doc.)*	Jonathan Nossiter	Greycat
Mindwalk	Bernt Capra	Triton [S]
Hearts of Darkness *(doc.)*	Fax Bahr/ George Hickenlooper	Triton

Key Foreign Films: La Femme Nikita, Life Is Sweet *(a bad year)*

1992

TITLE	DIRECTOR	DISTRIBUTOR
Daughters of the Dust	Julie Dash	Kino (AP) [S]
Thank You & Goodnight! *(doc.)*	Jan Oxenberg	Aries [S]
Mississippi Masala	Mira Nair	Goldwyn [S]

TITLE	DIRECTOR	DISTRIBUTOR
The Player	Robert Altman	Fine Line
American Dream *(doc.)*	Barbara Kopple	Miramax [S]
All the Vermeers in New York	Jon Jost	Strand [S]
The Waterdance	Michael Steinberg & Neal Jimenez	Goldwyn [S]
Night on Earth	Jim Jarmusch	Fine Line [S]
Incident at Oglala *(doc.)*	Michael Apted	Miramax [S]
One False Move	Carl Franklin	IRS
Monster in a Box *(doc.)*	Nick Broomfield	Fine Line [S]
Bob Roberts	Tim Robbins	Miramax/ Paramount
Gas Food Lodging	Allison Anders	IRS [S]
Johnny Suede	Tom DiCillo	Miramax [S]
The Living End	Gregg Araki	October [S]
A Brief History of Time *(doc.)*	Errol Morris	Triton [S]
Laws of Gravity	Nick Gomez	RKO
Mistress	Barry Primus	Rainbow
The Tune	Bill Plympton	October [S]
Brother's Keeper *(doc.)*	Joe Berlinger & Bruce Sinofsky	self (AP) [S]
Swoon	Tom Kalin	Fine Line (AP) [S]
Simple Men	Hal Hartley	Fine Line (AP)
My New Gun	Stacy Cochran	IRS
Claire of the Moon	Nicole Conn	self/Strand
In the Soup	Alexandre Rockwell	Triton [S]
Zebrahead	Anthony Drazen	Triumph [S]
Reservoir Dogs	Quentin Tarantino	Miramax [S]
Bad Lieutenant	Abel Ferrara	Aries
Passion Fish	John Sayles	Miramax

Key Foreign Films: Howards End, The Crying Game, Enchanted April

1993

TITLE	DIRECTOR	DISTRIBUTOR
Gun Crazy	Tamra Davis	First Look
Watch It	Tom Flynn	Skouras
Joey Breaker	Steven Starr	Skouras
Mac	John Turturro	Goldwyn [S]
El Mariachi	Robert Rodriguez	Columbia [S]
Bodies Rest & Motion	Michael Steinberg	Fine Line [S]
Ethan Frome	John Madden	Miramax (AP)
Just Another Girl on the IRT	Leslie Harris	Miramax [S]
Equinox	Alan Rudolph	IRS
Menace II Society	Hughes Bros.	New Line
The Music of Chance	Philip Haas	IRS (AP)
Delivered Vacant *(doc.)*	Nora Jacobson	Cinema Guild [S]
Road Scholar *(doc.)*	Roger Weisberg	Goldwyn [S]
Chain of Desire	Temistocles Lopez	Mad Dog
Amongst Friends	Rob Weiss	Fine Line [S]
From Hollywood to Hanoi *(doc.)*	Tiana	self [S]
The Wedding Banquet	Ang Lee	Goldwyn
Hold Me Thrill Me Kiss Me	Joel Hershman	Mad Dog
Boxing Helena	Jennifer Lynch	Orion Classics [S]
Praying with Anger	M. Night Shyamalan	Cinevista
The Ballad of Little Jo	Maggie Greenwald	Fine Line
Household Saints	Nancy Savoca	Fine Line
Ruby in Paradise	Victor Nunez	October [S]
Twenty Bucks	Keva Rosenfeld	IRS [S]
Inside Monkey Zetterland	Jefery Levy	IRS [S]
Combination Platter	Tony Chan	Arrow [S]
American Heart	Martin Bell	Triton [S]
The War Room *(doc.)*	D.A. Pennebaker	October

Key Foreign Films: Much Ado About Nothing, Orlando, Like Water for Chocolate, The Piano, Naked

1994

TITLE	DIRECTOR	DISTRIBUTOR
Red Rock West	John Dahl	Roxie Releasing
Golden Gate	John Madden	Goldwyn (AP) [S]
Sankofa	Haille Gerima	self/Mypheduh
Aileen Wuornos *(doc.)*	Nick Broomfield	Strand [S]
Suture	David Siegel & Scott McGehee	Goldwyn [S]
Naked in New York	Daniel Algrant	Fine Line [S]
You So Crazy	Martin Lawrence	Goldwyn
Even Cowgirls Get the Blues	Gus Van Sant	Fine Line
Fear of a Black Hat	Rusty Cundieff	Goldwyn [S]
Where the Rivers Flow North	Jay Craven	self/Caledonia [S]
Grief	Richard Glatzer	Strand [S]
Go Fish	Rose Troche	Goldwyn [S]
My Life's in Turnaround	Don Ward/ Eric Schaeffer	Arrow
Spanking the Monkey	David O. Russell	Fine Line [S]
Mi Vida Loca	Allison Anders	Sony Pictures Classics [S]
Barcelona	Whit Stillman	Fine Line
Eat Drink Man Woman	Ang Lee	Goldwyn
Fresh	Boaz Yakin	Miramax [S]
Killing Zoe	Roger Avary	October [S]
Totally Fu**ed Up	Gregg Araki	Strand [S]
What Happened Was...	Tom Noonan	Goldwyn [S]
Oleanna	David Mamet	Goldwyn
Pulp Fiction	Quentin Tarantino	Miramax
Hoop Dreams *(doc.)*	Steve James	Fine Line [S]
Clerks	Kevin Smith	Miramax [S]
The Last Seduction	John Dahl	October
Vanya on 42nd Street	Louis Malle	Sony Pictures Classics

TITLE	DIRECTOR	DISTRIBUTOR
Federal Hill	Michael Corrente	Trimark
Mrs. Parker and the Vicious Circle	Alan Rudolph	Fine Line

Key Foreign Films: Red, Belle Epoque, Farewell My Concubine

1995

TITLE	DIRECTOR	DISTRIBUTOR
The Secret of Roan Inish	John Sayles	First Look
Martha & Ethel *(doc.)*	Jyll Johnstone	Sony Pictures Classics [S]
The Last Good Time	Bob Balaban	Goldwyn
Amateur	Hal Hartley	Sony Pictures Classics
A Great Day in Harlem *(doc.)*	Jean Bach	Castle Hill
Blessing	Paul Zehrer	Self [S]
Clean, Shaven	Lodge Kerrigan	Strand [S]
Basketball Diaries	Scott Kalvert	New Line [S]
Crumb *(doc.)*	Terry Zwigoff	Sony Pictures Classics [S]
Swimming With Sharks	George Huang	Trimark
Picture Bride	Kayo Hatta	Miramax [S]
Search and Destroy	David Salle	October [S]
The Perez Family	Mira Nair	Goldwyn
Nina Takes A Lover	Alan Jacobs	Triumph [S]
Bulletproof Heart	Mark Malone	Keystone
Little Odessa	James Gray	Fine Line [S]
The Glass Shield	Charles Burnett	Miramax
Smoke	Wayne Wang	Miramax
Wigstock *(doc.)*	Barry Shils	Goldwyn [S]
Party Girl	Daisy Mayer	First Look [S]
The Incredibly True Adventure of Two Girls in Love	Maria Maggenti	Fine Line [S]

TITLE	DIRECTOR	DISTRIBUTOR
Safe	Todd Haynes	Sony Pictures Classics (AP) [S]
Living in Oblivion	Tom DiCillo	Sony Pictures Classics [S]
Kids	Larry Clark	Shining Excalibur [S]
Crude Oasis	Alex Graves	Miramax
Lie Down with Dogs	Wally White	Miramax
Postcards From America	Steve McLean	Strand [S]
Art for Teachers of Children	Jennifer Montgomery	Zeitgeist
Jeffrey	Christopher Ashley	Orion
Unzipped *(doc.)*	Douglas Keeve	Miramax [S]
River of Grass	Kelly Reichardt	Strand [S]
The Brothers McMullen	Ed Burns	Fox Searchlight [S]
The Usual Suspects	Bryan Singer	Gramercy [S]
Nadja	Michael Almereyda	October [S]
Jupiter's Wife *(doc.)*	Michel Negroponte	Artistic License [S]
Theremin *(doc.)*	Steve Martin	Orion [S]
Tie-Dyed *(doc.)*	Andy Behar	ISA [S]
A Reason To Believe	Doug Tirola	Castle Hill
Kicking and Screaming	Noah Baumbach	Trimark
The Addiction	Abel Ferrara	October [S]
Blue in the Face	Wayne Wang/ Paul Auster	Miramax
Doom Generation	Gregg Araki	Trimark [S]
Rhythm Thief	Matthew Harrison	Strand [S]
Reckless	Norman Rene	Goldwyn (AP)

[At the end of the year, Miramax released the following six productions with budgets up to $18 million: *Mighty Aphrodite, The Journey of August King, Crossing Guard, Two Bits, Things to Do in Denver When You're Dead, Four Rooms.* At that point, we threw in the towel on this log.]

APPENDIX II

INDIES IN RELEASE IN NEW YORK CITY
(See pages 204 and 335 in the text.)

	5/15/92		5/19/95
Miramax	Mediterraneo (Italy)	**Miramax**	The Englishman Who Went Up a Hill but Came Down a Mountain (UK)
	Incident at Oglala (US)		
	Delicatessen (France)		
	The Double Life of Veronique (France)		Muriel's Wedding (Australia)
	American Dream (US)		Picture Bride (US)
	Hear My Song (UK)		Priest (UK)
			Exotica (Canada)
			Pulp Fiction (US)
			Heavenly Creatures (NZ)
Goldwyn	The Waterdance (US)	**Goldwyn**	The Perez Family (US)
	The Playboys (UK)		The Madness of King George (UK)
	Rockadoodle (UK)		
	Mississippi Masala (US)		
Sony/Orion Classics	Howards End (UK)	**Sony Classics**	Burnt by the Sun (Russia)
	Raise the Red Lantern (China)		Amateur (US)
	A Woman's Tale (Australia)		Crumb (US)
	Europa, Europa (France)		Satyajit Ray retrospective (India)
			Farinelli (Belgium)

5/15/92		5/19/95	
New/Fine Line	The Player (US) Night on Earth (US) Proof (Australia) Edward II (UK) Where Angels Fear to Tread (UK)	**New/Fine Line**	Once Were Warriors (NZ) Little Odessa (US) The Basketball Diaries (US) My Family (US)
October	Adam's Rib (Russia)	**October**	Search & Destroy (US)
Trimark	The Favour, the Watch, & the Very Big Fish (UK)	**Trimark**	Swimming with Sharks (US)
Castle Hill	Othello (US-reissue) Who Shot Patakango? (US)	**Gramercy**	The Underneath (US) Panther (US)
Triton	Toto le Heros (France)	**Triumph**	Nina Takes a Lover (US)
Aries	Lovers (France)	**Arrow**	Ermo (Japan)
Kino	Daughters of the Dust (US)	**First Look**	The Secret of Roan Inish (US)
Skouras	Highway 61 (Canada)	**First Run**	Dreaming of Rita (Sweden)
Roxie	Good Woman of Bangkok (Australia)	**Northern Arts**	Dirty Money (US)
Concorde	Cabeza de Vaca (Mexico)	**Group One**	Erotique (Canada)

APPENDIX III

SHE'S GOTTA HAVE IT
starring TRACY JOHNS as NOLA DARLING
A SPIKE LEE JOINT

TOTAL GROSS=$6,125,000

TOP THEATRES

#1	Cinema Studio	361,208
#2	QUAD	299,039
#3	Fine Arts/Chi	233,931
#4	West End/DC	213,662
#5	Ritz/Phil	202,205
#6	Sunrise/VS	174,275
#7	Royal/LA	170,019
#8	RKO 86th	166,908
#9	Gr.Lake/Oak	142,683
#10	Gateway/SF	136,865
#11	Baldwin Hills	130,383
#12	Metro	125,892
#13	Nick/Bos	112,331
#14	Outer Cir/DC	105,943
#15	Harv Sq/Bos	99,536
#16	Tara/Atl	93,050
#17	Warner Twin	87,885
#18	Act/Berk	84,560
	TOTAL	$2,940,375
		(48% gross)

FORTY ACRES AND A MULE
YA-DIG   SHO-NUFF
DO THE RIGHT THING ©1986

TOP 20 MARKETS:12/11/86

#1	NY	$1,852,749
#2	SF/BAY	623,092
#3	DC	588,825
#4	LA	509,831
#5	CHI	395,308
#6	BOS	264,820
#7	PHIL	229,081
#8	ATL	138,138
#9	DET	134,183
#10	HOU	76,504
		$4,812,531
#11	DAL	76,400
#12	SEAT	67,726
#13	BALT	67,396
#14	SAN D	58,069
#15	MINN	49,620
#16	MILW	48,155
#17	ST.L	48,023
#18	CLEV	47,056
#19	SACR	38,165
#20	NHAV	33,669
		$5,346,810
		(87% gross)

BY ANY MEANS NECESSARY BY ANY MEANS NECESSARY BY ANY MEANS NECESSARY BY ANY MEANS NECESSARY

ISLAND
PICTURES

See page 75 in the text

INDEX

Aaronson, Bob, 256
ABC, *see* American Broadcasting Company
Abramowitz, Richard, 37, 42, 219, 224
Academy Awards, 29, 30, 58, 61, 77, 90–91, 98, 113, 139, 148, 166, 168, 170, 171, 173, 174, 194, 321, 326, 327, 329
Adams, Randall Dale, 104, 105, 109, 110, 111, 112, 113
Adams v. Texas (Adams), 113
Adjuster, The, 196
Affleck, Ben, 242
After Hours, 64
Agee, Arthur, 325, 326
Aguirre, the Wrath of God, 19, 214
Ahearn, Charlie, 17, 25
Aidikoff screening room (LA), 144, 145
A.J. Bauer, *see* Bauer International
Alambrista, 26
Aldrich, Robert, 216
Alexander, Jane, 76
Alice in Chains, 297
Alice in the Cities, 13
Alice Tully Hall (NYC), 97, 145–46, 150
Aliens, 69
Alive Pictures, 29, 107, 120; *see also* Island–Alive
"All the Young Dudes," 268
Allen, Woody, 72, 120, 219, 304, 333
Almereyda, Michael, 251
Almodovar, Pedro, 120, 195
Alternate Current, 84
Altman, Robert, 8, 38, 151, 171, 203, 308
Amateur, 335
American Broadcasting Company (ABC), 149
American Dream, 320–21
American Film Institute, 47
American Film Market, 309, 315
American Friend, The, 13
American Graffiti, 8, 196

American Heart. 286
American Hot Wax, 17
American Mavericks, 14, 15, 16, 26, 116
American Playhouse, 15, 98, 106, 111, 116, 119, 206, 209, 210, 321, 322
American Psycho, 245, 249
AMLF (French distributor), 128
Amnesty International, 84
Amongst Friends, 233, 237–38, 240, 241, 242, 243–45, 246, 249–60, 262–78, 279, 282, 287, 288, 296, 308, 323
    postproduction, 254–55, 258–59, 268
    production, 249–54
    release, 265–74
    seeking distributor, 252, 256–57, 259, 262–65, 307
    at Sundance, 257–60, 262–63, 274
    video release, 278
Anders, Allison, 27, 102, 202, 210, 211, 296, 334
Anderson, John, 328
Anderson, Kevin, 119
Angelika Films, 28
    Angelika Film Center (NYC), 28, 177, 178, 191, 194, 208, 222, 224, 309
Animal House, see *National Lampoon's Animal House*
Animals, 222–24, 226
Anna, 90, 91–94, 97–98
Annie Hall, 304
Antonioni, Michelangelo, 183, 186
Apartment Zero, 127
Apocalypse Now, 321
Araki, Gregg, 27, 43, 210, 211, 234, 236, 334
ARD (German TV), 37
Arkoff, Samuel Z., 104
Armatage, Kay, 100, 281
Armstrong, Gillian, 40

Arnold, Gary, 196
Arquette, Rosanna, 76
Arrow Releasing, 309, 310
Asbury Park (N.J.) *Press*, 125
Atlantic Records, 268
Atlantic Releasing, 61, 119, 262
Atomic Cafe, The, 19
Au Revoir les Enfants, 120
Austin Chronicle, 175, 196
Austin Film Society, 21, 180, 197
Avenue Pictures, 77, 142, 143, 145, 149, 150,
    151, 188
Avventura, L', 4

B, Scott and Beth, 19, 25
Babette's Feast, 120
Baby It's You, 19
Bac Films, 65
Back to the Future Part II, 183
Bacon, Kevin, 116
Bafaloukos, Ted, 106
Balance, La, 118
Balint, Eszter, 25
Ballad of Little Jo, The, 258
Band, The, 268
Banning, Bill, 153, 173, 309
Baraka, Larry W. (Texas judge), 111, 112
Barcelona, 202, 335
Barenholtz, Ben, 16, 28, 57, 58, 62, 86, 87, 94,
    118
Barker, Betsy, 188
Barker, Michael, 15, 17, 39, 40, 43, 61, 93, 120,
    129–30, 179, 187, 188, 189, 191, 193,
    194, 286, 293, 334, 335
Barnes, Paul, 106
Bartel, Paul, 17, 18, 26
Barton, Jerry, 161
Barton Fink, 129
Basinger, Kim, 262
Basketball Diaries, The, 226
Batman, 123, 124, 135, 136
Battle of Chile, The, 54
Bauer International, 9, 10, 12, 13, 118
BBC, 39, 58
Beastie Boys, The, 259, 268
Beat, The, 120
Beath, Linda, 17
Beaton, Jesse, 55, 58, 61, 66, 83
Beatty, Warren, 187
Bedlam, 15
Before Sunrise, 197
Before the Revolution, 12
Belizaire the Cajun, 65
Bell, Martin, 28, 286
Belushi, John, 100
Bender, Lawrence, 218, 260
Bennett, Tony, 259
Benson, Sheila, 143, 146
Bergman, Ingmar, 4
Berlin Film Festival, 7, 173, 296, 300, 315
Berlinger, Joe, 211, 321, 322, 326

Bernard, Jami, 167, 328
Bernard, Tom, 13, 15, 17, 40, 61, 120, 130–31,
    143, 188, 188, 189, 191, 193, 194, 233,
    286, 325, 334, 335
Bernstein, Fred, 162
Bertolucci, Bernardo, 12
Best Boy, 36
Beverly Hills 90210 (TV series), 240, 251
Big Audio Dynamite, 255
Big Dis, The, 127
Big Picture, The, 122
Biskind, Peter, 207
Black Filmmaker Foundation, 68
Blacklight film festival (Chicago), 69
Blackwell, Chris, 53, 62, 76, 130, 145, 192–93,
    220, 221, 222–23, 224
Blades, Ruben, 84
Blanco, Ray, 9, 12, 13
Blank, Les, 14, 104, 321
Blank Generation, 7
Blatt, Neil, 42
Bleecker Street Cinema (NYC), 15–16, 19, 26,
    45–46, 61, 104, 336
Blessing, 307
Block, Mitchell, 148, 173
Blodgett, Susan, 195
Blood 'N Donuts, 307
Blood Simple, 28, 55
Bloom, Marcie, 188, 194, 256, 291, 296, 309
Blow Dry, 14
Blue Collar, 46
Blue Velvet, 121
Blumberg, Matt, 249, 251–52, 253, 254, 255,
    256, 259, 260, 262–63, 265, 266, 268, 274
Bodies, Rest, and Motion, 286
Bogayevicz, Yurek, 90, 91, 92
Bogdanovich, Peter, 8, 61
Bolger, John, 36
Bono (U2), 221
Bonvillain, Mike, 253, 255, 268
Boomerang, 14, 202, 207
Borden, Lizzie, 27, 46, 54, 65, 83–88, 92,
    95–97, 98, 102, 115
Born in Flames, 46, 84, 87, 95
Boschwitz, Rudy, 174
Boston Film Festival, 224
Bowles, Eamonn, 291, 293, 297
Bowles, Jane, 86
Boxcar Bertha, 9
Boxing Helena, 261
Boyle, Lara Flynn, 177
Boys in the Band, The, 35
Boyz N the Hood, 192
Bradford, Gary, 51
Brady Bunch, The (TV series), 186, 261
Brahms, Johannes, 36
Brakhage, Stan, 2–3
Branagh, Kenneth, 262
Brantley, Alison, 128, 188
"Brass Monkey," 268
Brattle Theater (Boston), 20

Breathless (1959), 20
Breathless (1983), 20, 261
Brenner, David, 73
Bresson, Robert, 12, 186
Brest, Martin, 8
Brickner, Howard, 130
Brief History of Time, A (film), 113, 321
British Broadcasting Corporation, *see* BBC
Broderick, Peter, 229, 230, 234, 284
Brodie, V. S., 280
Brokaw, Cary, 29, 59, 61, 62, 65, 67, 76, 77, 142, 149, 150
Bronski Beat, 36
Brooks, Albert, 159
Brooks, Mel, 118
Brother from Another Planet, The, 28, 47, 50
Brother's Keeper, 321–22, 326, 329
Brown, Barry, 15, 46, 70, 226, 258, 294, 321
budgets of independent films, 234–38; *see also individual films*
Buñuel, Luis, 13, 186
Burden of Dreams, 321
Burg, Mark, 145, 193
Burnett, Charles, 205
Burns, Edward, 19
Burton, Tim, 55, 110
Buscemi, Steve, 35, 36, 39, 41, 43, 158, 189, 209

CAA, *see* Creative Artists Agency
Caddyshack, 306
Cage, Nicolas, 90, 128
Cage aux Folles, La, 35
Cahiers du Cinema, 131
Cameron, James, 237
Campbell, Tisha, 77
Campion, Jane, 335
Can I Watch Pictures, 311, 313–15; see also *Go Fish*
Canadian Bacon, 175, 256
Canby, Vincent, 27, 50, 92, 97, 146–47, 149, 153, 167, 168, 191, 220, 221
Canessa, Carlos, 70
Cannes Film Festival, 17, 24, 26, 34, 53, 54, 55, 59, 61, 62, 64–66, 77, 83, 85, 86, 109, 129, 179, 192, 212, 220, 231, 254, 291, 309
  Camera d'Or, 26, 66, 130, 132, 297
  Certain Regard, Un, 65, 107
  Directors' Fortnight (Quinzaine), 24, 53, 54, 65, 84, 107, 128, 129, 153, 208, 221
  International Critics' Week, 65, 86, 296
  Palme d'Or, 128, 193
  Prix de la Jeunesse, 66, 297
Cannon Films, 84
Canton, Mark, 159
Canyon Cinema, 14
Carnegie Hall Cinema (NYC), 15–16
Carpenter, John, 14
Carpenter, Richard, 208
Carpenters, the (band), 208
Carrey, Jim, 225, 333

Carson, L. M. Kit, 261, 263
Cassavetes, John, 5, 9–10, 12, 13, 18–19, 26, 89, 218, 332
Cassel, Seymour, 10, 209
Castle Rock Productions, 190, 197, 242
Castro Theater (San Francisco), 20
Cates, Phoebe, 308
CB4, 268
CBS/Fox Home Video, 28, 42, 75–76, 91, 131
Celluloid Closet, The (Russo), 35
Chameleon Street, 206
Chan, Tony, 262
Chan Is Missing, 17, 41
Channel 4 (U.K.), 37, 138, 164
Chaplin, Charles, 129–30
Charbonneau, Patricia, 39
Chariots of Fire, 161, 171
Charlottesville (Va.) Film Festival, 160, 167
Chase, Chevy, 163
Chicago Film Festival, 160, 167
Chicago Film Letter, 280
Chicago Tribune, 71, 296
Child Is Waiting, A, 10
Children of a Lesser God, 115
Chilton, Eve, 294
Chipmunk Adventure, 65
Chong, Rae Dawn, 62
Choose Me, 28, 120
Cinecom, 17, 26, 28, 29, 37–41, 42, 44, 50, 84, 91, 115, 119, 139, 141, 150, 151, 203, 219, 224, 264
Cinema 5, 11, 12, 118
Cinema Paradiso, 110, 143
Cinemax cable network, 42
Cineplex distributors, 118
Cineplex Screening Room (Toronto), 143
Cinevista, 17
Circle Films, *see* Circle Releasing
Circle Releasing, 28, 39, 57, 61, 62, 86, 87, 90, 118
City of Hope, 138
City on Fire, 176
Claire of the Moon, 286
Clapton, Eric, 87
Clash, the, 255
Clean Shaven, 225–26
Cleopatra (1963), 299
Clein & Feldman, 67, 68
Clein and White, 193, 266, 293
Clerks, 2, 4, 5, 21, 22, 79, 80, 124–25, 133, 134, 137, 178, 183, 184, 199, 200, 215, 216, 228–33, 279–88, 291–98, 300, 301, 304, 313, 324, 330, 333, 335, 336
  budget, 228–31
  at Cannes, 296–97
  release of, 297–98
  seeking distributor, 285–87, 293–96
  and Sundance, 282, 286–88, 291–96
Clinton, Bill, 104, 183
Clockers, 333
Clockwork Orange, A, 11

Coen, Ethan, *see* Coen brothers
Coen, Joel, 8; *see also* Coen brothers
Coen brothers, 16, 21, 28, 62, 87, 90, 106, 121, 129, 334; *see also* Coen, Joel
Cohen, Howard, 222
Cohen, Maxi, 15
Cold Spring Film Workshop, 175, 334
Collective for Living Cinema, 189
Collins, Glenn, 142, 145
Collins, Phil, 87
Color Purple, The, 47
Columbia Pictures, 77, 102, 122, 127, 128, 163, 192, 232, 235, 237, 263
Columbia/TriStar Video, 131–32, 195, 329
Combination Platter, 262
Come Back to the Five & Dime Jimmy Dean, Jimmy Dean, 38
Comic Magazine (film), 66
Common Threads, 174
Concept Arts agency, 93
Conformist, The, 11
Conn, Nicole, 286
Cooder, Ry, 27
Cook, the Thief, His Wife, and Her Lover, The, 88, 143
Cooley High, 47
Cooper, Karen, 77, 208
Coppola, Francis Ford, 8, 13, 108, 321
Corman, Roger, 8, 9, 18
Corporation for Public Broadcasting, 324
Corr, Eugene, 65
Corrente, Michael, 218, 334
Costner, Kevin, 194
Cotton Comes to Harlem, 70
Cottrell, Pierre, 64, 84
Coupland, Doug, 197
Cowan, Noah, 142
Cox, Alex, 85
Craig, Tim, 277
Creative Artists Agency (CAA), 287, 308
Crossover Dreams, 84
Crowe, Cameron, 259
Cruise, Tom, 264
Cruising, 35
Crumb, Robert, 95, 327, 328, 329
Crumb, 95, 313, 319–20, 325, 326, 327–29, 335
Crush, The, 266, 276
Cry Baby, 22
Crying Game, The, 203, 227, 294
Cundieff, Rusty, 269, 334

Dahl, John, 336
Dallas Observer, 269
Dalsimer, Susan, 116, 152, 160
Daly, Bob, 163
Dana, Jonathan, 222, 223, 286
Dances with Wolves, 194, 195
Dangerfield, Rodney, 274
Daniel, Lee, 191
Daniel, Sean, 128, 182

Dargis, Manohla, 220, 240
Dark Backward, The, 177–78
Dark Circle, 138
Dark Star, 14
Dash, Julie, 98, 100, 102, 208, 211
Daughters of the Dust, 98, 100, 207, 208
David Brenner Show, The, 73
David Letterman, Show, The, 136, 170
Day Lewis, Daniel, 39–40
Day Trippers, The, 132
Dazed and Confused, 182, 193, 196, 197, 202, 242
Dead, The, 119
DEG, *see* De Laurentiis Entertainment Group
Deitch, Donna, 39
De Laurentiis Entertainment Group (DEG), 120
Del Byzanteens, the, 25
Deleau, Pierre-Henri, 54, 84, 220, 221
Delivered Vacant, 322
Demme, Jonathan, 28, 50, 126
Denby, David, 169, 224
De Niro, Robert, 218, 219
Denver Film Festival, 160
De Palma, Brian, 17
Depp, Johnny, 19
Dern, Laura, 118
Dershowitz, Alan, 108, 231
de Segonzac, Jean, 219, 221
Desert Bloom, 65
Desert Hearts, 39, 40, 42, 55, 115
Destiny Turns on the Radio, 216
Details magazine, 266
Detour Productions, 185, 195
Deutchman, Ira, 10, 11, 17, 128, 141, 186, 335
   at Cinecom, 37–38, 39, 40, 41, 42, 50, 115
   at Fine Line, 194, 202–3, 220, 221, 262, 263, 264–65, 266, 278, 282, 293, 325, 326
Devine, Zanne, 90, 91, 92, 94, 98, 102, 126, 256
DiCillo, Tom, 24, 208, 209, 211, 334
Dick Tracy, 187
Dickerson, Ernest, 28, 47, 77
Dill, Bill, 130
Dillon, Matt, 142, 143, 255
Dim Sum, 115
Diner, 304
Dinger, Scott, 7
Dinkins, David, 143, 206
Di Palma, Carlo, 219
Direct Cinema, 148, 173
Dirty Dancing, 97, 119
Dirty Dozen, The, 9
Discreet Charm of the Bourgeoisie, The, 186
Disney Channel (cable), 294
Disney Company, *see* Walt Disney Company, the
distribution deals, for indie films, 29–30; *see also individual films*
Diva, 17
Do the Right Thing, 22, 23, 78, 79, 80, 105, 128–29, 131, 159, 171, 205, 285

Dobie Theater (Austin), 7, 187, 188, 189, 194
Dog Eat Dog Films, 150, 175; see also *Roger & Me*
Dogs in Space, 119
Doherty, Shannen, 239–42, 244, 245, 246, 247–48, 249, 277
Doren, Judy, 67
Douglas, Illeana, 5
Douglas, Kirk, 6
Dowd, Jeff, 55
Dowell, Raye, 64
Down by Law, 32, 59, 65, 76, 130, 223
Doyle, Cathy, 87, 94, 119
Drazen, Anthony, 209, 211
Driller Killer, 14
Driver, Sara, 24–26, 65, 86, 94, 102
Driving Miss Daisy, 171, 174
Drugstore Cowboy, 142, 171, 255
DuArt FIlm Lab, 36, 50, 51, 53, 84, 138, 143, 190, 205, 236
Dubinet, Ann, 224, 256, 262
Dunne, Griffin, 64
Dylan, Bob, 268
Dyson, Ronnie, 51

Early Frost, An, 41
Eastwood, Clint, 64, 159, 161, 205
Easy Rider, 8
Eat Drink Man Woman, 209, 336
Eating Raoul, 17
Ebert, Roger, 27, 65, 109, 110, 141, 142, 146, 168, 210, 324–25, 326, 331–32
Edelstein, David, 49, 69
Edinburgh Film Festival, 225
Edison, Thomas, 7
Edson, Richard, 25
Edward Scissorhands, 110
Egoyan, Atom, 22, 88, 195–96, 225, 334
Eisner, Eric, 220–21, 222, 223, 224, 256
Eisner, Michael, 144–45
Elgin Theater (NYC), 8, 15, 16
Ellis, Bret Easton, 249
Ely and Max, see *Go Fish*
Embassy Home Video, 87, 94, 95; see also Nelson Entertainment
Embassy Theater (NYC), 50
End of the Line, 120
End of the Night, 179, 208
Entermedia Theater (NYC), 14, 16
Entertainment Tonight, 170
Entertainment Weekly, 269, 293
Entre Nous, 17
Epstein, Rob, 174
Eraserhead, 16
Erendira, 84
Esposito, Giancarlo, 46, 74
Esquire magazine, 175
Estes, Larry, 128, 131
Eubanks, Bob, 193
Eustache, Jean, 64
Ewing, Patrick, 77
Exotica, 88, 334

F Troop (TV series), 143
Fab Five Freddy, 47
Faces Films, 10, 12, 89
Falco, Edie, 219
Falk, Leon, 28
Fall Time, 263
Far North, 120
Farewell, My Concubine, 110
Fassbinder, R. W., 12, 19, 129, 186
Fast Times at Ridgemont High, 196
Fedak, Suzanne, 120
Fellman, Dan, 159, 160, 161
Ferrara, Abel, 14
Ferrigno, Lou, 64
Field, Arabella, 219
Film Comment magazine, 160, 167, 168, 174, 186–87
Film Dallas, 118
Film Forum (NYC), 19, 26, 51, 59, 61, 77, 84, 98, 146, 192, 206, 208
Film House, 110
Film Odyssey (PBS series), 4
Film Society of Lincoln Center, 168; see also New Directors/New Films; New York Film Festival
Film Threat magazine, 177, 239
Filmex, 26, 27, 53
Filmmaker magazine, 138, 229, 230, 234, 312
Films, Inc., 15, 20, 24, 37, 77
Finch, Nigel, 43
Fine Line Features, 141, 194, 203, 204, 209, 210, 221, 256, 262, 263, 264, 268, 269, 276, 277, 282, 285, 288, 293, 296, 297, 310, 320, 325; see also New Line Cinema
First Run Features, 15, 45–46, 61, 87, 94
Fishburne, Laurence, 46, 74, 78
Fisher, Lucy, 152, 153, 159, 160, 161, 163
Five Easy Pieces, 8
Five Heartbeats, 70
Flash of Green, 29
Flea, 268
Flicker, Norman, 59
Fly, The (1986), 69, 91
Foote, Horton, 29, 106, 115, 121
For All Mankind, 127
Forrest Gump, 232
Fort Lauderdale Film Festival, 160, 167
40 Acres and a Mule Filmworks, 10, 57, 71, 99, 226; see also Lee, Spike
48 Hours, 34
400 Blows, The, 88, 124
Fourth Man, The, 118
Fox, Michael J., 119
Fox Television Network, 307, 308, 310, 331
Frankfurt, Garbus, Klein, and Selz, 40, 77, 152, 160, 189, 277
Franklin, Carl, 61, 210, 334
Frears, Stephen, 39
Fresh, 296
Fried, Rob, 260
Fried/Wood Films, 260

Friedman, Jeffrey, 174
Friedman, Rob, 161
Fuller, Samuel, 117
Funsch, Howard, 51

Gainor, Deirdre, 91
Gal Young Un, 15
Gallagher, Peter, 124
Ganoung, Richard, 36, 42
Garcia, Alberto, 190, 205
Gas, Food, Lodging, 210
Gates, William, 326
Gates of Heaven, 104, 109
Gavin, Bill, 166
Geffen, David, 221
Geffen Sid, 336
Geffen Company, 220
  Geffen Records, 221
General Motors, 144, 145, 150, 163, 166, 169,
  173
Genet, Jean, 208
George, Nelson, 49, 100, 122
Gere, Richard, 20, 119
Get Rollin', 50
Gibson, Mel, 205
Gigliotti, Donna, 13, 17, 40, 61, 120, 146, 188
Gilbert, Peter, 320, 322, 324
Gilmore, Geoff, 7, 208, 210, 213, 219, 257,
  258, 263, 282, 294, 324
Girl Can't Help It, The, 6
Girl 6 (S. Lee project), 333
Girlfriends, 12
Gladstone, Andi, 84, 92
Glass, Philip, 106, 107, 110
Glass, Schoor Production House, 108
Gleiberman, Owen, 269
Globus, Yoram, 84
Glover, Danny, 55, 205
Glynn, Kathleen, 142
Go Fish, 44, 227, 236, 276, 279–82, 285–94,
  296–97, 304, 311–18, 324, 333, 336
  at Berlin Film Festival, 296, 315
  financial breakdown, 311–18
  release, 296–97
  seeking distribution, 285–88
  at Sundance, 282, 286, 293, 296
  video release, 317
Godard, Jean-Luc, 7, 10, 17, 20, 175
Godfather, The, 8
Godmilow, Jill, 115
Golan, Menahem, 84
Gold, Joel, 15
Gold, Richard, 143
Goldberg, Whoopi, 55, 129
Goldwyn, Samuel, Jr., 59, 70, 222, 225
Goldwyn Company, *see* Samuel Goldwyn
  Company
Gomez, Nick, 98, 218, 219–24, 226, 234, 255,
  256, 269, 334
Gone with the Wind, 337
GoodFellas, 82, 250, 251

Gordon, Jon, 295
Gordon, Shep, 107
Gosse, Bob, 219, 223, 255
Gottlieb, Meyer, 149, 150–51
Grainy Pictures, 236, 311, 333; *see also* Island
  World: Islet division
Gramercy Pictures, 196, 256, 262, 263, 264
Grant, Lee, 12
Gray, Spalding, 218
Gray City Films, 13, 26
Great Jones Cafe, 49
Great Wall, The, 39, 61, 115, 141
Greenaway, Peter, 57, 88, 141, 143
Greene, Peter, 219, 225–26
Greenwald, Maggie, 211, 258
Gregory, Andre, 18
Greystoke: The Legend of Tarzan, Lord of the Apes,
  133
Grief, 43
Griffith, D. W., 7
Grigson, James, 103–4, 105
Grillo, Janet, 86, 282, 288
Groening, Matt, 327
Grokenberger, Otto, 26, 27, 86, 95, 243
Gross, Larry, 34
Guber, Peter, 163
Guest, Christopher, 122
Gumbel, Bryant, 45
Guns N' Roses, 256
Guy, Jasmine, 74

Haigis, Jack, 200, 246
Haines, Randa, 115
Hair, 51
Hairspray, 19, 22, 117, 205, 206
Halloween, 14
Hamilton, Peter, 18
Hammett, 13–14, 159
Hamptons Film Festival, 309
Handling, Piers, 309
Hangin' with the Homeboys, 207–8
Hanson, John, 15
Hardison, Kadeem, 74
Haring, Keith, 67
Harlan County, U.S.A., 11, 321
Harlin, Renny, 92
Harmetz, Aljean, 208
Harold Clurman Theater (NYC), 6–7, 16–17,
  34, 37
Harris, David, 106, 111–12, 113
Harris, Leslie, 98–100, 102, 166, 261–62
Harris, Wendell B., Jr., 205–6
Harron, Mary, 43
Hartl, John, 42, 187
Hartley, Hal, 4, 22, 95, 143, 180, 194, 195,
  202–3, 211, 216, 219, 334, 335
Hartley, Ted, 219
Hawk, Bob, 282, 284
Hawking, Stephen, 9, 113, 321
Hawkins, Screamin' Jay, 17, 27
Hawks, Howard, 16

Haynes, Todd, 43, 115, 194, 208, 211, 334
HBO cable network, 164
HBO Home Video, 111, 195
Hearts of Darkness, 321
Heat and Sunlight, 117
Heathers, 127, 240
Heaven, 107
Heffner, Richard, 68
Heller, Richard, 152, 163–64
Hemdale Pictures, 128
Hemingway, Mariel, 35
Henry, Lenny, 130
Henson, Lisa, 141, 159
Hersh, Andrew, 144
Herzog, Werner, 12, 19, 27, 104, 105, 129, 214, 321, 336
Hester Street, 12, 89
Heyman, John, 193, 220
Hicks, Tommy Redmond, 47, 57, 64, 67, 69, 77
Hildebrande, Lee, 56
Hill, Derek, 138
Hirsch, Mark, 249, 251, 252, 253, 254, 255, 256, 259, 260, 262–64, 265, 266, 268, 274
Hirschberg, Lynn, 334
Hitchcock, Alfred, 146, 147, 254, 261
Hoberman, J., 7, 22, 177, 220
Hof Festival, 26
Hoffman, Peter, 116
Holland, Agnieszka, 90, 91, 92
Hollywood Reporter, 165, 277, 294
Hollywood Shuffle, The, 70, 95, 235
Holt, Cinda, 173, 205
Hoop Dreams, 168, 189, 232, 281, 286, 319–20, 323–27, 329, 335, 336
Hope, Ted, 209
Horton, Robert, 187
Horwits, Mitch, 159–60
Hotel Terminus, 107, 139
House Party, 14, 75, 202, 205, 206, 207
House Party 3, 282
Hoving, Trea, 128, 153, 288, 294
Howards End, 194, 203
Hu, Marcus, 229
Hudlin, Reggie, 47, 211; *see also* Hudlin brothers
Hudlin, Warrington, 68; *see also* Hudlin brothers
Hudlin brothers, 14, 202, 205, 206, 207, 334; *see also* Hudlin, Reggie; Hudlin, Warrington
Hughes Brothers (Allen and Albert), 334
Hulce, Tom, 36
Hunt, Linda, 115
Hunter, Holly, 90
Hunter, Tim, 115
Hurston, Zora Neale, 57
Hurt, William, 29
Husbands and Wives, 219
Huston, John, 119
Hyams, Joe, 152, 161, 170, 171–72

"I Could Have Lied," 259
I Like It Like That, 102

"I Put a Spell on You," 27
"I Shall Be Released," 268
I Shot Andy Warhol, 43
ICM, *see* International Creative Management
IFEX, 86
IFFM, *see* Independent Feature Film Market
IFP, *see* Independent Feature Project
Illusion Travels by Streetcar, The, 13
Iltis, John, 324, 327
In a Lonely Place, 15
In the Soup, 10, 158, 209, 225
Incredibly True Adventure of 2 Girls in Love, The, 297
Independent Feature Film Market (IFFM), 37, 39, 116, 122, 137, 138, 153, 160, 164, 178, 185, 186, 194, 208, 231, 251, 282, 299–300, 307
Independent Feature Project (IFP), 15, 37, 317, 333
   Midwest, 322
   Program Committee, 106
Inkwell, The, 199
Inside Monkey Zetterland, 263, 286
International Creative Management (ICM), 237, 263
Into the Night, 179
Ireland, Dan, 93, 94
IRS Pictures, 210
Irvin, Sam, 17
Irving, Judy, 138–39
Ishtar, 299
Island/Alive, 26, 28; *see also* Alive Pictures; Island Pictures; Island World
Island Pictures, 29, 30, 37, 74, 83, 84, 91, 93, 107, 119, 130, 145, 150, 192, 221
   and *She's Gotta Have It,* 53, 55, 58, 59, 61, 62, 64, 65, 66–67, 68, 70, 71, 75, 76, 77, 122
   see also Island/Alive; Island Records; Island World
Island Records, 53, 192, 259
Island World, 192–93, 220–21, 222, 223, 224, 226, 256, 257, 262, 264, 274, 277
   Islet division, 193, 209, 210, 220, 249, 251, 252, 253, 255, 268, 269, 274, 276, 277, 286, 311, 313–15, 318; *see also* Grainy Pictures
   see also Island/Alive; Island Pictures; Island Records
I've Heard the Mermaids Singing, 119
Ives, John, 40
Ivory, James, 42, 91, 194, 203

J&M International, 109
Jackie Robinson (S. Lee project), 333
Jacks, James (Jim), 21, 28, 141, 151, 158, 159, 162, 182, 196, 246, 296
Jackson, George, 47, 53
Jackson, Larry, 59, 66
Jackson, Pamm, 58, 64, 71
Jacob, Gilles, 128

Jacobs, Jeffrey, 194, 222, 224, 309
Jacobs, Susan, 67
Jacobson, Harlan, 160, 167, 168, 169
Jacobson, Nora, 322
Jaglom, Henry, 10, 14, 142, 304
Jahan, Olivier, 54, 84, 220, 221
James, Caryn, 291, 294
James, Steve, 323, 324, 326
Jarmusch, Jim, 4, 8, 10, 19, 22, 23, 24–28,
    31–33, 40, 46, 56, 59, 64, 65, 66, 86, 95,
    106, 121, 130–31, 152, 202, 203, 209,
    216, 223, 226, 262, 334
Jaws, 8, 21, 186, 246
Jerome Foundation, 51
Jesus of Montreal, 195
Jet magazine, 71
JFK, 58
Jimenez, Neal, 209, 211
Jimi Plays Berkeley, 7
Jimmy Hollywood, 277
Joanou, Phil, 254
Joe & Maxi, 15
Joe's Bed-Stuy Barbershop: We Cut Heads, 46, 47,
    54, 78
Johnny Suede, 43, 209, 225
Johns, Tracy Camila, 50, 55, 64–65, 77
Johnson, Aryan, 99
Joint Adventure, 237
Jones, Duane, 17
Jones, Loretha, 70, 74, 76, 77
Jones, Mick, 255
Jones, Quincy, 59, 321
Jones, Robert, 262
Jordan, Neil, 227
Jost, Jon, 234
Jugular Wine, 307
Julia, Raul, 29
Jules and Jim, 20
Jungle Fever, 56, 129, 192
Just Another Girl on the IRT, 99–100, 193, 251, 262
JVC corporation, 130

Kadakawa corporation, 223
Kael, Pauline, 5, 168
Kafka, 202
Kalin, Tom, 43, 193, 209, 211, 223, 280, 281,
    314, 315; *see also* Kalin Vachon
    Productions, Inc.
Kalin Vachon Productions, Inc. (KVPI), 311,
    313–15; see also *Go Fish*
Kaplan, Paul, 35, 43
Kardish, Larry, 191
Karl Lorimar Home Video, 87, 118
Kartemquin Educational Films, 323, 327
Katzenberg, Jeffrey, 144
Keaton, Buster, 16, 19, 26
Keaton, Diane, 107
Kehr, Dave, 66, 71, 293, 328
Keitel, Harvey, 216, 218, 227
Kemper, Julie, 91
Kemper Insurance Group, 91

Kentucky Fried Movie, 183
Kerrigan, Lodge, 225
Keshishian, Alek, 321
Keys, Wendy, 150
Kid 'n Play, 205
Killer of Sheep, 205
King, Andrea, 165
King of the Hill, 131
Kings of the Road, 12
Kinks, The
Kino International, 98, 328
Kirkland, Sally, 90, 91, 92, 93, 97–98
Kirkley, Marcia, 295
Kiss Me Deadly, 216
Kiss of the Spider Woman, 29, 30, 66, 76, 203
Kitt, Sam, 14, 15, 16, 20, 26, 37, 128, 159,
    190–91, 226
Klein, Arthur, 109, 163
Klein, David, 200, 243
Kluge, John, 194
Koch, Ed, 309–10
Koch, Joanne, 168
Konk, 25
Kopple, Barbara, 102, 320–21, 322, 324
Koppel, Ted, 45
Kotto, Yaphet, 121
Krim, Arthur, 194
Krush Groove, 47
KTCA-TV (Minneapolis), 323, 327
Kubrick, Stanley, 161
Kuhn, Michael, 263, 264
Kureishi, Hanif, 39, 43
Kurosawa, Akira, 16, 59, 61, 150
Kurys, Diane, 17
KVPI, *see* Kalin Vachon Productions, Inc.

LA Weekly, 69, 265
Labadie, Jean, 65
Lam, Ringo, 176
Lancaster, Burt, 6
Lancelot du Lac, 186
Landis, John, 179, 182–83
Landmark Films, 61
Landmark Theater chain, 20, 58, 297
Lane, Charles, 129–30, 153, 192
Lang, Fritz, 7
Lange, Jessica, 120
Largo Entertainment, 264
Last Metro, The, 17
Last Outlaw Films, 252, 253, 254, 255, 256,
    265, 268, 276, 277; see also *Amongst
    Friends*; Weiss, Rob
Last Picture Show, The, 8
Last Seduction, The, 336
Last Tango in Paris, 11
Late Show, The, see *David Letterman Show, The*
Lathan, Stan, 55
Laurel and Hardy, 77
Law, Lindsay, 106, 206
Laws of Gravity, 180, 218–27, 229, 234, 235,
    237, 255, 256, 285, 309, 336

budget, 219, 227, 229, 234
  at festivals, 219, 224
  release, 224–26
  seeking distributor, 220–24
Layton, Charles, 128
Lee, Ang, 209, 336
Lee, Bill, 47, 49
Lee, David, 55, 79
Lee, Spike (Shelton J. Lee), 8, 10, 26, 27, 45,
  103, 106, 130, 131, 152, 189, 196, 200,
  220, 225, 232, 236, 258, 297, 331
  as "black Woody Allen," 61, 65, 69
  at Cannes, 64–66
  Clockers, 333
  Do the Right Thing, 78, 79, 80, 105, 128–29
  as inspiration to K. Smith and others, 4, 19,
    22, 23, 79–82, 216
  Joe's Bed-Stuy Barbershop, 46, 47, 53, 78
  Jungle Fever, 22, 56, 129, 192
  Malcolm X, 78
  as mentor, 99, 121, 192, 226
  Messenger (aborted project), 46, 47
  post-Clockers projects, 333
  School Daze, 73–74, 75, 76–77, 78, 82, 122, 128
  She's Gotta Have It, 32, 44, 46–73, 74–78,
    79–80, 81–82, 85, 87, 91, 92, 95, 121,
    167, 170, 174, 234, 235, 317–18
Leguizamo, John, 207, 223
Leigh, Janet, 27
Leigh, Mike, 58
Leipzig Film Festival, 160, 167
Lemon Sky, 116
Leno, Jay, 136
Leonard, Sugar Ray, 147
Leone, Sergio, 20
Lesher, John, 257, 260, 264, 268, 277
Lethal Weapon, 205
Let's Get Bizzee, 306
Letter to Brezhnev, 118
Letterman, David, 73
Levin, Doron, 145
Levin, Lloyd (of Largo), 264
Levine, Scott, 13
Levine, Sydney, 87
Levinson, Barry, 277–78, 304
Levy, Jefery, 286
Lewis, Claudia, 142
Lianna, 17, 35
Liberty Films, see Bauer International
Libra Films, 16, 26
Life and Tales of Tony D., The, 304
Life of Brian, The, 11
Lightning over Water, 25, 57
Linde, David, 295, 297
Linklater, Richard, 4, 21, 22, 180–81, 182, 183,
  184, 185–91, 193–97, 202, 211, 216, 220,
  234, 236, 331, 334
Lion King, The, 232
Lipsky, Jeff, 10, 12, 26, 27–28, 40, 56, 59, 66,
  89–90, 95, 107, 115, 118–19, 145, 210,
  295, 306, 328, 335

Lipsky, Mark, 87, 88, 89, 92, 111
Lipson, Mark, 106, 108, 110, 111, 112
Liquid Sky, 17
Listen Up, 321
Live Home Video, 213, 218
Living End, The, 43, 210, 229, 234, 301
Living in Oblivion, 209
Living on Tokyo Time, 88, 89–90, 95, 119, 237,
  320
Livingston, Jennie, 192, 211
Loader, Jayne, 19
Lolita, 16
Lollobrigida, Gina, 6
London, Barry, 264
London Film Festival, 160, 167, 309
Lonesome Dove (miniseries), 317
Longtime Companion, 43, 206
Los Angeles Film Critics Association, 168
Los Angeles Times, 42, 86, 143, 194, 291, 294
  Calendar section, 147, 173
Louie Bluie, 328
Lounge Lizards, 25
Love Crimes, 98
"Low Spark of High-Heeled Boys, The" 259
Lucas, George, 8, 59
Luddy, Tom, 328
Lugo, Mary, 266
Lumière, Louis and Auguste, 7, 173
Lurie, John, 7, 25, 333
Lynch, David, 16, 251, 261, 327
Lynch, Jennifer, 261, 262
Lynch, Kelly, 142, 143

Mac, 132, 286
MacArthur Foundation, 113, 281, 320, 323,
  324, 327
McCarthy, Todd, 42
McCormick, John, 89
MacDowell, Andie, 124, 133, 134
McElwee, Ross, 107, 115
McHenry, Doug, 47
McLean, Steve, 43, 312, 318
McNally, Keith, 179, 208
Macpherson, Elle, 93
Madonna, 187, 193–94, 210, 321
Madsen, Michael, 227
Magno Sound, 254
  Screening Room, 220
Maine Photographic Workshop, 138, 186, 188
Making Love, 35
Making of Michael Jackson's Thriller, The (video),
  93
Malcolm X, 58, 78
Malin, Amir, 38, 39, 40, 119, 151
Malle, Louis, 17, 120
Mallrats, 2, 21, 181–82, 183, 200, 239–41, 242,
  243, 247, 248, 296
Malta, Kathy, 259
Mamet, David, 293, 304
Man Who Fell to Earth, The, 11
Mandel, Yoram 34, 43, 50

Mann, Michael, 254
Manne, Liz, 325
Mansfield, Jayne, 6
Mansour, George, 71
Manzari, Bert, 297
Marchese, John, 175
Mariachi, El, 229, 232, 235, 237–38, 261, 263
Marky Mark, *see* Wahlberg, Mark
Marley, Bob, 53
Marriage of Maria Braun, The, 12
Martesko, Karol, 138
Martha and Ethel, 291
Martin, Darnell, 99, 102
Marx, Fred, 323, 324
Mask, The, 225
Maslin, Janet, 42, 97, 122, 296, 333
Maysles, Albert and David, 14
Maysles Films, 321
MCA, 221; *see also* Universal Pictures
MCEG, 132
Mean Streets, 8, 9, 11, 215, 218, 245, 253, 269
Meistrich, Larry, 219, 223, 224, 225
Menace II Society, 75
Mencken, H. L., 335
Merchant, Ismail, 42, 91, 194, 203
Meteor Man, 70
Metro-Goldwyn-Mayer, *see* MGM
Metropolitan, 141, 186, 190, 191, 195, 203, 251
Metzger, Tory, 287
Meyer, Gary, 58
Meyer, Russ, 16
MGM, 73, 76, 126, 161
Mi Vida Loca, 202
"Michael and Me" (Jacobson), 167
Michaels, Lorne, 73
Michaelson, Herb, 54, 92, 147
Michelson, Annette, 34
MIFED, 87
Mifune, Toshiro, 16
Miles from Home, 119
Milgrom, Al, 13
Minnelli, Vincente, 49, 73, 197
Miramax Films, 7, 84, 100, 114, 128, 130, 143,
    170, 188, 192, 202, 203, 204, 208, 209,
    251, 256–57, 288, 294, 310, 334, 336
  and *Clerks,* 229, 231, 232, 233, 281, 285,
    287, 293, 295, 296, 298
  interest in *Anna,* 92–93, 97
  interest in *Roger & Me,* 143, 147–48, 150,
    151, 152, 153, 158, 161–62, 166
Miramax International, 297
  as part of Walt Disney Co., 260, 294, 332
Prestige Films, 320
  and *Pulp Fiction,* 214, 298, 332–33
  and *Reservoir Dogs,* 213, 224, 226–27, 256
  and *sex, lies, and videotape,* 127, 128, 131,
    132, 161
  and *The Thin Blue Line,* 108, 109, 110, 111,
    112, 139
  and *Working Girls,* 85, 87–88, 92, 93, 95, 147
  see also Weinstein, Harvey; Weinstein brothers

Mississippi Masala, 202, 262
Mitchell, Eric, 25, 208
Mitchum, Robert, 161
Moderns, The, 107, 120
Modine, Matthew, 77, 296
MOMA, *see* Museum of Modern Art
Mona Lisa, 59
Monmouth (N.J.) *Courier,* 125
Montreal Film Festival, 160
Moore, Michael, 1, 4, 132, 136, 137–75, 186,
    191, 194, 205, 220, 236, 256, 326, 331,
    334
Morehouse College, 73, 77
Morgan Creek Productions, 266
Morris, David Burton, 117
Morris, Errol, 26, 102, 103–13, 139, 152, 220,
    321
Morrison, Toni, 98, 208
Morrison, Van, 14
Morrow, Vic, 183
Morton, Joe, 28, 50
Mosier, Scott, 21, 183, 287, 288, 294, 295, 296,
    298
Moss, Hajna, 74, 78
Mother and the Whore, The, 64
Motion Picture Association of America (MPAA),
    68, 69, 70, 329
Motion Picture Corporation of America/TriStar,
    308
Mott, Stewart, 145–46
Mott the Hoople, 268
Mottola, Greg, 132
Mound, Fred, 158
Movie Brats, The (Pye & Myles), 8
MPAA, *see* Motion Picture Association of
    America
Munich Film Festival, 216
Murphy, Eddie, 70, 202
Murphy, Karen, 142
Museum of Modern Art (NYC), 46, 85, 86, 190,
    191. 219, 221, 226; *see also* New
    Directors/New Films
My Beautiful Laundrette, 39–40, 41, 42, 188
My Brother's Wedding, 205
My Dinner with Andre, 17, 18
My Left Foot, 143, 171
My Life as a Dog, 95, 118–19, 145
My Life's in Turnaround, 18, 198, 276, 284,
    308–10, 333
My New Gun, 225
My Own Private Idaho, 203
Myles, Lynda, 8
Myron, Ben, 61
Mystery Train, 32–33, 130–31, 152
Mystic Pizza, 120–21

Nader, Ralph, 173
Nadja, 251
Nair, Mira, 202, 262
Naked in New York, 304
Nanook of the North, 173

Nashville, 8
National Board of Review, 168
National Lampoon's Animal House, 182, 183, 196
National Society of Film Critics, 27
Nava, Gregory, 17–18, 334
Navy Seals, 32
NBC Evening News, 71
Neighbors, 246
Nelson, Judd, 177
Nelson Entertainment, 94, 119; *see also* Embassy
    Home Video
New Directors/New Films, 46, 85, 86, 189,
    190–91, 219, 220, 222, 223, 291, 296, 309
New Jersey Drive, 226
    Animals project as precursor to, 222–24, 226
New Line Cinema, 10–11, 12, 17, 19, 29, 86,
    87, 92, 117, 188, 191, 203, 205, 206, 207,
    282, 308, 328, 333
    New Line Video, 195
    see also Fine Line Features
New School for Social Research, 124, 250
New York Daily News, 14, 92, 293, 328
New York Film Critics Circle, 168, 170, 171
New York Film Festival, 27, 36, 53, 57, 66, 85,
    97, 109, 120, 131, 189, 224, 226, 309,
    322, 324, 325, 327, 328
    American Independent sidebar, 15
    Roger & Me at (1989), 139, 145–47, 149–50,
    152, 161
New York Gay Film Festival, 36
New York magazine, 209–10, 224, 334
New York Post, 65, 167, 205, 294
New York State Council on the Arts, 46–47
New York Times, The, 51, 53, 69, 86, 122, 125,
    170, 183, 189, 190–91, 208, 217, 220,
    222, 253, 261, 274, 287, 291, 294,
    299–300, 326
    reviews by Canby, 27, 50, 92, 191
    reviews by Maslin, 42, 97, 333
    on *Roger & Me*, 142, 145, 146, 149, 150, 153,
    171, 174
New York University Film School, 2–3, 8, 11,
    25, 27, 30, 34, 44, 45, 46, 47, 62
New Yorker, The, 5, 173
New Yorker Films, 11–12, 13, 17, 89, 107, 120
Newman, Robert, 237
Newsday, 294, 328
Ney, Joanna, 161, 220
Nicholson, Jack, 8
Night in the Life of Jimmy Reardon, A, 93
Night of the Hunter, The, 161
Night of the Living Dead, 17
Night of the Shooting Stars, The, 191
Night on Earth, 203
Nightmare Before Christmas, The, 284
Nightmare on Elm Street, Part 3, A, 92
Nightmare on Elm Street series, 11, 29
Nilsson, Rob, 15, 117, 332
1900, 20
1918, 29
"No Expectations," 13

Nobody's Fool (1986), 59, 76
Noir et Blanc, 66
Nola Darling: N'en Fair Qu'a Sa Tête, see *She's
    Gotta Have It*
Noonan, Tom, 296, 335
Norte, El, 17–18, 39, 83, 141
Northern Arts, 206
Northern Lights, 15, 26, 192, 332
Novikoff, Mel, 15, 58
Nunez, Victor, 15, 29, 262

Oblivion Records, 53
Ocasek, Ric, 92
October Films, 43, 107, 151, 175, 204, 209,
    210, 222, 251, 262, 264, 285, 286, 295,
    328
O'Donnell, Lynn, 88, 89, 90, 95, 102, 320, 327,
    328
Off-Hollywood (Rosen & Hamilton), 18
Ohasi, Minako, 88, 89
Okazaki, Steven, 88, 89
Old Enough, 120
Olmos, Edward James, 116
Olsberg, Jonathan, 61
Olvidados, Los, 196
On Valentine's Day, 115
Once upon a Time in the West, 20
One False Move, 61, 210
Ontkean, Michael, 35
Ophuls, Marcel, 107
Ophuls, Max, 186
Orion Classics, 13, 17, 39–40, 41, 61, 93, 120,
    131, 139, 204, 325, 328
    interest in *Roger & Me*, 143, 146, 150, 151, 176
    and *Slacker*, 179, 186, 187, 188, 189, 190,
    191, 193, 194, 195, 196
Orion Pictures, 19, 194, 195
    Orion Home Video, 184, 195
    see also Orion Classics
Oscars, *see* Academy Awards
Ozu, Yasijuro, 12

Pacific Film Archive (PFA), 104–5
Pacino, Al, 35
Page, Geraldine, 29
Pak, Ho-Sung, 303
Palace of Fine Arts (San Francisco), 55, 56–57,
    58, 92, 107
Palace Productions, 128
Paramount Pictures, 9–10, 19, 193, 202, 207,
    264, 277
    Paramount Home Video, 264
Paris Is Burning, 192, 207, 321
Paris, Texas, 27, 28, 210
Parker, Laurie, 55, 61, 74, 77
Parlavecchio, Steve, 258
Parsons School of Design, 250
Parting Glances, 34–44, 46, 49, 50, 85, 115, 264
    distribution deal, 36–39
    legacy of, 42–43
    release, 40–42

"Passing Me By," 268
Pastime, 208
Patterson, Alex, 167
Patti Rocks, 117
Paxton, Bill, 177
PBS, *see* Public Broadcasting System
Peckinpah, Sam, 8
Pedas, Ted, 28, 62
Pelle the Conqueror, 88
Pena, Richard, 146, 324
Pence, Bill, 141
Pennebaker, D. A., 107
Pereths, Joy, 86
Perlberg, Janet, 13, 19, 44, 51, 56, 70, 74, 77,
    78, 84, 85, 105, 113, 146, 169, 285, 288,
    291, 323
Permanent Vacation, 25
Persona, 91
Personal Best, 35
Peters, Jon, 163
Pets or Meat, 136, 175
PFA, *see* Pacific Film Archive
Pharcyde, 268
Philadelphia Inquirer, 147
Phillips, Don, 183, 240
Phillips, Julia, 120
Phoenix, River, 93, 203
Piano, The, 203, 294, 335
Picker, David, 77
Picture Bride, The, 117
Pierson, Georgia, 78, 106, 109
Pierson, Janet, *see* Perlberg, Janet
Pierson, John:
    and *Amongst Friends,* 249–60, 262–78, 287,
        308, 323
    and *Anna,* 90, 91–94, 97
    on budgets, 234–38
    and *Clerks,* 2, 137, 279–81, 284–88, 291–97,
        313, 324
    and *Crumb,* 95, 313, 319–20, 328
    and *Delivered Vacant,* 321
    early career of, 8–9, 12–14, 19, 53, 54, 104, 335
    education of, 2–3, 7, 8, 105
    and *Go Fish,* 2, 43, 279–82, 285–91, 293,
        296, 311–18, 324
    and Grainy Pictures, 236, 333; *see also* Island
        World: Islet division
    and *Hoop Dreams,* 189, 232, 281, 286,
        319–20, 323–24, 326–27
    and *Just Another Girl on the IRT,* 98–100,
        193, 251
    and *Laws of Gravity,* 219–26, 237
    and *Living on Tokyo Time,* 88–90, 237
    and *My Life's in Turnaround,* 308–10
    and *Parting Glances,* 36–39, 42–44, 46
    and Roadmovies, 6–7, 16–17
    and *Roger & Me,* 1, 137–75, 186, 205, 237
    and *She's Gotta Have It,* 1, 49–77, 291
    and *Sidewalk Stories,* 129–30, 145
    and *Slacker,* 1, 137, 186–91, 193–95
    and *Sleepwalk,* 86, 94

on Sundance selection committee, 114–16
    and *Swoon,* 193, 209–10, 251
    and *The Thin Blue Line,* 1, 106, 107–8,
        110–11, 112
    and Wenders, 13–14, 189
    and *Working Girls,* 85, 86–87, 94, 97
Pierson, Wyatt, 186
Pilgrims, 116
Pilzer, George, 85
Pink Flamingos, 10, 16, 19, 22
Pitre, Glenn, 65
Pitt, Brad, 209
Planet of the Apes, 177
Platoon, 58
Player, The, 151, 203, 308
Playing for Keeps, 87
Plimpton, Martha, 308
Plummer, Amanda, 98
Plympton, Bill, 209
Poe, Amos, 7, 17, 25
Poison, 43, 115, 194, 207, 208, 209
Pollock, Tom, 131, 144, 159, 162, 163, 174,
    196, 196, 247
PolyGram, 256, 262, 263, 264, 277
    Records, 192–93
    see also Gramercy Pictures
Pomposello, Tom, 53
Porizkova, Paulina, 90, 91, 92, 93
Postcards from America, 43, 287, 312, 318
P.O.V. (TV series), 322, 323
Powwow Highway, 127
Prassis, Tom, 13, 49
Premiere magazine, 148, 207, 250, 265–66, 286,
    324
Presley, Elvis, 305–6, 308
Pressman, Ed, 249
Prestige Films, *see* Miramax Films
Price, Ray, 55, 56, 58, 64
Priest, 251
Prime Time Live, 149, 150, 170
Prisoners of Inertia, 98, 126
Producers, The, 118
Promised Land, 116
Public Access, 263
Public Broadcasting System (PBS), 4, 15, 104,
    111, 148, 175, 322, 323, 324
Public Theater (NYC), 106
Pulp Fiction, 2, 8, 203, 212, 213–14, 215, 216,
    225, 298, 320, 325, 326, 332, 333, 334,
    335, 337
Pumping Iron 2, 29
Putney Swope, 11
Puttnam, David, 77
Pye, Michael, 8

Quigley, Bill, 61, 93, 94, 97
Quinn, Aidan, 41
Quinn, Gordon, 323

Rachel River, 116
Rafelson, Bob, 8

Rafferty, Pierce and Kevin, 19
Raging Bull, 8
Raising Arizona, 21, 87, 90
Rajski, Peggy, 126
Ran, 76, 150
Rapaport, Michael, 209
Rappaport, Mark, 14
Rapture, The, 132
Rashomon, 32, 46
Ray, Bingham, 15–16, 43, 44, 89–90, 107, 120, 142, 145, 149, 150, 210, 295, 328
Ray, Nicholas, 15, 25
RCA Columbia Video, 127, 128, 131, 138; *see also* Columbia/TriStar Video
Rear Window, 146
Reardon, D. Barry, 159, 161, 164, 170, 173, 264
Red Hot Chili Peppers, 88, 256, 259, 268
Red Rock West, 153
Redford, Robert, 114
Reefer Madness, 10, 11
Reeves, Keanu, 203
Reichardt, Kelly, 307
Reitman, Ivan, 182
Rene, Norman, 206, 211
Renoir, Jean, 12
Reservoir Dogs, 80, 176, 210–11, 212–13, 216, 217, 218, 219, 221, 224, 226–27, 233, 250, 251, 254, 256, 257, 259, 269, 277, 297
Resnick, Gina, 128
Return of the Secaucus Seven, The, 16, 18, 41
Reversal of Fortune, 152
Reynolds, Burt, 180
Rich, B. Ruby, 282
Rich, Matty, 192, 195, 198–99, 200, 211, 250, 262
Richert, Bill, 93
Rickey, Branch, 299
Rickey, Carrie, 147, 150, 167
Rifkin, Adam, 177
Rio Bravo, 16
Ripploh, Frank, 41
Risher, Sara, 206
River of Grass, 230, 307
River's Edge, 115, 196
Rivette, Jacques, 26, 32
RKO Pictures, 219, 222, 224–25
Roadmovies, 6–7, 16–17, 30, 34, 37, 49
Roberts, Eric, 76
Roberts, Julia, 121
Rock, Bobby, 119, 222, 223
Rockwell, Alexandre, 10, 209, 211
Rocky, 237
Rocky Horror Picture Show, The, 11
Rodriguez, Robert, 235, 237, 261, 262, 263, 334
Roger & Me, 1, 123, 132, 134–36, 137–46, 148–75, 179, 186, 205, 206, 207, 237, 264, 288, 309, 319, 320, 321, 322, 326, 327, 334
  budget, 139

deal with Warner Bros., 159–65
  at film festivals, 141–43, 145–46, 149–50, 152
  release, 165–75
  seeking distributor, 137–46, 148–64
Rohmer, Eric, 214–15
Rolling Stone magazine, 221, 261
Rolling Stones, 10, 13, 17
Romero, George, 14, 17
Ronde, La, 186
Rondo Productions, 34–35, 42, 44
Room with a View, A, 41, 42, 91, 203
Rosemary's Baby, 9
Rosen, David, 18
Rosen, Gus, 112
Rosenblatt, Michael, 61–62
Rosenfeld, Keva, 286
Rosnell, John, 199
Ross, Monty, 47, 71, 74, 81, 82
Ross, Steve, 166
Roth, Tim, 227, 250
Rothman, Tom, 40, 77, 127, 149, 150, 165, 170, 206, 264–65, 288, 291, 297, 333
Roxie Releasing, 153, 160, 309
Royal Ontario Museum, 142, 143
Ruby in Paradise, 262, 263, 264, 286, 335
Rudolph, Alan, 28, 107, 120, 335
Rugoff, Don, 11, 15, 118
Russell, David O., 282, 334
Russo, Vito, 35
Ryder, Winona, 76

Safe, 43
Safford, Tony, 114, 116, 117, 127, 205
Safire, WIlliam, 183
Salaam Bombay, 202, 262
Salazar, Wayne, 50
Salvador, 58
Samuel Goldwyn Company, 37, 39, 40, 65, 66, 89–90, 107, 120–21, 132, 138, 192, 202, 204, 205, 209, 222, 224, 307, 310, 325, 333
  and *Go Fish,* 285–65, 288, 291, 293, 296, 297, 312, 314, 315, 317, 318
  interest in *Amongst Friends,* 256, 262, 264, 265
  interest in *Clerks,* 285–86
  interest in *Roger & Me,* 139, 141, 149, 150–51, 165
  interest in *She's Gotta Have It,* 56, 58, 59, 152
  and *The Hollywood Shuffle,* 70, 95, 235
  and *Longtime Companion,* 43, 206
  and *Stranger Than Paradise,* 26, 27–28
San Francisco Chronicle, 54, 55, 90, 92, 110
San Francisco Examiner, 55, 58
San Francisco Gay and Lesbian Film Festival, 297
San Francisco International Film Festival, 53–54, 55, 58–59, 88, 91, 92, 107–8, 147, 234
San Giacomo, Laura, 124
Sandlot, The, 193

Sassy magazine, 266
Saturday Night Live, 73, 100
Savage Nights, 305
Savoca, Nancy, 102, 126
Savoy Pictures, 260
Sayles, John, 16, 17, 18–19, 28, 35, 47, 50, 126, 138, 189, 308, 334
Scandal, 128, 143
Scarlet, Peter, 57
Scenes from a Marriage, 11
Schaefer, Stephen, 67
Schaeffer, Eric, 18, 308–10, 331, 334
Schaffer, Randy, 111, 112
Schamus, James, 209–10, 223
Scher, Jeff, 98
Schickel, Richard, 168
Schiff, Stephen, 67
Schneider, Ellen, 322
School Daze, 73–74, 75, 76–77, 78, 82, 122, 128
Schulberg, Sandra, 15, 317
Schulman, Cathy, 257, 258, 282, 285–86
Schulman, John, 163
Schultz, Michael, 47
Schulze, Paul, 219
Schulze, Rob, 119
Schwartz, Russell, 29, 59, 61, 62, 65, 66, 69, 71, 75, 76, 150, 151, 256
Sciorra, Annabella, 126
Scorsese, Martin, 5, 8, 9, 10, 13, 19, 26, 64, 215–16, 218, 220, 250, 265, 269, 277
Scott, Jay, 166
Scott, Ridley, 90
Scott, Tony, 90
Screaming Mimi, 15
Screen Actors Guild, 25, 91
Sea of Love, 144, 159
Seagal, Steven, 171
Searchlight Pictures, 333
Season of Change, 306
Seattle Film Festival, 93, 187
Secret of Roan Inish, The, 19
Secret Policeman's Ball, The, 84
Secret Policeman's Other Ball, The, 85, 110
Seidelman, Susan, 8, 17
Seifert, Steve, 37–38, 40, 41, 42
Seitz, Matt Zoller, 269
Seize the Day, 115
Seltzer, Nancy, 37
Sembène, Ousmane, 12
Semel, Terry, 163
Seven Beauties, 11
Seven Chances, 19
Seven Samurai, The, 4, 61
sex, lies, and videotape, 2, 123, 127–28, 129, 131, 132, 133–34, 138, 143, 161–62, 171, 203, 204, 210, 301
Sexual Perversity in Chicago (Mamet), 304
Shadows, 9, 10, 26
Shampoo, 14
Shapiro, Rachael, 282
Shawn, Wallace, 18

Shaye, Robert, 11, 19, 92, 328, 333
Shepard, Sam, 120
Sherman's March, 107, 115
Sherwood, Bill, 27, 34–36, 42–43
She's Gotta Have It, 23, 32, 46–78, 79–80, 84, 85, 89, 92, 95, 121, 129, 137, 145, 162, 167, 174, 200–201, 207, 264, 286, 288, 317
budget, 46–47, 226, 234
at Cannes, 62–66, 83, 291
deal with Island, 62, 65, 130, 291
foreign sales, 65
JP invests in, 1, 49–51, 77
and later career of S. Lee, 78, 333
MPAA rating, 68, 69–70
postproduction, 50–53
production, 25, 46, 99
release, 66–75, 81–82, 150
San Francisco premiere, 53–58
seeking distributor, 50–62, 152
video release, 75–76
Shock Corridor, 117
Shooting Gallery collective, 219, 221, 222, 223; see also *Laws of Gravity*
Shorter, Wayne, 130
Sid and Nancy, 85
Sidewalk Stories, 129–30, 145, 153, 221, 243
Sievernich, Chris, 27
Sikich, Dave, 324, 326
Silber, Glen, 15
Silberman, Mark, 128
Silence at Bethany, The, 116
Silver, Casey, 159
Silver, Joan Micklin, 12, 89
Silver, Marissa, 120
Silver, Raphael D., 12, 89
Silverman, Arthur, 34, 36
Silvers, Dean, 282
Simmons, Russell, 47
Simon, Neil, 4
Simple Men, 202–3, 225
Singer, Bryan, 261, 263, 334
Singer, Mark, 111
Singles, 259
Singleton, John, 71, 192, 200
Sinofsky, Bruce, 320, 321
Sirk, Douglas, 106
Siskel, Gene, 168, 210, 324–25, 326, 331–32
60 Minutes, 107
Skouras, Marjorie, 127
Skouras, Tom, 89, 145
Skouras Pictures, 89, 90, 95, 97, 115, 118–19, 127, 145, 264
Slacker, 1, 22, 137, 177, 178, 179, 180, 183, 185–91, 193–97, 198, 207, 210, 220, 233, 236, 253, 276, 282, 286, 304, 309, 334
budget, 234
at festivals, 187, 189, 191–92
postproduction, 189–90
production, 185
release, 186, 192, 193–95

seeking distributor, 186–89
video release, 195, 317
Slam Dance, 119
Sleep with Me, 216
Sleepwalk, 64, 86, 88, 89, 94, 95, 243
Sloss, John, 13, 189, 190
Smilow, Margie, 84, 92
Smith, Earl, 49, 70, 81–82
Smith, Kevin, 2, 18, 27, 98, 186, 189, 236,
     279–88, 291, 293–98, 300, 310, 323, 324,
     331, 332, 334
   conversations with JP, 4–5, 21–23, 31–33,
     79–82, 123–25, 133–36, 177–85,
     198–201, 212–17, 228–33, 239–48, 330
   see also Zeher, Costa
Smith, Liz, 241
Smith, Lory, 114
Smith, Roger, 136, 144, 149, 160, 166, 167,
     169, 170, 173
Smithereens, 17, 27
Smooth Talk, 115, 118
Snipes, Wesley, 209
Soderbergh, Steven, 2, 127–28, 129, 131,
     133–34, 138, 185, 202, 204, 205, 206,
     209, 211, 334
Soldier's Story, A, 47, 70, 82
Some Came Running, 197
Sony Corporation, *see* Columbia Pictures; Sony
     Music; Sony Pictures Classics; TriStar
     Pictures
Sony Music, 232, 259, 274, 277, 297
Sony Pictures Classics, 194, 203, 233, 256, 285,
     287, 288, 291, 293, 296, 309, 320, 325,
     328–29, 334–35
Sorvino, Mira, 249, 252
Sorvino, Paul, 249, 252
Soul Asylum, 297
Soul Man, 62, 130
Sound One, 110
South of Reno, 116
Spader, James, 129, 134
Spanking the Monkey, 282, 288, 296, 336
Spectrafilm, 17, 29, 39, 61, 118, 119
Spelling International, 263
Spielberg, Michael, 128
Spielberg, Steven, 8
Spielman, Fran, 11, 46, 61
Spines, Christine, 286
Square Dance, 76, 119
Stalker, The, 105
Stallone, Sylvester, 64
Stand and Deliver, 116
Stanzler, Wendey, 138, 149, 175
Star Wars, 8, 134
Starks, John, 78
Starstruck, 40
State of Grace, 254
State of Things, The, 25–26, 104
Steel, Dawn, 122
Steel Helmet, The, 117
Steinberg, Michael, 209, 286

Stern, Howard, 98, 293
Sternhell, Jeff, 252, 274
Stewart, James, 146, 331
Stickney, Phyllis, 74
Sticky Fingers, 119
Stillman, Whit, 186, 189, 190, 200, 202, 336
Stoltz, Eric, 209
Stone, Judy, 54–55, 90, 92
Stone, Oliver, 58, 277
Stone, Shelby, 37
Stone Temple Pilots, 256
Stonewall, 43
Stop Making Sense, 28, 50
Straight Out of Brooklyn, 192, 195, 198–99, 200,
     207, 246, 250
Strand Releasing, 228–29
Stranger Than Paradise, 2, 14, 22, 23, 24–29, 32,
     34–35, 39, 41, 46, 53, 56, 67, 76, 86, 95,
     133, 203, 333
Streetwise, 28
Stroszek, 104, 105
Subway Riders, 7
Sugarland Express, The, 7
Sundance Film Festival, 2, 7, 36, 41, 88, 102,
     114, 133–34, 173, 202, 296, 309
   1987, 115
   1988, 115–17
   1989, 10, 126–28, 131, 161
   1990, 186, 205–7
   1991, 98, 138, 190, 190, 207–8
   1992, 158, 204, 209–11, 213, 218, 219, 254,
     308, 321
   1993, 237, 257–65, 274, 279
   1994, 117, 225–26, 230, 282, 284–88, 291,
     293–95, 297, 298, 307, 313, 318, 324. 325
   1995, 117, 312, 336
Sundance Institute, 116, 117
Superstar: The Karen Carpenter Story, 208
Surf Nazis Must Die, 254
Sweet Sweetback's Baadasssss Song, 8
Swept Away, 11
Swinging Cheerleaders, The, 112
Swoon, 43, 193, 209–10, 223, 225, 251, 301,
     336
Sympathy for the Devil, 10, 17

Talbot, Dan, 11, 12, 15, 41, 67
Talking Heads, 28
Tarantino, Quentin, 175–76, 211, 212, 213,
     214–16, 217, 218, 221, 224, 227, 250,
     260, 331–32
Tarkovsky, Andrei, 105
Taubin, Amy, 100, 194, 209, 220, 282, 284
Taviani, Paolo and Vittorio, 191
Taxi Driver, 8, 215
Taxi zum Klo, 35, 41
Taylor, Elizabeth, 223
Teen Wolf, 62, 119
Telluride Film Festival, 27, 36, 38, 71, 85, 86,
     139, 141, 162, 189, 309, 328
Templeton, Anne, 141

Tenenbaum, Nancy, 132
Terrell, John Canada, 64, 68
Thelma and Louise, 281
They All Laughed, 61
Thief, 254
Thielen, Laura, 54
Thin Blue Line, The, 1, 104, 105, 106–13, 114,
    139, 171, 195, 319, 320, 321, 324
  and Adams's appeal, 111–13
Thin Blue Line, The (*cont.*)
  and American Playhouse, 106
  at festivals, 107, 109
  postproduction, 105–7, 109–10
  release, 109–11
  seeking distributor, 106–8
35 Up, 322
Thomas, John, 200
Thomas, Kevin, 86
Thompson, Anne, 69, 91, 293
THX 1138, 8
Time magazine, 168, 187
Time Warner Inc., *see* Warner Bros.
To Sleep with Anger, 205, 206
Today show, 71, 170
Todd-AO, 258, 268
Tokyo Pop, 119
Tolkin, Michael, 132
Tommy: The Amazing Journey, 294
Too Late Blues, 10
Too Something (TV series), 308
Topo, El, 16
Toronto Film Festival, 28, 36, 85, 100, 139,
    141, 142–44, 145, 153, 159, 166, 189,
    224, 251, 281, 309, 327
Total Recall, 213
Toumarkine, Doris, 277–78
Towne, Robert, 35
Townsend, Robert, 70, 95, 234–35
Townshend, Pete, 87
Toxic Avenger, The, 254
Toy Soldiers, 224
Traffic, 53, 259
Trapeze, 6
Travers, Peter, 261, 269
Travolta, John, 332, 333
Trese, Adam, 219
TriBeCa Film Center, 219
Triboro Home Video, 225
Tricontinental, 54
Trip to Bountiful, The, 29, 30
TriStar Pictures, 249, 252, 260, 308, 332
Triton Pictures, 158, 209, 222, 223, 286, 321
Triumph Pictures, 209
Troche, Rose, 227, 279–82, 287–93, 296, 298,
    311–15, 317–18, 322, 324
Troma Films, 254, 255
Trombetta, Leo, 254, 255, 258
Trouble with Dick, The, 115
True Love, 126, 161
Truffaut, François, 8, 17
Trust, 22, 180, 194, 195, 203, 219

Truth or Dare, 321
Tune, The, 209
Turan, Kenneth, 291
Turner, Guin, 227, 279–82, 287–93, 296, 298,
    311, 313–15, 317, 322–23
Turner, Kathleen, 19
Turner, Ted, 11
Turner Entertainment, 325, 328; *see also* Fine
    Line Features; New Line Cinema
Turturro, John, 132, 286
Tusk, Mark, 100, 128, 188, 285, 287, 294,
    295
TVC Film Lab, 251
Twentieth Century-Fox, 13, 17, 90, 333; *see also*
    Fox Television Network; Searchlight
    Pictures
Twenty Bucks, 286
Twilight Zone (TV series), 112
Twist and Shout, 84
200 Motels, 15

Ulmer, Edgar G., 185
Unbelievable Truth, The, 22, 143
Uncle Buck, 131
Underground USA, 25
Underneath, The, 131, 334
Underworld U.S.A., 117
United Artists, 10
  United Artists Classics, 13, 15, 17, 20, 26, 37,
    40, 118
United Talent Agency, 257, 264
Universal Pictures, 17, 28, 87, 98, 170, 182,
    183, 190, 196, 247, 256, 268
  interest in *Roger & Me*, 141, 144, 151, 153,
    158–59, 161, 162, 163
  and S. Lee, 122, 128, 130, 131, 226, 333
  and R. Weiss, 246, 249, 260, 263, 276
  see also Gramercy Pictures; MCA
U.S. Film Festival, 36, 41, 42, 88, 89, 114
  see also Sundance Film Festival
U.S.A. Film Festival, 107, 187
Usual Suspects, The, 263
Utah Film Commission, 114
U2, 53, 221

Vachon, Christine, 43, 44, 209, 280, 281, 314,
    318; *see also* Kalin Vachon Productions, Inc.
Valentino Returns, 116
Vampire's Kiss, 128
Vancouver Film Festival, 160
Van Peebles, Melvin, 8
Van Sant, Gus, 55, 190, 203, 260, 334
Van Wagenen, Sterling, 30
Variety, 42, 54, 59, 92, 143, 147, 291, 294
Vasquez, Joseph, 207–8
Verhoeven, Paul, 118
Vernon, Florida, 104
Vestron, 61, 92, 93–94, 97, 98, 116, 119–20,
    132
Viacom corporation, 336
Video Software Dealers Association, 174, 329

Vikings, The, 6
Village Voice, The, 7, 49, 67, 69, 125, 145, 167, 177–78, 194, 209, 220, 250, 265, 282, 284
Virgin Video, 127, 132
von Sydow, Max, 88

Wahlberg, Mark (Marky Mark), 223, 226, 256
Waiting for the Moon, 115
Walkow, Gary, 115
Walt Disney Company, the, 28, 130, 144–45, 153, 161, 170, 294, 332; *see also* Disney Channel
Wanderers, The, 261
Wang, Peter, 61
Wang, Wayne, 17, 115, 119
War Room, The, 107
Ward, Don, 18, 308, 310
Warhol, Andy, 7, 91
Warner Bros., 20, 58, 78, 116, 123, 134, 135, 136, 137, 141, 153, 159–67, 170–72, 205, 206, 264, 266, 321
    Warner Home Video, 174
    Warner Special Products, 259, 277
Washington, Denzel, 202
Washington Post, 65
Waterdance, The, 209
Waters, John, 10–11, 18, 19, 22, 117, 206, 303
Waterworld, 299
Waverly Theater (NYC), 17, 224–25
Wayne, Joel, 161, 167
Weber, Bruce, 266
Wedding Banquet, The, 209
WEG, *see* Weintraub Entertainment Group
Weill, Claudia, 12
Weinstein, Bob, *see* Miramax Films; Weinstein brothers
Weinstein, Harvey, 7, 110, 124, 130, 143–44, 153, 162, 165, 219, 221, 232, 287, 293, 294, 295, 296, 334, 335; *see also* Miramax Films; Weinstein brothers
Weinstein brothers, 84, 85, 87, 88, 92, 93–94, 97, 108, 128, 143, 147, 170, 227, 265; *see also* Miramax Films; Weinstein, Harvey
Weintraub Entertainment Group (WEG), 120
Weisman, David, 30
Weiss, Carl, 250, 251, 274, 277
Weiss, Rob, 218, 237–38, 239, 240, 241, 242–26, 247, 248, 249–64, 266–78, 279, 331
    Murder Inc. project of, 260
Welles, Orson, 254, 319
Wells, Junior, 13
Wenders, Wim, 9, 12, 13–14, 16, 25, 27, 49, 57, 104, 120, 129, 179, 189, 191, 210
Werner Herzog Eats His Shoe, 104
Wes Craven's New Nightmare, 333

Westby, Jay, 310
What Happened Was, 296, 336
White, Cara, 190
Wiggens, Wiley, 196
Wild at Heart, 251
Wild Bunch, The, 8
Wild Style, 17
Wilhite, Tom, 117
Willenson, Seth, 210
William Morris Agency, 46, 260, 308
Williams, Erwin, 99
Williams, Treat, 118
Williams, Vanessa, 74
Williamson, Bruce, 67
Willis, Bruce, 332
Wilmington, Michael, 42
Wilson, Lanford, 116
Wings of Desire, 120, 129, 191
Wish You Were Here, 119
Wishman, Seymour, 46, 87
Wizard of Oz, The, 49, 73, 169
Wojnarowicz, David, 312
Woman under the Influence, A, 9, 10, 19
women filmmakers, difficulties facing, 102
Women on the Verge of a Nervous Breakdown, 120, 195
Women's Prison Massacre, 71
Wonder, Stevie, 56
Woo, John, 303
Woods, Cary, 260, 294
Woodstock, 159, 173
Working Girls, 54, 65, 84–88, 89, 90, 92, 93, 94, 95, 97, 115, 147, 284
Wright, N'Bushe, 209
Written on the Wind, 106

Yakin, Boaz, 296
Yo! MTV Raps (TV series), 205
Yojimbo, 16
You Are Not I, 86
You Only Live Once, 7
You Only Live Twice, 7
Young, Irwin, 50, 51, 190, 205
Young, Neil, 221
Young, Robert, 26

Z, 11
Zappa, Frank, 15
Zarpas, Chris, 27, 90, 145, 221
Zebrahead, 209
Zeher, Costa (pseud.), 231, 300–301, 310
Zehrer, Paul, 307, 308
Zeitgeist Pictures, 208, 328
Zoetrope Studios, 13, 159
Zwigoff, Terry, 95, 320, 327–28, 335